Sir William Hamilton

Envoy Extraordinary

SIR WILLIAM HAMILTON

ENVOY EXTRAORDINARY

BRIAN FOTHERGILL

NONSUCH

by the same author

THE CARDINAL KING

NICHOLAS WISEMAN

MRS JORDAN: Portrait of an Actress

First published 1969
Copyright © in this edition 2005
Nonsuch Publishing Ltd

Nonsuch Publishing Limited
The Mill, Brimscombe Port,
Stroud, Gloucestershire, GL5 2QG
www.nonsuch-publishing.com

British Library Cataloguing in Publication Data.
A catalogue record for this book is available from the British Library.

1-84588-042-0

Typesetting and origination by Nonsuch Publishing Limited
Printed in Great Britain by Oaklands Book Services Limited

CONTENTS

LIST OF ILLUSTRATIONS

Sir William Hamilton. (By William Thomas Fry. National Portrait Gallery, London.)

Sir William Hamilton and his First Wife. (By David Allan. Blair Castle, Perthshire.)

Dedicatory Plate from Hamilton's 'Greek and Roman Antiquities'. (By courtesy of the Trustees of Sir John Soane's Museum)

Wedgwood's First Day's Vase with designs from Hamilton's 'Greek and Roman Antiquities'. (Reproduced by permission of the Wedgwood Museum Trust)

Naples from Posillipo. (Plate by Pietro Fabris from Hamilton's 'Campi Phlegraei'. By permission of the British Library.)

Venus disarming Cupid, attributed by Hamilton to Correggio. (Reproduced by permission of the late Earl of Radnor, K.G.)

View of Lake Avernus. (Plate by Pietro Fabris from Hamilton's 'Campi Phlegraei'. By permission of the Britsh Library.)

Sir William Hamilton in the robes of a Knight of the Bath. (By David Allan. National Portrait Gallery, London.)

Vesuvius in Eruption. (Plate by Pietro Fabris from Hamilton's 'Campi Phlegraei'.By permission of the British Library.)

Sir William Hamilton in 1777. (By Sir Joshua Reynolds. National Portrait Gallery London.)

Plate from Hamilton's 'Collection of Engravings from Ancient Vases' (Photograph by Raymond Earles. By courtesy of the Trustees of Sir John Sloane's Museum.)

Emma Hart, later Lady Hamilton. (By George Romney. National Portrait Gallery, London.)

Excavation of the Temple of Isis at Pompeii. (Plate by Pietro Fabris from Hamilton's 'Campi Phlegraei'. By permission of the Britsh Library.)

Vice-Admiral Viscount Nelson. (By Sir William Beechey. National Portrait Gallery, London.)

The 'Hamilton Vase'

INTRODUCTION TO THE MODERN EDITION

William Hamilton may be one of the best-known cuckolds in history. His second wife, Emma, secured her own fame by becoming the mistress of Horatio Nelson, the greatest of Britain's naval heroes, but Hamilton's claim to posterity is based, rather more prosaically, on the fact that he was one of the foremost antiquarians and vulcanologists in the world, as well as Britain's envoy to the Kingdom of the Two Sicilies, which included Naples, for more than three decades.

Born in 1830, William Hamilton was the grandson of the third Duke of Hamilton on his father's side and the sixteenth Earl of Abercorn on his mother's. His father was variously a naval officer, an MP, a Lord of the Admiralty and Governor of Jamaica; his mother was reputedly the mistress of Frederick, Prince of Wales. Brought up with the future King George III and educated at Westminster School, he was commissioned into the 3rd Regiment of Foot Guards in 1747 and saw action during the War of the Austrian Succession and the Seven Years War. He resigned his commission and married an heiress, Catherine Barlow, in 1758, before being elected to Parliament in 1761. In 1764 Hamilton was appointed Envoy Extraordinary to the Court of Naples, in which capacity he would continue for the next thirty-six years.

In 1767 Hamilton was promoted to Minister Plenipotentiary and in 1772 he was created a Knight of the Bath in recognition of his service at the Neapolitan court. His wife died in 1782, following which he returned to England to bury her and to put her affairs in order, among other things. It was during this year away from Naples that he was to meet Emma Hart, three decades his junior, the mistress of his nephew, Charles Greville, and the mother of an illegitimate child. Born Amy Lyon in 1765, she was the daughter of a Cheshire blacksmith who started work as a nursemaid at the age of thirteen, changed her name and became the mistress of Sir Harry Fetherstonehaugh, a young and dissolute baronet, before being taken up by Greville when he tired of her. When Greville decided to go heiress-hunting Emma was despatched to Naples to join his uncle, becoming first his mistress and then his wife. Nelson visited the city briefly as captain of HMS *Agamemnon* in 1793, but it was not until he returned in 1798, an admiral, a Knight of the Bath, a peer of the realm and the victor of the Nile, that they began to set tongues wagging.

Hamilton's position as envoy to the Neapolitan court was ideal for him to indulge his interests in antiquity and volcanoes. Pompeii, Herculaneum and Vesuvius were all nearby and he began building a collection of antique vases; when he published a catalogue of his collection in 1766–67 it required four volumes. His first collection of vases was bought for the British Museum in 1772 and, in 1784, he sold to Margaret, dowager Duchess of Portland, what is now known as the 'Portland Vase.' Now in the British Museum, it is described as 'arguably the most famous and certainly the most influential piece of ancient glass in the world'. In 1798 Hamilton decided to catalogue his paintings: the list included works by Titian, Rubens, Raphael, Rembrandt, Canaletto, da Vinci, Van Dyck, Tintoretto, Rosa, Cuyp, and Romney. Fourteen of them were of Emma. Much of his second collection of ancient vases was lost when the ship carrying it to England sank off the Isles of Scilly in 1798, an occurence which greatly depressed him and which may have indirectly contributed to the marital troubles which were to beset him: his preoccuptation with his lost antiquities blinded him to his wife's scandalous behaviour with Nelson until it was too late.

Soon after his initial arrival in Naples Hamilton began sending letters to the Royal Society in London, and those describing the activity and eruptions of Vesuvius during 1765–67 attracted particular attention. They earned him his election as a Fellow of the Society in 1766, perhaps the highest honour that can be accorded to a British scientist, and Horace Walpole called him 'the Professor of Earthquakes.' He despatched samples of salts, sulphurs, lava and cinders, collected during his many ascents of the volcano, and would record two further massive eruptions, in 1779 and 1794. His research also took him to Sicily, where he climbed Mount Etna, and observed the volcanic island of Stromboli. In 1776 he published *Campi Phlegraei*, subtitled *Observations on the Volcanoes of the Two Sicilies*, which capitalised on the success of the letters which he had sent to the Royal Society during 1765–67.

William Hamilton, then, was more than simply the husband wronged by Nelson in his adulterous passion. He served for thirty-six years as George III's representative at the Court of the Two Sicilies, a period during which the Mediterranean Sea became increasingly important to Britain's naval and diplomatic strategies. He was an avid collector of paintings and antiquities and an eminent vulcanologist and a leading expert on Vesuvius. History, though, will remember him as the man cuckolded by Emma Hamilton.

Brian Fothergill was awarded the W.H. Heinemann Award in 1969 for *Sir William Hamilton: Envoy Extraordinary*. Presented by the Royal Society of Literature for a work, generally non-fiction, of outstanding literary distinction, he won it again in 1979 for *Beckford of Fonthill*, a biography of William Beckford, the hedonistic eccentric who wrote the Gothic novel *Vathek*. He was also the author of *The Cardinal King* (1958), about Henry, Cardinal Stuart, last legitimate descendent of James VII / II and, to the Jacobites, King Henry IX / I; *Nicholas Wiseman* (1963), about the first Cardinal Archbishop of Westminster; *Mrs Jordan: Portrait of an Actress* (1965), about the great Georgian actress and mistress of King William IV before he ascended the throne, Dorothy Jordan; *The Mitred Earl: An Eighteenth-Century Eccentric* (1974), about a school-friend of Sir William Hamilton, Frederick Hervey, Bishop of Derry and Earl of Bristol; and *The Strawberry Hill Set: Horace Walpole and his Circle* (1983).

FOREWORD

It has been the fate of Sir William Hamilton to appear as a background figure in many biographies and historical studies but never to stand alone in the centre of the stage, though much in his later life and the whole of his early and middle years make him a personality worthy of more detailed treatment than he has thus far received. It is for this reason that I have confined the present study to the limits of Sir William's life and have not continued the story to the deaths of those nearest to him at the time of his own death in 1803, his second wife and his friend Lord Nelson. Nelson's last years are sufficiently well known while Emma Hamilton's are of no great significance, at least in so far as her husband's life is concerned.

Hamilton was a many-sided and versatile character. To do full justice to all the activities in which he excelled would require the combined skills of a diplomatic and social historian, an art-historian, an authority on Greek and Roman antiquities, on eighteenth-century music, on volcanology and on natural history, to name but the chief of Sir William's interests. It would be too much in this present age for one man to claim to be an expert in all these fields; it is my intention to do no more than give a general picture of a remarkable and somewhat neglected personality, who, because of the unusual circumstances of his latter years, has rarely been studied except in relation to others perhaps more heroic or more romantic but not necessarily more admirable than he was himself.

Sir William's unique position at the Court of Ferdinand IV and Maria Carolina of Naples, his European reputation as collector and *dilettante*, his contributions to scientific knowledge and his high place in the cosmopolitan society of the eighteenth century would in themselves have made him a person of sufficient fascination to posterity even if he had never married Emma Hart or been the friend of Horatio Nelson. It is my hope to set these lesser known activities of Sir William Hamilton's life in their proper relationship to the more spectacular aspects of his last years as British Minister to the Court of the Two Sicilies.

I must thank Mr. Brian Connell, Messrs. André Deutsch Ltd., and Messrs. E.P.S. Lewin and Partners for permission to quote from *Portrait of a Whig Peer*; the Earl of Pembroke and Messrs. Jonathan Cape Ltd. to quote from *The Pembroke Papers*; and Mr. Romney Sedgwick and Messrs. B.T. Batsford Ltd. for permission to quote from *Lord Hervey's Memoirs*. I am also indebted to Messrs. Christie's for giving me access to their sale catalogues for the year 1801.

I am most grateful to Mr. Brinsley Ford for kindly allowing me to consult his material on British travellers to Italy in the eighteenth century. Material from this source is indicated in the footnotes by [F]. I must also acknowledge my thanks for advice or assistance from Mr. Harold Acton, Professor P.E. Corbett, Dr. Kenneth Garlick, Mr. Cecil Gould, Mr. Jonathan Griffin, Dr. Leslie Hotson, Miss Dorothy Stroud, and Mr. Oliver Warner. Finally I must express my warm thanks to Miss Edith Clay for much valuable help and many useful suggestions.

PART ONE
1730—1783

CHAPTER I

Hamilton's Early Life

There are many hazards, unsuspected by the living, that can intervene between death and the final verdict of history. When Sir William Hamilton died in the fullness of years and fame, in the very early days of the nineteenth century, distinguished in so many fields, cultivated, urbane, the very epitome of eighteenth-century sensibility, few would have suspected that more than a hundred and fifty years would pass before his biography would be written; before he would be assessed on his own merits and not considered merely as the husband of a beautiful adventuress or the best friend of a hero destined to supplant him in the affections of his wife. Sir William Hamilton died in the arms of Emma, his second wife, clutching the hand of Lord Nelson, his greatest friend. These figures, who jointly dominated the last decade of his existence, have overshadowed him ever since. Their presence at his death-bed created a situation in which irony, rather than tragedy or grief, would have been the foremost emotion to strike anyone who might have chanced to witness the scene.

The man who died on that April day in 1803 had so many claims on the interest of posterity that it seems almost incredible that he should be remembered chiefly as a complacent husband, the eldest, and, therefore least romantic member of a celebrated *ménage à trois* that scandalised and titillated society in its own day and has not ceased to fascinate the world since.

The opinion of his times, especially in that longer period of life before he made his second marriage, held him in very different esteem from that accorded to him since his death. His career was one of so many facets that he seemed to sum up all that was best in the much vaunted Age of Reason which was to crumble, in his own lifetime and almost before his very eyes, in the shambles of the Age of Revolution. He was nurtured in the shadow of the Court. In his early years he served as a soldier and sat in the House of Commons. For thirty-seven years he represented his country at the court of the King of the Two Sicilies where his embassy became the acknowledged centre of the artistic and cultural life of the capital. He was a distinguished archaeologist; his scientific studies secured his election as a Fellow of the Royal Society; he became a connoisseur of art and patron of artists, an amateur of music, an enthusiast of volcanoes, an active sportsman, a man 'whose taste and zeal for the Arts' as Dr. Charles Burney testified, 'and whose patronage of artists, are well known throughout Europe'.

If his diplomatic duties were none too arduous in the tranquil years that characterised the greater part of his long mission, he was none the less punctilious and successful in their performance. Lady Craven, later Margravine of Anspach, declared that 'no foreign minister ever enjoyed in so particular a degree the confidence and affection of the King of Naples'; and Hamilton himself, a dozen years after his appointment,[1] was able to tell Lord Dartmouth, 'It is singular but certainly true that I have become more a *ministre de famille* at this Court than ever the ministers of France, Spain and Vienna'.

No person of any consequence who visited Naples between the years 1764 and the outbreak of the Revolution of 1799 would have cared to miss the opportunity of meeting the British envoy. To make one's bow at the Palazzo Sessa, to attend one of the Minister's musical concerts, to be allowed to inspect his collection of Greek vases, to accompany him on an expedition to the crater of Vesuvius or to the excavations at Pompeii, these were distinctions coveted by every visitor to the Neapolitan capital. To fail to gain so highly prized an honour was failure indeed. Edward Gibbon, the future historian of the Roman Empire, visited Hamilton in the year of his appointment, and even at that early date commended him for 'wisely diverting his correspondence from the Secretary of State to the Royal Society and British Museum', for by so doing he 'elucidated a country of such inestimable value to the naturalist and antiquarian'. Over twenty years later on his celebrated Italian journey, Goethe, describing a picture painted by his friend Tischbein, declared that any artist capable of such work would be more than welcome in the distinguished circle of Sir William Hamilton. Nor was it only the great and famous who respected and honoured the British Minister. Michael Kelly, the Irish singer and composer, recalled how Sir William was a favourite with the *lazzaroni*, the half-naked beggars who swarmed the slums of the city, and who 'often lamented that so good a man *must* be eternally punished, since he was a heretic'. This verdict would no doubt have amused the affable ambassador, but the verdict of history has been no less unjust, for it remembers him primarily as a cuckold.

William Hamilton was born at Park Place near Henley[2] on the 18th of December 1730. His ancestry was distinguished, for he descended on both sides from branches of the Hamilton family, among the most noble blood in Scotland. It was fortunate that he was destined to live in an age when such breeding counted as an asset, for he could not claim to have been born to wealth. 'I know what it is for an honest man to be distressed in his circumstances', he confessed many years later to his favourite nephew, and he added the sound advice: 'If you find that your house is too expensive, get rid of it as soon as you can.'[3] Such advice sprang from his own experience as a younger son who had position rather than means. In later years he was accustomed to remark that he had started in life with an ancient name and a thousand pounds.

His father was Lord Archibald Hamilton, who was nearing sixty and in his third marriage at the time of William's birth. Lord Archibald was the seventh son of the third Duke of Hamilton, and had in his time served in the Royal Navy and in Parliament, and was to be a Lord of the Admiralty, Governor of Greenwich Hospital, and Governor of Jamaica. At the time of his son's birth he represented Lanark in the House of Commons. Despite these public offices he seems to have been a person of little or no consequence; indeed, it must be confessed that he, too, is chiefly remembered, rightly or wrongly, as *un mari complaisant*.

If Hamilton's father passes as something of a cipher, the same cannot be said of his mother. Lady Archibald was herself a Hamilton, being the daughter of the sixth Earl of Abercorn. She was married in September 1719, her husband having been twice left a widower without children. His third marriage was certainly to make up in fruitfulness what the previous two had lacked, for Lady Jane Hamilton was to bring ten children into the world, of whom William was the fourth and youngest son.

Whether Lady Archibald was in the fullest sense the mistress of Frederick, Prince of Wales, is a fact which has never been completely proved. That she enjoyed the reputation of being his mistress is a fact which has been well established on the evidence of the far from friendly memoirs of John, Lord Hervey. Her attachment to the Prince began when her youngest son was little more than an infant, and reached its triumph in 1736 when she became Lady of the Bedchamber and Mistress of the Robes to the Princess of Wales at a salary of nine hundred pounds a year. That she succeeded in winning the friendship of the Prince's young bride is perhaps an indication of the basic innocence of her relationship with the Prince. Lord Hervey would have us believe that it was simply due to the lady's cleverness, or rather to her cunning and ability at intrigue; but Lord Hervey is a most unfriendly witness.

Horace Walpole, on the other hand, who was to live on the most cordial and friendly terms with William Hamilton, had no hesitation in including his friend's mother among the favourite mistresses of the Prince of Wales, adding in his *Memoirs* that she had been 'neither young nor handsome' within the memory of her lover. She was, he declared, 'very agreeable and artful', and 'governed absolutely at the prince's court'. Walpole's description can hardly count as flattery, but might almost seem so in comparison with what Lord Hervey had to say: 'Lady Archibald Hamilton was not young, had never been pretty, and had lost at least as much of that small share of beauty she once possessed as it is usual for women to do at five-and-thirty, and after having lain many years by a man old enough to be her father and being the mother of ten children'. Of the poor husband he merely says that he was 'of so quiet, so secure and contented a temper, that he seemed cut out to play the passive character his wife and the Prince had graciously allotted him'.[4]

It was in the shadow of the court of Frederick, Prince of Wales, with its background of scandal, intrigue, and bitter enmity, that William Hamilton formed his earliest impressions of life and of human nature. It was a court entirely dominated by the unedifying quarrel between the Prince and his royal parents, a quarrel so degrading and squalid as to be unsurpassed in the annals of royalty generally and of the House of Hanover in particular, a dynasty in whose service Hamilton was destined to spend the whole of his adult life. The atmosphere, however, was not entirely clouded by stormy and cantankerous exchanges between the King, the Queen, and the Prince. Even Frederick had his moments of grace. When not quarrelling with his father he was collecting pictures; during intervals of argument with his mother he found time to play the 'cello. If his character as a man of taste, a patron of art and literature, has perhaps been exaggerated, it cannot be denied that it existed, and under happier circumstances might have had the chance to develop and flourish. Lady Archibald was a cultivated and educated woman who could appeal to this side of the Prince's nature, and in her son, whose life was to be spent in courts and in coping with the foibles of royalty, a love of art and music was to predominate.

For all her encouragement of the Prince's more intellectual interests, Lady Archibald was fully involved in the machinations of his court, and was present on the most deplorable occasion of all when Frederick rushed his pregnant wife from Hampton Court to St. James's Palace after she had started her labour, in order that his child should not be born under his parents' roof. In her favour it must be said that Lady Archibald begged the Prince to abandon this foolish and cruel plan; but when he insisted she followed the grim procession and was able, by borrowing warming-pans and napkins from neighbouring houses, and by putting the Princess to bed between tablecloths because there were no sheets in the deserted palace, to make such arrangements as were possible for her mistress to be delivered of what the Queen later described as a 'poor, little, ugly she-mouse'.

Queen Caroline, when she arrived on the scene, bitterly admonished the Mistress of the Robes for having permitted the Prince to act with such madness, but Lady Archibald was able to turn aside the royal rebuker by looking hard in the direction of the Prince and saying: 'You see, Sir', in an audible voice. This reply, as Lord Hervey pointed out, 'was so prudent and judicious an answer, as it intimated everything that could be urged in her justification, without directly giving him up'. Hervey, who did not admire Lady Archibald, was compelled to add that he could not help thinking that chance put the reply into her mouth. In fact she showed herself fully qualified to become the mother of a diplomatist.[5] As for the unfortunate 'she-mouse' whose entry into this world was so unpropitious, she was destined to live for seventy-six years, marry Prince Charles of Brunswick, and become the mother-in-law of King George IV.

It was, however, the Prince's second child and eldest son who was to be most closely associated with the fourth son of the Mistress of the Robes. The future King George III was born on the 4th of June 1738, and William Hamilton was always to be known as his foster-brother. He was so described at the time of his death, as well as on several other occasions during his lifetime. It was this childhood relationship with his future monarch which, according to the author of his obituary notice in the *Annual Register*, 'laid the foundation of that gracious attachment and friendship with which he was honoured by the King, through the whole of his public service.' Hamilton was seven and a half years older than the young Prince George, but his mother's influential position at the Court of the Prince's father brought him into close contact with this lonely and rather timid child. The Prince had, indeed, little chance of meeting anyone who was not a nominee of the all-powerful Lady Archibald. By 1741 she had placed so many members of her family at the court that Frederick told Sir William Stanhope that whenever he met anyone at Canton House whom he did not know, he simply said 'your humble servant, Mr. Hamilton', on the fairly certain assumption that they would answer to that name.

The association between Hamilton and the Prince was to remain close until the former left for Naples at the age of thirty-four to take up his post as Envoy, an appointment which also sprang from the 'immediate protection'[6] of King George III. It was only in the very last years of his life, when the relationship between his second wife and the hero of the Nile had become too notorious to pass unobserved, that a decided coolness was noticeable on the part of the King towards his old friend.

When Hamilton was nine years old he was sent to Westminster School. The choice was fortunate, for during a period when flogging seemed to be the chief occupation of English school masters, Westminster, under the guidance of Dr. John Nicoll, enjoyed a rare reputation for enlightenment. It was of this school, where he was a pupil some two years after Hamilton left, that Edward Gibbon wrote: 'I shall always be ready to join in the common opinion that our public schools, which have produced so many eminent characters, are the best adapted to the genius and constitution of the English people.' Unfortunately he modified this high opinion by adding that 'our seminaries of learning do not exactly correspond with the precept of the Spartan King "that the child should be instructed in the arts which will be useful to the man" since a finished scholar may emerge from the head of Westminster or Eton in total ignorance of the business and conversation of English Gentlemen in the latter end of the eighteenth century.'

Here Gibbon was being rather hard on his old school, where he spent only a very brief time, and that constantly interrupted by periods of illness. In fact, under Nicoll, Westminster seems to have been a comparatively civilised place. If Hamilton began to develop his tastes as an amateur of the arts during this period at school (and this seems very likely), it may be said of Westminster, if only as a somewhat negative compliment, that at least it did not attempt to flog these tastes out of him, as many English public schools, both then and since, would have considered it their duty to do.

That Hamilton did indeed begin to develop his artistic and scientific interests while still at school may be surmised from a close attachment he made there, which was to last until the close of his life. This, surprisingly enough, was with the son of the same Lord Hervey whose venomous comments on Hamilton's mother have already been quoted. Fortunately for the friendship between William Hamilton and Frederick Hervey these *Memoirs* were to remain hidden from the world for another hundred years. The young Hervey, later to be Bishop of Derry and Earl of Bristol (thus, as Horace Walpole did not fail to observe, becoming the first Earl-Bishop since William the Conqueror's brother Odo, Bishop of Bayeux and Earl of Kent) was to develop into one of the most eccentric characters of the eighteenth century. But before all else he was to become one of the greatest collectors of *objets d'art* of his day, gathering up, and dispatching to his great mansion at Ickworth, innumerable specimens of statues, pictures, busts, vases and antiques of every description, which he bought at vast expense during his many absences from his diocese on prolonged European journeys.

It must surely have been a common taste in *virtù* which first brought these two boys together, for this was to be their common interest through life. Hervey always addresses his friend in his many letters as his dear old school-fellow, and their friendship survived the years despite the excessively odd behaviour of the Earl-Bishop (including an absence of eleven consecutive years from his diocese, an appearance at Rome in full Anglican canonicals, and a short spell in a Milanese prison) which must often have tried the patience of one of His Britannic Majesty's representatives at an Italian Court.

It was with such friends as Frederick Hervey, who combined a boisterous and excitable temperament with his love of art, and Lord Stormont, who like Hamilton was to make a career in diplomacy, that the years at school were passed. In Hamilton's last year at Westminster the country was convulsed by the invasion of Prince Charles Edward's army from Scotland, but such was the authority of the headmaster, and such the respect in which he was held, that the school remained calm and tempers under rigid control during those anxious but exciting months. The year 1745 was also to see the end of Lady Archibald Hamilton's rule over the court of the Prince of Wales. In June of that year Horace Walpole informed Mann that she left the Prince's household 'with a pension of twelve hundred a year'. As this sum was three hundred pounds in excess of her previous salary we must assume that Walpole was misinformed or that Lady Archibald was unusually fortunate.

One other family event which occurred during Hamilton's school days was, in the sequel, considerably to effect his future life. On the 16th May 1742, his sister Elizabeth was married to Francis, Lord Brooke, afterwards first Earl of Warwick. The connection between this marriage and Lord Nelson's mistress may seem remote, but it was the second son of Lord and Lady Warwick, William Hamilton's favourite nephew Charles Francis Greville, born on the 12th of May 1749, who would be the link connecting the obscure Amy Lyon with the man who raised her from mistress to wife, a position which she was her self to change for that of mistress to the most famous sailor of the age, with results so unfortunate to the fame and reputation of her husband.

When Hamilton left school he knew that he would have to make his own way in the world. It was true that he belonged to the ruling aristocratic class whose position and authority in the middle of the eighteenth century were still impregnable and unassailed. It was also true that he had virtually no income, and no settled position or inheritance waiting for him. There was an alarming tradition of younger sons going to the bad, and the debtors' prison was no respecter of rank. At school he had developed cultivated tastes and interests which would greatly have enhanced and adorned a life of elegant refinement and leisure. Such an existence, so agreeable to contemplate, was not to be his lot. He knew that if he were to enjoy the pleasures of connoisseurship and collecting, of scientific observation or philosophical speculation, the means had either to be earned or the desire denied.

For a penniless sprig of the nobility in those days there were only two alternatives open to him if he were to survive in the environment into which he had been born and within the limits of which he hoped to live; he must either marry an heiress or find some secure and lucrative place. In due time William Hamilton was to do both.

1. 16 January 1776.
2. *Vide Glenbervie Journals*, Vol. I, p. 340. According to DNB he was born in Scotland.
3. Morrison, 95.
4. *Lord Hervey's Memoirs*, Vol. II, p. 475.
5. *Vide Lord Hervey's Memoirs*, Vol. III, p. 762.
6. *Annual Register* for 1803, p. 503.

CHAPTER II

Soldier to Statesman

On leaving school William Hamilton went into the army. He did not attend a university. In this he suffered no great loss for at this period the ancient seats of learning were not notable for intellectual activity. Their slumber was deep and profound. For young men from humbler spheres than Hamilton's they served a certain purpose, for at College a man might find an aristocratic patron who could supply the first step on the ladder of ecclesiastical preferment, or who might be looking for a companion for the Grand Tour, or a Tutor for his younger brothers. The grandson of the Duke of Hamilton and foster-brother of Prince George of Wales had no need to hunt for patrons. As for his intellectual tastes, already formed, these would have found little encouragement among the dons of Oxford whose 'dull and deep potations' were shortly afterwards to engage the ironic attention of Edward Gibbon. The idea of entering one of the Scottish universities, where the light of learning still shone, might have been more profitable, but does not seem to have occurred to his parents, though their ancestry should have encouraged them to consider it.

Hamilton began his career as a soldier just over a month after his sixteenth birthday, being commissioned as an ensign in the Third Regiment of Foot Guards on the 27th of January 1747. It was by no means unusual for boys to enter the services at this tender age; indeed, both the army and the navy would accept lads even younger. Nelson was only twelve years and three months old when he was first rated as a midshipman, and this was almost a quarter of a century after Hamilton's military career had begun.

The war of the Austrian Succession was still in progress. Hamilton served in Holland under the Duke of Cumberland, who had returned to the command of the continental army after defeating Prince Charles at the battle of Culloden in the previous year, when he earned for himself the lasting title of 'Butcher'. Not much is known of Hamilton's service in the last year of this war, but he was very probably present when Cumberland met the redoubtable Marshal Saxe and was defeated at the battle of Lauffelt in July 1747. It was the great Marshal of France's last victory but an occasion of no very great distinction for the Duke of Cumberland, who was driven from the field. Perhaps this was why, if present, Hamilton did not refer to it in later years.

When the war ended with the Treaty of Aix-la-Chapelle, Hamilton, though continuing his life as a soldier, was able to devote his attention once more to the arts of peace. He was already an accomplished violin player, and in 1750, began to take lessons from the great Giardini, who first came to London in the same year. This distinguished artist had previously played in the orchestra of the San Carlo opera house at Naples where his extraordinary virtuosity had been rewarded by the composer Jommelli with a box on the ear after the violinist had interpolated a brilliant but unsolicited cadenza into one of the master's works. Giardini is said never to have forgotten this lesson, but it is to be hoped, at least for his young pupil's sake, that he spared his own scholars the same treatment. Hamilton remained devoted to the violin all his life. Later on, in Naples, he would always have one or two musicians among his servants, so that he could entertain himself and his guests to trios and quartets.

His interest in the arts soon brought him into contact with Horace Walpole and his circle, especially after he became aide-de-camp to Walpole's favourite cousin Henry Seymour Conway, afterwards Field-Marshal. Walpole described Hamilton as 'picture-mad', adding that he would soon 'ruin himself in virtu-land.'[1] These words were written at the time of Hamilton's appointment as envoy to Naples and after his financial position had been improved by marriage to an heiress. Probably Walpole did not know that Hamilton had in fact almost suffered this fate in his young bachelor days, when the little collection of pictures he had made had to be sold to pay his debts. He never forgot this sad episode and referred to it when, as a man of fifty, he wrote some sound advice to his nephew Charles Greville, another impoverished younger son: 'I was obliged to sell my collection of pictures once, on which I doated, rather than bear to be dunned.'[2] Only those who are themselves 'picture-mad' can appreciate what this must have meant to the youthful dilettante.

The year 1751 saw the death of Frederick, Prince of Wales, the 'poor Fred' of the song, 'who was alive and is dead' and who was not greatly mourned either by those who would have been his subjects or by his august parent. The King, on hearing the news while playing cards, contented himself with the remark '*Il est mort*' without adding any words of qualification or regret, though Walpole tells us that he looked extremely pale and shocked. As a result of this death Hamilton's 'foster-brother' became Prince of Wales and immediate heir to the throne, and shortly afterwards Hamilton was himself appointed as Equerry to the Prince, a post which he was to hold for five years, and to which he was reappointed when the Prince succeeded to the throne. This position brought him once more into close contact with his childhood's friend, though not so much as to prevent a visit to Paris to improve his knowledge of the French language. It was here that he met General Wolfe, the future conqueror of Quebec, who referred to the young man as his 'friend and companion'.

In June 1753, at the age of twenty-two years and six months, Hamilton was promoted Captain, which was to be the highest rank he would hold in the army. He was to see active service again with the outbreak of the Seven Years War, when he took part in the expedition against Rochefort in 1757. Perhaps 'active' is not the right word to describe this early attempt at amphibious warfare, which could hardly be called a success, but it was while serving in this affair as General Conway's aide that we get one of our few glimpses of Hamilton as a soldier. Once again it is Horace Walpole who tells the story. While they were on the isle of Aix 'Mr. Conway was so careless and so fearless as to be trying a burning-glass on a bomb—yes, a bomb, the match of which had been cut short to prevent its being fired by any accidental sparks of tobacco; Hamilton snatched the glass out of Mr. Conway's hand before he had at all thought what he was about'[3]. It would have been an unfortunate end to a promising career if he had been blown to fragments through the careless and absent-minded conduct of a senior officer. Walpole describes this story as showing Conway as being 'more like himself', an opinion which suggests that the job of being his aide-de-camp was not without its risks and dangers. Fortunately Hamilton survived both the war and the appointment.

In fact Hamilton resigned his commission before the war was over, an act which in those more civilised days of professional wars and professional soldiers did not give rise to any special comment from the non-combatant part of the population. He had decided that the army was unlikely to offer him the sort of position for which he hoped. An itinerant and unsettled life, which was all a military career had to offer, was unsuitable to a man whose interests lay in the picture gallery and the study, and who had political rather than warlike ambitions. Furthermore Hamilton was about to take a step which would greatly improve his financial situation and make him independent; he was about to marry an heiress.

The young lady in question was Catherine Barlow, the daughter of Hugh Barlow of Lawrenny Hall, Pembroke. The family also had a house in Clarges Street, and it was in London that the couple met. The Barlows came from a family of Pembrokeshire squires, and Catherine was heiress to an estate which was estimated to bring in an income in the neighbourhood of eight thousand pounds a year. For the bride's family it was undoubtedly satisfactory to form a connection with a young man so closely allied to the nobility, and for the bridegroom the promise of an inheritance which would bring him financial security was sufficient compensation for taking a step which in other respects was not particularly welcome, though the bride's family was certainly a respectable one and the young lady herself accomplished and cultivated if not particularly beautiful. It was a thoroughly eighteenth-century arrangement.

Hamilton frankly admitted in later years that he had made a marriage of convenience, a confession he could make with all the more sincerity since he came to respect and admire a wife for whom he had never felt romantic love. But money was not the only thought that influenced his choice; he knew that in Catherine Barlow he would have a sympathetic companion whose tastes were compatible with his own. 'A disagreeable rich devil the Devil himself cou'd not have tempted me to marry,' he told his nephew Charles Greville over twenty years later,[4] 'but

I have really found a lasting comfort in having married (something against my inclination) a virtuous, good-temper'd woman with a little independent fortune to which we cou'd fly shou'd all other dependencies fail, and live decently without being obliged to anyone.'

The reader must not blame Hamilton for holding a view of marriage which was entirely accepted in his own day and generation. He would have been dismissed as a fool had he married a penniless beauty; as it was, he could be congratulated on finding a companion in life who could be expected to support him in so many other ways than those which sprang simply from her financial inheritance. In fact, the marriage was a successful one. Before condemning the system under which Hamilton made his first marriage the romantically inclined critic should consider very carefully how it compared with his second.

It would be difficult to find anyone more completely different than Catherine Barlow from the boisterous beauty who would eventually succeed her. She was not remarkable in her personal appearance; indeed, she was rather plain, and her nature was gentle, retiring, and deeply religious. She shared with Hamilton a love for music, being generally accepted as one of the best harpsichord players of her day. Her personality was sympathetic and young people, especially those like William Beckford who considered themselves star-crossed and misunderstood, felt strongly drawn to her. To such people she was able to give help and understanding as well as sound advice, and they loved her in return. Beckford called her an angel of purity. Describing her as he had first known her at Naples he recalled how she lived uncorrupted in the midst of that easy-going court. 'You must have known what that court was', he added, 'to comprehend this in its full meaning. I never saw so heavenly-minded a creature.' Of her playing he wrote: 'Her power of musical execution was wonderful—so sweetly soft was her touch—she seemed as if she had thrown her own essence into the music. I used to listen to her like one entranced.'[5]

Hamilton's first wife never enjoyed good health. She seems always to have been delicate though the exact nature of her complaint remains a mystery. Horace Walpole declared at the time of their departure for Naples that she was 'dying of an asthma', while others spoke vaguely of 'nerves'. It was generally considered that Catherine's health was one of the factors that determined Hamilton to accept the post at Naples when it was offered to him, as it was felt that the mild southern climate would prolong her life, a hope which fortunately proved true, for she was to survive at Naples for another eighteen years for all Walpole's sombre reports.

They were married in January 1758. In May of the same year Hamilton resigned his commission. At that time there was no question of his adopting a diplomatic career. His father-in-law died shortly after the marriage and for some time Hamilton was occupied in the management of his wife's estates in Wales, which lay in the neighbourhood of Milford Haven. Their time was divided between London, with its busy social life as well as its picture sales which so interested

Hamilton, and the rural life of Pembrokeshire, where he enjoyed the occupations of a squire and land-owner eager to improve his property. It was an agreeable existence but not one that would content indefinitely a man of Hamilton's energy and intellectual adventurousness. After almost three years of marriage, however, the chance of greater opportunities occurred for him when in the autumn of 1760 the aged King died and Hamilton's 'foster-brother' succeeded to the throne as King George III.

The King's dislike for the existing Ministry of Pitt and Newcastle, perhaps the most competent that the country had experienced, was well known, as was the ambition of the Earl of Bute, the new monarch's friend and mentor. The death of the old King was a signal to many people in the world of politics and the Court that the time had come for them to retire graciously or make terms as best they could with their new master. For others it meant that their moment had come at last.

In the election that followed the accession it was clear that those in the confidence of the young King, who might form a Court party in Parliament, would be in a strong position, in that age of patronage, if they wished to be nominated as candidates for the House of Commons. It was natural that the twenty-two-year-old King should welcome Hamilton, now rising thirty, as one who could be relied upon to vote in his interest in the new Parliament which was elected in 1761. Hamilton was adopted as one of the two candidates for Midhurst in Sussex, and was duly returned by an electorate who knew what was expected of them by their patron and landlord Viscount Montague, who controlled the borough. Hamilton's fellow member was the soldier-dramatist General John Burgoyne, later to achieve fame in the war of American Independence as he had already achieved notoriety by eloping with a daughter of the Earl of Derby.

Hamilton passed four years as a member of the House of Commons where he does not seem to have distinguished himself in any way except, like Gibbon, by supporting his party 'with many a sincere and *silent* vote'. But he must have enjoyed his time as a member, for twenty years later he wrote to Charles Greville from Naples saying that he had some notion of offering himself as Member for Pembroke,[6] though it must be admitted that the reason he then gave for this move was that if he were again in Parliament he might be allowed to stay longer in England when he came there on leave.

His interest in domestic politics certainly did not cease when he took up his post as an ambassador. He remained eager to know of the ebb and flow of the political tide as well as the rise and fall of individual reputations. He relied on his nephew Greville to keep him well informed about 'who loses and who wins: who's in, who's out'. Official news of Parliamentary happenings, which it was his duty to know about, he could obtain from the circulars of the Secretary of State. Greville provided him with glimpses behind the scenes and could describe, not always without malice, the intrigues of members, their hopes and fears, their successes and failures. The fact that so many of those involved were Hamilton's close relatives or friends added considerably to the interest and enjoyment he derived from these bulletins of Parliamentary news.

It cannot be said, however, that Hamilton made any mark as a Member of Parliament. His wife's delicate health was undoubtedly a handicap, and must quite soon have made him consider the possibility of taking a post abroad, should a suitable opening occur. By 1763 she was enough of an invalid to prevent a visit to Scotland. In May of that year Hamilton's niece, Lady Garlies, wrote to him from Edinburgh: 'I am sorry Mrs. Hamilton's health is such as makes it impossible for one to hope to see you here. Lady Cathcart[7] mentions her having been plagued with the asthma. I hope she has got the better of it now, at least for some time.'[8] Duty to his ailing wife as well as inclination and ambition would help him to reach a decision when the promotion of James Gray to be Minister Plenipotentiary at the Court of Spain left a vacancy at Naples early in 1764. A successful career in politics would require a greater fortune than Hamilton could command, despite his many influential connections. A post as envoy abroad would offer scope for his energy as well as additional emoluments; the mild climate of Naples would be ideal for his wife's fragile health. He applied for the post, and, sure of the benevolent interest of his royal foster-brother, was duly appointed. In August his credentials and instructions as Envoy Extraordinary to the Court of Naples were handed to him, and on the 17th of November he arrived in the city where he was to remain *en poste* for a period of nearly thirty-seven years.

Shortly after the first rumours of Hamilton's new appointment were whispered he received a letter that gives us a vivid glimpse of the world of place-seekers who surrounded the Court, which had been the background of his life for as long as he could remember. 'Am I to wish you joy of going to Naples?' the writer, who signed himself H. Minchin, began by asking. 'I hear from so many people that it is to be so, that I cannot help giving credit to it and I beg you will inform me about it as it will give me much pleasure to hear that it will turn out to your satisfaction.' After this polite flourish the writer came straight to the point of his letter. 'It occurred to me yesterday in talking to a friend of yours on this subject that I might perhaps do you some service in this affair and at the same time a thing which would be agreeable to me. You told me that if your Naples scheme should succeed you wished to change your Rank of Equerry to that of Groom of the Bedchamber as abroad *Chambellan* sounds much better than *Ecuyer*, but not to ask for the additional salary and only to have your present Pay as Equerry. The only objection the Ministry could possibly make to granting this at once and naming you of the Bedchamber is that it would lessen the number of Equerries or put them to the additional expense of an Equerry's pay. Now if it would be of any sort of use to you and forward your scheme you may inform Mr. Grenville that if he will have you appointed of the Bedchamber I will succeed to your place as Equerry and take upon me the Trouble, the Expence and the Attendance *with out drawing any salary at all.* (By the Bye) ask him if this is not the first offer of this sort he has had since he came into the Ministry . . . '[9]

History does not relate whether in fact Hamilton became 'of the Bedchamber' or Mr. Minchin achieved his ambition of becoming an unpaid Equerry, but the scene of ministerial and court intrigue which the letter depicts was no less typical (though a good deal less innocent) of the Court of King George III, which Hamilton was now leaving, than of the Court of King Ferdinand IV of Naples, at which he was about to make his bow.

1. Walpole to Mann, 8 June 1764.
2. Morrison, 95.
3. Walpole to Mann, 20 November 175.
4. Morrison, 95.
5. Lewis Melville: *Life and Letters of William Beckford*, p. 94.
6. Morrison, 92.
7. Hamilton's sister Jane had married the ninth Lord Cathcart in 1753.
8. Morrison, 4.
9. British Museum: Add. MSS 42096, f. 5.

CHAPTER III

The Two Sicilies

The Kingdoms of Naples and Sicily, or the Two Sicilies,[1] though claiming a history that went back to the ancient Norman and Swabian dynasties, had only known independence as a modern Kingdom for about thirty years when William Hamilton began his residence as British Envoy in November 1764.

They were fated always to be governed by foreign dynasties. The Swabians had given place to the House of Anjou, and the Angevins in their turn to the short-lived rule of the Aragonese. Normans, Germans, French and Spaniards had in turn occupied the throne of this Italian realm. Frederick of Aragon, driven from his throne in 1501, was the last king to hold personal court in Naples until the arrival of Charles of Bourbon over two hundred and thirty years later. For this long period (from 1501 until 1734) the Kingdoms had been ruled by Viceroys, first of Spain and then of Austria, during which time they had become little better than provinces, the once proud title of King being swallowed up in the sonorous dignities borne by the reigning monarchs in Madrid or Vienna.

The two Sicilies owed the return of an independent King to the ambition of an Italian princess. Elizabeth Farnese, descendant of a Pope, last of the ducal house of Parma and Piacenza, wife of the King of Spain, had spent many years and much energy, with which nature had plentifully endowed her, in the pursuit of thrones for her children, the Infants Don Charles and Don Philip. As the second wife of Philip V, this formidable princess had the mortification of seeing the throne of Spain and the Indies descending to the son of her predecessor as Queen, while her own children, in the normal course of events, were unlikely to inherit more than a younger son's portion. It was therefore in her native Italy that she sought a patrimony for them, and more especially for Don Charles, the elder. In the dynastic game that dominated the affairs of the Italian peninsula she held two trump cards. The reigning families of Parma and Tuscany were in rapid decline, ruled by effete and childless princes. As a Farnese her title to Parma was clear; as a descendant also of the House of Tuscany she cast covetous eyes in the direction of Florence where, hidden from the public gaze in the recesses of the Pitti Palace, the last of the Medici, fat and indolent, ruled his subjects from his bed, from which he was rarely, if ever, known to rise.

After much diplomatic activity the Duchy of Parma was secured to Charles and the Grand Duke of Tuscany was persuaded to adopt him as his heir. The powers recognised these settlements by the second treaty of Vienna in 1731. Spain, however, had never reconciled herself to the loss of Naples, which had been handed over to the Habsburgs under the terms of the treaty of Utrecht, so when the death of Augustus II in 1733 plunged Europe into the war of the Polish Succession, the Infant Charles, encouraged by Elizabeth Farnese and with his father's blessing, set out to conquer the southern kingdom.

His campaign was successful and on 10 May 1734, the eighteen-year-old prince entered Naples amidst the rejoicings of the people who were glad to see the departure of the Austrian Viceroys and to welcome once more a king of their own. 'Their hopes in the new sovereign were great', wrote the Neapolitan historian Pietro Colletta, 'and their joy was increased by the gold and silver which the treasurer scattered profusely in the streets of the city.' On 15 June Charles published a decree of his father Philip V in which the King of Spain ceded his rights in the kingdom to his son, who was forthwith proclaimed King of the Two Sicilies. The following year, on 3 June, he was solemnly crowned in the cathedral of Palermo as Charles III.

It was the intention of Charles III to rule as a benevolent despot, but unlike that other philosopher-King, his almost exact contemporary Frederick II of Prussia (who ascended his throne in 1740) Charles's rule in Naples was peaceful. He had no military tastes, could only with difficulty be persuaded to review his troops, and seldom wore uniform. The Kingdom of the Two Sicilies was to know a long period of peace under this king and his successor, though it must be admitted that the peace of the Kingdom during the war of Austrian Succession was due not so much to the pacific intentions of Charles III as to the arrival of the British fleet in the Bay of Naples with the threat to bombard the city if the King refused to remain neutral. Neutrality was observed, but when the fleet sailed away the King greatly strengthened the fortifications of his capital.

Charles III's reign was one of mild reform in the political sphere and of gradual growth and prosperity in the economic. The Marquis Tanucci, a Tuscan professor of law who had first served Charles in Parma, was appointed Minister of Justice and was soon to become the King's most powerful servant. Born in 1698, appointed Minister in 1734, Tanucci would still be in power when Hamilton presented his credentials to Charles's successor in 1764. He continued to hold office until 1776.

A great period of building followed the restoration of independence to the Kingdom of Naples, while the city was embellished with the treasures of the Farnese family which had been removed from Parma when that Duchy was ceded to Francis of Lorraine in 1737. To these great works of art were added those revealed by the excavations of the buried cities of Herculaneum and Pompeii which were carried out under the direct patronage of the King. In 1755 he founded the Royal Herculanean Academy to supervise and co-ordinate the work and to undertake the issue of a regular catalogue of discoveries. Meanwhile he had built himself a country palace at Portici, close to the menacing slopes of Vesuvius, and work was started on a royal villa at Capodimonte, with its splendid view of the city and bay of Naples, and the vast palace of Caserta, some sixteen miles from the capital. In the surrounding game preserves Charles could indulge in his untiring love for the chase, that characteristic passion of the House of Bourbon. In Naples itself he built an opera house next to the royal palace. It was the largest theatre in Italy and was named San Carlo in honour of the patron saint of its founder.

Charles III reigned as King of the Two Sicilies for twenty-five years. His reign was ended not by his own death but by that of his half-brother Ferdinand VI of Spain. This event was not unexpected at the Neapolitan court for the Spanish monarch had for some time been completely insane. A profound melancholy had descended on him after the death of his wife, though even before this he had been subject to fits of depression when the only thing which brought him any solace had been the voice of Farinelli, the famous *castrato*, who had been his favourite singer for many years. But now violence had replaced melancholy and no song, however sweet, could bring order to his distracted mind. In this pitiable state the King of Spain died on 10 August 1759. By his death Charles succeeded to the Spanish dominions.

The death of Ferdinand VI placed Charles in a dilemma. By international agreement it was decreed that the thrones of Spain and the Two Sicilies should remain separated. By his marriage with Maria Amalia of Saxony, which had taken place in 1738, Charles had three sons, but the elder, Don Philip, had been an imbecile from birth. In order to settle the succession to his various kingdoms it became the sad duty of the King to show publicly the inability of his eldest son ever to undertake the duties of sovereignty. The Prince was therefore examined by a commission of the leading nobles, foreign ambassadors, and eminent physicians, who pronounced his imbecility to be of such a nature as to disqualify him for ever from the throne, and this decision was, by the King's order, published to the world.

This painful business settled, Charles III declared his second son, the Infant Charles Anthony, heir to the throne of Spain and the Spanish dominions in the New World, and formally abdicated the Kingdom of the Two Sicilies to his third son the Infant Ferdinand, who became thereby Ferdinand IV of Naples and III of Sicily was well as King of Jerusalem, Infant of Spain, Duke of Parma, Piacenza and Castro, and hereditary Grand Duke of Tuscany. The ceremony which bestowed these splendid titles (half of which were empty ones) on the new King took place in the Royal Palace of Naples on 6 October 1759. The Prince who succeeded to them was eight years old.

Before he sailed for Spain Charles III appointed a Council of Regency to govern in his son's name until he reached his majority, which was fixed at the age of sixteen. Of the members of this council, which numbered eight in all, only two need be brought to the attention of the reader. One was Tanucci, who would not only be the virtual ruler of the country but who would also act as the personal agent of the King of Spain; and the other was the Prince of San Nicandro, who was appointed tutor to the young King.

Before wholly condemning this last nobleman for his almost total failure in his task as royal mentor one important fact must be remembered. The terrible threat of madness hung over the head of the young King of Naples like the ominous cloud that hovered above the crater of Vesuvius. His grandfather Philip V had ended his days in mental stupor; his uncle Ferdinand VI had died insane; his elder brother was an imbecile. His father, who himself dreaded this frightful family inheritance, believed that an open-air life, hunting, and plenty of wholesome physical exercise, was the best safeguard against the hereditary malady. The formal education of Ferdinand IV was sadly neglected, and it has been held against the regents—and even against his father—that they encouraged this in order to consolidate their own power at the expense of an almost illiterate monarch. The subject of the King's neglected education was to feature prominently in Hamilton's early dispatches. Before passing judgement on the tutor for his undoubted negligence, the responsibility thrust on him by his knowledge of the mental history of the Spanish Bourbons must not be forgotten.

At the time when William Hamilton arrived in Naples it was, after Paris, the largest city on the European continent, and by its position amongst the most beautifully situated in the world. In its crowded streets rich and poor lived in close and lively proximity. In order to call on some great noble the visitor often had to pass through squalid scenes of poverty and filth even in the lower regions of the *palazzo* itself until, on reaching the *piano nobile*, the door would be flung open onto a suite of apartments of indescribable luxury. The King of Naples was said to number among his subjects, who totalled in all about four million, over a hundred princes, more than one hundred and fifty dukes, one hundred and seventy-three marquesses, and an even vaster number of counts, barons, and lesser nobles. The richer of these lived with ostentatious outward display in their splendid palaces, attended by regiments of flunkeys; the lesser nobility often had few worldly possessions beyond their title and pride of birth. Between these nobles of greater or lesser degree and the teeming multitude of the poor, whose only refuge was a mild climate, came the black throng of the clergy. In the whole kingdom twenty-eight out of every thousand were, according to Pietro Colletta, ecclesiastics of one sort or another, whether priest, monk, or nun. In Naples alone, he claimed, there were more than sixteen thousand of these subjects of the Church. Of all classes of society it was the lowest, the despised *lazzaroni*, upon whom Ferdinand IV could rely for his most loyal support.

The King was thirteen years old and already looking forward to the proclamation of his majority in three years time when Hamilton drove in state to the Royal Palace to present his credentials. The Envoy conveyed the good wishes of his sovereign in a short speech in French, and left thoroughly satisfied by his reception. Of the young King he was to write: 'He is certainly a most gracious Prince, and the goodness of his heart is conspicuous in his countenance.'[2] Of this countenance the most prominent feature, even at this age, was a very large and rather bulbous nose, which was to gain for Ferdinand the name of *Il Re Nasone*. Hamilton was to attribute the 'particular attention' shown to him to 'the respectable Character His Majesty has been pleas'd to honor me with at this Court', little thinking that he was to remain at this post for the next thirty-seven years.

After these ceremonies Hamilton turned his attention to the more prosaic duties of his profession and drew up a memorandum 'Relative to the Revenues of the Kingdom of the Two Sicilies'.[3] Noting that five and a half Neapolitan ducats represented one pound sterling, he recorded that 'the annual sum raised upon the Kingdom of Naples is Ten Millions of Ducats, four of which only go into the King's Coffers. The rest is appropriated to the discharge of the large National debt of about Nineteen Millions Sterling contracted by large donations to Charles the fifth, Philip the second and their successors to assist them in their many expensive Wars and Enterprises.'

He next noted the way in which the money was raised. 'The greatest part of the Revenues are duty and customs. There are also three other articles called, *Dogana di foggia*, the *Adora* and the *Fuochi*. The first is a tax upon Sheep, at so much a head when they pass from the mountains to the plains of Apulia and produces Two Hundred and fifty thousand Ducats per Annum. It was practised by the Romans. The *Adora* is a sum paid by those who hold Fiefs of the Crown in lieu of personal service. The *Fuochi* is hearth money and produces about a million Ducats per annum'. It was typical of the antiquarian in Hamilton to mention in an official memorandum that the method of taxing sheep had been used by the Romans. He completed his report with a few more notes of a financial nature: 'The maintenance of the Fleet and Army amounts to above Two Millions of Ducats yearly. The expenses of the King's Household is reckoned about Four Hundred Thousand Ducats. The Government of Sicily three hundred and fifty thousand Ducats yearly.'

The cordiality which was to exist over so long a period between Hamilton and the King and government of Naples was expressed even before he arrived in a note to the Marquis Tanucci from the Secretary to the Neapolitan embassy in Paris, who had already made the acquaintance of the new British Envoy. The secretary was the Abbé Galiani who, though less than five feet in height, towered over his contemporaries in wit, scholarship and *esprit*. 'I was enamoured of him,' he told the Minister. 'Either I am grossly deceived or your Excellency will love him greatly, even more than Gray. He has more innocence and candour, and no less ability.'

With this friendly testimonial to herald his arrival Hamilton was soon able to establish himself as British Envoy, and he was quickly on excellent terms with the all-powerful Tanucci. But his happy relations with the government did not blind his eyes to the general state of the kingdom or prevent him from forming a dispassionate view of affairs. A severe famine had caused great distress in Naples in the year of his arrival. A letter addressed to Henry Seymour Conway almost a year later gives us a glimpse of some of the after-effects of this disaster, and also a view of the more sinister side of life in the capital.

'The Police is so bad here and justice so slack', he wrote on 1 October 1765, 'that irregularities of every kind gain ground daily, scarcely one day passing without two or three assassinations in this Capital. It is remark'd that since the late Scarcity (I may almost say Famine) Assassinations have been much more frequent owing to the common people at that time having resumed the custom of wearing long knives in their pockets which they then found necessary to make their way to the bakehouses and to protect their bread after they had purchas'd it, which custom (though directly contrary to law) they have not dropped, so that upon the slightest offence every man without ceremony revenges himself upon the spot. On Sunday last there were no less than five Assassinations, in, or near this City.'[4]

Naples then, as now, was a city of contrasts. The bay of serene beauty, the threatening volcano; the elegant palaces, the squalid slums; the cultivated and polished nobles, the sudden acts of violence or revenge. Hamilton was soon enslaved by the fascination of the place. At first, no doubt, he was startled and even possibly shocked by much of what he saw, at court no less than in the streets and alleyways of the city. Soon he got used to it; eventually he became a part of it.

For some years he would apply from time to time for other posts of more consequence and fret at the political inactivity and unimportance of his post. But it was his fate to remain where he was. Commenting on the well-known aphorism 'See Naples and die', the eighteenth-century traveller Henry Swinburne was to write: '*Vedi Napoli e poi mori* is the Neapolitan proverb; but I say, on the contrary, that after living in Naples it is impossible not to wish to *live* that one may return to it'[5] and soon his friend Hamilton would come heartily to agree with this sentiment. At length he was to become so much a part of the life of the city that he would probably also have agreed with the verdict of another British traveller who, many years later and meaning to pay him compliment, would write of the Envoy to the Court of King Ferdinand: 'As to Sir William Hamilton, he was a perfect Neapolitan both in mind and manners.'[6]

1. The mainland being 'Sicily beyond the Pharos' as distinct from Sicily proper.
2. B.M. Egerton MSS 2634 f. 91.
3. B.M. Add. MSS 42096 ff. 35-6.
4. B.M. Egerton MSS 2654 f. 84.
5. H. Swinburne: C*ourts of Europe at the Close of the Last Century*, Vol. I, p.141.
6. P. Lockhart Gordon: *Personal Memoirs*, Vol. II, p. 386.

CHAPTER IV

Discovering the Past

Shortly after reaching Naples Hamilton wrote a letter to his friend Lord Palmerston (father of Queen Victoria's Prime Minister) giving some impressions of his new home. No one doubted, when it was announced that William Hamilton had been appointed to Naples, that he would find much to interest himself there in addition to his official duties, and in this letter we get the first glimpse of the dilettante as opposed to the diplomat.

'I am much obliged to you for your kind remembrance of us and for the letter you was so good as to send me,' he wrote.[1] 'We had indeed a very rough passage and for Mrs. Hamilton, to whom the sea was quite a new object, it was dreadful. I found it very unpleasant though I have been more used to it. However here we are safe in a most delightful climate indeed and now the ceremony of presentations and visitings are over I begin to enjoy the many curiosities of nature and art with which you know this country abounds. I obeyed your commands and have got drawings of the Mausoleum and Triumphal Arch of St. Remy from Joli and will send it you the first good opportunity. I am heartily glad you found those ruins as well as I described them, for they pleased me much. When I am more settled and make any new discoveries here I will take the liberty of troubling you with a letter, and if there is anything in this part of the world that you think I can serve you in, I hope you will always command me. Mrs. Hamilton (who desires to be kindly remembered to your Lordship) is amazingly recovered since she came here. I am sure this mild climate will re-establish her entirely. I have just begun to look about me as I was determined to see nothing till I had finished all ceremonials; I admire the bronzes of Herculaneum most exceedingly, and the tour from the point of Micana to Pozzuoli is very classical and entertaining.'

This letter gives a good indication of the direction Hamilton's life was to take in the future. The 'many curiosities of nature and art' of which he wrote were to occupy all his leisure; he was to approach them not as an amateur (in the derogatory sense) passing away a few idle moments, but as a very intelligent and experienced observer. Soon the Royal Society and the Society of Antiquaries of London were to receive the first of a long series of letters and papers which were to add considerably to the store of human knowledge on those subjects in which he was especially interested. He brought with him to Naples an established reputation as a connoisseur and man of taste; to this he was to add very soon an interest amounting almost to a passion in the activities of Vesuvius, which in time made him an expert in volcanology respected by all the savants of his age. 'He laboured harder on the slopes of Vesuvius', wrote the author of the *Lives of the Founders of the British Museum*, 'than an exceptionally diligent craftsman would labour in a factory—had Naples possessed any. Within four years he ascended the famous mountain twenty-two times.'[2]

If the presence of Vesuvius was responsible for a new interest in Hamilton's life, everything in and around Naples encouraged his fascination for antiquity; volcanic eruptions as well as ruins and classical inscriptions were even to find their way into his diplomatic dispatches. His old friend Henry Seymour Conway was now one of the Secretaries of State and so was perhaps less surprised than might otherwise have been expected to receive a report on the all-powerful Neapolitan minister which referred only to his activities with regard to the excavations at Pompeii. 'The Marquis Tanucci,' Hamilton informed Conway on 12 November 1765.[3] 'who has the direction of the Antiquities here, has lately shewn his good taste by ordering that for the future the workmen employed in the search of Pompeii should not remove any inscriptions or paintings from the walls, nor fill up after they have search'd so that travellers will soon have an opportunity of walking the streets and seeing the houses of this Ancient City (which is infinitely more considerable than Herculaneum) as commodiously as Naples itself. The buildings are only bury'd in the ashes of pumice stone of Mount Vesuvius and not cover'd with Lava as Herculaneum is, so that when they are removed the City will be once more above the ground. The principal Gate of the town, a curious temple, and part of the Theatre are already clear'd; they are in wonderful preservation.'

In spite of Tanucci's orders the work was only carried on in a dilatory way, much to Hamilton's impatience. By the May of 1767 work on the excavations seemed to have slowed down considerably, though Hamilton was present at the discovery of a temple dedicated to Isis, and saw the ashes of the victims visible on the altars and the paintings 'as fresh as when they were first painted.'

In describing this discovery to Dr. Robertson, a Scottish clergyman who had formerly been tutor to his nephew Lord Greville, Hamilton did not disguise his irritation at the way things were being done. 'It would grieve you to see the dilatory and slovenly manner in which they proceed in the researches at Herculaneum and Pompeii' he told the Doctor.[4] 'Were they to proceed as they should do, every day might bring to light matter sufficient for a new volume. At Herculaneum they have in a manner given over searching, tho' it is very certain further discoveries might be made, and they have filled up every part which they had cleared. Except the theatre at Pompeii they employ about ten or twelve men only, and these improperly, for instead of entering the principal gate of the Town which was discovered about five years ago, they dip here and there in search of pieces of antiquity and then fill up.'

Hamilton had good reason to be angry at this, for not only was it futile, from the point of view of study, to fill up the excavations, it was also contrary to the orders issued by the Marquis Tanucci only three years before. After describing the 'pumice stones and light calcined matter' which covered the site, 'Judge, Sir,' his letter continues in an outburst of enthusiasm, 'how curious and interesting it would be were they to disclose the whole city, which I am convinced might be done at a very trifling expense, as this rubbish is removed with infinite care. I am at present at a little Villa between these Towns, and often visit them. This very day I was at Pompeii, and found them very little advanced since I was there about a month ago, the principal Gate still untouched. They had just cleared a square which certainly had been a sort of Barrack for the infantry, having found helmets and armour in several of the rooms. Several skeletons were found in one room and fetters of iron were also found in the same room which leaves no doubt of its having been their prison. A curious chapel of Isis was found very entire last year and is still left open, tho' they have carried off the paintings of the walls to the King's museum at Portici where they are confounded with the rest of the paintings. I would have wished that before they were removed an exact drawing of the Temple had been taken and the position of the paintings expressed therein, as they all related to the Cult of Isis, and would have been much more interesting published together than at random which will, I fear, be their fate. . .'

He ended his letter by saying 'I perceive this subject has carried me away.' It was to carry him a good deal further. His interest in the buried cities and in the treasure unearthed from them was not merely antiquarian. He tended to despise the collector whose interest in any *objet d'art* was bounded solely by an appreciation of its beauty or curiosity, and went so far as to train a pet monkey, in whose antics he delighted, to study a vase through a magnifying glass in mockery of these aesthetes. Hamilton believed that modern arts and modern craftsmen and designers could benefit by a more profound study of the antique and that a practical usefulness could result from the knowledge so gained. He was himself soon to take a hand in this work.

Pictures of Hamilton at this period show a distinctly aristocratic cast of countenance, a slightly hooked nose, and bushy eyebrows. His expression is intelligent and distinguished, but there is a hint of remoteness or reserve about him. The only picture of him with his first wife shows him sitting beside her as she plays the clavichord. His attitude is rather languid, with an elegant hand resting on the arm of the chair. On the table are a bundle of papers and his violin, which he appears just to have put down. A messenger crosses an open door in the back ground through which we catch a glimpse of the volcano with its plume of smoke.

The artist who painted this charming picture was David Allan, the Scottish portrait and *genre* painter who had arrived in Italy in 1768 with a recommendation to Hamilton from his sister Lady Cathcart. The Envoy, who was to extend his patronage to many other British artists during his years in Naples, clearly took to 'Lady Cathcart's little painter Allan', as he described him, adding generously that he was 'one of the greatest geniuses I ever met with; he is indefatigable.' The picture of Hamilton and his wife must have been painted at this time; the star and red riband of the Order of the Bath are a later addition, painted in after Hamilton had been raised to this dignity in 1772.

Sir Nathaniel Wraxall said of Hamilton after fifteen years in Naples that 'in his person, though tall and meagre, with a dark complexion, a very aquiline nose, and a figure which always reminded me of Rolando in *Gil Blas*, he had nevertheless such an air of intelligence, blended with distinction, in his countenance, as powerfully attracted and conciliated all who approached him.'[5] It was this gift of making himself approachable without loss of dignity which also struck Lady Craven. Though finding him 'a finished courtier' he had, she declared, 'none of that servility of manners, or that species of adulation, which is generally to be met with, but he preserved an independence which seemed to qualify him particularly for the diplomatic profession.'

Diplomatic duties were not excessively heavy during the early years at Naples, and there was plenty of time for agreeable expeditions to Pompeii or Herculaneum, descriptions of which as we have seen, would occasionally find their way into his dispatches. As the date for the proclamation of the King's majority drew near, however, there seems to have been something of a scramble among the Regents to feather their nests while the going was good. In September 1766 Hamilton felt obliged to comment on this to Lord Shelburne who had succeeded Conway as Secretary of State. His message was sent in cipher, prefaced with the explanation: 'I should not make so much use of the Cypher did not I plainly see that of late my letters from your Lordship's office have been opened.' The regency, he wrote, was due to expire in the following January. Faced with the possibility of future unemployment the Regents, Hamilton reported, making use of a quaint eighteenth-century expression, 'lose no time in winding up their bottoms and making themselves rich, and I am well assured that such a scene of bribery and corruption can be scarcely paralleled in History.' The Envoy found only one member of the regency council whose conduct escaped condemnation. 'The Marquis Tanucci', he concluded, 'is alone excepted; his character in that particular is unblemished.'[6]

Before he could regale the Secretary of State with accounts of the celebrations in honour of King Ferdinand's majority an event occurred which required Hamilton's close attention. On 1 January 1766, James Stuart, son of King James II, ended his long life of exile in his Roman palace. Britain had no representative at the Papal Court, which still recognised James as King, so that Sir Horace Mann at Florence and Hamilton at Naples were the closest British diplomats to the shadow court which had for so long surrounded the sad figure of the 'Old Pretender'.

The exiled Stuarts, though now of little or no political importance, were still something of a problem to British diplomats in Italy. Their presence attracted the interest and curiosity of English travellers who were eager to see them but careful not to be thought guilty of Jacobite sympathy. A motley entourage moved round them, some shady, some mere adventurers, others deeply sincere, but all likely to be of considerable embarrassment to a British ambassador loyal to the House of Hanover. Wherever the Stuarts went intrigue and plots followed them, and even Hamilton himself, 'foster brother' to King George, would have to defend his reputation, in later years, from a half-serious charge brought by an enemy of showing a little too much interest in one of the Pretender's agents.

The death of James Stuart caused Hamilton a certain anxiety. The Court of Spain had made use of the exiled royal family according to its own political purposes, and the Court of Spain was all-powerful at Naples so long as Ferdinand was a minor and Tanucci ruled. And Charles III was still King of Spain, who when he sailed to conquer the Kingdom of Naples as a young man had taken Prince Charles Edward with him. On their voyage the young Stuart Prince's hat had blown overboard, but when the sailors had tried to retrieve it Charles of Bourbon had stopped them; 'It floats towards England,' he had cried, 'and the owner will soon go and fetch it.' He had then flung his own hat after it so that he too might have something to fetch from England.

The owner of that first hat was now a disillusioned, drunken, middle-aged man, living in Florence, from which he refused to budge even for his father's funeral; while in Rome itself his younger brother the Cardinal-Duke of York fussed and fluttered about the Papal Court hoping to persuade the Pope to extend to his sad wreck of a brother the royal recognition which had been enjoyed by his father. But Clement XIII was in no hurry to move. He would wait and see what course the King of Spain would take before committing himself to the anxious Stuart Cardinal or to a world which waited, with very little curiosity, on the outcome of the issue. The Cardinal, meanwhile, drew up a letter in support of his claims for the Papal eye. Very soon a copy of it was in Hamilton's hands.

'I have been so lucky as to procure a true copy of the Letter that the Cardinal, Son to the late Pretender, wrote to the Pope immediately upon his Father's death. . . ' Hamilton was able to inform the Secretary of State on January 14, barely two weeks after the Stuart Prince's death.[7] 'I am told that the Pope has desired the Young Pretender to defer his intended journey to Rome. I shall, I dare say, be able to give you for His Majesty's information the best and earliest intelligence of whatever steps are taken at Rome in regard to the Pretender. . . The Cardinal has, I hear, notified the death of the Pretender his Father to this Court, but no notice will be taken of it here till they have instructions from Spain.'

The ink was hardly dry on this dispatch when further information reached Naples, which Hamilton added in a hasty post-script. 'I have this minute seen a letter from Rome dated the 10th of Jan. 1766 which says that the contents of the Pretender's Will are still kept secret. That the French Ambassador there insists upon the Pope's acknowledging the Pretender as King, saying that France and Spain would as soon as the situation of affairs should permit, but the Pope does not chuse to be the first to acknowledge him. It is thought that the Pretender will not be suffered to come to Rome till that ceremonial is adjusted.'

In fact the French Ambassador had no authority from his Court to make this recommendation, and was shortly afterwards to receive a smart rebuke from Versailles for his pains. By the fourth of February Hamilton was able to announce that notice had been given by the Cardinal Secretary of State that the Pope was not expected to give Prince Charles the title of Majesty or treat him in any respect as a King. This would prevent the Cardinals from visiting him, for, as Hamilton pointed out, 'they could not pay him, as Baron Douglas, the first visit'. Etiquette appeared to have come to everyone's rescue.

So the matter might have ended had not Cardinal Orsini, the Neapolitan Ambassador at Rome, called on Prince Charles when he arrived in that city, though he tried to excuse himself on the grounds that he had only given the Prince the title of Monsieur. Hamilton lost no time in making his Court's displeasure known to the Neapolitan government, who were as much embarrassed by the episode as he was, and was able to report on 10 February: 'Cardinal Orsini's visit to the Pretender was without the authority of his Court, the Marquis Tanucci was pleased to tell me so himself last Sunday, and that His Sicilian Majesty had greatly disapproved of it. The Pope continues firm in not allowing any of his subjects to give the Pretender the title his Father enjoyed at Rome.'[8]

So the comedy ended. The Neapolitan Court was not prepared to countenance any encouragement of the exiled house of Stuart. Its fortunes would continue to fade until, thirty-five years later, the proud Cardinal-Duke of York himself, by then sadly impoverished and far advanced in old age, would seek refuge in Naples from the victorious French and be cheered in his exile by the news of Nelson's victory. That day would find Hamilton still at his post.

As the year 1766 drew to its close the Neapolitans began to make preparations for the celebration of the young monarch's majority. As the various foreign embassies would be expected to take part in these festivities Hamilton grew a little apprehensive at the extra expense which this would involve. His rank at this moment was that of Envoy Extraordinary. On 16 December he addressed a letter to the Secretary of State[9] asking for promotion to the additional rank of Minister Plenipotentiary, explaining that even with the addition of the whole of his private fortune his present salary 'would scarcely suffice for the numberless expenses in servants, equipages, etc., which the fashion of this Country render absolute necessity.' He foresaw 'many additional expenses that His Sicilian Majesty's approaching Majority must necessarily occasion' and ended his letter: 'May I entreat of your Lordship most humbly to lay me at the King's feet, and to represent again to His Majesty my real situation as above described which indeed is not exaggerated.' His letter received a favourable hearing. On 10 February 1767 he was able to acknowledge his promotion and ask for his humble thanks to be returned to the King who had not only granted him his request for 'the additional Character of Plenipotentiary' but also expressed his royal approbation of the new Minister's conduct at the Neapolitan Court. 'I am at a loss', Hamilton wrote, 'for words to express what I felt upon reading the letter.'

Hamilton took the occasion of the King's Majority to send what he described as a 'succinct account of the King and Minister who govern here' in a dispatch to Lord Shelburne dated 17 March 1767. As Ferdinand's character matured but little over the years, and as his reign was to out-last Hamilton's time at Naples, the dispatch must be quoted at some length not only for the picture it gives of the young monarch but also for the light it throws on the British Minister as a judge of character.

'His Sicilian Majesty', Hamilton wrote,[10] 'is of a constitution extremely delicate which with his brother he inherited most probably from his great-grandfather of his mother's side. Unhappily for himself and his people he has neither had Masters capable of instructing him nor Governors who have studied to inspire him with ideas worthy of his rank. He is beloved by the vulgar Neapolitans merely from his having been born amongst them, and if he loves them as he seems to do, it is perhaps because, by the distance which they have always carefully placed between him and his Nobility of his own age, he has been drove rather to seek company of menial servants and people of the very lowest class than those of a better education; and indeed it is in the company of the former that he is the best pleased whilst he treats the latter as if there was no difference between the one and the other. It is easy to imagine what sort of Principles he must have imbibed in such a school, and to what low flatterers he has been accustom'd.

'While he was yet a Minor they had great hopes from him; these hopes were neither founded upon the goodness of his own education nor upon any word or remarkable action of his, but having felt all the weight of the past bad Administration, they imagine that as they could not be in a worse state any change would lead to a better. As yet, however, they have not found it so. Ambitious to come out of his Minority, the young King who had been counting the days of it for a year past, seems to have been more desirous of becoming his own Master to follow his caprices than to govern his Kingdoms, neither has he given the least attention to business, wholly giving himself up to his pleasures which he shares with people of the very lowest class whose manners he imitates. His most intimate friend and favourite is, as I am credibly informed, one who serves in the Palace even below the degree of a Livery Servant. He is thought not to have a great share of sensibility, is cholorick, obstinate and capable of bearing resentment; yet from a child he was always thought to have a better temper than any of his brothers.'

This picture of Ferdinand IV could hardly be described as encouraging, but subsequent events were to prove the essential justice of Hamilton's unflattering description. Only on the point of the King's delicacy was he at fault, for

Ferdinand was to grow into a man of robust health. Unfortunately his mental equipment was never to match his physical vigour. The most unhappy item in this catalogue of unimpressive qualities was that of the King's inability to form any sort of understanding of the habits of mind of his own social equals. The 'distance which they have always placed between him and his nobility', of which Hamilton complained, was to grow wider with the years. The more intellectual of the Neapolitan aristocracy could find little in common with this uncouth and ignorant monarch, and the King on his side would grow to fear and distrust those whose minds were so obviously superior to his own. The lack of *rapport* between King and nobility would in due time have tragic results.

The King's laziness and love for low company were also to remain characteristics of his personality. The former fault was to play into the hands of his minister Tanucci, who had no fear of his power being superseded when the Council of Regency was disbanded, and who continued to govern the country as he had done before. If anything his power increased with the declaration of the royal majority. 'The Regency being changed into a Council of State, the Marquis Tanucci has united in his person all the authority that was divided among the Regents, and by that means is become Prime Minister', was Hamilton's opinion. He finished his dispatch with a few comments on this powerful Minister, whose personality had not entirely shed the characteristics of the former professor of law, and who, if he escaped the charge of peculation, was to be condemned on the score of vanity. 'He piques himself more upon being a learned man than a Statesman', Hamilton observed, 'his followers praise, and he himself applauds, his skill in Letters. . . '

On the more important point of policy, however, Hamilton could report that the Minister's heart was in the right place so far as England was concerned, even though the motives did not necessarily spring from any disinterested love for Great Britain. 'The Marquis Tanucci hates the French', the dispatch ends, 'because their Ministers have shown too openly that they have not the good opinion of him which he has of himself; and if he agrees with us, it is perhaps because we agree so little with the French. Indeed, I believe he rather fears than loves us, but I believe him capable of doing much in our favour provided that, taking advantage of the fear he has of our power, one has always the precaution of showing a great regard for him in his private capacity. He is more jealous of his power than taken up with his affairs, but he loves to appear to have great application to them and requires being treated by foreign Ministers with a gravity that can give him no room to believe that he has an ascendancy over them.'

In spite of these blemishes Hamilton considered this Minister as the only person among those employed in the royal service who knew anything of business, but he added a warning that if Tanucci was independent of the will of the King of Naples he was in the entire confidence of the King of Spain, 'who would have great need of him should any accident happen to His Sicilian Majesty'.

Such an eventuality was never entirely to be ruled out among a people somewhat given to conspiracy or to sudden acts of violence. Less than six months after the general celebrations in honour of Ferdinand's majority Hamilton was reporting the rumour of a plot to assassinate the King. He had been informed 'with great secrecy', and hastened to pass the information on to London, that a man had demanded to speak with Tanucci in private and on being admitted into the presence of the Minister had fallen onto his knees and in this theatrical pose had promised to reveal a secret of the greatest importance in exchange for a pardon for his own part in the business. Having received an assurance on this point he then confessed that he was one of twelve people who were sworn to murder the young King. As a result of this confession it was said that the other conspirators were caught the very same day, and as Hamilton wrote, were already languishing in the castle of St. Elmo, the formidable fortress that frowned over the city from above the monastery of San Martino.

Hamilton was unable to discover any further details of this grim plot, but when he was next at court he noticed that the second-in-command of the military never stirred from the King's side, a point of court etiquette which had not been observed before. No more was heard of this affair. It was a tiny cloud in the bright Neapolitan sunshine. The days when serious conspiracies would darken the brilliance of the court, bringing fear and suspicion into the very corridors of the palace, were still very far away. The young King, for all his neglected education and gross manners, was still regarded by the majority of his subjects as a symbol of hope.

But if Ferdinand could be looked upon in this hopeful light (for when all was said and done he was still little more than a boy) Hamilton did not fail to observe the ill effects of his neglected upbringing. Under the system of enlightened despotism which the King had inherited from his father, and which was the accepted form of government in most European monarchies of the day, a just rule could only result from an alliance between the throne and the best elements among the nobles, who in Naples still wielded almost feudal power.

The King's scanty education and distaste for the responsibilities of power made any such alliance impossible. Almost exactly a year after rumours of assassination had reached the ear of the British Minister the country was *en fête* for the celebration of the King's marriage to a daughter of the Empress of Austria. In reporting these festivities Hamilton noted: 'The Neapolitan nobility do not conceal their indignation at the neglect of their Sovereign's education and the Foreigners, of which there are many here at present from all parts of Europe, are struck with amazement. The Prince of Nicandro, His Sicilian Majesty's late Governor, hangs his head and those very courtiers who lately encouraged their Master in his youthful behaviour I see are shy of appearing near His Majesty in public lest his familiarity with them should convey (which is but too true) that they have had a share in His Majesty's education.'[11]

The nobility who turned from the King in disgust in 1768 under the wax candles of a court ball would turn against him in the streets of his capital thirty years later with a more bitter disgust and send him hurrying in flight to Palermo under the protection of Lord Nelson's guns. Had Ferdinand's natural talents and abilities been better developed in his impressionable years, many of the tragedies that later befell his Kingdom might have been avoided.

1. *Vide* B. Connell: *Portrait of a Whig Peer*, pp. 58–9.
2. E. Edwards: *Lives of the Founders of the British Museum*, Vol. I, p. 350.
3. B.M. Egerton MSS 2634 f. 93.
4. National Library of Scotland, MS 3942.
5. Wraxall: *Historical Memoirs*: pp. 163–4.
6. B.M. Egerton MSS 2634, f. 192.
7. B.M. Egerton MSS 2634, f. 112.
9. B.M. Egerton MSS 2634, f. 128.
10. B.M. Egerton MSS 2634, f. 215.
11. Ibid., f. 245.
12. B.M. Egerton MSS 2635 f. 11.

CHAPTER V

Hamilton's First Collection

Almost exactly a year after Hamilton had arrived in Naples Samuel Sharp wrote of the British Envoy: 'It is the custom when neither the Opera, nor any particular engagement prevent, to meet at his house, where we amuse ourselves as we are disposed, either at cards, the billiard-table, or his little concert; some form themselves into small parties of conversation, and as the members of this society are often Ambassadors, Nuncios, Monsignoris, Envoys, Residents, and the first quality of Naples, you will conceive it to be instructive as well as honourable.'[1] Such agreeable gatherings soon became a regular feature of Hamilton's embassy. His house was the particular meeting-place for those Neapolitans or foreign visitors whose interests embraced the world of art and music, who enjoyed the pleasure of civilised conversation and were able to appreciate the growing collection of pictures and antiques which was the special pride of their distinguished host. For a British embassy to have the reputation of being a centre of intellectual life is rare; Hamilton's house was to be known to scholars, artists, antiquarians and men of science from all parts of Europe, and even the great Goethe was to confess, after discussing many topics with the British Envoy, that he 'learned a great deal from him, and looked forward to learning more in the future'.

There was no official residence for the ambassador.[2] The Hamiltons eventually settled themselves into the Palazzo Sessa which had been converted into a private house from a former monastic building by the family from whom it derived its name. It was to remain in Hamilton's hands until he was forced to abandon it in December 1798 when he accompanied the royal family on their flight to Palermo. The palazzo was in the Pizzofalcone quarter of Naples, built on steeply rising ground so that it towered above the surrounding houses and commanded a splendid view towards the bay. The outside was not particularly prepossessing, but the interior contained a suite of rooms which provided a gracious and dignified background for the display of Hamilton's celebrated collection of works of art. As befitted his official station, however, he did not forget to introduce a certain English note as a contrast to the Italian splendours that surrounded him. This was an 'English Room' decorated with designs by Robert Adam, and Lady Anne Miller, who visited the Palazzo Sessa in January 1771, declared that she could have fancied herself at an assembly in London.

Whether it was the Adam decorations or the fact that she 'was surprised at the appearance of two English ladies . . . who were dressed as they would have been for a court-day at St. James's' that made Lady Anne Miller fancy herself to be in London we do not know. On the quality of the music heard at the British embassy she fortunately leaves us in no doubt. 'Mrs. Hamilton's musical assembly', she wrote,[3] which she gives once a week, is rendered perfect by her elegant taste and fine performance; it is called an *Accademia di Musica*; and I suppose no country can produce a more complete band of excellent performers.'

William Beckford was one of the many English visitors to enjoy the hospitality of the Palazzo Sessa, where he was especially welcome for his brilliant though somewhat hectic personality as well as for the fact that he was one of Hamilton's close relatives. After being presented to the King of Naples he tells us how glad he was to return to Sir William Hamilton's 'where an interesting group of lovely women, literati, and artists were assembled.' Among these was the Abbé Galiani who 'happened to be in full story, and vied with his countryman Polichinello, not only in gesticulation and loquacity, but in the excessive licentiousness of his narrations'. Fortunately before the tiny Abbé was completely carried away 'beyond all bounds of decency and decorum, at least according to English notions' the situation was saved by the diplomatic tact of the ambassadress, who quickly sat down at the harpsichord, thus imposing a polite and expectant silence on the company. The recollection of her playing made Beckford indulge in one of those rhapsodic passages which always flowed from his pen at the memory of Hamilton's gentle and charming first wife. 'Her plaintive modulations' (in comparison with the *risqué* rhetoric of Galiani) 'breathed a far different language. No performer that I ever heard produced such soothing effects; they seemed the emanations of a pure, uncontaminated mind, at peace with itself and benevolently desirous of diffusing that happy tranquillity around it; these were modes a Grecian legislature would have encouraged to further the triumph over vice of the most amiable virtue.'[4]

Perhaps Beckford, who was himself soon to be involved in a serious scandal, was a little hard on the brilliant and vivacious Abbé; but in administering his rebuke he gives us one of our rare glances of Catherine Hamilton exercising a subtle influence which would have been very much beyond the reach of her down-to-earth successor. Catherine came very much into her own as mistress of the Palazzo Sessa and earned the gratitude of her husband. Charles Duclos, the author of *Voyage en Italie*, who visited the Hamiltons in Naples and saw them in their family circle as well as at their formal and official receptions, said of them: 'They are the happiest couple I ever saw.'

Catherine Hamilton's musical gifts never failed to delight those who heard her play, and brought compliments even from professional musicians. When Dr. John Moore came to Naples with the British Minister's cousin the Duke of Hamilton, he found no house there where the company was more numerous or brilliant than they were at the Palazzo Sessa, and observed that the Minister met with every mark of regard from the Neapolitan nobles 'on account of the high favour in which he stands with their Sovereign'. Like everyone else he was charmed by Catherine Hamilton's harpsichord playing, declaring that she 'understands music perfectly and performs in such a manner as to command the admiration even of Neapolitans'. Hamilton's own efforts on the violin did not escape his notice either. He was, said Moore, 'the happiest-tempered man in the world, and the easiest amused.' He 'performs also, and succeeds perfectly in amusing himself, which is a more valuable attainment than the other.'[5]

In addition to the Palazzo Sessa Hamilton had two small Villas in the country outside Naples, one to the north at Posillipo (this was later to be known as the Villa Emma), and the other south of the city at Portici, close to the Royal Palace. This, the Villa Angelica, was at the foot of Vesuvius, and it was from here that Hamilton began most of his volcanic expeditions and from where he could observe the behaviour of the volcano which so fascinated him. When Lord Herbert, the son of Hamilton's old friend the Earl of Pembroke, visited Naples in 1779, he described the former villa as being 'the last house a carriage can arrive at', which suggests that it was somewhere in the neighbourhood of Capo di Posillipo. One tradition claims that the villa was destroyed during the period when Murat was King of Naples when a new road was being built, but its exact position is now unknown. 'It is built on a small rock', Lord Herbert recorded in his diary, 'and consists of three rooms and a kitchen with a very diminutive garden. There are two flights of stairs to come up to it. When the weather is fine a small terrass before the building constitutes the Setting Room (sic.) with a large Venetian blind over it to guard it from the heat of the sun.' Hamilton often dined at this villa at the early hour which was customary in the eighteenth century, 'for at two', as Lord Herbert observed, 'the sun is off and while everybody is broiling at Naples he is enjoying the cool of the said cassino'.[6]

The Villa Angelica at Portici had the fertile slope of Vesuvius behind it and to the front one of the most splendid views which that beautiful part of the world could provide. Lord Herbert, who reckoned that he had seen all the fine views that offer themselves from every spot in the neighbourhood of Naples, considered that the one from Hamilton's front window at Portici surpassed any he had seen before. Dr. Charles Burney came to dine at this villa when he visited Naples in 1770 to collect material for his *History of Music*, and noticed the 'glasses of all sorts' which his host used for his scientific observations of the volcano. 'His Villa Angelica is but a small house which he fitted up himself,' Burney recorded in his *Musical Tours in Europe*. It was 'situated opposite and within two miles of the foot of Mount Vesuvius, in a very rich and fertile spot, as every one hereabouts is that is not covered with fresh Lava. He has a large garden, or rather vineyard, with most excellent grapes.' Hamilton and his wife provided a musical entertainment for Dr. Burney which was occasionally interrupted with fiery displays from the crater of the volcano 'then very busy.' The Hamiltons were by now hardened to such interruptions from their volcanic neighbour. Catherine, in a letter to a friend, had described 'an exhibition of the most splendid cluster of fiery red stones' sent up from the crater one evening. 'It was an astonishing sight', she added, 'but we went on playing, just as you would have done if you heard a pop-gun in the street.' It is Burney who tells us that Hamilton employed two pages in his household who performed, one on the violin, and the other on the 'cello, and described them as excellent performers.

Dr. Burney was the sort of visitor the Hamiltons particularly liked to welcome, and they went out of their way to entertain him and help him in his musical researches. His arrival in Naples was greeted with a 'very obliging letter' from Hamilton inviting him to dine and asking him to stay at the Villa Angelica. In order to 'gratify his musical curiosity' a great concert was arranged at the Minister's house at which the chief performers in Naples took part. Among them were Barbella and Orgitano, the latter being described by Burney as one of the best players and writers for the harpsichord in Naples, and who was later to direct the music at His Majesty's Theatre in London. But in spite of the presence of this *virtuoso* it was Dr. Burney's opinion that Catherine Hamilton was 'herself a much better performer on that instrument than either he or anyone I heard there'.

The day following this concert, 30 October 1770, Burney called at the Palazzo Sessa, but was told that the Minister was out. The Minister's wife, however, was at home, and the Doctor was shown to her room. 'She is very intelligent,' he noted, 'shewed me pictures and music—and told me of Paesiello's Burletta called I' Idolo Chinese, and played some of the airs.' Burney was enchanted with the music and said he would like some of it copied; Mrs. Hamilton 'immediately called for one of the pages to enquire after a copyist for me—then invited me to her toilet in order to finish our chat. She had a pretty Sicilian girl waiting upon her, whom she desired to sing, and accompany herself on the Tambour de basque; the air was simple and national.' Remembering his role as historian of music, Burney noted down the tune. This reminded him that Hamilton had promised to give him his notes on a visit to Sicily, and he expressed his regret that the Minister was out, but to this his hostess answered: 'No, he is not out to you—he is writing in his study and you may go to him,' and Burney left, escorted by the 'Sicilian songstress' to show him the way.

He found Hamilton busy at his dispatches, but he at once put down his pen in order to show Burney his collection of Greek and Etruscan vases and other antiques, and lent the historian a manuscript 'by a French gentleman of his acquaintance' describing a voyage to the Levant which gave an account of the music of the Turks and Greeks. He also signed an order to permit his visitor to see the Royal Museum at Portici, offered him the use of his box at the San Carlo to hear a new opera by Jomelli, at that time considered the leading composer in Naples, and finally invited him 'to hear a remarkably fat Dominican sing Buffo songs' on the following

Saturday. On another occasion some days later Hamilton and Burney sat talking until two in the morning. 'It was very cheerful, and the conversation, much of it, to my purpose.' They discussed a trumpet recently unearthed at Pompeii. 'Mr. Hamilton says it was discovered in the Corps de Garde Room,' Burney wrote in his account, 'which proves it to have been a military instrument, the true *Clangor Tubarum* of the ancients.'

On the Saturday, after the fat Dominican had given his performance, Burney was conducted round the already famous collection. 'The curiosities both of art and nature in Mr. Hamilton's possession are numberless and inestimable,' he wrote. 'The examination of his immense collection of Etruscan vases, and other varieties of the highest antiquity, was of the utmost importance to the subject of my enquiries. But by these precious remains of art I was not more enlightened concerning the music and instruments of the ancients than by his conversation and counsel.' To provide such knowledge and instruction to scholars and artists was, of course, one of the chief reasons why Hamilton made his collection, and he must have welcomed the opportunity to display it to one so learned and appreciative as Dr. Charles Burney. 'I took leave of Mr. Hamilton and his lady with infinite regret,' Dr. Burney concludes, 'as the countenance and assistance with which I was honoured by them during my residence at Naples were not only of the utmost utility to me and my plan, but such as gratitude will never suffer me to forget.'[8]

The collection of vases and antiques which Burney saw and admired had been assembled by Hamilton with the discrimination and taste of a scholar. He began to collect as soon as he reached Naples and quickly established his reputation as a leading connoisseur. He was not, of course, the first person to collect Greek vases, but, it has been claimed, 'to Hamilton belongs the merit of being the first to appreciate with warmth the severe beauty of their shapes, colouring and drawing, the mingled simplicity and feeling of the designs figured upon them; and it was he who recognised the value of these unpretentious vessels for forming and ennobling modern art-taste.'[9] In an age when fantastic nicknames were very much in vogue (like his own contemporary and namesake 'Single-Speech' Hamilton) it is a wonder that the British Minister at Naples was not known as 'Vase' Hamilton— and perhaps he only escaped this sobriquet because 'Volcano' Hamilton would have suited him just as well. His passion for collecting became famous and in later years a somewhat startled visitor would relate how he had seen His Majesty's Minister Plenipotentiary in a back street of Naples in full court dress with his star and riband helping a local peasant to carry home some dusty vases which he had just purchased.

The collection, or 'cabinet' as the contemporary phrase went, was greatly enriched in 1766 when Hamilton bought the Porcinari collection of Greek vases. By the year 1771 when negotiations were in progress for its purchase by the nation the museum of antiquities which he had assembled consisted of seven hundred and thirty vases, one hundred and seventy-five terracottas, three hundred specimens of ancient glass, over six hundred bronzes, one hundred and fifty ivories and the same number of antique gems, more than a hundred gold ornaments and over six thousand coins. When this collection was sold he immediately began to assemble a second which included, in addition to the Etruscan vases, such objects as Greek and Roman helmets, a gilt horse's head, three military hatchets, bronze and iron swords of Roman work, spurs, chains and fragments of horse's harness, gold necklaces and ear-rings, 'a most curious fillagree ladies ornament', a topaz in a curious setting representing a star, the head of a bodkin, sixteen gold and silver rings 'in the state in which they were found', a bronze distaff, a Roman foot rule and pair of compasses, a bronze instrument described as 'probably for keeping accounts', three little hammers and fourteen bronze dice.[10] Hamilton was lucky in that he began his collection at a time when Greek and Etruscan vases were not greatly sought after. His own publications, however, were to effect a change in taste, and towards the end of his time in Naples he was to lament to his nephew Charles Greville: 'I am sure the mine of these vases lately discovered must fail soon, and therefore I must not let one essential vase escape me, tho' the price is much higher than it was formerly. The King of Naples has now began to purchase them, but my harvest luckily was in first. . . '[11]

Like many people of scholarly tastes Hamilton derived a certain malicious pleasure in exposing the errors of pedants and rival collectors. An opportunity of this sort, which he clearly relished, came his way when he acquired a vase which represented the theme of Silenus, the merry drunken companion of Bacchus who, if clothed at all, is generally depicted as finding a few vine leaves as a sufficient covering—and these very often only adorning his brow. This particular vase, when it came into Hamilton's possession, showed Silenus decently draped, and had been the subject of a learned article by one Passeri who (in Hamilton's words), 'had displayed in his dissertation much of his erudition to explain the reason why a Silenus was represented thereon completely clothed, and not naked, as in most monuments of antiquity'. The real reason for this unwonted prudery on the part of the demi-god was quickly discovered by Hamilton. 'I soon perceived that the drapery on the Silenus had been added with a pen and ink', he explained, 'as was the case on the figures of many other vases in the same collection, the late possessor, being very devout, having caused all nudities to be covered. However, as soon as the vase was mine, a sponge washed off both modern drapery and Passeri's dissertation!'[12]

In the years 1766–7 Hamilton brought out four sumptuous folio volumes illustrating his collection. The text was written by Pierre François Hugues, the art-historian better known by his *nom de plume* of D'Hancarville. The introductory matter and description of the plates were printed in both French and English in the first volume, issued in 1766, but in the three subsequent volumes which came out in the following year only French was used. The plates were engraved and hand-painted, their form usually consisting of a drawing of the vase in perspective, a sectional plan giving its measurements and proportions in detail, and a coloured drawing showing the full design of the vase at the bottom of the plate. The text is set up in a fine clear type, the English in italic and the French in roman, on opposite pages. In the first volume a splendidly designed and engraved plate carries a dedication to King George III, and is itself a fine example of the neo-classical taste which Hamilton hoped to foster and encourage. The chief engravers employed were Antoine Cardon, Carmine Pignatoro, Giuseppe Bracci and Carlo Nolli.

The purpose which inspired Hamilton to issue these beautiful folios is set out in the Preface to the first volume. 'Our aim has certainly been to shew a considerable collection of exquisite Models', D'Hancarville wrote, very clearly expressing the ideas of his patron, 'but we likewise have proposed to ourselves to hasten the progress of the Arts, by discussing their true and first principles. It is in this respect that the nature of the work may be considered as absolutely new, for no one has yet undertaken to search out what sistem (*sic*) the Ancients followed, to give their Vases that elegance which all the World acknowledges to be in them, to discover rules the observation of which conduct infallibly to their imitation, and in short to assign exact measures for fixing their proportions; in order that the artist who would *invent* in the same stile, or only *copy* the Monuments which appeared to him worthy of being copied, may do so with as much truth and precision, as if he had the Originals themselves in his possession. It is by this means, that the present work may contribute to the advancement of the Arts, and make the masterpieces of Antiquity, that are worthy of imitation, understood as they deserve to be, for we believe it will be readily acknowledged that it is not sufficient to have a general idea of the vases of the Ancients, as they are given to us in the Books of the Count de Caylus and Father Montfaulcon: These works at the utmost only shew what members the Ancients employed in the composition of their Vases, but do not indicate their relative proportions, and one should succeed as ill in copying them after these vague notions, as one should in attempting to imitate Greek Architecture with success, without having first studied its proportions. We should think that we had not advanced one step forwarder, if the Monuments we publish were to the Artists merely the object of fruitless admiration, but shall think we have gone something farther if it should prove that we revive an ancient Art, and explain its first rudiments and the successive discovery of its fundamental Maxims, and if there should result from that part of our work which relates to the forms such a theory, that to reduce it to practice, nothing more will be necessary than the faculty of execution which labour and experience give to the hand of the meanest Artist.'

The whole of Hamilton's aesthetic theory, and his self-justification as a collector and connoisseur of the antique, is summed up in the idea that works of art should not be 'merely the objects of fruitless admiration' but must serve some purpose of utility, especially in the example and practical inspiration they can provide for modern artists and craftsmen. It is on this note that the Preface ends: 'In every Art good models give birth to ideas by exciting the imagination, theory furnishes the means of expressing those ideas, practice puts these means in execution, and this last part which is always the most common is also the easiest. If we complete our design, we shall have done what is insisted upon by *Longinus*, who thinks with reason, that when one treats of an Art, the principal point consists in shewing how, and by what means, what we teach may be acquired.'

Hamilton set so high a standard in the production of these volumes, having type specially imported from Venice, that by the time they were completed he was six thousand pounds out of pocket. Their influence was, however, fully to justify the care and expense he had expended on them. Even before the books were published his brother-in-law Lord Cathcart lent some proofs of the plates to Josiah Wedgwood just at the time the celebrated potter was building his new factory at 'Etruria' near Burslem, and they had a profound effect on the work of this artist-craftsman, having been described as one of the earliest influences in forming his neo-classical style. When the famous pottery works was opened in June 1769 Wedgwood and his partner Thomas Bentley celebrated the occasion by throwing six black vases which were handpainted in red encaustic enamel with three figures taken from Hamilton's book.[13] Wedgwood had every reason to refer to the British Minister at Naples (as he did in a letter to Bentley of 18 April 1772) as 'our good friend Sir William Hamilton'.

Other more distinguished if perhaps less practical persons wrote to congratulate him when the volumes appeared. 'I have got the first volume of the Etruscan vases, which I like much', Lord Bessborough wrote from London,[14] 'it is a very fine work, and must do you honour in the world, and particularly among the virtuosi, and I give you joy of it.' More to the point was a letter from Sir Joshua Reynolds in which he informed Hamilton that he had just been elected President of the newly formed Royal Academy of Arts (adding that 'it is only honour for there is no salary annex'd to this dignity'), and praising the usefulness of Hamilton's publication. 'I admire the work which is published under your Patronage exceedingly, it is not only magnificent as it should be, being published with your name but it is likewise useful to antiquarians and will tend to the advancement of the Arts, as adding more materials for Genius to work upon. . .' and he commented on the 'grace and genteelness of some of the figures', which he found 'much in the Parmegian stile'.[15]

The four volumes entitled *Collection of Etruscan, Greek and Roman Antiquities from the Cabinet of the Honourable William Hamilton*, with the volumes which Hamilton issued twenty-five years later in the years 1791 to 1795, were to fulfil his hopes in respect of the influence they were to have on the neo–classical movement in art. Not only was Wedgwood to make considerable use of these books in his famous Jasper vases and Black Basaltes, but artists such as John Flaxman and Henry Fuseli came directly under their influence. The neo-classical movement had, of course, already started before Hamilton's volumes made their influence felt. They cannot be said to have started any new trend in art. What they did do was to encourage a more exact and scholarly approach to the favourite subjects of the artists of this school, and this is perhaps as much as Hamilton himself would have hoped or desired. It is ironical that this movement should have found its ultimate expression in the works of the artists of revolutionary France, for the French Revolution was something which Hamilton would spend his last years trying to frustrate, and whose principles he always held in contempt.

Nothing, however, could have seemed more remote than revolution in the late sixties and early seventies of the eighteenth century, especially to a dilettante placed in an agreeable situation close to the most beautiful bay in Europe. If Hamilton had any feelings of disappointment over the publication of his *Greek and Roman Antiquities* it was only that the high price of the volumes put them beyond the reach of young artists, for these were the people he most wished to help and guide. There was undoubtedly something of the pedagogue about Hamilton, though the desire to impart knowledge was hidden behind the mask of an urbane courtier and man of the world. He was never happier than when some young artist or musician asked for his help or advice. If they arrived expecting to be met by a disdainful or remote aristocrat they soon learnt their mistake. He would go to great lengths and take infinite trouble to help them, as the obscure fifteen-year-old Michael Kelly was to discover. Hamilton had the gift of winning the confidence and trust of young people, especially those who showed signs of sharing his artistic interests, whose taste he could form and develop.

He was fortunate in finding just such a kindred spirit in his own family circle. In the spring of 1769 he received a visit from his twenty-year-old nephew Charles Greville, then making his Grand Tour, that essential part of the education of an eighteenth-century gentleman. No doubt the young man had pored over the fascinating descriptions and pictures of Greek vases from his uncle's collection when the large volumes had reached Warwick Castle some two years before, for he already had the air of a young *Conoscente* when he presented himself at the Palazzo Sessa. A friendship which was to last a lifetime began at that moment. The formal relationship of uncle and nephew was abandoned at once and in the letters that followed the visit the two men were already addressing each other on terms of easy equality as 'My dear Greville' and 'My dear Hamilton', while the London wits, hearing of their relationship of taste as well as of blood, would refer to them as 'Pliny the Elder' and 'Pliny the Younger'.

Greville was to grow into a rather cold and calculating man for whom self-interest seemed to be the dominating passion. He has been described as a 'queer compound of the Pharisee and the Publican, something between a Charles and a Joseph Surface.'[16] Like his uncle he became an assiduous collector, but while Hamilton collected from zeal Greville, one cannot help feeling, always had an eye open for a good investment. In his first letter after leaving Naples he ended with the request: 'By the bye, if you can pick up any vases of which you have duplicates, lay them aside for me; don't buy them if not well conserved and good, nor many of a shape—a few elegant and good.' The request must have delighted his uncle, but the qualifying phrase strikes one as a little over prudent, perhaps, for an enthusiast of twenty years of age. It was the beginning of a long correspondence which would cover much more than Greek vases and include, in just over fifteen years' time, perhaps the strangest series of letters ever known to pass between an uncle and a nephew.

1. S. Sharp: *Letters from Italy*, p. 76 [F].
2. The term ambassador as applied to Hamilton here and elsewhere is used in the general sense of a diplomatic representative. His rank remained that of Minister Plenipotentiary.
3. Lady A. Miller: *Letters from Italy*, Vol. II, p. 224-6.
4. W. Beckford: *Italy, Spain and Portugal*, p. 121-2.
5. J. Moore: *A View of Society and Manners in Italy*, p. 279.
6. *Pembroke Papers*, Vol. I, p. 225.
7. C. Burney: *Musical Tours in Italy*, Vol. I, pp. 264-7.
8. Op. cit. p. 281.
9. A. Michaelis: *Ancient Marbles in Great Britain*, p. 110.
10. B.M. Dept. of Greek and Roman Antiquities: Hamilton Papers 4-21.
11. Morrison, 182 (1790).
12. W. Hamilton: *Collection of Engravings from Ancient Vases*, Vol. I, p.10
13. *Selected letters of Josiah Wedgwood*, pp. 62, 75.
14. Morrison, 19.
15. *Letters of Sir Joshua Reynolds*, pp. 20-3, Letter XIII.
16. W. Sichel: *Emma Lady Hamilton*, p. 38.

CHAPTER VI

A Royal Wedding

Vases and volcanoes were all very well for leisure hours, but the work of diplomacy had to go on. While Hamilton was seeing his volumes of *Greek and Roman Antiquities* through the press the King of Naples was busily occupied in getting married. Since attaining his majority at the age of sixteen Ferdinand IV had been impatient for the celebration of this event. Hamilton sent his first report of a possible royal marriage as early as December 1765, when in denying the rumour that Ferdinand was about to be betrothed to a Princess of Savoy, he confirmed the more promising proposition 'that there is great reason to believe that His Sicilian Majesty has been long engaged to one of the Archduchesses'.[1] It was not, however, until March 1767 that the marriage treaty was concluded, and the King was able to announce his forthcoming union with Maria Josepha, daughter of the formidable Empress Maria Theresa, who had selected this child from among her considerable progeny as part of her plans for improving relations between the Habsburgs and the Bourbons by the well-tried Austrian policy of dynastic marriages, a policy which in this instance had the full support of the Court of Spain. After informing his household that the marriage treaty was concluded Ferdinand summoned the diplomatic corps of Caserta where he proudly displayed a portrait of the young Archduchess for their admiration. In Hamilton's opinion the future bride was very handsome 'if one may judge from a portrait', and the King appeared greatly satisfied with the choice which had been made for him.

Fate, however, had not intended that Maria Josepha should become Queen of Naples. In August, following the announcement of the marriage, Hamilton was asking the Secretary of State with reference to the ceremonies about to take place, if he 'would be so kind as to acquaint me whether His Majesty will expect that I should give any particular entertainment upon that occasion'; a month later he had to announce that the marriage was postponed until the following spring as 'on Friday last a Courier from Vienna brought the account of the future Queen of Naples having been seiz'd with the smallpox, at the same time assuring His Sicilian Majesty that it was happily of the most favourable sort . . .'; on October 27 he had to inform his government of the fatal outcome of this attack: 'A Courier from Vienna arrived here on Saturday last with the melancholy account of the death of the Archduchess Maria Josepha. The Court and City are in the utmost consternation upon this unlucky event; the grief of His Sicilian Majesty is strongly painted in the Marquis Tanucci's billet to me upon the occasion.'[2] To add to the confusion Vesuvius was in full eruption creating, in Hamilton's phrase, 'a perpetual scene of horror'.

The death of the young Archduchess was hardly a personal tragedy for Ferdinand as he had never set eyes on his intended bride. His chief cause for grief, in fact, was that the etiquette of court mourning prevented him from engaging in his favourite sport of the chase. Deprived of fresh air and game to slaughter, and soon tiring of billiards and leap-frog, the King was almost distracted by boredom until some courtier with a morbid sense of humour suggested that they should divert themselves by acting in mime the funeral of the unfortunate Maria Josepha. A pretty youth served as the corpse, his complexion disfigured with chocolate drops to represent the pustules of the fatal disease, while the King, draped in black, posed as the chief mourner. His boon companions followed with simulated grief as the macabre procession wound its way through the interminable halls and corridors of the palace. Hamilton, who had gone there to make his condolences, was the unwilling witness of this extraordinary and bizarre spectacle.

After an interval of less than three months news reached Naples that the Empress in Vienna had selected another of her daughters for the fate from which Maria Josepha had been so suddenly deprived by death. This time her choice fell on Maria Carolina. A year and a half junior in age to Ferdinand, this princess had been brought up in close companionship with her younger sister the Archduchess Maria Antonia who was also to marry a Bourbon, become Queen of France, and as Marie Antoinette end her life on the scaffold. Maria Carolina showed so little enthusiasm at the thought of becoming Queen of Naples that when the news was first brought to her she considered she might just as well have been thrown into the sea. Her enthusiasm would probably have been even less had she known of the mock funeral procession by which the youth she was about to embrace as a husband had so unfeelingly celebrated the death of her elder sister. It was not, however, for her to question what the Empress had decreed for her future; if she accepted her fate without enthusiasm she was none the less determined to make the best of it. The girl of fifteen was to grow into a woman of remarkable determination.

The choice of a Habsburg princess as their future Queen was popular to the people of Naples. Her brother Leopold, who had succeeded the last Medici in Florence as Grand Duke of Tuscany, and who accompanied Maria Carolina on the last stages of her journey to Naples, was at that time the most enlightened ruler in Italy, and in the words of the liberal-minded historian Colletta (later a bitter critic of the Queen) 'the whole progeny of Maria Theresa appeared to us as a family of philosophers in high places, sent by God to regenerate the human race'. The young Archduchess had set off for her new country carrying a letter of good advice from her mother. 'Do not be always talking about our country or drawing comparisons between our customs and theirs', the Empress-Queen had written. 'There is good and bad to be found in every country. . . In your heart, and in the uprightness of your mind be a German; in all that is unimportant, though in nothing that is wrong, you must appear to be a Neapolitan.'[3] As advice it was certainly sound though hardly flattering to Maria Carolina's future subjects, who were only to be imitated in what was unimportant.

While the Neapolitans, happily ignorant of the low place they occupied in the estimation of the Empress of Austria, were busily preparing to welcome their new Queen, the British Minister was mainly concerned with the thought of the financial burden which the wedding celebrations would add to his expenses. 'The Neapolitan nobility and gentry whose predominant passion is exterior show of magnificence', he informed the Secretary of State on 3 May 1768, 'have eagerly embraced this opportunity of vieing with each other in rich clothes, equipages and liveries, by which many families will be greatly distress'd, and the entertainments which this Court and the Spanish Minister, by order of His Catholick Majesty, are preparing for the Populace will cost the lives of many. . . I shall take care upon this occasion to make a figure adequate to the honorable situation in which his Majesty has been graciously pleased to place me at this Court. At the same time I shall carefully avoid every expense that is unnecessary, regulating myself by my colleagues who are not *Ministres de Famille*.'[4]

The financial problem was an acute one for Hamilton at that moment, even though he had recently received an increase in his salary. He knew that he would have to meet the extra expenses of the wedding celebrations out of his own pocket, trusting in the Government at home to reimburse him later on. He also knew that Governments were never in any particular hurry to fulfil this obligation, sometimes quibbling for months and even years over the details of payments, and not always meeting them in the end. This was particularly worrying as he had just spent six thousand pounds of his own money on the production of his four volumes of *Greek and Roman Antiquities*.

These considerations account for the note of anxiety in the dispatch which he sent to Lord Shelburne in the following July, when the period of festivity was at last over. 'His Sicilian Majesty's wedding', he explained, 'has actually put me to an Extraordinary expense of upwards of one thousand pounds sterling, four hundred of which indeed are not sunk as they were for an addition of Jewels which were necessary for Mrs. Hamilton's appearance at Court. Illuminations, balls, masquerades, etc., which have continued almost without interruption for these two months past, with a dinner and concert which I had the honour of giving to their Royal Highnesses the Great Duke and Duchess (in a Manner at their own request) have swallow'd up the remainder of the sum. . . I only wish that the King may be informed of these circumstances leaving it afterwards entirely to the decision of His Majesty whether the whole of this extraordinary expense is to fall upon me or not.'[5] Clearly Hamilton thought that his best hope lay in trusting to the generosity of his foster-brother, upon whose benevolent interest he knew he could rely. This was Hamilton's first experience of such matters, but he was to discover that it needed more than royal protection to move a Government when it came to a question of reimbursement. Though settlements were made from time to time he would still be pursuing a recalcitrant Government to within the last year of his life on the thorny issue of extraordinary expenses.

Meanwhile the wedding celebrations themselves had not been without moments of embarrassment for the members of the diplomatic corps. In a dispatch of 18 May 1768 Hamilton complained of the confusion which had surrounded the ceremony of presentation of himself and his colleagues to the King and Queen after their marriage. Tanucci had arranged for them to go out to Caserta, but then seemed to have forgotten all about it, so that when the ambassadors arrived they found themselves unexpected and everything in a state of incredible confusion. The diplomats, considerably ruffled by what appeared as an affront to their dignity, made a vigorous protest to the Minister, and Tanucci, in Hamilton's words, 'much embarrassed probably from being sensible of his neglect, went into the King's Closet and returning soon after took me by the hand and told us that the King was too much taken up to receive us'. They could, however, be presented to the Queen on her way to Mass. This makeshift arrangement did not satisfy the ambassadors who 'wished to have a particular distinguished presentation as due to [their] character', and they decided to withdraw 'and shew, without shocking any one in particular, some sort of resentment for these repeated neglects'.

The diplomats returned in a body the following Saturday only to be thrown into further confusion by the action of the Ambassador of France. As a 'family minister' he had the right to be presented first, and it was arranged that his presentation should take place in another room just before the other ministers made their bow. On arrival at the Palace, however, Maria Carolina appeared in the room where they were all assembled upon which the French Ambassador 'perceiving that the Queen was passing on and that nobody offered to present him, placed himself directly before Her Majesty and made his compliments without any presentation', and the other Ministers had no choice but to follow suit, though Hamilton declared that had he known what was going to happen he 'should certainly not have followed the French Ambassador's example as it appears to me that there is a want of dignity in his proceeding'. He concluded his dispatch to Lord Shelburne by expressing the hope that the Secretary of State would 'approve of my having avoided making an *éclat* upon this occasion' as he was convinced that no offence was intended and that his example was followed by the representatives of Denmark, Turin, Portugal, Malta, Venice and Genoa 'who are pleased to say that they will continue to act as I do throughout this affair'.[6]

These nice points of etiquette may seem very trivial to us now after the passage of two hundred years, but they were of considerable importance at the time, and Hamilton would have been considered remiss in his duties had he not joined with his colleagues in protest. The life of a Court was like some intricate ballet in which everyone had a proper place and function; a false move might disrupt the whole game. An ambassador had to keep a keen eye on the elaborate ceremonial in which he was involved, for not only was his own position threatened if he allowed the rules to be broken, but the prestige of the country he represented might suffer, and this was something he could never allow. As the members of the diplomatic corps retired from the Queen's presence after the high-handed action of the French Ambassador they were all aware that the matter could not be allowed to rest at that, and it is a tribute to the position which Hamilton had achieved for himself after less than five years at Naples that those who were not 'family ministers' already looked to him for leadership. The *impasse* was fortunately settled by a move on the part of the Court. On 23 May Hamilton was able to report to London that the matter was cleared up: 'I was appointed with the rest of Foreign Ministers on Sunday last to meet Their Sicilian Majesties at a house in the harbour from whence their Majesties made their public entry into this Capital. We had there the honor of Complimenting His Sicilian Majesty upon his Marriage, after which His Majesty was pleased to present us himself to the Queen.'[7] Everyone could now pretend that the bungled presentation at Caserta had never happened, and honour was satisfied on all sides.

Poor Hamilton was soon to find himself in another scrape, though on this occasion it was certainly through no fault of his own. The episode took place at one of the court balls in celebration of the royal wedding. 'As I could not learn the etiquette at this Court with respect to Foreign Ministers dancing with Her Sicilian Majesty', he reported on June 7, 'I avoided the first Ball night placing myself forward, as did the rest of my colleagues. I acted in the same manner the first part of the second night. When Their Sicilian Majesties went in to supper the Prince Belmonte Pignatelli, who acts as Master of the Ceremonies at these balls, came up to me and asked me why I did not dance with Her Majesty. I naturally told him my reason for having kept at a distance, when he assured me not only that it would be proper for me to dance with the Queen but that I should pay my court to Her Majesty, who loved dancing, by so doing, and concluded by desiring me to ask the Queen as soon as Her Majesty should return. As I made no doubt but that the Master of Ceremonies had his instructions to speak to me in this matter I went forward in the circle and the Queen came up to me immediately upon her return from supper. After some little conversation I said to Her Majesty that I did not know whether I might presume to offer myself to have the honor of dancing with Her Majesty. The Queen went directly to the King, and after some consultation it was decided that none but the Family Ministers and *Chambellans* were to have that honor. I complain'd to the Prince Belmonte who excused himself for having led me into this scrape by assuring me he understood that all the Foreign Ministers might have the honor of dancing with the Queen. I desired, however, Count Kaunitz to assure Her Majesty that I should never have dreamt of taking the liberty of asking her had I not been directed to do so by the Master of the

Ceremonies. I also desired Prince San Nicandro to tell His Sicilian Majesty the same. Prince Belmonte is generally blamed. The Queen at the ball last night said very obligingly in my hearing that she could not abide the word *Etiquette*.'[8]

This little episode seems amusing enough now, but must have been very mortifying to Hamilton at the time, knowing, as he did, how much some of his colleagues would enjoy what appeared as a *gaffe* on his part. The remark the Queen later made in his hearing no doubt restored his spirits and shows that Maria Carolina, for all her extreme youth, was not lacking in tact and diplomacy.

The same, alas, could not be said of the King. Marriage had failed to improve his character and he continued to act as some thing between a lout and a buffoon. He caused the greatest scandal during the marriage festivities by playing every sort of youthful trick even to the extent of tripping up the ladies of his Court as they danced and then mocking their confusion when they attempted to rise. He constantly left the Queen on her own so that it appeared as though he positively disliked her. Hamilton reported that the Grand Duke and Duchess of Tuscany were 'shocked beyond measure' at his behaviour. To Sir Nathaniel Wraxall he later disclosed more intimate details of the King's coarse and disagreeable conduct. 'Ferdinand manifested on his part neither ardour nor indifference towards the Queen', Hamilton recalled.[9] 'On the morning after his nuptials. . . when the weather was very warm, he rose at an early hour and went out as usual to the chase, leaving his young wife in bed. Those courtiers who accompanied him, having enquired of his Majesty how he liked her, "*Dorme com un amazzata*", replied he, "*e suda com un porco*".'[10] His behaviour at table was equally uncouth. After consuming a large meal with evident relish he was accustomed to place his hand on his belly and announce that having eaten well his next immediate need was to relieve nature, and he would then select those of his courtiers whom he considered worthy to accompany him while he performed in their presence what most people prefer to do in private.

A more sinister side of his character was displayed on the hunting expeditions which filled so large a part of his life. Hamilton, who enjoyed the sport, very often went with the King, though his enjoyment was not increased by the indiscriminate slaughter he generally had to witness. It was his duty, however, to make the best use of these outings to win the confidence of the young King, while they offered him an unrivalled opportunity to observe Ferdinand in his unguarded moments far from the trammels of the Court and the promptings of his Ministers. One such opportunity occurred early in May 1768, 'I was on Sunday last above three hours with the King of Naples on one of these parties when away from his courtiers and surrounded by his menial servants,' Hamilton reported to London.[11] 'I was grieved to see in him a disposition to tyranical cruelty both towards his servants and the animals which unfortunately fell into his hands. It proceeds, I really believe, rather from a want of reflection and from the very bad education they have given His Majesty than from a natural bad disposition or want of understanding. This disposition must prove fatal to his subjects if it should take root.' The Envoy was clearly trying to make the best of the situation by blaming the bad education, so often invoked in excuse for the King's shameful conduct, but he was sufficiently alarmed at Ferdinand's manifestation of cruelty to feel obliged to send an account of it to his Government, and took the precaution of doing so in cipher. Fortunately it did not take root. The King's character developed very little, but like many men of limited understanding and scanty education he only became cruel when he was afraid or felt his position threatened or insecure, and this happened rarely enough in the early years of his reign. For the rest he remained through life good-natured, affable, and stupid.

Lady Craven gives us what is, perhaps, the most sympathetic picture of Ferdinand in his prime. 'His features were coarse and harsh', she wrote, 'yet the general expression of his countenance was rather intelligent, and perhaps even agreeable, although, separately taken, every feature was ugly. His conversation, his deportment, his manners, were from an unpolished simplicity, rude in their nature, though rather pleasing; as they removed from the mind what is always to be expected from a sovereign—that habit of disguise, artifice, and concealment, which accompany the possessor of a throne. If he did not converse much with strangers, yet he always appeared to say what he thought; and, although destitute of art or elegance, he did not betray a want of understanding or of information. He reminded one of a rustic elevated by accident to the crown; but then it was an honest well-intentioned countryman, not entirely unworthy of such an honour.'[12]

Lady Craven's comparatively flattering portrait of the King was due, to some extent, to his undoubted gift of making himself agreeable to women. They found him decidedly *simpatico* and could even discover points to admire in his very considerable ugliness. His lack of education would be less noticeable to them in a conversation which consisted chiefly in the exchange of gallantries. On the other hand his bigotry and superstition made him an object of ridicule in an age which boasted of its enlightenment; he was 'covered with relics and charms and. . . during thunderstorms he [would] walk about his apartments ringing a little bell taken from the Holy House of Loreto'.[13] There can be no doubt that nature had endowed him with very few of the qualities necessary for the exercise of royal power in an age of absolutism.

Maria Carolina was the thirteenth of the sixteen children of the Empress Maria Theresa and Francis of Lorraine, and was herself to be the mother of eighteen children, most of whom died in infancy or early youth. Like all the children of Maria Theresa she had received a sound education, was strong willed and imperious, but had a deeply passionate nature which often placed her reason at the mercy of her emotions. This was to result in the frustration of many of her political designs and was later to make her arch-enemy Napoleon ask the shrewd question: 'Is your Majesty's mind, so distinguished amongst women, so unable to divest itself of the prejudices of your sex that you must treat affairs of state as if they were affairs of the heart?' The French Emperor, who represented all that Maria Carolina most hated, had put his finger on the one great weakness in the character of the woman who was to become, by an ironical trick of fate, his own grandmother-in-law. At the time of her wedding, however, Napoleon Bonaparte had not quite completed his first year and the young Queen of Naples looked forward to a future in which revolutions and usurpations were not included. She looked no further than the birth of her first son, for her marriage treaty stipulated that after that event she would take her seat in the Council of State. As a woman with political ambitions, married to a weak husband, she awaited this moment with impatience.

People were to differ considerably in their opinions of the Queen's personal appearance. Lady Anne Miller, who saw her three years after her marriage, considered the Queen a beautiful woman with the finest and most transparent complexion she had ever seen. 'Her hair is of that glossy light chestnut I so much admire,' she wrote,[14] 'it is by no means red; her eyes are large, brilliant, and of a dark blue, her eyebrows exact and darker than her hair; her nose inclining to the aquiline, her mouth small, her lips very red (not the Austrian thickness) her teeth beautifully white and even, and when she smiles she discovers two dimples which give a finishing sweetness to her whole countenance. Her shape is perfect; she is just plump enough not to appear lean; her neck is long, her deportment perfectly easy, her walk majestic, her attitudes and action graceful.' Less enthusiastic in his description was Henry Swinburne, who found that 'the Queen has something very disagreeable in her manner of speaking, moving her whole face when she talks and gesticulating violently. Her voice is very hoarse, and her eyes goggle. She has acquired a roundness in her shoulders and is very fond of showing her hand, which is beautiful.'[15] Michael Kelly confessed that he did not think her particularly handsome, while Lady Craven somewhat confusedly declared that 'though her face was neither beautiful nor her person lovely, yet she was not altogether deficient in either point. Her figure might be esteemed too large, but it wanted neither dignity, grace, nor attraction.' It was inevitable that she should be compared with her sister Marie Antoinette, and was generally found to be less beautiful. That she was considerably more intelligent was not always noticed.

Hamilton was soon to appreciate the young Queen's quality of mind, as she herself was quick in discovering the limits of her husband's mental range. The question of Naples joining in the Bourbon Family Compact had been at issue since this agreement had been reached between France and Spain in 1761, and had been brought up again when France purchased the island of Corsica from the Genoese Republic in the year of Ferdinand's marriage. 'The following is a curious, true, and interesting anecdote', Hamilton reported in July 1768,[16] 'as it shews the character and penetration of the young Queen of Naples and His Sicilian Majesty's way of thinking with respect to the French, as well as his thoughts and those of the Marquis Tanucci upon the Family Compact, which in the circumstances of Corsica may prove of consequence hereafter.

The Queen, speaking confidentially to a Lady, said "Tanucci must be an able man since he can persuade the King that he acts for himself, for he told me lately that he had not sign'd the Family Compacts, not he truly, nor would he ever sign them. I should have greatly puzzled him I believe (added the young Queen) if I had ask'd His Majesty what these Family Compacts were".'

Maria Carolina had obviously taken her husband's measure. Indeed many people were to be hard put to it to find qualities to admire in this monarch beyond a general amiability and rather boisterous sense of fun which often took the form of crude and sometimes dangerous practical jokes. All that Dr. John Moore could find to praise, apart from Ferdinand's prowess at 'waging war against the beasts of the field and the birds of the air' was his proficiency at billiards. 'No King in Europe', wrote the Doctor, 'is supposed to understand the game of billiards better. I had the pleasure of seeing him strike the most brilliant stroke that perhaps ever was struck by a crowned head.'[17] Unfortunately Ferdinand's political skill did not match his ability with the billiards cue. He allowed the management of affairs to pass more and more into the hands of his wife, who even contrived to arrange for her husband to keep slightly better company than had been the case in his bachelor days. Her brother the Grand Duke Leopold was the agent through whose influence at the Court of Spain this transformation was brought about. By the middle of November Hamilton was able to comment on Ferdinand's 'great grief for the loss of some of his principal favourites who were in the lowest offices about the court and have been remov'd last week by a positive order from His Catholic Majesty. . .'[18] The influence of Maria Carolina was already being felt at the Neapolitan Court.

This ill-assorted couple were to remain on the throne of Naples through many vicissitudes for the whole of William Hamilton's long period as British Minister, and for many years afterwards. Their three lives were to be strangely, and at times dramatically, interwoven.

1.   B.M. Egerton MSS 2634 f. 105.
2.   B.M. Egerton MSS 2634 f. 316, 350 and 357.
3.   Bearne: *A Sister of Marie Antoinette*, p. 65.
4.   B.M. Egerton MSS 2634 f. 409.
5.   B.M. Egerton MSS 2635, f. 26.
6.   B.M. Egerton MSS 2635, f. 1.
7.   B.M. Egerton MSS 2635, f. 7.
8.   B.M. Egerton MSS 2635, f. 13. Kaunitz was Austrian Ambassador to Naples.
9.   N. Wraxall: *Historical Memoirs*, p. 173.

10. 'She sleeps like one slaughtered, and sweats like a pig.'
11. B.M. Egerton MSS 2634, f. 413.
12. Margravine of Anspach: *Memoirs*, Vol. I, pp. 291-2.
13. C. Giglioli: *Naples in 1799*, p. 16.
14. A. Miller: *Letters from Italy*, Vol. II, p. 234.
15. H. Swinburne: *The Courts of Europe at the Close of the last Century*,
     Vol. I, p. 132.
16. B.M. Egerton MSS 2635, f. 30.
17. J Moore: *A View of Society and Manners in Italy*, p. 284.
18. B.M. Egerton MSS 2635, f. 53.

CHAPTER VII

'Professor of Earthquakes'

In the year 1766 William Hamilton was elected a Fellow of the Royal Society. In those days the Fellows could be divided into two distinct groups, the first consisting of eminent men of science, the second and more numerous group consisting of men elected for their wealth, influence, or position in the world. When Sir Joseph Banks was elected President twelve years after Hamilton had first become a Fellow, there were over two hundred of these 'non-scientific' members as compared with a mere one hundred and thirteen professed scientists, while another forty-seven members were Peers of the Realm.[1] Hamilton was in the unique position of belonging to both of these groups, for if he seemed, as a man of birth, to find his place among the second, the contributions which the Society were very soon to receive from his pen quickly put him among the first.

Hamilton's reports on the activities of Vesuvius in a series of letters addressed to the President, Lord Morton, were what first distinguished him as a Fellow of the Royal Society. The proximity of this volcano was not a matter which every visitor to Naples could view with the calm curiosity of the British ambassador; to some, indeed, its very presence was considered a good reason for quitting the city as quickly as possible. This was to be the opinion of Madame Vigée-Le Brun. Driven from Paris to Naples by revolution, she was soon driven from Naples to Rome by eruptions, or the fear of them. 'Magnificent as is the country I was leaving', she confessed in her *Souvenirs*, 'I should not have liked to spend my life there. In my opinion Naples ought to be seen, like an enchanting magic-lantern, but to pass one's days there one must have overcome the terror inspired by the volcano. . . ' Vesuvius held no terror for Hamilton; it fascinated him. Any sign of activity would find him on its slopes taking notes, making sketches, digging up samples of earth, venturing as near as he dared to the smoking crater or to the streams of molten lava, often at the risk of his life. To Horace Walpole he became 'the Professor of Earthquakes' and he welcomed one of Hamilton's visits to England (for such was his reputation as an authority on earthquakes and eruptions) by the remark that he would not be quite out of his element 'for we have had pigmy earthquakes, and much havoc by lightning, and some very respectable meteors'.

Vesuvius, after centuries of quiescence, began its modern history in the great eruption of 21 August, A.D. 79, when the cities of Herculaneum and Pompeii were destroyed and the elder Pliny lost his life. From the time of that great disaster the volcano was never again thought to be dead, though there were long periods, sometimes as much as a hundred years, when there were no manifestations of violence. Between the years 202 and 1136 there were occasional disturbances causing considerable damage, and in 1631 there had been a very fierce eruption when eighteen thousand lives were said to have been lost. Since then the volcano had never been wholly quiescent, but it was not until the end of Hamilton's second year of residence at Naples that it began another period of special activity, with great eruptions, all of which he witnessed, in 1767, 1779, and 1794, the latter being considered one of the worst in the recorded history of the volcano.

Hamilton noticed the first changes in the volcano's behaviour during the month of September 1765 when the smoke issuing from the crater became more considerable, and continued even in fair weather. In October, as he later reported to Lord Morton, he 'perceived sometimes a puff of black smoke shoot up a considerable height in the midst of the white, which symptom of an approaching eruption grew more frequent daily; and soon after, these puffs of smoke appeared in the night tinged like clouds with the setting sun'.[2]

At the end of November, when the mountain was covered with snow, Hamilton decided on a climb in order to take a closer look at things: 'I perceived a little hillock of sulphur had been thrown up, since my last visit there, within about forty yards of the mouth of the Volcano; it was near six feet high, and a light blue flame issued constantly from its top. As I was examining this phenomenon, I heard a violent report, and saw a column of black smoke, followed by a reddish flame, shoot up with violence from the mouth of the volcano; and presently fell a shower of stones, one of which, falling near me, made me retire with some precipitation, and also rendered me more cautious of approaching too near, in my subsequent journies to Vesuvius.' His old school-fellow Frederick Hervey, future Bishop of Derry, was less fortunate, or perhaps just less nimble, for on one of these subsequent visits he was actually struck by one of the stones, receiving a wound in the arm of which he was not a little proud.

From November 1765 until March 1766 the smoke from the crater continued to increase and was accompanied by occasional falls of ashes which did much damage to the vineyards that grew on the slopes of the mountain. Towards the end of March Hamilton witnessed a sight which made him sure that a new phase had started and that things would soon begin to get more lively; 'A few days before the eruption I saw (what Pliny the younger mentions having seen before the eruption of Vesuvius which proved fatal to his uncle) the black smoke take the form of a pine tree.' On Good Friday, 28 March, at seven o'clock at night, the lava 'began to boil over the mouth of the Volcano. . . It was preceded by a violent explosion, which caused a partial earthquake in the neighbourhood of the mountain, and a shower of red hot stones and cinders were thrown up to a considerable height.' The first of the three great eruptions which Hamilton was to witness had started; the activity was to continue until the end of October of the following year.

Hamilton's reaction to the eruption was characteristic of his active curiosity. 'Immediately upon sight of the lava,' he continues in his letter to Lord Morton, 'I left Naples with a party of my countrymen whom I found as impatient as myself to satisfy their curiosity in examining so curious an operation of nature. I passed the whole night upon the mountain; and observed that, though the red hot stones were thrown up in much greater number and to a more considerable height than before the appearance of the lava, yet the report was much less considerable than some days before the eruption. The lava ran near a mile in an hour's time, when the two branches joined in a hollow on the side of the mountain, without proceeding farther. I approached the mouth of the Volcano, as near as I could with prudence; the lava had the appearance of a river of red hot and liquid metal, such as we see in the glass-houses, on which were large floating cinders, half lighted, and rolling one over another with great precipitation down the side of the mountain, forming a most beautiful and uncommon cascade. The color of the fire was much paler and more bright the first night than the subsequent nights, when it became of a deep red, probably owing to its having been more impregnated with sulphur at first than afterwards. In the day-time, unless you are quite close, the lava has no appearance of fire, but a thick white smoke marks its course.'

The next day the activity died down, but the lava appeared again on the 30th. On the last day of March Hamilton again spent the night on the mountain when he found that 'the lava was not so considerable as on the first night, but the red hot stones were perfectly transparent, some of which, I dare say of a ton weight, mounted at least two hundred feet perpendicular, and fell in or near the mouth of a little mountain that was now formed by the quantity of ashes and stones, within the great mouth of the Volcano, and which made the approach much safer than it had been some days before, when the mouth was near half a mile in circumference, and the stones took every direction'. Safe or not, it was on this occasion that Frederick Hervey was hit, though the stone that winged him was mercifully not one weighing a ton, or the Irish hierarchy might have been deprived of one of its more eccentric ornaments, for the wounded clergyman was within a year of his consecration as a bishop. Hamilton, however, had little time for his friend's plight; he was far too taken up with the strange scene before him. 'It is impossible to describe the beautiful appearance of these girandoles of red hot stones, far surpassing the most astonishing artificial fire work,' he concluded, though Hervey, after a more direct contact, was perhaps a little less enthusiastic.

It was ten days before Hamilton was able to climb the volcano again, but he kept it under constant observation, noticing 'a kind of intermission in the ferver of the mountain, which seemed to return with violence every other night'. The whole day and night of 12 April was spent on Vesuvius when he followed the flow of lava to its source, seeing it burst out of the side of the mountain within half a mile of the summit 'attended with violent explosions which threw up inflamed matter to a considerable height, the adjacent ground quivering like the timbers of a water-mill.' Following the lava course as it descended he saw two places where the liquid lava totally disappeared and ran for a while in a subterraneous passage, reappearing pure having left the scum and cinders behind it in the earth. On another visit just before finishing his letter to Lord Morton (which is dated 10 June) Hamilton reported that 'this eruption seems now to have exhausted itself, and I expect in a few days to see Vesuvius restored to its former tranquillity.'

During the brief period of quiescence before the volcano became active again Hamilton collected some specimens of salts and sulphurs which were dispatched to the President of the Royal Society. These he put into bottles actually on the mountain itself in the hope 'that they might not lose any of their force'. Examples of lava and cinders were also packed off to London, Hamilton expressing the polite hope: 'I shall be very happy if these trifles should afford your Lordship a moment's amusement', and added that he had been unable to find any chemist in Naples who had ever been to the trouble of analysing the productions of Vesuvius. The collection of these salts had not been without risk. 'The deep yellow, or orange-color salts' he explained, 'of which there are two bottles, I fetched out of the very crater of the mountain, in a crevice that was indeed very hot.' His expedition for this purpose had been carried out in the nick of time, for within three days fire appeared again on the top of the mountain and Hamilton, who was there with his elder nephew Lord Greville, heard 'the most dreadful inward grumblings, rattling of stones, and hissing, and we were obliged to leave the crater very soon on account of the emission of stones.' A new eruption was about to begin, but by December the volcano had settled down again for a few months of deceptive quiet, only to burst forth once more in October 1767, just at the time when the Neapolitan Court had learnt of the death of the Archduchess Maria Josepha.

The first news of this eruption to reach London came with Hamilton's dispatch of 20 October, which was primarily concerned with the account of the Archduchess's illness. As usual he tried to get as close as he could to the scene of volcanic activity (which seems to have interested him a good deal more than the activity of the Court) but, as he told the Secretary of State, 'prudence soon obliged me to retire, for I saw the sides of the Mountain split in many places and throw up fountains of liquid matter many feet high which afterwards formed rivers or rather torrents of fire. In an instant ashes of pumice stones caused almost a total darkness. I hastened from this curious but horrid scene and at my return the conflagration having increased and my Villa, which is at the foot of the mountain, being too much agitated by the explosions, I returned to Naples.[3] On his way he warned Tanucci that the King should leave Portici, where the Court was then in residence, as the palace might be in danger from the lava, but his warning was not immediately taken. By two o'clock in the morning, however, repeated explosions shook the palace so much that the King and Minister were compelled to take the British Envoy's advice and make a hasty retreat. The lava did, in fact, come close to the royal domain, and only a sudden change in the direction of its course saved the palace from the immediate possibility of destruction.

The eruption was very much more violent than that of the previous year, reaching its peak at the moment when the news of Maria Josepha's death was confirmed. Hamilton's dispatch announcing this sad event closed with a description of the confusion and terror which reigned in Naples. 'This last week exhibited a perpetual scene of horror', he wrote,[4] 'the eruption of Mount Vesuvius having continued with great violence. Many fine vineyards are destroy'd, but fortunately His Sicilian Majesty's palace and the museum at Portici have escaped by the lava's having taken another course when it was within a mile and a half of them. . . The streets of Naples have been full of processions attended by women with bare feet and their hair loose. On Tuesday the mob set fire to the Cardinal-Archbishop's gate, His Eminence having refused to bring out the Relicks of St. Januarius; and the same night the prisoners in the city gaol having wounded the jailer attempted to escape but were prevented by the troops. On Thursday the mob was so increas'd and tumultuous that His Sicilian Majesty thought proper to order the procession; it was attended by twenty thousand people at least. They went as far as the Porta Maddalena, the very extremity of Naples towards Mount Vesuvius, and if the noise had not happen'd to cease it is imagined they would have obliged the Cardinal to have gone to the Lava itself. After having loaded their Saint with the greatest abuse for having suffered the mountain to give them these alarms, this tumultuous mob (as soon as the noise ceas'd as usual after five or six hours) fell on their faces and afterwards returned to the Cathedral singing the praises of the Saint for the late Miracle. Vesuvius is now calm'd and the Lavas no longer run.'

To the Royal Society Hamilton sent a more detailed account of the impact of this new eruption. In a further letter to Lord Morton he described how he made an ascent of the mountain accompanied by a peasant only, whom he does not name, but who was very probably Bartolomeo Pumo, an old familiar of the volcano called by Hamilton the Cyclops of Vesuvius, who was his usual companion on these expeditions. 'I was making my observations upon the lava . . .' the letter records,[5] 'when, on a sudden, about noon, I heard a violent noise within the mountain, and at the spot about a quarter of a mile off the place where I stood, the mountain split; and, with much noise, from this new mouth a fountain of liquid fire shot up many feet high and then, like a torrent, rolled on directly towards us. The earth shook, at the same time that a volley of pumice stones fell thick upon us; in an instant clouds of black smoke and ashes caused almost total darkness; the explosions from the top of the mountain were much louder than any thunder I ever heard and the smell of sulphur was very offensive. My guide, alarmed, took to his heels; and I must confess that I was not at my ease. I followed close, and we ran near three miles without stopping. As the earth continued to shake under our feet, I was apprehensive of the opening of a fresh mouth, which might have cut off our retreat. I also feared that the violent explosions would detach some of the rocks off the mountain of Somma, under which we were obliged to pass. Besides, the pumice-stones, falling upon us like hail, were of such size as to cause a disagreeable sensation upon the part where they fell. After having taken breath, as the earth still trembled greatly, I thought it most prudent to leave the mountain and return to my Villa, where I found my family in great alarm at the continual and violent explosions of the Volcano which shook our house to its very foundation, the doors and windows swinging upon their hinges.' The relief of Catherine Hamilton can well be imagined when she saw her husband return none the worse except for a few bruises.

A particular feature of this eruption was 'a continued subterraneous and violent rumbling noise' which on the first night lasted for more than five hours on end. It was Hamilton's opinion (as he explained in his letter) that this strange noise 'might be owing to the lava in the bowels of the mountain having met with a deposition of rain water; and that the conflict between the fire and the water may, in some measure, account for so extraordinary a crackling and hissing noise.' In defence of his theory he quoted the example of the great eruption of 1631 when, he said, 'it is well attested that several towns, among which Portici and Torre del Greco, were destroyed by a torrent of boiling water having burst out of the mountain with the lava, by which thousands of lives were lost'. A similar phenomenon had been observed at Mount Etna in Sicily, which 'threw up hot water' only four years before the date at which Hamilton wrote.

From the 19th of October until the eruption ceased Hamilton kept a daily record of the volcano's behaviour, though on the 20th, after reaching Naples, it became impossible to judge the situation as the dense clouds of smoke and ashes completely obscured the mountain, the sun 'appearing as through a thick London fog or a smoked glass'. Ashes fell on the city all day. The thundering noise which he had heard on the first day returned on the morning of the 2nd with even greater violence, the oldest men declaring that they had never heard the like before; 'and indeed', Hamilton commented, 'it was very alarming; we were in expectation every moment of some dire calamity'. Ashes continued to fall and were very offensive to the eyes; people who had to go out were obliged to use umbrellas 'or flap their hats' as a protection. On the 23rd the noise ceased and few ashes fell, but they came again on the 25th. 'They issued from the crater of the Volcano', wrote Hamilton, 'and formed a vast column as black as the mountain itself, so that the shadow of it was marked out on the surface of the sea. Continual flashes of forked or zigzag lightning shot from this black column, the thunder of which was heard in the neighbourhood of the mountain, but not at Naples. There were no clouds in the sky at this time except those of smoke issuing from the crater of Vesuvius. I was much pleased with this phenomenon which I had not seen before in that perfection.'

On the 26th the smoke continued though less thick and without the dramatic accompaniment of thunder and lightning, and the flow of lava came to an end, a fact which puzzled Hamilton. 'As no lava has appeared after this column of black smoke, which must be occasioned by some inward operation of fire,' he wrote, 'I am apt to think that the lava, which should naturally have followed this symptom, has broke its way into some deeper cavern where it is silently brooding future mischief, and I shall be much mistaken if it does not break out a few months hence.' In fact the eruption had exhausted itself. On the 27th Hamilton commented: 'no more black smoke nor any signs of eruption'. No happening, however quaint, was overlooked by Hamilton if he thought it might contain a grain of scientific interest. He followed up his own personal observations of the eruption by an enquiry among the inhabitants of the neighbourhood of the volcano, and incorporated the results in a further letter addressed to Dr. Thomas Maty, the Secretary of the Royal Society.[6] A peasant whom he interrogated had lost eight hogs when these animals had eaten food which had become mixed with volcanic ash which had fallen into their trough. As a result of devouring this strange mixture the unfortunate hogs had become giddy and died within a few hours. Other informants told him that as well as forked lightning they had seen 'many meteors, like what are vulgarly called falling stars'. He had noticed that on the last day of the eruption the ashes which had fallen were almost as white as snow and was interested to discover that the old people considered this a sure symptom of the eruption being at an end.

'It would require many years close application', Hamilton wrote in the course of this letter, 'to give a proper and truly philosophical account of the volcanoes in the neighbourhood of Naples, but I am sure such a history might be given, supported by demonstration, as would destroy every system hitherto given upon this subject.' Hamilton's own observations, continued over the years, and regularly reported to the Royal Society, were in fact to make a major contribution to the study of volcanology, at that time a much neglected science. Despite all the advances that have since been made in this field his work still has value as well as interest to the scientist no less than to the historian. His published letters on Vesuvius have been described as the first noteworthy contribution on the subject since the Renaissance, and a recent writer has declared that 'his firsthand accounts of eruptions of the volcanoes of Italy still provide a valuable source of information'.[7]

In his own day Hamilton's letters to the Royal Society caused the liveliest interest. Lord Mountstuart who, as eldest son of the Earl of Bute, had known William Hamilton since his boyhood days at the court of the Prince of Wales, wrote in September 1766 to say how much he envied his old friend the night he had spent on Vesuvius. 'It must have been glorious', he continued, 'I think you richly deserve F.R.S. for the pains you have been at to send a description of it.'[8] Another friend added a word of caution to his congratulations after the last letters of the series describing the eruptions of 1765–7 had been published. 'I saw Mr. Simms lately, who has the honour of being known to you,' Charles Yorke wrote on 20 October 1769.[9] 'He was full of admiration at your philosophic fortitude in the midst of the Horrors of Vesuvius. I told him with what Tranquillity you had exprest your *hopes* to me that another *concussion* would lay the mountain open to the observation of the curious. We could not help fearing that you would suffer the fate of Pliny; and agreed that on such occasions the better part of *philosophy* is *discretion*, whatever it may be of valour; which you certainly have not wanted.' Sir Joshua Reynolds also wrote after the account of Hamilton's visit to Sicily had been added to the other letters to congratulate him 'on the honour you have acquired by the account you have given to the Royal Society of Vesuvius and Etna. I hear everyone speak of it with the highest enconiums as the best account that has hitherto appeared. I find that you are not contented with the reputation of being at the head of the Virtuosi but are extending your views to all kinds of knowledge.'[10] Sir Joshua went on to enquire whether Hamilton had heard of the report in the newspapers of his having been 'cast away in some of your excursions in hunting for Burning Mountains'. The thought of the death of the elder Pliny, Reynolds concluded, had once again put the idea into somebody's head. 'I hope you will never suffer for your eagerness after knowledge', the letter ends, 'but that you will live and return to be the Mecaenas to the rising generation of artists.'

As far as Hamilton was concerned any plea for discretion would have fallen on deaf ears; he was to continue to make ascents of the volcano in all its moods, and often at some peril, until he was well over sixty years of age. He was never an armchair scientist. Like his friend Sir Joseph Banks he believed in direct observation on the spot. Indeed, when the latter's scientific voyages were over and he was settled in London as President of the Royal Society, he could not but envy his friend who was so fortunate as to have a live volcano almost on his doorstep. When Hamilton wrote to congratulate him on his election as President the great botanist replied: 'That I envy you your situation within two miles of an erupting volcano you will easily guess. I read your letters with that kind of fidgetty anxiety which continually upbraids me for not being in a similar situation. I envy you, I pity myself, I blame myself and then begin to tumble over my Dried Plants in hopes to put such wishes out of my head, which now I am tied by the leg to an armchair, I must with diligence suppress.'[11]

Hamilton had an opportunity to observe another volcano at close quarters when he visited Sicily in the Spring of 1769. It was his first visit to this island which formed a part of the kingdom to which he was accredited as ambassador. His party consisted of his wife and Lord Fortrose. Catherine Hamilton had recently received the news of her mother's death and was, as her husband informed Charles Greville, 'in a situation you can imagine, as you know the tenderness of her nature'. He had, he said, hastened his departure to Sicily in order to divert her. Lord Fortrose was an ideal travelling companion for them as he already shared Catherine's musical tastes and was prepared to share Hamilton's adventures on the slopes of Mount Etna. They were altogether three months away from Naples, being ready on 18 April 'to take advantage of the first wind', and reported their return home 'on Saturday last' in a dispatch of 5 July. The ascent to the crater of Etna (at ten thousand five hundred feet the highest volcano in Europe, over two and half times the height of Vesuvius) was to be one of the chief objectives of their trip, and was to be the subject of a further letter to the Royal Society written on Hamilton's return to Naples.

At Palermo the party were received with the utmost attention by the Viceroy for whom it was a rare enough honour to receive the ambassador of a foreign power. The Sicilian nobility, Hamilton discovered, were proud of showing great hospitality to strangers, and the Envoy was made to feel welcome in the city where he would one day come to seek refuge from revolution. He was clearly delighted with the reception he received in the great houses, though his admiration did not extend to the masses of the people. 'There is not much trade here', he reported, 'and the people seem to me as indolent and inactive as at Naples, but the Nobility are better educated and much more conversable than at Naples.'[12] It was in the house of one of these Sicilian noblemen that he came across a book which showed him that he was not the first British diplomat to visit Etna and write an account of what he had seen. Lord Winchelsea, returning from his post as ambassador to the Sublime Porte exactly a hundred years before, had witnessed the great eruption of 1669. He had just reached Catania, where he was the guest of the Bishop, when chance made him an eyewitness of what he described as 'the late prodigious earthquake and eruption of Mount Etna'. Hamilton found the book in the library of Prince Torremuzzo's house in Palermo and read it with the greatest interest. Nothing could have been better calculated than the discovery of this curious book to whet his appetite for the adventure that lay ahead.

In order to reach Catania Hamilton and his party decided to sail round the southern coast of Sicily, but between Palermo and Agrigento they encountered strong contrary winds and were driven so far off course that they were forced to put into the port of Valetta. A visit to Malta had not formed part of the original plan, but the opportunity to see so interesting a place was too good to miss, and ten days were spent on the island. In 1769 Malta was still in the hands of the knights of the Sovereign Military Order of St. John of Jerusalem, who had held it since they had been driven from Rhodes in 1522, and were now, at the time of Hamilton's unexpected arrival, nearing the end of their time on the island by whose name their Order was popularly known. The Grand Master of the Knights of Malta, like the Viceroy of Sicily, received the party with all possible hospitality, as did the principal officers of the Order. The venerable Grand Master was over ninety years of age, but the English visitors found that he enjoyed 'a perfect state of health, and neither his understanding or eyesight have failed him in the least'. Hamilton was impressed with all he saw at Valetta and left the island with regret having formed a high opinion of its industrious inhabitants. 'I found in general at Malta a spirit and industry and action seldom seen in these warm climates', he reported with approval to the Secretary of State. He would see Malta again many years later from the deck of Nelson's flagship when the tricolour of republican France had replaced the cross of St. John over the ramparts of the citadel of Valetta.

Catania was at length reached, a city, as Hamilton described it, 'so often destroyed by eruptions of Etna and totally over thrown by earthquake', as to have been more or less completely rebuilt within the last fifty years and was by then a considerable town of at least thirty-five thousand inhabitants. The persistence with which people returned to rebuild and re-establish themselves on land so often devastated did not cause him any surprise after his experience of life in Naples. 'I do not wonder at the seeming security with which these parts are inhabited, having been so long witness to the same near Mount Vesuvius,' he wrote[13]. 'The operations of Nature are slow; great eruptions do not frequently happen; each flatters himself it will not happen in his time or, if it should, that his tutelar saint will turn away the destructive lava from his grounds; and indeed the great fertility in the neighbourhoods of Volcanoes tempts people to inhabit them.' With regard to the tutelar saints, he was already familiar with the faith the Neapolitans placed in their patron St. Januarius. The inhabitants of Catania, under similar misfortunes, had recourse to the veil of St. Agatha. Hamilton did not scoff at these pious practices for he realised that they had value for the scientist as well as the superstitious. 'Till the year 252 of Christ the chronological accounts of the eruptions of Etna are very imperfect', he commented, 'but as the veil of St. Agatha was in that year first opposed to check the violence of the torrent of lava and has ever since been produced at the time of great eruptions, the miracles attributed to its influence, having been carefully recorded by the priests, have at least preserved the dates of such eruptions. The relicks of St. Januarius have rendered the same service to the lovers of natural history by recording the great eruptions of Vesuvius.' From these sources he was able to account for twenty-seven eruptions of Etna and twenty-nine of Vesuvius.

The expedition to the summit of the volcano began on 24 June. With Hamilton and Lord Fortrose was Canon Recupero, described as 'an ingenious priest of Catania who is the only person there that is acquainted with the mountain'. This excellent ecclesiastic must have jumped at the opportunity offered him for his life so far, at least with regard to his volcanic studies, seems to have been rather a discouraging affair. Of this enthusiast of Etna Hamilton wrote: 'He is actually employed in writing its natural history; but, I fear, will not be able to compass so great and useful an undertaking for want of proper encouragement.'

Two days were taken in the ascent, and the top of the mountain was reached on the early morning of the third day. At one point they explored a cave in the lava left by the eruption of 1669. 'By means of a rope', said Hamilton, 'we descended into several subterraneous caverns, branching out and extending much farther and deeper than we chose to venture, the cold there being excessive and a violent wind frequently extinguishing our torches.' On the second day they passed through an area covered with the largest oak, chestnut and fir trees that the English climbers had ever seen. It was from here, Hamilton noted, that the King of Naples' dockyards were supplied with timber for ship-building. As they began to reach the higher slopes of the mountain the air began to get sharper 'so that', Hamilton's letter records, 'in the same day the four seasons of the year were sensibly felt by us on this mountain; excessive summer heat on the *Piemontese*, spring and autumn temperature in the middle, and extreme cold of winter in the upper region. I could perceive, as we approached the latter, a gradual decrease of vegetation, and from large timber trees we came to small shrubs and plants of the northern climates.' When night came on they pitched a tent and made a good fire without which, in Hamilton's opinion, they would have perished with cold. In the course of the next day they passed valleys of snow as they set out at the early hour of one o'clock in the morning, so as to reach the crater before sunrise.

'Soon after we had seated ourselves on the highest point of Etna the sun arose and displayed a scene that indeed passes all description,' Hamilton's letter continues. 'The horizon lighting up by degrees, we discovered the greatest part of Calabria, and the sea on the other side of it; the Phare of Messina, the Lipari Islands; Stromboli with its smoking top though above seventy miles distant seemed to be just under our feet. We saw the whole island of Sicily, its rivers, towns, harbours, etc., as if we had been looking on a map.' Their Italian companion told them that Malta, too, was often visible, though on this occasion the island was obscured by haze. The shadow of the mountain on whose summit they sat 'reached across the whole island and far into the sea on the other side'.

After feasting their eyes on this scene they turned their attention to an examination of the crater. Hamilton describes it as being, as near as they could judge, about two miles and a half in circumference, though they did not think it safe to go round and measure it as some of the surrounding ground appeared to be very unsafe. 'The inside of the crater', he recorded, 'which is incrusted with salts and sulphurs like that of Vesuvius, is in the form of an inverted hollow cone, and its depth nearly answers to the height of the little mountain that crowns the great volcano. The smoke, issuing abundantly from the sides and bottom, prevented our seeing quite down, but the wind clearing away the smoke from time to time, I saw this inverted cone contracted almost to a point; and, from repeated observations, I dare say, that in all volcanos the depth of the craters will be found to correspond nearly to the height of the conical mountain of cinders which usually crowns them. In short, I look upon the craters as a sort of suspended funnel under which are vast caverns and abysses.'

After spending three hours on the crater they began the return journey, passing on the way the remains of an ancient building which Canon Recupero, much encouraged, it is to be hoped, by the adventures he had shared, told them was called the Philosopher's Tower, according to tradition once inhabited by Empedocles. This philosopher is supposed to have wished to demonstrate his godlike power over death by casting himself into the flaming crater; the volcano, however, had replied by throwing back one of his sandals to show that it could devour philosophers with as much ease and appetite as ordinary mortals. Hamilton, recalling that the ancients used to sacrifice to the celestial gods on top of Etna, thought that the ruin showed the remains of a temple once dedicated to that purpose. The remainder of their descent passed without incident until they reached the foot of what Hamilton was to refer to, perhaps in comparison with the smaller size of his neighbour Vesuvius, as 'this respectable volcano'.

One more volcano, no less respectable, was to come under Hamilton's observation as they sailed back from Messina to Naples. Their course took them through the Lipari islands, all 'evidently formed by explosion', and there they saw Stromboli 'existing in all its force'. An illustration to the book containing Hamilton's volcanic letters, which was published in 1772, shows this volcano as an almost perfect cone with immense clouds of black smoke bursting from its top and covering half the sky. 'This volcano differs from Etna and Vesuvius,' Hamilton observed, 'by its continually emitting fire, and seldom any lava; notwithstanding its continual explosions this island is inhabited, on one side, by about an hundred families'. To a man of Hamilton's enthusiasm he might almost have thought it a pleasant spot to retire to, but it is doubtful whether Catherine Hamilton, for whose diversion the tour had originally been undertaken, would have shared this opinion. It is to be hoped that she returned to Naples restored in health and spirits. Hamilton certainly returned with his reputation as an authority on volcanoes fully established.

1. *Vide* H. C. Cameron: Sir Joseph Banks, p. 133.
2. W. Hamilton: *Observations on Mount Vesuvius*, Letter I.
3. B.M. Egerton MSS 2634, f. 350.
4. Ibid., f. 357.
5. W. Hamilton: *Observations on Mount Vesuvius*, Letter II, p. 26.
6. W. Hamilton: op. cit. Letter III, pp. 46–7.
7. *Vide* F. M. Bullard; *Volcanoes in History, in Theory, in Eruption* (Edinburgh, 1962) p. 17.
8. Morrison, 9.
9. B.M. Add. MSS 42069, f. 70.
10. *Letters of Sir Joshua Reynolds*, p. 28, Letter XVI, 17 June 1770.
11. B.M. Egerton MSS 2641, f. 130.
12. B.M. Egerton MSS 2635 f. 85.
13. W. Hamilton: *Observations on Mount Vesuvius, etc.*, Letter, IV.

CHAPTER VIII

Hamilton's Influence Extended

The Bourbons were great hunters. Had they devoted the same energy to the welfare of their subjects that they expended in the almost daily pursuit of wild animals and game the history of their dynasty, in its latter days, might have been more fortunate. Whether in France, Spain, or Naples the Royal Hunt occupied a place of first importance in the annual routine of the court. Ferdinand IV, like his father, was no exception to this family predilection for the chase; indeed, it might be described as the predominant passion of his life. But he differed from his father in that he was quite prepared to allow others, whether the Queen or the chief Minister, to occupy themselves with the affairs of the Kingdom so long as he was free to follow his favourite sport. 'Give him a boar to stab, a pigeon to shoot at, a battledore or an angling rod', wrote William Beckford after meeting the King, 'and he is better contented than Solomon in all his glory, and will never discover, like that sapient sovereign, that all is vanity and vexation of spirit.'[1]

The King's conduct on the field of sport was not especially endearing. 'The sport was a sad sight—a mere butchery of hogs', wrote Henry Swinburne, a witness of the royal huntsman at work. 'The King and several of his courtiers were stationed on horseback in the plain in front with large spears in their hands. A body of hunters drove all the game from the hanging woods which line the sides of the immense crater to the spot where the King was placed; and this was the best part of the sport, for it was a cheerful scene to see such crowds beat the thicket, and to hear their continued firing, shouting and hallooing. The boars ran down into the open grounds and there large hounds were let loose to stop them, in order that the horsemen might come up and spear them; but as the dogs were too large and too numerous for these tame animals, the poor beasts generally tumbled about sprawling for the royal hero to drive his spear into them at his leasure.'[2]

Hamilton was a constant companion of the King on these hunting expeditions. Though often repelled by the wholesale slaughter in which he was compelled to take part, he enjoyed the exercise, the opportunity to observe the countryside, and the less sanguinary aspects of the sport itself. It also presented him with a splendid chance to get on to terms of close friendship with the King. If he soon came to hold a unique place among the Ministers attached to the Court of Naples he owed this very much to the long and often tedious days spent in Ferdinand's company in the game preserves of the royal estates. His diplomatic colleagues were often too old, too unfit, or too obtuse to see the advantage to be gained from taking part in these holocausts of hogs. By sharing in them and vieing with the King in athletic skill, Hamilton was able to establish an intimate relationship with this rather stupid young monarch who was so incapable of appreciating the Minister's intellectual interests. Ferdinand tended to distrust clever men. That he came to respect Hamilton and to rely on his judgement was due almost entirely to the many hours the British envoy was prepared to spend in the hunting field. That Hamilton himself would gladly have sacrificed much of this time to his other pursuits is obvious, but the time was not wasted. The close relationship he forged with the King was worth all the time away from his pictures, his vases, and his papers. It was thanks to this that he became indispensable as the representative of his country at Naples. Even so he was not to escape a smart rebuke from his nephew Greville for the hours he appeared to waste in the hunting field.

'To hear of your comfort and happiness will always give me pleasure', that young man wrote rather smugly,[3] 'and, as I suppose you will find in every season of the year some unfortunate animals to torture and extirpate, I shall beg you to give me the short intervals of rationality, and describe either your acquisitions or your satisfaction from the works either of art or nature which shall present themselves to your observation.' That diplomatic advantage could also be gained in every season of the year from these outings in the forests and game preserves does not seem to have occurred to Charles Greville.

Hamilton sketched a scene typical of one of these hunting expeditions in a letter written to Sir Joseph Banks in January 1778, at a time when he had long become familiar with the routine. 'I am here leading as Wild a life as you can conceive, which I like exceedingly—for a short time. His Sicilian Majesty, whose particular kindness to me is visible to everyone, has taken me on this private party and indeed he has invited me once for all to every party. We are lodged in a dreary village at the foot of the Appenines surrounded with mountains whose tops are cover'd with snow and lower parts with thick woods which are full of the largest and fiercest Boars. . . Every day a district of these woods is surrounded with Peasants intermixed with Soldiers to oblige them to go into the thick Bushes, 2000 men at the least are every day employed. The Chasseurs (which are 14) draw up in a line at a proper distance one from another. The Peasants contract their semicircle and three or four hundred Dogs are continually hunting the game and give you notice of the approach of a Boar, etc. The Chasseurs have a parapet of trunks of trees before them as I assure you that these Boars attack without any ceremony. As it takes time to place the people we do not go to the Woods till after dinner, but our Dinner is never later in the morning than half past 10 o'clock. At night we return with seldom less than 40 or 50 Boars. . . No expence is spared, good roads are made to communicate to all the Mountains; we have the King's carriages and Post horses to carry us as far as is coach-road, and then his saddle horses. There is no dress, for the rule is to be in frock and boots, and the King and

Queen will have no ceremony, nay, we dine with them with our hats on when in a cold place, which sometimes happens. We had no less than 1336 Dogs when we came here and as there are generally a dozen killed or wounded every day such a supply is necessary. In short, these parties are so singular that no description can give an idea of them. The King of Naples never does lose a moment that can be employed in shooting, fishing, or what relates to one or the other. The regular lists of every piece of game are sent to the King of Spain. The King weighs himself every Boar as soon as we have come home, the largest we have killed, without his guts, weigh'd 280 lbs. As my great pleasure is in the observation of Nature I have an ample field here besides the real pleasure I have in the shooting. I am constantly remarking some very singular characters, as savage as many you met with in the South Sea Islands. . . '4

Given the King's tastes it is not surprising that when the question came up of King George III sending him a present, Hamilton at once suggested that he be sent an Irish Wolf-hound, as he had discovered that Ferdinand was eager to have a dog of this breed. In a dispatch on this subject to Lord Shelburne he added the note in cipher: 'This affair, trifling as it may appear, is certainly of consequence to me as I am convinced that his Sicilian Majesty would have more pleasure in the possession of these Dogs than the Empress-Queen in the restoration of Silesia. Would not His Majesty think proper to make such a present to the King of the Two Sicilies, who has receiv'd one of the like nature from the Emperor and the Great Duke, which gives him much satisfaction.'5 The British Government were less appreciative of the sporting habits of the King of Naples than was their Envoy, and Hamilton was still pressing for the gift of a wolfhound when Lord Shelburne had been replaced as Secretary of State by Lord Weymouth.

Fishing no less than hunting occupied the idle hours of the King of Naples, and as Hamilton was all his life a keen fisherman he probably enjoyed their days out in the bay in the royal fishing boat as much as any of these sporting activities. Wraxall described the British Envoy 'laboriously engaged in an open boat, exposed to the rays of a burning sun, harpooning fish in the bay of Castellammare', and declared that on these occasions the King 'neither regards heat, nor cold, nor hunger, nor danger'. It was Ferdinand's eccentric habit to sell his catch in the open market when he returned from a day's fishing. Mrs. Piozzi witnessed this bizarre spectacle and described in her *Glimpses of Italian Society* how the King got as big a price as he could, 'but gives away the money they pay him for it, and that directly, so that no suspicion of meanness, or of anything worse than a little rough merryment, can be attached to his truly honest, open, undesigning character'.

The King's favourite companions on these fishing expeditions were the inhabitants of the Lipari islands who, according to Wraxall, 'have been in all ages most expert sailors, divers, and fishermen'. These were among the 'low companions' for whose company Ferdinand continued to show preference, much to the anxiety of Tanucci and the King of Spain. The Neapolitan monarch's increasing independence from the restraining influence of his father and chief minister was reflected in a dispatch of Hamilton's, dated 15 August 1769. The King, he reported, 'continues his usual life of dissipation and notwithstanding the remonstrances of the Marquis Tanucci passes whole nights in a boat in this bay, disguised like a fisherman drawing nets of stinking fish. I am told that His Majesty has now very little regard for the orders from Spain which used to keep him in great awe, in short the worst consequences may be expected from the very bad education they have given this Prince, who had naturally a good disposition. The Queen is so young that she rather seemingly joins in and encourages these puerilities than checks them'.[6]

The Court and diplomatic corps had particular reason to be apprehensive on the matter of the King's uninhibited behaviour just at this time as Naples had been much in the public eye owing to the royal marriage, and earlier in the year had experienced the mixed blessing of a visit from that paragon of monarchs, the Emperor Joseph II. Few brothers-in-law can have been more ill-assorted than the meticulous, dry, high minded, reforming Emperor and the rustic, uncouth and unpolished King of Naples. The Emperor reached Naples at the end of March 1769 and summed up its monarch in a curt and illuminating sentence: 'Although an ugly Prince, he is not absolutely repulsive: his skin is fairly smooth and firm, of a yellowish pallor: he is clean except for his hands; and at least he does not stink.'[7] The Emperor had clearly expected the worst.

The arrival of Joseph II was so sudden and unexpected that he found his brother the Grand Duke of Tuscany still in bed. His suite consisted of only five people, and he refused all honours and ceremonies, preferring to stay with his ambassador in his villa at Portici instead of occupying the rooms prepared for him in the royal palace. He travelled incognito and insisted on this unofficial status being observed throughout his stay in his brother-in-law's capital.

Hamilton had two reasons for ingratiating himself with the Austrian Emperor. In the first place it was important to discover the disposition of so powerful a monarch towards the policies of the British government and to pass on such information as he could glean to the Secretary of State in London; and secondly he had himself ambitions to succeed as British Ambassador in Vienna when that post became vacant, and the visit of Joseph gave him a splendid opportunity to make himself agreeable to a sovereign who might express a desire flattering to Hamilton's plans for his own future. He quickly gained the goodwill of the Emperor by offering him one of his coaches so that Joseph could visit all the sights of the city without his identity being discovered. The serious-minded Emperor was naturally attracted to an Envoy who enjoyed Hamilton's reputation for scholarship and taste. 'He talked to me',[8] Hamilton reported, 'for near an hour mostly upon the subject of the antiquities and natural curiosities of this country and was pleased to say that his brother the Great Duke had so often mention'd to him the pleasure he had in seeing some of them with me, that he hoped I would not deny him the same satisfaction. . . ' The reception given him was so cordial that Hamilton had to confess that it had caused a good deal of jealousy among his colleagues. The Emperor, he said in the same dispatch, 'is rather low in stature, is robust, well made, and has a Martial appearance. There is a remarkable sweetness in his countenance and vivacity in his eyes. His conversation is easy and unaffected and, if I may be allowed to judge in so short a time, I believe him to be a Prince of great discernment and full of humanity and goodness.'

The desire expressed by the Emperor to be shown some of the natural and artistic curiosities of Naples in the company of the British Envoy had not been mere politeness. On 11 April Hamilton was able to report that the Emperor had spent the entire day with him visiting the various historic sites in the neighbourhood of the city, including Herculaneum and Pompeii. In fact Joseph could hardly have chosen a better guide, but Hamilton was flattered by so marked an attention, and wrote full of enthusiasm. 'He seems to me of a most humane disposition,' he declared; 'simple in his manner, exalted in his ideas, and as he despises singularly all little actions I believe him capable of doing very great ones.'

After five years at the Court of the oafish Ferdinand the thought of a possible transfer to Vienna, to a court presided over by this philosopher among monarchs, must have presented itself to Hamilton's imagination in the liveliest of ways, when the Emperor, paying a visit to the Palazzo Sessa, dropped a hint which the Envoy lost no time in passing on to London. 'He is well inclined to Great Britain,' Hamilton continued in his dispatch of 11 April,[9] 'and I know for certain that in a confidential discourse with a person who repeated it to me, he discover'd a very particular personal regard and esteem for the King our Master. My house is the only one, positively, that the Emperor has honour'd here with his presence, and what appear'd to me extraordinary, having no reason to be expected, he said: "We hope and wish to see you one of these days at Vienna." I repeat the very words, and the Foreign Ministers have all made me their Compliments upon the honors I have received, and they look upon the very distinguished manner in which the Emperor has treated His Majesty's Minister at this Court as a certain sign of the great regard he has for His Majesty himself.' In attempting politely to pass all the compliments paid him as being due to King George III Hamilton could not hide the elation he felt at the triumphal conclusion of his meetings with Joseph II, or of the hopes, in fact never to be fulfilled, which they seemed to hold out for the future.

A more personal account of the Emperor's private visit to the Hamiltons' house was sent in a letter to Greville from his proud uncle. Joseph, like all who heard her, had praised Catherine's playing on the harpsichord, and had then gone into what Hamilton described as his 'lumber room', where his celebrated collection was on display. ('But by the bye', he adds, 'I had put my collection in a little better order than when you was here.') The imperial visitor remained half an hour in this sanctum and expressed the greatest satisfaction with all he saw. 'He allowed the pictures to be the best he had ever seen,' Hamilton informed his nephew. 'I will tell you what he said when he went away, taking me by the hand, tho' I wouldn't to anybody else lest they should think me vain. *On vous rends justice, on vous estime, vous êtes honête homme, c'est tout dire*. These were his very words. . . .'[10]

The Emperor must certainly have found the cultivated atmosphere of the Hamilton's *ménage* a pleasant change from the somewhat grotesque displays of buffoonery he had been compelled to witness at the royal palace, where the King would chase his elderly ministers and courtiers down the corridors, administering slaps and pinches to any who got in his way, and even inflicted what Joseph described as 'a great salute' on the Imperial behind when the Emperor had been least expecting so familiar or painful a salutation. Reticence was not a quality the King cultivated. Henry Swinburne described an extraordinary episode of this visit which was related to him by Hamilton. 'His Majesty's manners are not very refined,' he wrote of Ferdinand; 'when the Emperor was here, and standing at a balcony with his brother-in-law, the latter made a very unwarrantable noise and, by way of apology, said, "*E necessario per la salute, fratello mio*".'[11] The Emperor's only consolation came from the thought that his sister would easily be able to manage so absurd and foolish a husband.

The Emperor's kind words, and the marked attention he had paid to the British Envoy and his wife, encouraged Hamilton's hopes for a change to a post of greater responsibility and importance. Now in his fortieth year, he was by no means reconciled to the thought of remaining always at Naples, despite all it had to offer to a man of his tastes. Charles Greville had been staying with the Hamiltons just before Joseph II arrived in Naples, and when he answered his uncle's letter describing the Imperial visit to the Palazzo Sessa he was in fact in Vienna, through which city he was passing on his journey home. His reply served to increase Hamilton's hopes that he might himself go there soon as his Sovereign's representative. 'I must now inform you what I have done and do at present at Vienna,' Greville wrote.[12] 'I must begin with wishing that you could contrive to come here as Ambassador, as I am sure you would like it extremely, and be adored. . . ' Lest political ambition should not be a sufficient incentive he added another bait which he knew his uncle would find it hard to resist: 'If you was here, for a mere trifle you might pick up pictures, as the taste for them is now gone, and good and bad are in the same estimation.' In March 1770 Hamilton had hopes that just such an opportunity had occurred for him to 'contrive' to secure the Vienna appointment. The Imperial Ambassador at Naples told him that the Emperor was thinking of reorganising his embassy at London on a new basis, and Hamilton at once sent a report of the conversation to Lord Weymouth, putting in his own plea at the same time. 'Count Kaunitz, the Imperial Ambassador at this Court, having assured me that the Court of Vienna would for the future send only a Minister Plenipotentiary to that of Great Britain, may I beg the favour of your Lordship if you should not think it improper, to mention in my name to the King most humbly that I should be very happy if my poor abilities could be employ'd for His Majesty's Service in a more active scene than this Court affords, and that in case the King should not think proper to continue his Ambassador at the Court of Vienna I should esteem the character of His Majesty's Envoy Extraordinary and Plenipotentiary at that Court as a singular honor and favor. I am more encouraged to take this liberty with your Lordship as the Emperor himself was graciously pleas'd to tell me when at Naples, that in case Lord Stormont should quit Vienna, he hoped that I might succeed his Lordship.'[13] Lord Stormont, in fact, was to remain for a further two years at Vienna, and Hamilton's first request for a transfer to another post fell upon deaf ears.

In the year following the visit of Joseph II Hamilton found his position gaining, if only temporarily, a little more of the political influence he coveted and generally found wanting in his present post. In disputes between great powers it often happens that minor ones, if they are able to remain neutral, can exert an influence out of proportion to their strength. When two powers have severed diplomatic relations their only means of communication is through their respective representatives at a neutral court, and Hamilton saw himself cast in this role when war threatened between Great Britain and Spain over the question of the possession of the Falkland Islands. The fact that the King of Naples was still very much in awe of Tanucci, (despite occasional efforts to show some independence), and that that Minister still took his orders from the King of Spain, made Neapolitan neutrality by no means certain, nor was the attitude which the French Government would adopt immediately clear.

In urging neutrality upon the Neapolitan Government Hamilton had to exploit as best he could the vanity of Tanucci and his known dislike of the French, as well as his reluctance to join the Family Compact, an issue which was again being raised by the other Bourbon Courts. His task, fortunately, was made all the easier by Tanucci's own desire to keep Naples out of a war from which she could expect to gain no advantages. 'The Marquis Tanucci is very anxious His Sicilian Majesty should be allow'd to preserve a Neutrality if the War should take place,' Hamilton wrote in a dispatch of 8 January 1771,[14] 'and I have been confidentially assured by the person charged with the affairs of the Court of Vienna at this Court, who had it from the Queen of Naples, that His Catholic Majesty[15] had consented to the above mentioned Neutrality, but that His Sicilian Majesty is at present greatly disturb'd at a fresh injunction from his Father that in the case of War any British ships coming into his ports should on no account be assisted with either stores or provisions. I have been told likewise that the Duke of Choiseul, who has a great aversion to the Marquis Tanucci is, in order to distress him, ever insisting upon the King of Spain's obliging the King of Naples to accede to the Family Compact.'

It was in fact Louis XV's Minister Choiseul whose intervention prevented war from breaking out between Britain and Spain, but before the issue of peace or war was settled Hamilton set down what he considered his own position would be should general hostilities result. 'In the case of a war', his dispatch continues, 'I flatter myself that my having the good fortune to be personally well with His Sicilian Majesty, his Ministers, and the French Ambassador here (who is so very particularly connected with those Ministers who govern at the Court of France)[16] may be of some little service should His Majesty at any time think proper to make use of such a channel when most others will be shut.' Spain's agreement to cede the Falkland Islands to Great Britain would soon remove the danger of war—and also his hopes of being able to represent his Government in a position of inflated importance. From the point of view of Lord North's government, which had recently come to power in England, Hamilton's obvious and growing influence at the Neapolitan Court was a strong argument in favour of leaving him where he was and not transferring him, as he wished, to some other post.

In comparison with questions of war and peace some of the other issues which formed the subject of Hamilton's dispatches seem trivial enough, but they help to give us a picture of the sort of problems he had to deal with against the background of the vivid and colourful life of the city of Naples. There was, for example, the case of Mr. Fothergill's leg, which Hamilton brought to the attention of a surprised, but possibly not very interested Secretary of State on the 9th of April, 1771. 'Some days ago', wrote the Envoy, 'as Mr. Fothergill and Mr. Stepney, Member of Parliament, were returning from Portici in an open Chaise, they were overturned and Mr. Fothergill's leg was unfortunately broken, but Mr. Stepney receiv'd no hurt. His Sicilian Majesty was pleas'd to tell me as soon as he heard of the accident that his Surgeon should attend Mr. Fothergill if he chose it, and indeed I believe by His Sicilian Majesty's goodness Mr. Fothergill's leg will be saved as there were symptoms of an approaching mortification when the King's Surgeon first attended him, and which are now vanished.' If the Secretary of State breathed a sigh of relief at the prospect of vanishing mortification he was in for a shock when Hamilton's next dispatch arrived. 'Mr. Fothergill, the unfortunate young gentleman mentioned in my last,' the Minister read under the date of 23 April, 'was obliged to submit yesterday to the amputation of his broken leg, in order to prevent if possible more fatal consequences. Their Sicilian Majesties have shown great goodness of heart upon this occasion having order'd that every assistance should be given him, and seem much interested in the fate of the unhappy Patient.'[17] Here Mr. Fothergill and his one remaining leg disappear from official correspondence, so it is to be hoped that fatal consequences did not ensue. Perhaps the unfortunate young gentleman's greatest misfortune had been his acceptance of the ministrations of the King's surgeon.

Of more importance was the unpleasant experience which befell Mr. Boscawan, for it raised the religious question, which was always a delicate point in the relations between Catholic and Protestant Courts, and often caused Hamilton alarm, for the English 'milords' who came to Naples in increasing numbers were not always tactful in criticising what they regarded as Popish superstition. 'On Friday last',

Hamilton informed London on 15 May 1770, 'Mr. Boscawan was at the Cathedral of this Capital with Monsieur de Crillon, a French Officer, whilst the ceremony of the liquifaction of St. Januarius's blood was performing; the blood remaining hard longer than usual the Mob began to take exception at Mr. Boscawan and M. de Crillon as thinking them Hereticks, and they prudently retired, but passing by the same Church some time after as the people were coming out some Women more zealous than the rest threw stones at them but without having hurt either of them.'

The incident in itself was sufficiently slight, but Hamilton knew the temper of the Neapolitans, especially when the honour of their Patron Saint was concerned, and decided to warn his compatriots against any provocative acts. 'The story is told very differently here,' his dispatch continues, 'I have related it to your Lordship as I have it from the two gentlemen above-mentioned. However having been inform'd that many of the Lower Class of people had arm'd themselves and had determin'd to insult any Hereticks that should dare to come to the Cathedral the next day when the same ceremony was to be performed, I took care that none of His Majesty's subjects (of whom there are no less then 40 here at the moment) should be present.'[18] There can be no doubt that Hamilton's prompt action prevented what might have developed into an ugly situation calculated to inflame the worst prejudices of both countries concerned. His own view of the situation was summed up in a single phrase: 'There is no conceiving the enthusiastick Madness of the common people of Naples called *Lazzaroni* at the time this pretended Miracle is performing.'

The opening months of the year 1771 saw Hamilton on the eve of departure for his first leave in England since taking up his post. Though he knew that he would be returning to Naples and not to some other appointment he could still congratulate himself on the achievements he had made during the past seven years, though these had been mainly in fields outside diplomacy. The comparatively obscure Member of Parliament who had left England in 1764 was now very much a personality in his own right. The reputation he had gained from his published volumes of *Greek and Roman Antiquities* as well as his letters on volcanic subjects to the Royal Society assured him of a welcome in London in the artistic and scientific circles he most loved to frequent, while he had no reason to be ashamed of his conduct as Envoy Extraordinary and Minister Plenipotentiary. Indeed he had already, almost unwillingly and against his own wishes, made himself indispensable to his country at the Neapolitan Court. His high standing there was made clear enough in the last dispatch he sent to London before himself leaving on that long and still sometimes perilous journey. 'The Marquis Tanucci,' he wrote,[19] 'altho' indisposed, has done me the honor of calling at my door to wish me a good journey which, as I am informed, he has never done upon the like occasions except to Ministers of the first order.'

If Tanucci's ceremonious leave-taking left the ambassador with some feelings of complacency there were other considerations calculated to cause apprehension as he set out for home. He was considerably in debt. The dispatches he had addressed to the Secretary of State on the question of the extraordinary expenses incurred at the time of the marriage of Ferdinand and Maria Carolina had remained unanswered. The heavy expenses which the production of his volumes of *Greek and Roman Antiquities* had cost him had still to be met. Hamilton realised that unless he was to fall yet more deeply into debt the collection which he had so lavishly illustrated, as well as some pictures, would have to be sold. This was a sad thought, for when Joseph II had told him that his collection of pictures was the best he had ever seen he could hardly have paid a greater or more flattering compliment to the man who had been described 'picture-mad' when he first came to Italy, and who had been collecting assiduously ever since.

By the year 1798 when he was compelled to quit Naples for Palermo Hamilton had over two hundred pictures and drawings in the Palazzo Sessa including works attributed to such masters as Canaletto, Rembrandt, Raphael, Veronese, Rubens, Velazquez, Claude Lorraine, Poussin, Tintoretto, Titian and van Dyck, as well as the works of many of his own contemporaries such as Reynolds, Romney, Mengs, Gavin Hamilton, Le Brun, Rosalba, Philipp Hackert, Angelica Kauffmann, Battoni and his own protégé Pietro Fabris whose lively *gouache* sketches of Neapolitan life were to establish a popular *genre*. Hamilton's correspondence is full of details of purchases made on behalf of other people, for like most diplomats of his day in Italy he acted as a sort of unofficial art dealer, but unfortunately he makes few references to his own purchases, and it was not until he was forced to leave Naples in the face of revolution that he drew up a catalogue which shows his collection as it was hung in the various rooms of the Palazzo Sessa on 14 July 1798. But of the dates at which the pictures were acquired, or of the dealers or fellow–collectors from whom they were purchased, he unfortunately gives us no hint.

As a man without private fortune, Hamilton looked upon his purchases of pictures and antiques as a form of investment. Being a person of taste and discernment fortunately placed in a country where works of art could be picked up comparatively cheaply he hoped, when the time for retirement came, to be able to dispose of his collection at a considerable financial profit. He now found that he would have to begin selling a part of what he had amassed in his 'lumber room' in order to relieve his immediate financial difficulties, and the process he had hoped to put off until retirement began, in fact, on his first leave. He continued to buy and sell in this way throughout his career, for if it sometimes saddened him to part with a masterpiece, he was stimulated by the thought of being able to indulge once more, Out of the proceeds of the sale, in his passion for collecting. 'It is my nature to collect, and has been all my life. . . ' he wrote to his agent in England when he was in his sixty-third year.[20] 'I am convinced that in Pictures and *Virtù* I have now in my house here as much as has cost me £10,000 and I am sure will always be money's worth, so that rather than be distressed in the latter part of my life I will down with my pictures and paint my walls in fresco which they do here admirably and at a cheap rate.' It was this attitude, no doubt, which caused a French acquaintance of the ambassador to remark that it was not so much that Sir William Hamilton supported the arts but that the arts supported Sir William. He might have added that by purchase, recommendation, and encouragement, Hamilton also supported a good many artists.

The picture which he hoped to sell on this first leave had been seen by Dr. Charles Burney when he visited the Hamiltons in the autumn of 1770. His host, Dr. Burney recorded, 'was so obliging as to show me his charming picture painted by Correggio (sic); the subject is a naked Venus who has taken Cupid's bow from him, which he is struggling for, while a satyr is running away with his quiver. It is a wonderful performance and reckoned equal, for the number of figures, with the St. Jerome at Parma.'[21] Hamilton must have been very reluctant to part with this picture which responded so admirably to the taste of his generation, for it appears that he had a copy made of it before the original was sent to London, where it was seen and admired by Horace Walpole in November 1771, for over sixteen years later Lord Gardenstone, after visiting Hamilton's house in Naples, wrote 'here he has a very choice collection of paintings, ancient and modern. I was particularly pleased with a delight fully wanton Venus, struggling to hold cupid's bow, which she had stolen from him; while a salacious satyr steals his arrows. It is a rare painting, by Correggio.'[22] The same writer also recorded seeing some painting by Fabris which represented 'in a very pleasing stile the characters and humours of the people of Naples,' several fine Gavin Hamiltons, a Reynolds of 'distinguished gaiety and spirit', and a picture of 'a sweet smiling boy at his play' which he described as 'a rare painting by Leonardo da Vinci'. This is presumably the picture described by Hamilton as 'Laughing boy—Leonard da Vinci' in his catalogue of July 1798, but which does not appear in the inventory made when his collection was packed for shipment between the months of October and December of the same year.

Hamilton had spoken of his Correggio[23] to Sir Joshua Reynolds when he had sent some casts of antique bas reliefs as a present to the newly founded Royal Academy of Arts in 1770. The President's reply, thanking him for his gift, must have raised the Envoy's hopes for the sale of this picture. 'I beg leave to thank you as President,' Reynolds wrote,[24] 'you will receive with this an Official Letter of thanks from the Academy. I must acquaint you that in speaking to His Majesty some time ago of the Present you had made and mentioning some other particulars in the Letter, he asked me if I had the Letter about me and if he might see it. I had it in my pocket and put it in his hands. You have no reason to be displeased on any account but there was one circumstance rather fortunate, your having mentioned His Majesty in it with great affection and certainly without any expectation of his seeing it. I wonder he was not tempted by your lively description of the Correggio. Was I King of England I certainly would have it at all events; there is no Master that one wishes so much to see. . . ' Alas for Hamilton, the King did not share the

enthusiasm of the President of the Royal Academy. Had Hamilton seen the letter
Horace Walpole wrote on the same subject he might have had his hopes dashed,
for though Walpole admired the picture he found the price quite prohibitive,
and few people knew the market value of works of art better than he did. 'Mr.
Hamilton's Correggio is arrived,' he told Horace Mann.[25] 'I have seen it: it is
divine—and so is the price; for nothing but a demi-god, or a demi-devil, that is,
a Nabob, can purchase it. What do you think of three thousand pounds? It has all
Correggio's grace, but none of his grimace, which, like Shakespeare, he is too apt
to blend and confound.'

The arrival of the Hamiltons in England after nearly seven years' absence caused
a good deal of interest and curiosity among their friends. Lady Mary Coke saw
them in August at a musical party at Lady Hertford's and declared that Catherine
Hamilton had never looked so well in her life, though she was 'much discontented
with our climate and seems to say she will be glad to return to Italy'. Hamilton,
on the other hand, she considered to look a good deal older than the seven years
he had been away.[26] Perhaps it was the sunburn which made Lady Mary think
that Hamilton looked so much older, for to be sunburnt was highly unfashionable
in the eighteenth century. 'Vesuvius has burnt him to a cinder,' was Walpole's
comment after meeting his old friend again in October.

One of Hamilton's main objects was, of course, to sell his collection of Greek and
Roman Antiques. The appearance of his volumes describing the vases had aroused
considerable interest in advance and Horace Walpole, as may well be imagined,
was among the first to wish to inspect the treasures when the collection, carefully
packed and crated, reached England late in November. It was barely unpacked
before a note addressed from Strawberry Hill was delivered to Hamilton asking
for permission to view these spoils of antiquity. 'I have no scruple in shewing
you my collection', Hamilton replied,[27] 'tho' it is not yet in the order fit for the
regular eye. I shall be at Lord Cowper's on Friday mornings from 10 till 3 and
shall be happy to give you some idea of what the collection will be when properly
arranged.'

In appearing to make a special exception for Walpole to see his treasures
while still not properly arranged for public display, Hamilton must have realised
his good fortune, for he knew that he could rely upon the most articulate and
intelligent gossip of the day to describe with the authority of an acknowledged
connoisseur what he had been allowed to see at Lord Cowper's house; and that
those to whom this information would be imparted were the ones most likely to
realise the value and importance of the collection. Everyone enjoys the privilege of
a private view and no one savoured so select an occasion so much as did Horace
Walpole. Hamilton's letter to him was dated 10 December; four days later Walpole
was busily describing all he had seen to the Countess of Ossory. 'If Lord Ossory
has a mind to enrich Ampthill', he told her, 'Mr. Hamilton has brought over a
charming Correggio, and a collection of Tuscan vases, idols, amulets, javelins and

casques of bronze, necklaces and ear-rings of gold from Herculaneum, Pompeii, and Sicily; sacrificing instruments, dice of amber, ivory, agate, etc., in short, enough antiquity to fill your whole gallery at least. Your Lord must make haste, or those learned patrons of taste, the Czarina, Lord Clive, or some Nabob will give £50,000 for the collection, though the picture may as yet be had for £3,000 and the antiquities for £8,000. They are a little dear, but the first is delightful and the latter most entertaining.'[28]

The collection was, in fact, bought in 1772 by the Trustees of the British Museum with a Parliamentary grant for the sum of eight thousand four hundred pounds, and was to form the basis of the department of Greek and Roman antiquities. The Museum had been founded in 1753 and the idea of such a purchase from public funds was something of a novelty and not without its critics, but the wisdom of the Trustees was shown later, and their expenditure justified, when Josiah Wedgwood was able to point out that in two years he had himself brought into England by the sale of Wedgwood copies of the Hamilton vases three times as much money as had been paid by Parliament for the collection. The satirists, however, led by 'Peter Pindar', had their own ideas as to how Hamilton's collection had been made:

> Sir William, hand in glove with Naple's King,
> Who made with rare Antiques the Nation ring,
> Who when Vesuvius foam'd with melting matter
> March'd up and clapp'd his nose into the crater,
> Just with the same *sang froid* that Joan the Cook
> Casts on her Dumplings in the Pot a look:
> But more, the world reports (I hope untrue)
> That half Sir William's mugs and gods are new;
> Himself the baker of th'Etruscan Ware
> That made our British Antiquarians stare;
> Nay, that he means ere long to cross the main
> And at his *Naples oven* sweat again,
> And, by his late successes render'd bolder,
> To bake new Mugs and Gods some ages older.

Hamilton's success in disposing of his collection of vases and antiquities did not extend to the picture of *Venus disarming Cupid*. Despite the high praise bestowed upon it by Sir Joshua Reynolds and Horace Walpole it did not find a purchaser. When Hamilton left England it was still unsold and was left in the care of Charles Greville. Many must have been daunted by the price, which was considerable for that day and age; others, perhaps, were dubious as to the attribution in spite of Hamilton's reputation as a connoisseur. In fact the attribution to Correggio has since been disputed and the picture is now generally considered to be the work of Luca Cambiaso. Hamilton had hoped to sell it to the Empress of Russia, and the knowledge that this august patron of the arts, with legendary wealth at her command, was interested in the picture may have been another cause which made more cautious purchasers hold back. 'To be sure I am a little disappointed that my Correggio is not sold', Hamilton wrote to his nephew on returning to Naples,[29] 'as it would so nicely free me from debt, tho' I will answer for it no one will ever enjoy it more than I have, or shall still if it remains mine.' It was to remain his for many years, hanging in a place of honour on his nephew's wall.

Hamilton received official recognition for his work as Envoy at Naples when he was created a Knight of the Bath on in January 1772. The Order, founded by George I in 1725,[30] consisted at that time of the Sovereign, a Grand Master, and thirty-six knights companions (its expansion and division into three classes did not take place until 1815) so that appointments could only be made to its distinguished ranks when a vacancy occurred through death. The Duke of Chandos had recently died occasioning such a vacancy and it was this riband which the King now bestowed on his foster-brother. For the privilege of wearing the red riband and star Hamilton had to pay the sum of three hundred and forty-three pounds, sixteen shillings and fourpence in official fees, the list including, among other things, such interesting and curious items as payments to the Officers of the Order (£151), to the Heralds for supporters to his coat of arms (£40), to the Jewel Office (£21 10s. 6d.), to the Treasury (£2 2s. 0d.), while the lesser expenses included one guinea each to the Gentleman Porter, Marshal's men and Ringers, half a guinea to the Under Porter, and the bizarre addition of another half-guinea for 'Marrow Bones and Cleavers'.[31]

If the expense was irritating in his present state of financial embarrassment the honour done him was great, and must have consoled Hamilton for the disappointment he certainly felt at having to return to Naples as Envoy and not to some more important and influential post. Honours of this sort were granted sparingly in those days and the Order of the Bath was still more or less exclusively aristocratic; few people would wear its riband with a greater air of distinction than 'Il Cavaliere Hamilton' as he would be known to the Neapolitans when he got back there, and would continue to be known for the remaining years, more than a quarter of a century, that he was to spend in the Kingdom of the Two Sicilies.

1. W Beckford: *Italy, Spain and Portugal*, p. 121.
2. *The Courts of Europe at the Close of the Last Century*, Vol. I, pp. 201–2.
3. Morrison, 102.
4. B.M. Add. MSS 34048, ff. 2–3.
5. B.M. Egerton MSS 2635, f. 43.

6. B.M. Egerton MSS 2635, f. 91.
7. *Vide* H. Acton: *The Bourbons of Naples*, p. 138.
8. B.M. Egerton MSS 2635, f. 79.
9. B.M. Egerton MSS 2635, f. 82.
10. Morrison, 18.
11. 'It is necessary for the health, brother.' Swinburne: *The Courts of Europe at the Close of the Last Century*, Vol. I, p. 144.
12. Morrison, 20.
13. B.M. Egerton MSS 2635 f. 129.
14. B.M. Egerton MSS 2635, f. 198.
15. The King of Spain.
16. The French Ambassador was Choiseul's nephew.
17. B.M. Egerton MSS 2635, ff. 217 and 218.
18. B.M. Egerton MSS 2635, f. 141.
19. Ibid,. f. 228.
20. B.M. Add. MSS 42096, f. 148.
21. Burney: *Musical Tours in Europe*, Vol. I, p. 281.
22. *Travelling Memorandums made in a Tour upon the Continent of Europe*, Vol. III, p. 98 [F].
23. Hamilton's spelling of this artist's name varied between 'Correggio' and 'Corregio'.
24. *Letters of Sir Joshua Reynolds*, pp. 26–8, Letter XVI.
25. Walpole to Mann, 18 November 1771.
26. Lady M. Coke, *Letters & Journals*, Vol. III, p. 442.
27. Fitzwilliam Museum, Percival Bequest MSS.
28. H. Walpole: *Letters*, Vol. V., pp. 356–7.
29. Morrison, 30.
30. The creation claimed to revive an Order of doubtful historical authenticity said to date from 1399.
31. B.M. Add. MSS 37077, f. 2.

CHAPTER IX

Triumphs and Disappointments

The Hamiltons returned to Naples in the autumn of 1772 by easy stages, during the course of the journey paying their respects to both Voltaire and the Pope. The seventy-eight-year-old philosopher took the ambassador to a window of his house at Ferney to show him the view of mountains which it commanded (a compliment, no doubt, to the 'Professor of Earthquakes') but Hamilton, when writing to Voltaire the following June, told him that these summits were '*d'un goût tout opposé*' to Vesuvius and Etna.[1]

At Vienna, where Hamilton's old friend Lord Stormont was still Ambassador, they remained for three weeks being greatly fêted in official circles. In a letter to Greville[2] describing their adventures Sir William recounted with pardonable pride the very gratifying welcome they had received from the Imperial Court. The Emperor and Empress gave a dinner in their honour at Laxenburg where the Archduchess Elizabeth sang to them and Catherine Hamilton's playing on the harpsichord 'so tickled their Majesties' ears' that the Empress gave her both a kiss and a gold enamelled snuff-box with the royal cipher set in brilliants. It would be difficult to say which was the greater honour, the snuff-box or the kiss, and Lady Mary Coke, perhaps a little jealous, reported that Lady Hamilton became rather proud after her great success with the Empress. Proud or not, Catherine caught a cold in Vienna which became so bad after they had resumed their journey that she was laid up with fever for five days in the Tyrol. Hamilton undertook the cure himself, and while his wife was recovering he passed his time on a lake close by where he amused himself catching pike.

Their last evening in Vienna had been the occasion of a particular compliment on the part of Joseph II, who seems to have had a genuine regard for the Hamiltons. It has been noted that theirs was the only foreign embassy which he had visited during his stay in Naples, and in his own capital he had never been known to set foot in a Minister's house. On this evening, however, contrary to his maxim, the Emperor suddenly appeared at Lord Stormont's with some letters from the Empress addressed to the Grand Duke and Duchess of Tuscany. These he begged Lady Hamilton to deliver when they passed through Florence, 'and with this pretence', wrote Sir William, he 'passed the evening with us'.

Continuing their journey towards Venice they found much to interest them. At Verona Hamilton met 'a delightful fossil man' and told Greville that the British

Museum would do well to take him into their service to arrange the Natural History department: 'he is ready to sell himself and his collection, which is admirable'. Between Trent and Verona Sir William observed 'most noble havock made certainly by volcanick explosion'. Unfortunately nobody was able to tell him anything about it and he had no time to explore on his own account. 'Had I been alone', he assured his nephew, 'I shou'd have stopped and, I am sure, have had matter for a letter to the Royal Society.'

Venice was reached in November, and it was from this city that Hamilton sent the account of his journey to Greville, who had disported himself there on his own Grand Tour. It was to this, no doubt, that the uncle referred when he told his nephew, 'I can conceive that a gondola with a fine woman in it must seem a most luxurious conveyance for a young man in his prime; but as I mean only to satisfy my eyes I think a week here will be sufficient, and am in no fear of following your example.' Instead of such Casanova-like adventures his time was spent in pursuits more in keeping with his character as a Minister Plenipotentiary and Knight of the Bath, though it would be many years yet before it could be said that Hamilton was past his prime. He examined the old master pictures and other curiosities of art in which Venice was so richly endowed and was delighted with Paul Veronese though, surprisingly, somewhat disappointed with Titian. Writing of these artists made him think of his own Correggio which he had left in Greville's keeping. 'How does my dear *Venus?*' he asked: 'There is nothing like her, believe me.'

From Florence Sir William wrote to the firm of Wedgwood to tell them that the Ambassador from Malta to the Court of Rome wished to procure a complete service of their white ware with the purple edge. Nothing pleased him more than an opportunity of this sort to promote the work of a firm which succeeded so well in pursuing his own principles of applying the lessons of art to the needs of industry, and he must have taken some credit to himself when he assured them that their Etruscan ware was universally admired. He had, in fact, hopes of adding another two volumes to those already published illustrating his own collection, which had had such an influence on Wedgwood's designs, but in Florence he discovered to his dismay that the 'rogue' he had employed for this purpose had pawned the plates and was languishing in prison. Hamilton had to apply to the Grand Duke before his property was restored to him. He promised to send Wedgwood drawings of some finely shaped vases. 'Continue to be very attentive to the simplicity and elegance of the forms, which is the chief article,' he urged, adding the admonition: 'You cannot consult the originals in the museum too often.'[3]

There were two personalities in Rome whom English visitors wished to see in the latter half of the eighteenth century, though for the most part they owed allegiance to neither of them; they were the Pope and the Pretender. The hospitality which the Sovereign Pontiffs of this period offered to British visitors was considerable, and a public or private audience was one of the coveted honours which travellers hoped to secure during the course of a visit to the Eternal City. The Popes put few difficulties in the way of receiving these pilgrims from a Protestant nation, while heretic lords and ladies were seen thronging the splendid ceremonies in the Basilica of St. Peter's. The Pretender created a more difficult problem for it was still dangerous, or at least unwise, to show too keen an interest in him, though curiosity could hardly resist the chance of seeing the exiled monarch or his Cardinal brother when they chose to appear in public. Prince Charles Edward, broken by disappointment and frustration, was now living at the Palazzo Muti with Louise of Stolberg, a princess thirty years his junior, whom he had married this very year.

Hamilton saw the Count and Countess of Albany (as the Pretender and his wife were called) and also spoke with the Abbé Peter Grant, as he wished to thank this Jacobite agent, whom he had previously met in Naples, for the help and kindness he had shown to English travellers who had passed through Rome on their way to the Kingdom of the Two Sicilies. On reaching the Palazzo Sessa early in January 1773, Sir William thought it prudent to send an account of what he had witnessed in Rome to Lord Rochford, the Secretary of State. 'Whilst I was at Rome', his dispatch began,[4] 'I had an opportunity of seeing the Pretender and his Wife at Church; the Pretender appear'd to me much thinner and more declining than when I saw him four years ago. A gentleman on whose veracity of judgement I can depend and who is with him frequently, assured me that his understanding was almost ruin'd, that his temper is grown so violent as to make his wife and every one about him unhappy. He takes every opportunity of abusing the Pope whom he calls a Heretick for not allowing him the titles he pretends to. His wife, as I am inform'd, is a very agreeable woman; she is about twenty years old and rather handsome. The Pretender talks of his return to England as being at hand. He says that his wife is six months gone with Child which she constantly denies (neither indeed is there the least appearance of it). He tells her that he understands these matters better than she can; in short, he is universally looked upon as in a great degree out of his Senses, and would be deserted if a few people did not go to him out of compassion for his Wife, whom he never quits a moment.'

Before he left Rome word was brought to Hamilton that the Pope wished to see him. Sir William's reputation as an aesthete and connoisseur was too well known for the Pontiff to allow him to pass through his dominions without first hearing his opinion of the Museum which had recently been established at the Vatican. A formal meeting presented problems as Great Britain did not have a representative at the Papal Court and Hamilton felt, in view of his own official status, that if His Holiness gave him an audience 'it might give room for news-mongers to form nonsensical conjectures'. He was most anxious to avoid any such situation, not only for the repercussions which might result in England, but also because relations between Naples and the Vatican were in a very delicate state. In concert with the other Bourbon Courts the Neapolitans were bringing every pressure they could to bear on the Pope to induce or, if necessary, force him to suppress the Society of Jesus, while Clement XIV was still hoping to postpone to the last possible moment a decision which he deplored, but to which he was, by his election, deeply committed.

In the face of this dilemma Hamilton had recourse to Thomas Jenkins, an Englishman who was employed to collect antiques for the Papal gallery, and explained his position. To decline Clement's invitation would be both uncivil and impolite; to accept might well be imprudent if Sir William was to be received as one 'employed in a Public Character'. Mr. Jenkins carried this message from the embarrassed diplomat to the Holy Father. Clement XIV was a man of comparatively humble origins (his father was a surgeon) and had spent the greater part of his ecclesiastical life in the cloister as a Franciscan friar. He saw not the slightest difficulty in receiving the British Minister to Naples any evening in his private apartments with a minimum of form or ceremony.

Reassured by this message Hamilton went the very next evening to the Apostolic Palace in the company of the accommodating Mr. Jenkins. 'We were immediately introduced by Father Buontempi, the Pope's friend and confidant,' Sir William reported in a subsequent dispatch.[5] 'I did not leave my hat and sword in the outward room as is usual in audiences of form. The Pope came forward, shook me by the hand and thank'd me for coming to him in the manner I did. I took this opportunity of expressing the grateful sense of my countrymen for the particular favours and distinctions they enjoyed at present at Rome. He assured me he would always endeavour to make it agreeable to them.' Having exchanged these courtesies the Pope and the Envoy talked for the best part of half an hour on the subject of antiquities, a subject, Hamilton could not help noticing, upon which the Pope appeared to know little, collecting only 'to curb the prodigious export of valuable monuments of antiquity which has prevailed of late years'. When the time came for Sir William to take his leave the Pontiff conducted him to the door which he opened himself. 'He is cheerful', Hamilton concluded, 'and appears to have a good understanding, but his ideas confined as might naturally be expected from the monastick life he has had, and which indeed he continues to lead as far as his high station will permit.'

This visit to Clement XIV was to have a sad sequel. In his dispatch the ambassador had described the Pope as one who 'seems healthy and likely to live as long as any man of his age'. The Pope was then in his late sixties. Within six months of his meeting with Hamilton he issued his brief *Dominus ac Redemptor noster* which abolished the Jesuit Order. Less than a year after this his health broke down completely and the last months of his life were passed in a morbid terror of poison. He died in the autumn of 1774, the rapid decomposition of his corpse being attributed by the superstitious to the sinister effects of a venom administered by the Society he had suppressed in defiance of the dictates of his conscience.

Hamilton had every reason to be pleased with the reception which greeted him upon returning to his post early in January 1773 after this long leave of absence. His welcome by the Court was highly flattering; at his first audience with Ferdinand the King showed evident pleasure at seeing the British Envoy once again, and raising his voice so that all could hear, declared: 'You have gained the hearts of the Neapolitans and you deserve them.'[6] The Marquis Tanucci, with whom the ambassador dined, was no less cordial, and Sir William noted that the Minister was in a much better state of health than he had been at the time when he had left Naples, and he professed his belief that Tanucci was certainly a remarkable man for his age.

It was unpleasant to have to pass from the enjoyment of these compliments to face a situation which had arisen, as it were, upon his own doorstep, and which was to develop over the next twelve months into an ugly quarrel. Since his return the British Consul in Naples had been behaving very strangely towards the Envoy and had caused him some considerable embarrassment. This official, whose name was Jamineau, had been difficult and jealous for some time, and had snatched at every chance offered him to encourage frivolous complaints from discontented English travellers. As there were always people who did not consider that they had received sufficient attention from the busy Minister, Jamineau's opportunities for inviting criticism and intrigue were not infrequent, and as a result a decided coolness had developed between the Consul and the Minister. This continued for some months.

Hamilton might well have accepted this as one of those annoying but inevitable dissensions which accompany public office. With his tact and urbanity he was well able to cope with such a situation, but unfortunately Mr. Jamineau eventually went too far, indulging, in the terms of the Minister's protest, in what could only be considered as great impertinence. The innocent cause of this storm was the Abbé Grant, that benevolent priest of Jacobite sympathies to whom Sir William had shown some kindnesses in both Naples and Rome. By some devious means a letter written by the Consul had fallen into his superior's hands and Hamilton found himself reading a description of the excellent Abbé which was decidedly unflattering both to Grant and to himself. This priest, wrote Jamineau, was 'a damn'd rascal tho' the chief favourite of His Britannick Majesty's Minister at Naples, which is a most absurd thing to all true Englishmen who have their eyes open'. In the Consul's opinion Hamilton should 'take no notice of him, for as he has the honour to serve the true King in a very important capacity he could have no intercourse with those who frequent the mock King and his Court'.

Sir William was furious at this thinly veiled accusation of being in sympathy with the Pretender or with those who frequented his Court. His association with Grant (who shared Hamilton's antiquarian tastes) had been entirely a matter of common courtesy, but even now, almost thirty years after the last attempt by the Stuarts to regain their throne, a career could still be damaged by hints as vague as those made by Jamineau. Reaching in great indignation for his pen Hamilton wrote a dignified protest to the Secretary of State, for absurd as the charges might seem it would not have been wise to have ignored them or treated them with the silent contempt they deserved. If there were moments for silence, this, Sir William decided, was not one of them.

> 'Your Lordship has, I dare say, heard, and every one of our countrymen who have been at Rome for several years past can certify', Hamilton wrote,[7] 'how very serviceable and obliging the Abbé Grant has been to them, and that without his assistance they would be at a great loss at Rome where we have no Minister. I therefore certainly did shew him civilities when he came to Naples. I do not mean to justify the Abbé's principles, but I have been confidentially informed that he never does go to the Pretender's Court. . . Tho' I have not the least fear that the malicious insinuations of Mr. Jamineau should induce anyone to call my principles in question or make them doubt one moment of the respectful and affectionate attachment that I have to our Gracious Sovereign and Royal Master whom I have had the honor of serving from his infancy; yet your Lordship will allow that such insinuations should not be pass'd over in silence, and as I cannot consistently with the character I am honour'd with at this Court, or indeed without demeaning myself, correct Mr. Jamineau for his malicious insolence, I hope your Lordship will excuse my having resolved to lay my complaint before your Lordship to whose candour and justice the whole is submitted.'

This letter had the desired effect. Lord Rochford replied on the 15th of March. He not only assured Hamilton that the Consul would be taken to task for his impertinence but also enclosed a copy of the letter which he had addressed to that erring official. It was a stinging rebuke. After the unpleasant experience of discovering the attack made on him and reading the false accusations in the purloined letter, Sir William must have felt a certain pleasant satisfaction as his eyes perused the following lines which he knew were also being read by the chastened Consul:

> *St. James's*, 18 *Feb*. 1774
>
> Sir,
>
> Having received Copy of a Letter wrote by you to Sir Wm. Hamilton dated the 29th of Decr. last, I am to acquaint you that the King has taken Notice of it, as not being couched in a Stile consistent with your Situation and with that Respect and Decorum due to his Envoy.
>
> The difference between your Station and that of Sir Wm. Hamilton is too obvious to make it necessary for me to point out a Line for your Conduct, and, without dwelling upon the Subject, which cannot but be painful to me, I am persuaded that this Intimation will have the desired Effect, and produce an Alteration in your Behaviour as may prevent any future Complaints.
>
> I am, etc.,
>
> ROCHFORD.'[8]

With this the unpleasant episode ended. 'I return your Lord ship my sincere thanks', Hamilton replied to Lord Rochford, 'and beg leave to assure you that it shall not be my fault if you are, troubled any more upon so disagreeable a subject.' In the following May Sir William was sent a special intimation of King George's 'most gracious approbation' of his work in the royal service which gave him such high satisfaction that he took occasion, in his answer, to hint that his only wish was that he had 'better opportunity of proving my attachment to His Majesty and His Government than are likely to offer at this Court',[9] a hint that was not taken up by His Majesty's Government who much preferred Sir William Hamilton to remain in Naples where he was so useful and well liked.

The person who might have been most interested in the exchanges between Naples and London on the subject of these flimsy charges was presumably unaware that they were taking place. Prince Charles Edward Stuart was busily engaged in removing his Court from Rome to Florence and still living in hope of providing his House with an heir. He would perhaps have been pleased, but certainly not surprised, had he known what a flutter the mere mention of his name could still cause.

Jamineau was for the moment silenced; but he continued to be a thorn in the side of Hamilton for some time, for two years after he had received Lord Rochford's rebuke Lady Hamilton was writing to warn Charles Greville against the Consul's evil influence. He was, she believed, spreading stories at home which might prove unpleasant to her husband, though with her usual charity she added 'but perhaps my own anxious mind may represent this in a blacker light than need be'.[10] The Consul's most foolish step had been to attack the Envoy on the grounds of Jacobitism, for as the foster-brother of George III and the son of Lady Archibald it would have been difficult to find anyone whose family background or professional ambitions were more closely tied to the House of Hanover than were Hamilton's. But whatever harm Jamineau's intrigue might have done in London (and it does not appear to have done any) it was certainly unable to damage Hamilton's reputation in Naples. He was now at the height of his power, influence and renown, and was perhaps the most prominent personality at the Court of Ferdinand and Maria Carolina.

That monarch was about to be presented with a son and heir by his wife, whose previous children had all been daughters. While the diplomatic corps waited in the vast palace of Caserta for the Queen's confinement at the beginning of 1775, the British Envoy passed the time in taking stock of his situation. Hopes for promotion to a more important post were not yet dead in spite of the agreeable life he lived in Naples. 'I have long been *Le Doyen du Corps diplomatique* at this Court', he wrote to Lord Rochford on 2 January. 'This is the third Minister from Spain, there have been three French Ambassadors, three Ministers from Vienna, as many from the Court of Turin and Copenhagen during my ten years residence at Naples. I have certainly reason to be pleas'd and flatter'd with my situation at this

Court, having the honor of being distinguish'd very particularly indeed by Their Sicilian Majesties who are pleased to call me *Paesano nostro*.[11] Yet I cannot help regretting that it is not in my power to exert my poor endeavours in His Majesty's Service to better purpose than my present situation will admit of.'[12] This was to be his regret for some years to come; indeed it was only after his first wife's death and the arrival of a beautiful young mistress answering to the name of Emma Hart that hopes of this nature were to be abandoned altogether.

Hamilton's reflections were cut short by the arrival of the infant prince. With his colleagues he saw the royal child being carried in the arms of its triumphant father whose behaviour, always eccentric, was somewhat startlingly so on this joyful occasion. 'His Sicilian Majesty', Sir William's dispatch recorded,[13] 'in a transport of joy lifting up with his finger the distinctive mark of the sex said, "Well, Gentlemen, are you convinced that it is a Male?"' Reassured by this simple demonstration the diplomats retired to their embassies to inform their several Governments of the arrival of an heir to the Sicilian crown. The young prince was at once privately baptised with fourteen names beginning with those of his grandfather, father, and the Patron Saint of Naples, but weighed down with this heavy burden of nomenclature was to survive for barely three years in an unwelcoming world. By the terms of her marriage treaty the birth of this prince gave Maria Carolina the right to a seat in the Council of State. Determined to achieve the downfall of Tanucci the Queen accomplished this end within the space of two years. The Minister had been in power for more than forty years; the banishment of the Society of Jesus was the only comparable event in the experience of most Neapolitans. Most, but not all. The Abbé Galiani found a different parallel. 'It has roused me somewhat from the depression in which the illness of my angora cat, reputed to be incurable, has plunged me,' he declared, 'and I see this world is only a perpetual chain of pleasures and sorrows.' Sir William himself was to regret the Minister's fall. 'It is true', he wrote, 'that with all his failings this Minister has great honesty and integrity and it will be difficult to find out another here endowed with these especial qualities.'

As *Doyen* of the Diplomatic Corps he was often presented with problems by his colleagues which required tact and patience as well as diplomatic skill for their solution. These very frequently revolved round obscure or disputed points of etiquette. The new Danish Minister came to him in great fury and indignation at the conduct of the French Ambassador. The Minister had been making his calls upon the other members of the *corps diplomatique* and had been received courteously by all his colleagues including the Papal Nuncio. All, that is, except the Baron de Breteuil, whose door was shut and who refused to receive the Danish Minister except at an hour named in advance by himself. Scandalised by this unexpected arrogance the Minister rushed with his complaint to Sir William.

Hamilton attempted to solve this problem by arranging for the Ambassador and Minister to meet on neutral ground. Brought thus face to face with his adversary he advised the Danish Minister to say how disappointed he was at not having met His Most Christian Majesty's representative and to ask when he might have the pleasure of finding him at home. The Minister agreed to this sensible solution provided that the Baron de Breteuil would not pin him down to any particular hour. Having secured agreement from the Danish side Hamilton called on his French colleague to propose the meeting, but only to have his plan rejected as His Excellency insisted upon naming the hour. Upon this all three diplomats retired in various states of indignation, frustration or infuriation to their embassies in order to report to their Governments. Sir William declared in his dispatch: 'I cannot but think that Monsieur de Breteuil has acted with hardship upon this occasion by having required more of the King of Denmark's Minister than he did of those of other Courts, and it certainly does not appear right that distinctions should be made in point of etiquette, tho' Monsieur de Breteuil says that Ambassadors have the right *d'insister ou de sélectionner* as they please.'[14] The truth of the matter was that Hamilton had a very poor opinion of the French Ambassador whom he considered to be plotting with some of the Neapolitan nobility to undermine the government. The present ridiculous *impasse* was unexpectedly solved without further intervention from the British Minister as the sudden death of Louis XV plunged the French Ambassador and the Neapolitan Court into mourning, and shortly afterwards the Baron was recalled.

Eighteen months later, in February 1776, Hamilton found himself once more involved in a dispute on a point of etiquette, though in this case his colleagues were united in the face of a common affront. The tale was unfolded in a long dispatch to Viscount Weymouth who had succeeded Lord Rochford as Hamilton's superior in London. When the King of Naples dined in public the Foreign Ministers, as representatives of crowned heads, always stood on his right in order of seniority, the Imperial Minister coming first and the Spanish next, as being *Ministres de famille*. The Pope's nuncio took his place with the rest. The dispute occurred when Cardinal Orsini and another Cardinal swept in and not only placed themselves above the ambassadors, but turned their backs on the representatives of Austria and Spain. The two ministers, their faces as scarlet as the Cardinals' birettas, promptly left the room.

The remaining diplomats were in some perplexity as to what to do next. They wished to support their Austrian and Spanish colleagues, but as their own view of the monarch had not been blocked by the ample figures of the two princes of the Church, and as they had no desire to offend the King, they decided to hold their ground until the ceremony was over. Once outside, however, a quick consultation took place between Hamilton and the representatives of Sardinia, Portugal and Denmark. Having discovered that the Cardinals had taken up their position 'with premeditation' they determined to leave the royal table on the next occasion (rather than attempt to maintain their ground by force) should their Eminences once more 'return to the charge'.

Before the King next dined in public one of the Cardinals had left Naples, but Orsini remained, determined to uphold the dignity of the Roman purple in the face of the diplomatic body. 'Cardinal Orsini returned to Court the following Thursday', Sir William reported, 'and, stepping forward to make his bow, turned his back on the Imperial and Spanish Ministers who left the table; but his Eminence retiring a little afterwards the other Ministers did not think it yet necessary to walk off, but the Cardinal having returned and placed himself before us also, we all went from the table to another part of the room.' The King, startled and annoyed by these strange manoeuvres, showed his displeasure by withdrawing also, upon which the ministers stormed into Tanucci's room with their angry complaints.

The old Minister was within a few months of his fall from power. Cardinals, he was told, though very great men at Rome, could not have the least just pretension to take precedence over representatives of crowned heads, much less turn their backs on them. To emphasise their case the ministers pointed out that when a similar dispute had occurred in Vienna the Neapolitan envoy had sided with his colleagues against the Red Hats. Tanucci replied that whatever their wrongs might be, by leaving the royal presence they gave the appearance of chastening the King rather than the Cardinal, but he agreed that Cardinals had no right of precedence over Foreign Ministers at any Court, and so their point was gained. In order to let the matter settle down Tanucci advised the King not to dine in public again until tempers had cooled. Excusing his raising the matter to Lord Weymouth, Sir William ended his dispatch: 'This occurrence, trifling as it must appear . . . makes a great noise here, particularly as there are many of the Nobility related to Cardinals, and are the more enraged as we have gain'd our point.'[15]

Life, however, did not consist wholly in solving nice problems of Court etiquette. While diplomats and prelates were jostling and pushing for position a more formidable game was being played in the world beyond the blue bay of Naples. In the years that immediately followed Hamilton's return from leave the revolt of the American colonists against their King gradually developed into a war in which the great Bourbon powers of France and Spain found themselves ranged with the Americans, whose principles they did not share, against Great Britain, whose growing power they resented. It was Sir William Hamilton's business to see that Naples, as a minor Bourbon Monarchy, did not join in with France and Spain in a general alliance against his country. The Kingdom of the Two Sicilies could hardly be regarded as a warlike nation and Hamilton's task was not one that was likely to put much strain on his powers as a diplomat. He did, however, manage to prevent the government from allowing 'gunpowder or any other warlike stores' from being sent to America. 'I have made the most diligent enquiry and I do not believe Warlike stores have as yet been exported from Naples or any other of his Sicilian Majesty's Dominions to our Colonies in America,' he reported[16] on

15 August 1775, and seven days later was able to assure the Secretary of State in London that as a result of his representations orders had been given to prevent all such exportations.

Hamilton, unlike his friend Horace Walpole, had no sympathy whatsoever with the cause of the American colonists. His attitude was summed up in a dispatch of this period in which he told the Secretary of State: 'I return your Lordship many thanks for the Gazette with the account of the defeat of a party of the Rebels in America and I trust in God that those unfortunate and deluded people will be soon brought to a just sense of their crimes, and submit again to the mild government of the Mother Country, the true value of which they do not seem to have known.' In common with many liberal-minded aristocrats Hamilton only believed in reforms that came from above; he was unable to appreciate or even comprehend a popular movement. He was to adopt the same limited attitude to the revolutionary party in Naples in the years after 1789. He often deplored the venal and corrupt government of Ferdinand IV; he sincerely hoped that it might be reformed; but he could only envisage such a reformation as taking place through the benevolence of the ruler. He could not distinguish between a patriot and a rebel (though both terms were to be greatly abused) and he abhorred revolution as something which overthrew ordered society and did infinitely more harm than good.[17] Acts of violence he held in contempt, and he would have applauded the verdict of Chateaubriand when he wrote: 'In my eyes murder will never be an object of admiration or an argument for freedom; I know of nothing more servile, contemptible, cowardly, and stupid than a terrorist.'

When, in 1778, France joined in the war, Hamilton continued his efforts to keep Naples out of the conflict. The Neapolitan Court had a double relationship with that of Versailles since the accession of Louis XVI, for the Bourbon monarchs were both married to Habsburg queens. Fortunately Maria Carolina was strongly Anglophile. In April Sir William was able to assure his Government that the Court of Naples intended to adhere to the strictest neutrality. 'I trust in God', he added, 'that France at least will soon have reason to repent bitterly of its low perfidy.' Two months later he passed on information received from Rome giving a warning that France was planning an attack on Ireland and 'that the Roman Catholicks there, worn out (as they say) with long and fruitless oppression, are eager for the event'.[18] Irish priests and friars had already left Rome, so his informant told him, and were bent on fermenting trouble at home.

When the King of Spain determined to join in the war against England Hamilton's battle at the Court of Naples was already won. The King of Naples was informed of his father's warlike intentions and promptly 'leaked' the information to the British Minister. Two days before the actual declaration of war by Spain (16 June 1779) Sir William wrote; 'The Queen of Naples on Wednesday last said with a very significant look that the Prime Minister of Naples was very ill, and I have since heard that his illness was occasion'd by a violent dispute he had with the French Ambassador. It is said here that the King of Spain's confessor has been gain'd by France and work'd up His Catholick Majesty against us, but that the Prince of Asturias, the majority of the Spanish Ministry and the nation in general are greatly disinclin'd to a War with Great Britain.'[19]

Hamilton's greatest diplomatic triumph came just after Spain entered the war, and was a resounding tribute not only to his success in dividing Naples from the other Bourbon Courts, but to his high personal standing with the King. 'On Saturday last', he informed Lord Weymouth in cipher on 27 July, 'His Sicilian Majesty being at a Concert of Musick did me the honor to call for me and place me next him. Between the acts His Majesty was pleas'd to tell me in the utmost confidence that His Catholic Majesty had distress'd him greatly by desiring that he would procure him intelligence from England through the channel of his Minister at the Court of London; that the professions he had so often made me of his desire of maintaining and cultivating the friendship of His Britannick Majesty were perfectly sincere. Nothing would induce him to act a dishonorable part towards Great Britain. He therefore wished I would inform my Court confidentially of his present dilemma, and as he was equally desirous of avoiding giving offence to his Father, if it would be agreeable to His Britannick Majesty he was ready to grant a leave of absence to Count Pignatelli for some time, and by that means remove all cause of jealousy. I returned His Majesty my humble thanks for the confidence he was pleas'd to repose in me and promis'd to make a faithful report of the same to your Lordship, and that I was persuaded so open and noble a proceeding would give the highest satisfaction to the King who was equally desirous of maintaining the good understanding between the Courts of Great Britain and Naples.'[20] Hamilton went on to tell Lord Weymouth of his surprise at the firm and clear manner in which the King expressed himself, for neither quality could be described as characteristic of Ferdinand IV, and he also believed the Chief Minister to have no very great love for Great Britain. Perhaps the secret of the King's sudden resolve lay hidden in the last paragraph of Sir William's dispatch. 'However,' he concluded, 'that Minister's power is now greatly on the decline and it is the Queen of Naples that actually governs this country. . . ' Maria Carolina was to become Sir William's staunchest ally.

In spite of these little triumphs Hamilton continued to feel that his post in Naples offered no real scope for his professional talents though, as he pointed out in March 1775, when applying unsuccessfully for the embassy at Madrid, 'my situation in point of self-comfort can never be more agreeable that it is at present'. The European repercussions to the war in America only emphasised the unimportance of his present post. As an antidote to the disappointment he clearly felt after failing to secure the posts in Vienna or Madrid upon which he had set his heart, he indulged with increased ardour in his passion for art, archaeology and science, adding to his collection of vases, pictures, and antiques, and gathering material for another lavishly produced work, this time on the volcanic curiosities of the neighbourhood of Naples, the *Campi Phlegraei* where, according to tradition, gods and giants had done battle in ancient times. If he could not become the head of a great embassy Sir William was determined, at least, that he would become one of the greatest *virtuosi* in Europe.

1. *Studies on Voltaire & the Eighteenth Century*, Vol. IV, p. 114.
2. Morrison, 26.
3. Morrison, 28.
4. B.M. Egerton MSS 2635 f. 232.
5. B.M. Egerton MSS 2635, f. 235.
6. B.M. Egerton MSS 2635, f. 237.
7. B.M. Egerton MSS 2635, f. 256.
8. B.M. Add. MSS 41197, f. 253.
9. B.M. Egerton MSS 2636, ff. 34, 51.
10. Morrison, 73.
11. Our Countryman.
12. B.M. Egerton MSS 2636.
13. B.M. Egerton MSS 2636 f. 101.
14. B.M. Egerton MSS 2636, f. 55.
15. B.M. Egerton MSS 2635, f. 170 et seq.
16. Ibid., 2636, f. 140.
17. Johnson's Dictionary gives as a definition of the word Patriot: 'A factious disturber of government.
18. B.M. Egerton MSS 2636, ff. 215 and 226.
19. Ibid., 2637, f. 16.
20. B.M. Egerton MSS 2657, f. 92. Pignatelli was Sicilian Minister in London.

CHAPTER X

Campi Phlegraei

The flattering reception which his volcanic letters to the Royal Society had received in London decided Hamilton that he would bring them out in an edition accompanied by detailed illustrations which would bear comparison with the splendid volumes devoted to his collection of vases. The result was three folio volumes (two published in 1776 followed by a supplement three years later) of a quite exceptional beauty. *Campi Phlegraei*, subtitled *Observations on the Volcanoes of the Two Sicilies*, as well as being the most exquisite, is also the most personal of the works issued under Hamilton's name, for not only are the text and descriptive matter his own, but the illustrations, finely executed and coloured, were made under his supervision in close collaboration with the artist he had specially selected and trained for the purpose.

Pietro Fabris, the artist chosen for this task, though he had spent most of his life in Naples was in fact a British subject and had exhibited in London in 1768. The first volume consisted of forty views of volcanic scenery in the neighbourhood of Naples; pictures of Vesuvius in eruption with streams of lava flowing from its crater over the fertile countryside, topographical views of Naples itself and other towns, lakes formed from old craters and other scenes of a volcanic or geological interest. A further plate illustrated the discovery of the Temple of Isis at Pompeii, and was followed by thirteen others showing specimens of minerals, curious volcanic matter, lava, marble, tufa, pumice and crystals thrown up by Vesuvius or collected by Hamilton from the live crater of the volcano. These the artist shows as they might have been displayed in Sir William's own cabinet in the Palazzo Sessa. The plates were finely engraved and coloured by hand. Before each illustration was a general description of the scene written by Hamilton, followed by comments on points of special interest under numerical headings which refer to corresponding numbers on Fabris's pictures. The text was printed in double column in English and French. The second volume, which contained the bulk of the text in the form of Hamilton's 'volcanic letters' to the Royal Society and his 'remarks upon the Soil of Naples and its Neighbourhood', was illustrated by a map of the area from the gulf of Gaeta to the gulf of Salerno, indicating further references to the text and plates.

The pictures which Fabris produced under Hamilton's guidance and supervision have a remarkable vitality. Their appeal is simple and direct, but while their main purpose is to illustrate the geological and topographical features of the landscape they are drawn with a fine artistic imagination and a vigorous dramatic sense. Though intended to demonstrate Hamilton's scientific theories and observations on volcanology and natural history the artist was allowed to introduce a human note which greatly adds to the charm of the plates. Sir William himself often appears in them on horseback, or leaning on his cane; in some he is alone, in others he is discoursing on the scene with a fellow antiquarian. One splended view shows a scene on the slopes of Vesuvius during an eruption. Clouds of vapour and ashes darken the sky while a stream of red-hot lava cuts across a devastated landscape. In the foreground, hat in hand, Sir William is showing the red river of fire to the King and Queen of Naples. Four royal guards with shouldered muskets stand at a respectful distance; the Queen's sedan chair waits nearby and a groom holds the horses from which the King and Minister have just alighted. As a final touch the artist has introduced himself sitting with legs crossed beneath a tree with his sketch book open on his knee.

Hamilton, in his descriptions of the plates, allowed himself to wander at times from the strictly scientific. A fine picture of Lake Avernus shows Sir William surveying the scene on horse back while a dog leaps along the road behind him. After commenting on the volcanic origin of the lake and recording other features of special interest, his note on this picture adds:

> 'This spot has been celebrated by many ancient Poets who brought their Heroes here to sacrifice to the Muses or consult the Sybil. Hercules, Ulisses, and Eneas are mention'd to have been at Avernus.'

Hamilton's purpose in issuing this further series of lavishly illustrated volumes is set out in the letter of dedication addressed to Sir John Pringle, President of the Royal Society. 'It is lamented', Sir William declares, 'that those who have wrote most on the subject of Natural History, have seldom been themselves the observers, and had too readily taken for granted the sistems which other ingenious and learned men have perhaps formed in their closets with as little foundation of self experience; the more such sistems may have been treated with ingenuity, the more have they served to mislead, and heap error upon error. Accurate and faithful observations on the operations of nature, related with simplicity and truth, are not to be met with often, and such only have I the honor of laying before the Respectable Society, at the head of which you, Sir, are so worthily placed.' If Sir William's own scientific system is no longer relevant to the requirements of modern knowledge, his 'accurate and faithful observation' remains enshrined in these three folio volumes, and the modern reader who turns the pages of *Campi Phlegraei* finds himself, thanks to the genius of Hamilton and Fabris in this happy collaboration, taking a fascinating and rewarding journey through the Neapolitan countryside as it appeared in the middle years of the eighteenth century. It is as though he had been transported back to those distant times and was able to follow, in company with some *milordo inglese*, in the progress of a Grand Tour.

Sir William's personal satisfaction in the production of this book with its delightful and informative illustrations 'giving the clearest idea of every stratum in this country of all the craters' was shown in a letter to Charles Greville in which he concluded:

> 'I wish every book of natural history was executed with such fidelity, and we shou'd not be so much in the dark as we are.'[1]

Fidelity was one thing but cost was another; once again Hamilton had to foot the bill, for the high standards he set could only be achieved at great expense. 'Considering the difficulty of printing in two foreign languages the edition promises well', he told his nephew in a further letter dated 12 March 1776, 'but the plates, which are the material, will I am sure surpass any thing of the kind. I have been obliged to be the translator, corrector, inspector, etc., etc. What is worse, the furnisher of the money; above £1300 already is gone but, thank God, the last plate is in hand which compleats 54. Nothing material has been omitted. I have secured the original drawings, tho' they have suffer'd much by handling, flies, etc.[2]

The third volume, which forms a supplement to *Campi Phlegraei*, came out in 1779 with a dedication to Hamilton's friend Joseph Banks who had been elected President of the Royal Society the previous year. The text consists of Sir William's long and detailed description of the eruption of Vesuvius in 1779, with two views of the erupting volcano by Fabris. The first of these two plates, made on the night of August the 8th, shows a great column of fire issuing from the summit, the bright scarlet flames shooting up in vivid contrast to the surrounding darkness. The other plate shows the same scene the following day, the clouds of smoke and vapour now appearing dark against the morning sky while red-hot stones fall like cannon-balls on every side. Vesuvius is viewed across the bay of Naples from Posillipo. In the foreground a peasant woman points towards the fearful sight while another joins her hands in prayer; above them a man throws out his arm in a theatrical gesture of admiration or defiance. These dramatic pictures of Vesuvius in full eruption seen in the contrasting circumstances of night and day were to become a regular feature of Neapolitan popular art. Fabris added two more plates, similar to those in the first volume, depicting the various minerals 'thrown out of Vesuvius during the last eruption'.

The three volumes of *Campi Phlegraei* together form a work of unusual beauty. Hamilton's text still conveys the enthusiasm he felt for the great volcano which, as he told Banks in the year that the last volume appeared, he had already climbed no less than fifty-eight times. But there can be no doubt that it is Pietro Fabris's illustrations that give this work its unique value. Their freshness, charm and feeling for human life as well as topographical detail are without equal, especially when it is remembered that the plates were originally intended to illustrate a book of scientific interest addressed by a Fellow of the Royal Society to the world of learning. This, of course, was exactly what Hamilton wanted and was the reason why he chose Fabris for the task. The marriage of art and science for the advancement of human knowledge was perfectly in line with his general theory of utility in the arts, which had been the theme of his previous volumes on his collection of antique vases, and was his own justification for his activities as a patron and connoisseur.

The dedication of the last volume to Joseph Banks was, in the circumstances, a happy chance. It was, of course, as the successor to Sir John Pringle as President of the Royal Society that Banks earned this distinction, but unlike his predecessor in the presidential chair he was also a close friend of Sir William's and it was to him that Hamilton addressed a whole series of letters on all matters concerned with his scientific as opposed to his strictly artistic interests. Joseph Banks was thirteen years junior to Hamilton in age, but became his life-long friend after they had first met as active members of the Royal Society. Both men were passionate believers in the value of first-hand experience and direct and accurate observation in the formation of scientific theory, and both held the 'arm-chair' scientist in contempt. It was to Banks that Hamilton communicated any detail of natural history, of botany, archaeology, or of general curiosity, which he thought might interest or entertain his friend. Among the more serious subjects which filled the pages of a correspondence of many years Hamilton found time to regale him with such diverse topics as the netting of birds, bubbles rising in Lake Agnano, double roses discovered at Paestum (he 'did not find them sweeter or better than the common ones'), Herschel's astronomical observations, Arabic chronicles found in Sicily, the manufacture of silk in Naples, the medal struck by Cardinal York to announce his 'accession' to the British throne, curious fish called *Angelino di Mare*, the habits of the sea-snail or slug, and the use of lightning conductors on ships. Drawings of specimens sometimes accompanied these letters, and not only drawings: 'Greville tells me you have thought of sending us over some serpents', Banks wrote in August 1778.[3] 'They will, I can assure you, be most welcome guests and most acceptable companions of my leasure hours.'

The money spent on the production of *Campi Phlegraei* served to remind Hamilton once again of the money still owed him by the Government. To Greville, now a Member of Parliament, he wrote asking him to 'get up when the Civil List is before the House and urge the necessity of paying the King's debts, or at least as much as will prevent foreign Ministers from being drove to expose themselves abroad'.[4] What he spent on books and vases and pictures was his own business, but the expenses of running the embassy increased as his reputation as a man of taste spread, for all who visited Naples wished to meet Sir William Hamilton, and all who entered the Palazzo Sessa expected His Britannic Majesty's Minister to entertain them, as a result of which the Minister found that he was having to cope with a constant flow of visitors from young noblemen on the Grand Tour to ageing savants or aspiring collectors, and it was a rare occasion when he and Lady Hamilton sat down with less than twelve to dinner, not counting their regular gala days when as many as sixty would have to be provided for. Mean while visiting royalty took it as a matter of course that Sir William Hamilton would conduct them round the ruins of Pompeii or Herculaneum or accompany them to within a safe distance of the crater of Vesuvius. To enjoy such a reputation was a mixed blessing, and after taking Duke Albert of Saxony and the Archduchess Maria Christina on one of these expeditions in April 1776 Sir William wrote rather wearily to the Secretary of State: 'The very long stay I have made in this country and my love for Antiquities and natural history have acquired me the character of the best *Cicerone* of Naples and its environs which has procured me a great deal of honor to be sure, but attended with some fatigue.'[5] And also, he might have added, with considerable expense.

Hamilton sent an amusing account of the English visitors in a letter to his favourite nephew written in March 1775. 'The English, of whom we have had a large flight this year,' he told Charles Greville,[6] 'have felt the good effects of my being on such a good footing at Court. I have remarked how one or two of the set always decide the rest whether they shall follow the Arts, gaming, whoring, or drinking. Last year the Arts and gaming were the prevailing passions with the English, this year it is drinking and gaming; and as they made their party at cards at the Festini at the palace the King looked on, liked their manner of playing, and as H.S.M. cares not for etiquette, but follows the dictates of Nature, he sat down with them without one of his courtiers, and this he did every night. I thought it prudent, to avoid any little disagreeable circumstances that might occur in the heat of the play, to be one of the party also; but I play'd low and my loss was small.' The other English players, who included Lord Monson and Lord George Cavendish, less prudent than their Minister, lost over two thousand pounds, most of which found its way into the pocket of the King of Naples 'who is quite fond of the English,' Sir William added dryly.

The task of preparing *Campi Phlegraei* for the press and keeping an anxious eye on the activities of the English visitors by no means exhausted Hamilton's energy. In November the composer Picini came to the Palazzo Sessa bringing three new songs which he rehearsed with the ambassador, who pronounced them to be delightful.[7] Earlier in the same year Sir William purchased for three hundred pounds a great vase 'far beyond any monument of the kind at Rome'. This vase had been discovered at Hadrian's Villa outside Rome in 1771. It was Hamilton's intention to have it restored and then to sell it to the British Museum. 'I was obliged to cut a block of marble at Carrara to repair it, which has been hollowed out and the fragments fixed on to it, by which means the vase is as firm and entire as the day it was made,' he told Charles Greville, to whom he left the details of the negotiations with the Museum authorities. However the 'old Dons' (as Greville described the Trustees) failed to agree over the price and the matter fell through. Sir William determined to send the vase home despite this set back, assuring his nephew that 'if the Museum do not take it I will have a good price for it, I promise you'. Before the vase left Italy on its long and perilous journey an engraving of it was made by Piranesi and dedicated to Sir William Hamilton whom the artist described very appropriately as *Amatore delle Belle Arte*. Eventually it was bought by his elder nephew after whom it has been known as the Warwick Vase.[8] Like the Portland Vase, which also came to England as a result of Hamilton's flair for collecting, it was not destined to be known by his name.

Sir William's interest in pictures is shown by the purchases he made over this period on behalf of his nephew. In October 1774 a crate of pictures was sent home destined for this budding collector. 'You will find in the case a hairy Magdalen of Cambiasi in the stile of Correggio which I make you a present of,' Greville was told, 'and will do well enough hung up high or over a door as the character is sweet but the picture has suffer'd a little, and was probably longer. You will likewise find the little St. Catherine of Siena by Parmegiano; it is sweetly painted and most undoubtedly original, and I do assure you that originals of this master are as rare as Correggio's. This is worth all your money. The little saint of Lod. Carracci is also original, but a little black. I have not attempted to clean either.'[9] At the bottom of the case Sir William had included the portrait of a Spanish boy in sixteenth-century dress, which, he declared, would do very well for Lord Warwick at the castle 'and may be christened *Fulk* [after Faulke Greville] as the Spanish dress was worn in England in Elizabeth's time'.

Little more than a year later (January 1776), Greville received more news of his uncle's picture-buying, which included the purchase of the picture described by Lord Gardenstone, when he saw it in 1788, as 'a sweet smiling boy at his play' by Leonardo. It is clear from Hamilton's letter that he was by no means convinced as to the authenticity of this attribution. 'I have this day got home', he wrote, 'the Guido Cagnacci, the Anibal Carach, the Albano, and the portrait called Leonardo da Vinci, from Coranello's Collection; the three first for you, and the last for me, as they would not fail from their demand more than selling the 4 for 1000 ducats. . . They are charming pictures and will do you credit. I shall pack them up frames and all, which are tollerably good, and send them off by the first ship.'[10]

In the middle of all these happy activities the Hamilton household was suddenly struck by tragedy. In 1775 a child, dear to both of them, died after a serious illness. A certain mystery surrounds this girl, whose name was Cecilia. She has been described as their daughter, though no record of her birth or of her age at the time of her death has survived. Indeed she passes from the world's stage leaving hardly a trace behind of her brief existence. In Charles Greville's letter written after his visit to Naples in 1769 is the phrase: 'I hope little Chechille (*sic.*) is quite recovered,' but this is the only reference to her in the correspondence of uncle and nephew. It seems more likely that she was an adopted daughter. Catherine Hamilton's delicate health makes it unlikely that she had a child of her own, and Sir William, despite infidelities and a second marriage, appears to have had no children. There is no record of his having illegitimate children in an age when men did not blush to acknowledge them, and though Emma had a daughter long before she knew him and was twice pregnant by Nelson, her marriage with Hamilton was childless. It is also curious that the Queen of Naples never mentions this child in her copious correspondence though she had great curiosity about all that concerned the offspring of her friends.[11]

The year following this sad loss the Hamiltons again visited England, but Horace Walpole, who in general curiosity about his friend's affairs could vie with Maria Carolina, has nothing to say about the death of their daughter, though he had much to say on the subject of Lady Hamilton's death nearly six years later. Indeed, the advice he sent her was hardly what would be expected for a woman only recently bereaved of an only child. After telling Sir William that he would subscribe for a copy of *Campi Phlegraei* but regretting that he had exchanged his taste in painting and antiquity for what he terms 'Phenomena' (he need have had no worries on this score) Walpole adds: 'I advise Lady Hamilton to beg, buy, or steal all the plumes from all the theatres on her road; she will want them for a single fashionable head–dress, nay, and gourds and mellons into the bargain. You will think like William the Conqueror that you meet marching forests.'[12] It is most unlikely that the death of a real daughter would pass so totally unrecorded in the correspondence of their friends. The existence of an adopted child, on the other hand, might well not have been widely known beyond the intimate circle of the Palazzo Sessa.

The Hamiltons left for England at the end of May 1776 and did not return to Naples until November of the following year. A reminder of Sir William's hopes for the Spanish embassy came when a letter reached him from London some months before he set off on leave (it was written on 4 January) from a certain Stephen Sullivan asking for the post of Secretary to the Embassy 'whenever your own appointment to Madrid is confirm'd'. No confirmation was to be made of this appointment, and one reason for this (as Sullivan mentioned in his letter) was the general opinion about Westminster and Whitehall that Sir William 'might have had Spain long ago, but [you] was then too immers'd in Volcanoes to bear the idea of quitting Naples'.[13] The arrival of the subscribed copies of the first two volumes of *Campi Phlegraei* at the same time as their author would do nothing to dispel this notion.

Distinctions of another sort were in wait for the returned Envoy. On his previous leave he had been elected to the council of the Society of Antiquaries of London; on this leave, in February 1777, he received a letter from Charles Crowle as Officiating Secretary informing him of his election as a Member of the Dilettanti Society and expressing the hope that he would 'attend a Call of the Society at the Star and Garter, Pall Mall, of which you will be properly informed'. [14]

Founded in the early years of the reign of George II this society consisted of a group of noblemen and gentlemen whose interest was in the promotion and patronage of the arts, and whose activities were very much after Hamilton's own heart. In 1764, by sending Richard Chandler on an expedition to make drawings of the artistic monuments of antiquity in Greece and Asia Minor, they had, in fact, anticipated something of what Sir William himself had attempted in the volumes illustrating his first collection. Their meetings were conducted with some formality, presided over by the officers of the society in splendid robes, but their deliberations were not without a degree of conviviality as befitted a society whose origins went back to the days of the Hell Fire Club.

Hamilton is the central figure in one of the two groups of members of the Dilettanti Society painted by Sir Joshua Reynolds. These pictures, representing together a single occasion, were commissioned in the year Sir William joined the society (though they were not completed until 1779) and it has been suggested that the scene represents the ceremony of his introduction as a new member.' It was a rule that the President should drink to the health of the newly elected and that as soon as the foot of his glass touched the table all the other members should join in the toast and 'with one universal loud Acclamation vociferate the name of the New Elected Member'. In Reynolds's picture the President, Sir Watkin Williams-Wynn, has just emptied his glass and all the other members have their glasses raised. Hamilton alone is without a glass in his hand but points to a Greek vase on the table in front of him on which also lies an open copy of his *Greek and Roman Antiquities*.

There is no doubt that Hamilton sat to Sir Joshua during this visit to England. A formal portrait of him, sitting by an open window commanding a distant view of Vesuvius, shows the Envoy in his star and riband with an open copy of his vase book on his knee. Other indications of his scholarly tastes in the form of antique vases and folio volumes complete the composition which shows Sir William more as amateur of the arts than as diplomatic representative. This portrait was first exhibited in 1777. It is interesting to note that the pose of the head and shoulders is identical with the figure of Sir William in the Dilettanti group, which suggests that the latter picture was still incomplete when Hamilton left London for his return to Naples (as indeed the records of the Dilettanti Society bear out) and that Reynolds had to rely on the sketches made for the first portrait in order to finish the second.

When Sir William and Lady Hamilton travelled back to Italy in the autumn of 1777 they were making the long journey together for the last time; Catherine Hamilton would never see her native land again. Another five years was all that remained to this gentle and charming woman in the country whose warm and temperate climate had already prolonged her existence. They reached the Palazzo Sessa once more towards the end of November, Hamilton reporting on the 25th that 'after a tedious and rather hazardous journey owing to uncommon inundations, Earthquakes, bad roads and worse horses we arrived here on Thursday last'. Even the 'Professor of Earth quakes' found these a little inconvenient when they interrupted a journey.

The returned ambassador discovered the government of Naples in a state of transition. The long rule of Tanucci was over; the day of John Acton had not yet dawned. For the moment the reins of government were held in the unsteady hands of the Marquis della Sambuca who had succeeded to office while Hamilton was on leave. In a long dispatch to Lord Weymouth written on Christmas eve Sir William painted a dismal picture of the political scene.

'While his Sicilian Majesty is trifling away his time in a continual round of dissipation. . . ' he informed the Secretary of State under cover of cipher,[16] 'the Marquis Sambuca is endeavouring to arrange the affairs of state which have been left in the utmost confusion by his predecessor the Marquis Tanucci, who for some years past would neither do business himself nor suffer any other Ministers to act in their departments; but I perceive already that the new Minister, tho' a very honest and well intention'd man, has neither parts nor resolutions enough to bring about any material change to extricate this Nation from the various difficulties it labours under; and, indeed, he has in some measure put it out of his power by giving up to each Minister the full powers in their respective departments which they enjoyed till it had been wrench'd from them by the late Minister, only reserving to himself the Foreign department and the Post Office. This step might have been very proper had the other departments been occupied by able and honest men, which is far from being the case. In short, a general corruption prevails in this country which has infected every class and the disease is so rooted that it must require a great length of time and very wise measures to bring about any essential alteration.'

Hamilton's complaint of general corruption in this dispatch is typical of his attitude to the sort of government which prevailed in Naples before Acton's attempts at reform. The advocates of the later revolutionary party have held up the British Envoy as exemplifying the conventional reactionary of the *ancien régime*. This is to misunderstand him completely, though without doubt he could in no sense ever be described as favouring revolution or revolt. It was no part of his mission to tell the King of Naples how to run his country, though his dispatches show very clearly how he deplored the general state of injustice, corruption, and inefficiency that seemed to hold sway throughout the kingdom. He welcomed the intervention of the Queen in affairs of state because he thought she represented a more liberal and intelligent influence than could be expected either from Ferdinand or from the Neapolitan aristocracy. He supported Acton for the same reason. Though he belonged to a generation and class which tended to regard an enlightened paternalistic régime as the most suitable form of government his main quarrel with the Neapolitan revolutionaries when they appeared on the scene was not so much their desire for reform (though he would have rejected their notions of egalitarianism out of hand) as that they sided with France in an ideological struggle in which Great Britain found herself on the other side.

For the moment, however, there was no need for people to concern themselves with ideological problems. The world was moving towards the last decade of tranquillity it was to enjoy before the events of 1789 would in due course deprive France of a King, Maria Carolina of a sister, the world of peace, and Hamilton of that calm and cultured atmosphere which had been the chief characteristic of his official residence at the Court of the Two Sicilies. For the present that Court was presented with no greater tragedy than the death of an infant prince.

In Hamilton's dispatch reporting the death of this three-year-old child he called the Prince 'one of the most amiable and beautiful children I ever beheld'. It was to the British Envoy and his wife that the bereaved Maria Carolina turned for consolation. 'The Queen was pleased to send for Lady Hamilton and me on Sunday last,' Sir William's dispatch, dated 2 December 1778, continues, 'and we had the honor of being with Her Majesty near two hours during which time Her Majesty would allow of no other topic of conversation but what had some relation to the departed Prince.'[17] The circumstances surrounding the Prince Royal's death were certainly extraordinary as they were described in a letter from Catherine Hamilton to Henry Swinburne. 'Never was anything more terrible than the combination of accidents which contributed to make the scene of the death of the Hereditary Prince of Naples more horrible', she wrote. 'The Queen did not suspect his danger till the moment the physicians declared there were no hopes, at which news one of the women, going to call the King, dropped down in convulsions; her companion fell into the same state, and they could not be removed out of the Queen's hearing. Six men could not hold them, and at that moment one of these was struck with apoplexy. It blew a dreadful hurricane from the mountains, the roof of the house took fire, and to add to the distress and danger, all the corridors had been filled with hay to prevent noise.'[18]

Shortly after these sad events a new inmate arrived at the Palazzo Sessa destined to cause the Hamiltons a good deal of amusement. This was an East Indian monkey called Jack. We first hear of him in February 1779 in a letter from Sir William to Joseph Banks in which Jack's antics are cited to confound the theories of the distinguished French naturalist the Comte de Buffon. 'He is black', we learn, 'with a light brown beard, his hands remarkably well made. He bites his nails and keeps them in charming order, and every motion genteel. But, Mr. President, the reason for my introducing my monkey is to prove Mons. Buffon but a poor naturalist, at least *sur le chapitre des singes*. He gives the Elephant, the Horse, and the Dog more sense than a Monkey. My monkey loves insects and flies of every kind. He caught a wasp in his hand last autumn which stung him; ever since, when he sees a wasp settle he takes up a stick or a stone and crushes it. If the rope that ties him is twisted ever so much he contrives to free himself. My wife retired into a closet lately, and I caught him with his eye to the key hole which he constantly repeats when any ladies go into that retreat—in short I could fill a volume with his gentleness, and he is wonderfully good humour'd, with the most laughing merry countenance you ever saw. He has a long tail like a lion's but no power of holding by it. When he walks on all fours he turns out his hands like the best French dancing master. . .   I wish you could see him for he really is the most amiable creature of his kind I ever saw, and was he not a little dirty at times I should be better directed in *tête à tête* with him than with half mankind. I should like to see Mons. Buffon's horse put his eye to the key hole! In short there is nothing like a close and impartial observation of nature itself free from prejudice and system.'[19]

We hear more of Jack's antics in a letter to Lord Herbert, the Earl of Pembroke's son, who had made the monkey's acquaintance when he visited Naples the year before. 'Jack is greatly improved', Sir William wrote on 11 July 1780, 'but bites now and then as Your Lordship may remember he could when you was here. The battles between him and my boy Gaetano (whom you may remember to have a St. Januarius, an I.C., and a Pulinchinello tattooed on his arm) when he is naked and going into the sea with me in the morning are really curious. He never bites him but plays him all sorts of tricks, his favourite one is to pull him by his — and then he always smells his fingers; the other day he pull'd rather hard and the boy clapped his two hands upon it whenever the monkey approached. Jack made use of a most excellent expedient to put the Boy off his guard. He passed by him and kept his hind parts close to the Boy who was sitting at the head of the boat, and who no longer fearing him removed his hands; Jack, who was squinting back, immediately seized his prey with one of his feet, which you know are equally handy, and held him fast to the great entertainment of the Waterman and myself.'[20] It is in this same letter that Hamilton describes how he taught the monkey to make fun of the pompous connoisseur: 'I don't despair of making him an Antiquarian for he manages a magnifying glass very well and will look at a Cameo or an intaglio very gravely through it.'

In spite of an assurance to Banks that good fires would keep the monkey alive during the cold weather while the Neapolitan sun would do for him in the summer, Jack did not survive the winter of 1780. On 26 December, Hamilton had to tell Lord Herbert of the death of this entertaining and intelligent animal:

> 'Our poor Jack, your Friend, alas! is dead. Nothing could be more moving than his illness and death; it half kill'd Lady H, for he never would leave her a moment. He grew quite gentle and for the last month was without a chain, and never attempted to bite. He shewed us that his disorder was in his breast. He would do anything for us, and finding that glisters did him good he would turn up his tail and ask for one every morning. He really was the most extraordinary animal, if it was one (for I am sure I have several servants in my house that deserve that appellation more than him) that I ever saw. He was ten times wiser than when you saw him, and was improving daily. His lungs were decay'd.'[21]

After this touching panegyric on Jack's almost human qualities Sir William's last word on the subject comes almost as a shock: 'I have preserved him in spirits and intend him for the British Museum.'

As well as receiving news about Jack, Lord Herbert was also kept informed about Hamilton's musical activities. Strong competition on the violin had decided him to abandon that instrument for the viola. 'I have left off the fiddle as Rosamowski and the Vienna Minister quite cut me out, and I have taken to the Tenor', Hamilton confided in the same letter in which he described Jack's tricks with the boy Gaetano. 'I should think some of Abel's musick for the Viol di Gamba wou'd do well on the Tenor if you cou'd get any old solos or pieces of his Musick copied for me out of Lady Pembroke's books. . . '

Sir William's knowledge of the musical life of Naples was much in demand just then, for a youth of unusual talent had arrived in the city in May 1779 and placed himself under the protection of the British Minister. Michael Kelly was later to become a musician of distinction both as singer and composer. He was the first British artist to appear in Italy when he sang at the Teatro Nuovo in Florence and later became a member of the Vienna opera and sang the part of Don Basilio in the first performance of *Le Nozze di Figaro*; he ended his days as musical director of the Theatre Royal, Drury Lane. At this period, however, he was an unknown youth of about fifteen whose only claim to fame was having a few appearances at the Smock Alley Theatre in his native Dublin.

Kelly's *Reminiscences* describe his first encounter with the British Minister who until that moment had never heard of the obscure Irish youth who presented himself at the Palazzo Sessa. Many a Minister Plenipotentiary would have taken little notice of such a lad, or quickly have perused his letter and passed him on to some minor official for a word of advice before turning him loose on the great city. Such was not the method of Sir William Hamilton. 'I immediately waited on Sir William and presented my letters', Kelly recalled: 'when he had read them he received me most kindly and assured me that he should be happy to give me any advice as to the line I ought to persue, and render me every service in his power.'

This was no mere formality. Next day the boy was bidden to dinner and introduced to Lady Hamilton. 'The taste and partiality for music of this highly-gifted person are too well known to need a remark from me', Kelly later wrote. 'At that period she frequently gave concerts, to which all the best performers were invited. She was herself considered the finest pianoforte player in Italy.' No doubt Catherine felt no nervousness when playing for this gifted young admirer. It had been a different case nine years previously when she had had to play in the presence of a more renowned child prodigy. Lady Hamilton 'trembled when she played before Wolfgang' Leopold Mozart had noted when the Ambassadress performed before his son during their visit to Naples in May 1770.[22]

After dining with the Envoy and his wife and being presented to the Duke of Bedford, who was also present, Michael Kelly was asked to sing. Perhaps Hamilton wanted to discover the quality of the boy's talent before recommending him to one of the Neapolitan academies of music. Kelly chose Rauzzini's *Fuggiam da questo loco* (hardly a tactful choice) and *Water parted from the Sea*. The effect on his audience, however, was all that could be wished—I seemed to give general satisfaction'—and the young singer was asked to call on the ambassador again next morning at eight o'clock. Elated, perhaps, by his success of the night before Kelly did not reach the Palazzo Sessa until a quarter to nine. On entering the breakfast room he found Sir William seated with his physician and a couple of antiquaries, the table covered with cameos, intaglios, and lava. Kelly recorded what followed in his *Reminiscences*: 'As soon as I entered the apartment, he said, "My good boy, you were to have been here at eight; it is now three quarters of an hour past"; and added, looking very seriously at me, "if you do not learn to keep time, you will never be a good musician." Through life I have recollected that hint.'

Having administered this firm but kindly rebuke Hamilton proceeded to give some more practical advice. Kelly had mentioned his wish to study with Finaroli. 'My good lad,' replied Sir William, 'it is impossible to choose a more able instructor or a better man. I know him intimately, and will introduce him to you, and recommend you to his care.' He then reminded the young musician that nothing could be done without steady application: 'your inclination for the stage you must smother for the present; your youth, and the unsettled state of your voice should preclude all thoughts of that; a year or two may do much for you'. He then suggested that Kelly take 'a fortnight's pleasure' in order to see the sights of Naples before getting down to work, adding: 'And recollect, as Grey says, "today for pleasure, tomorrow for business"—when once we begin we must work hard.'

Later on Sir William introduced his young friend to the King of Naples. On being told that he was a lad from Ireland come to study music Ferdinand looked hard at such a strange prodigy and asked '*Ne, siete Cristiano?*'—'Are you a Christian?'—and receiving a satisfactory reply asked him to sing in English. Kelly obliged with an air from *The Duenna* which he followed with another song in Italian. The King, delighted with such virtuosity, presented him to the Queen who rewarded the young singer with an ice-cream and a glass of Maraschino. Kelly, for his part, was to record 'how much my young mind was elated at her Majesty's condescension'. For the remainder of his time in Naples Sir William kept a fatherly eye on this gifted young man, not forgetting to take him on a climb up Vesuvius during the eruption which occurred during the year of his visit.'[23]

Hamilton's kindness to Michael Kelly and the care he took to advise him about his career were typical of the interest he always had for young people, especially if they showed some aptitude for the arts. It was the same with painters as with musicians; whether Pietro Fabris, Alexander Cozens, David Allan, Wright of Derby, or any of the other artists who flocked to Naples at this period. To one, Thomas Jones, he actually offered his palace for use as a studio while he was away observing the effects of an earthquake. To be a patron of the arts, in Sir William's eyes, did not merely mean the purchase of pictures; it meant giving practical help wherever possible to artists of every description.

1. Morrison, 54.
2. Morrison, 71.
3. B.M. Egerton MSS 2641, f. 127.
4. Morrison, 40.
5. B.M. Egerton MSS 2636, f. 185.
6. Morrison, 52.
7. Morrison, 58.
8. Morrison, 53, 59 and 71.
9. Morrison, 39.
10. Morrison, 62.
11. The author is grateful to Mr Harold Acton for this information.
12. Morrison, 70.
13. B.M. Add. MSS 41198, f. 8.
14. Ibid., f. 10.
15. Vide C. Harcourt-Smith: *The Society of Dilettanti, Its Religions and Pictures*, pp. 70-2.
16. B.M. Egerton MSS 2636, f. 195.
17. B.M. Egerton MSS 2636, f. 275.
18. Vide H. Swinburne: *Courts of Europe at the Close of the Last Century*, Vol. I, p. 223.
19. B.M. Add. MSS 34048, f. 7-8.
20. *Pembroke Papers*, Vol. I, p. 294.
21. Ibid: II, p. 76.
22. E. Schenk: *Mozart and His Times*, p. 133.
23. Vide M. Kelly: *Reminiscences*, Vol. I, pp. 28-30, 50-4.

CHAPTER XI

A Diplomat of Tact

A Diplomat in the course of his career has occasionally to deal with situations which require both tact and imagination. In such cases he must rely upon his own discretion if the matter is not one that comes within the immediate terms of his instructions. In these days if any unusual or delicate problem presents itself an ambassador can, by modern means of communication, get immediate guidance from his government; but in Hamilton's days an envoy had no choice but to act on his own initiative for a problem which might be settled within a week would be over and done with long before his dispatch on the subject (if it warranted one) had reached its destination. Hamilton had his share of these problems, two of which, of special interest, occurred one just before and the other shortly after his visit to England of 1776-7. Both concerned women; one a lady in distress, the other a rather distressing lady.

The first woman was beautiful, her story highly romantic, and her ultimate fate a sad one. She was also almost certainly an impostor. In helping her Sir William was the unintentional agent of her undoing. It was ironical for one so susceptible to feminine beauty that he never set eyes on her. How he first came to hear of this lady is told in a dispatch to the Earl of Rochford written on the 4th of January 1775. 'About a fortnight or three weeks ago there came to Naples a Lady from Ragusa with a suit of nine persons, some in Polish dress. She called at my door and left the name of Countess of Bamberg and desired that I would procure her passports for Rome, which I refused to do, as she had not brought a letter of recommendation, and I called at her door to make my excuse more civil, but did not see her. The next day she sent one of her suit to me and beg'd for God's sake I should procure her a Passport to go to Rome as her money was nearly expended and it might be of great detriment to her should she be detain'd longer in this Kingdom with her numerous suit having been obliged already to perform Quarantine at Taranto. In short, thinking it would be of no consequence, I from compassion applied to the Marquis Tanucci and having procured her a Passport for Rome she went off the next day leaving me a billet of thanks stiling her self the Princess Elizabeth, daughter of Elizabeth, late Empress of Russia, and desiring me to keep her secret. I then enquired of the Minister of Ragusa, and he told me that she was generally thought to have been Mistress to Prince Radziwill, but that he treated her always with respect.'[1]

While Sir William was still writing this dispatch a packet arrived for him from Rome which contained a long letter from the self-styled Princess and various enclosures consisting of copies of letters by herself to the Sultan of Turkey, and a message of passionate devotion to her cause and person over the signature of 'Montague' which she declared to belong to 'Milord de Montague' but appears in fact to have been the hand of Edward Montague, son of the famous Lady Mary Wortley Montague and no more a Lord than the lady he addressed as 'Your Highness' was a Princess. The letter which Hamilton read was a plea for help, and between flattering phrases addressing him 'as an enlightened and just Minister who on all occasions makes his noble and just character evident', told an extra ordinary and romantic story. It was sent to him, he discovered from the contents, because the 'princess' could address herself 'only to a Minister combining right, power and good intentions'.

She was, she declared, the daughter of the Empress Elizabeth by Count Rosomoski. 'The Empress my mother decorated M. le Comte de Rosomoski with the order of St. Andrew, made him Grand Hetman of all the Cossacks, and married him secretly.' Her mother died when she was eight and a half years old and made a will in her favour. It fell to Peter III to bring her up, but according to the Princess he packed her off to Siberia where she spent a year before escaping through the compassion of a priest. This pious man handed her over to friends of her father but an attempt was made to poison her by 'a kind of governess' after which she was sent for greater safety to Persia. Here she was looked after by a relative of her father's, and 'possessing great wealth he gave me the best possible education, sending for masters in various arts and science and in several languages'.

In Persia plots of all kinds took place and eventually her relative made her leave for Europe. She 'passed through all nations both pagan and Christian' and finally arrived 'absolutely incognito' in Berlin. Her stay there was not long, however, for on her journey she had taken counsel with many useful people and determined to go to Constantinople 'to treat in person with the Grand Seigneur'. With this splendid purpose in view she got as far as Venice where she met Prince Radziwill, who was on the point of leaving for Ragusa. 'Before my departure from Venice', Hamilton read, 'my Lord Montague came to see me. He is as judicious as wise, has an excellent heart, and is a good counsellor.' To this encomium the Princess added somewhat cryptically that Montague 'did for me what a brother would not do' ('*et pour moi ce qu'un frère ne ferait pas*') a phrase which leaves one in some doubt as to its exact interpretation. Prince Radziwill and the Princess arrived in Ragusa with a suite of eighty in attendance. Here they 'waited for two months and spent much money', hardly a surprising fact considering their mode of travel.

At Ragusa the Princess learnt that peace was about to be signed between the Russians and the Turks. 'What decision was I to take at such a critical moment?' she demands in her letter. 'A few weeks before I had written two letters to the Grand Seigneur. . . We had more to fear than to hope for. I continued my desire to go to Constantinople but could not do so as my funds were exhausted. We could only wait; everywhere were obstacles; the sea, the season, the long wait for fresh letters which were sometimes six weeks coming. . . ' Prince Radziwill, who was perhaps also exhausted, decided at this point that he had had enough, and prudently returned to Venice. As the Princess considered that her health did not permit her to expose herself to several weeks at sea she resolved to go to Naples.

Having left Naples for Rome with Sir William's help, why did she now address this long and rambling account of her adventures to him? She wished to continue her travels to Constantinople but could not go by way of Hungary (hardly a promising route) 'when that power was allied to Catherine'. But Sir William, she hoped, could give her a passport which would enable her to pass through Imperial territory, also some 'letters of recommendation for the Ministers of your court at Vienna and Constantinople'. Her lot, she told him, was cruel and crushing; 'soften it, worthy Minister, by the action of your generous soul; heaven will watch over you!' Descending from this lofty height the Princess pointed out that the best action his generous soul could take would be to send her a passport 'in the name of Mme. Walmod, or another, as if I were Hanoverian.'[2] In short, she was asking him to issue a false passport to someone who was making determined but not very practical attempts on the throne of a friendly sovereign. He was in the same position that a Russian ambassador might be in if one of the Young Pretender's followers, or even the Pretender himself, had asked him for a false passport to enter Great Britain.

Sir William had been in the middle of drafting his dispatch on the 'Princess's' first request for a passport to Rome when this packet arrived with its copies of the letters she had written to the Sultan of Turkey proclaiming herself heir to 'the late Empress Elizabeth of all the Russias'. He had copies made of the letters (the Princess's own letter was copied by Lady Hamilton and covers eight folio pages), and then returned them to the sender. Having done this he took up his pen and added a paragraph to his dispatch: 'Though I believe there can be no doubt of this woman being an adventuress I thought in consideration of the friendship that subsists between the Courts of Great Britain and St. Petersburg, Your Lordship would approve of my losing no time in giving notice of this affair to the Court of Petersburg through the channel of Count Orloff, who is now at Pisa, which I accordingly did by sending His Excellency copies of [letters] saying that I did not doubt that the King my Master would approve of the same.' By doing this he sealed the fate of the unfortunate adventuress.

Sir William then wrote to Count Orloff telling him how he had given a passport to Rome to this lady and how 'encouraged by the step which I took purely out of pity for a woman who I was told was beautiful, though I had never seen her' she had now sent him 'the singular papers' of which he enclosed copies. The Russian Count was, of course, delighted to receive information about this affair which, he declared in his reply, 'although based on chimeras and falsehood does not cease to interest me and is necessary for me to know'. He promised to make a full report to his Sovereign whom he would inform at the same time of the British Minister's devotion and care for her interest. He asked Hamilton to send him any more news he could discover about this person whom he considered to be either an adventuress (as Sir William had suggested) or else mad.

Another letter arrived from the lady, written from Rome on 10 January, once more asking Hamilton to facilitate the means for her to travel incognita through lands which she vaguely described as 'belonging to various nations subject to various laws, usage and customs'. Once again she had resort both to flattery and pity: 'My lot is worthy of compassion. I am speaking to a Minister who is as wise as he is enlightened; give me news when I may allow myself to be happy. . . ' To this Sir William again made no reply. Orloff, meanwhile, continued to press him 'to inform yourself in every possible way about her and to communicate everything you can learn about her; you will thus greatly oblige me'. The urgency the Russian now gave to the matter was clear from his letter. 'I shall not fail to be grateful', he assured his British colleague, 'and I am ready to be of service to you at the earliest opportunity in any way within my power; I beg you only to let me know how I can give you pleasure.'[3]

Hamilton certainly made some further enquiries about this strange individual. On 7 February he told the Secretary of State that he thought it possible that she might indeed be 'as she styles herself in private, the daughter of a great personage', and a fortnight later reported that she was still in Rome but 'intends leaving it soon having receiv'd a large supply of money which has relieved her from her great distress'. According to his information this much needed supply of funds came from a great northern power.

It would seem to have come, in fact, from Count Orloff. The next thing Sir William heard was that this nobleman had ingratiated himself with the 'princess' and prevailed upon her to visit Pisa where he treated her with the utmost respect, even going to the extent of standing in her presence when they appeared in his box at the opera. For some time he continued to flatter her in this way and to lull any suspicions she might still entertain against him. After a few days he proposed to the gullible lady that they should go on a 'party of pleasure' to Leghorn where, by a happy chance, some ships of the Russian fleet happened to lie at anchor. In no time the lady was inveigled on board the largest of these vessels where she was promptly handed over to the commanding officer and the party of pleasure ended with her in custody and the ship under weigh. A Russian prison awaited her at the end of her voyage. Sir William's last word on this picaresque episode came in a dispatch of 30 May 1775: 'The Person I mention'd to your Lordship in a former letter as having been decoy'd on board a ship of the Russian Fleet at Leghorn is, by what I can learn from Prince Orloff, the daughter of a Keeper of a Coffee-house in or near Prague. She is supposed by this time to be at St. Petersburg.'[4]

It might at first seem that Hamilton had behaved in a callous way towards the Lady from Ragusa. Having helped her in the first instance he then abandoned her to her fate, passing on to Count Orloff information fatal to herself and to her somewhat crazy pretensions to an imperial throne. In fact he could take no other course than the one he followed. His mistake, if he may be said to have made one, was to be beguiled by the thought of a beautiful woman in distress into giving her the first passport. If the unfortunate woman (about whom he then knew nothing beyond the fact that she called herself Countess of Bamberg) had been content to accept the passport and leave Naples in silence, no more would have happened. He asked for no more information. It was the lady herself who made the insensate mistake of sending to an ambassador whom she had never met highly treasonable letters against a sovereign with whom his Court was then on terms of friendship. British Ministers in Italy, whether at Florence, Turin or Naples, were highly sensitive on the question of Pretenders. Prince Charles Edward Stuart was not yet dead. Catherine II, after her succession, also had to contend with more than one Pretender to the throne she had seized. Having received the letters which this woman had been foolish enough to send him, Hamilton had no choice but to hand them on to his Russian colleague.

It is just as well that Sir William never set eyes on the Lady from Ragusa if she was indeed as beautiful as her reputation proclaimed her to be. It can hardly have been pleasant to imagine her fate when she fell into the hands of the relentless Catherine of Russia, to become an obscure victim in that monarch's ruthless process of establishing her claim to be known as 'the Great'.

The Case of Lady Maynard was very different from that of the *soi-disant* Princess Elizabeth. Lord and Lady Maynard were on a visit to Naples in the early months of 1778 and, like most English visitors, wished to be presented to the Neapolitan sovereigns. There was nothing to prevent the husband from making his bow to King Ferdinand but Lady Maynard's presentation to the Queen (which it would have been Lady Hamilton's duty to perform) raised difficulties of a most embarrassing nature. She had been born Nancy Parsons and was the daughter of a Bond Street tailor. There was nothing in this to prevent her presentation at Court; it was not her birth, but her reputation, that was in question. Lady Maynard, unfortunately, had a past. The nature of this past was nicely summed up by Horace Walpole. She had first lived with a West Indian merchant called Horton, whom she had left in order to enjoy the favours of a series of noblemen. She was, in Walpole's opinion, one of the commonest creatures in London: 'You know of no Mrs. Horton,' he told Horace Mann, 'but the Duke of Grafton's Mrs. Horton, the Duke of Dorset's Mrs. Horton, everybody's Mrs. Horton. . . ' Had her reputation been confined to England it might not have been quite so bad, but by now it had become international. 'His Sicilian Majesty', Hamilton was to write at the end of a long dispatch on this painful subject, 'ask'd me lately if it was not true that Lady Maynard was the very same person he had seen here in a box at the

Opera with an English Duke some years ago, to which I could only answer that it was but too true.'

Lord Maynard went to all the lengths to force Catherine Hamilton to receive his wife, a necessary first step before she could appear at Court. He even drove her up to the door of the Palazzo Sessa and demanded admission, only to be turned away. Henry Swinburne was in Naples at the time and noted that Maynard 'has left no stone unturned to get her presented, and poor Lady Hamilton has had a great deal of trouble about refusing it'. He added that the Queen was not unwilling to receive her, 'which is possibly true, for Maria Carolina had an unbounded curiosity about all members of her own sex, but the King would not hear of it. 'Lord Maynard asked him in the tennis-court', said Swinburne, 'and was refused plump'.

Eventually Lord Maynard went to see Hamilton on his own and a first-class row took place which Sir William afterwards recorded for the benefit of the Secretary of State. His dispatch gives a vivid impression of the scene. 'I am almost ashamed to trouble your Lordship upon so foolish an affair as that which I am going to relate', he began,[5] 'yet I think it right that you should be acquainted with the exact truth in case a complaint (which I am threatened with) should come before your Lordship.

'Lord and Lady Maynard arrived here some days ago. [The despatch is dated 6 January, 1778]. His Lordship left his name at my door, and I returned his visit a day or two after, as soon as I came from St. Leucio. He was invited to dinner the next day, which invitation his Lordship did not accept. Some days after whilst I had the honor of being again with Their Sicilian Majesties at St. Leucio, Lord and Lady Maynard drove into my Court at Naples. Notwithstanding that the porter had assured them that Lady Hamilton was not at home, they argued with him as they saw several other coaches in the Court, and insisted that Lady Hamilton was at home. The Porter, according to his instructions, was as firm in his denial, and they went away.

'As soon as I return'd to Town I received a Note from Lord Maynard desiring to see me, and the same evening Lord Maynard came to my house. When we were alone in my Closet Lord Maynard began by assuring me that what he was going to say was not meant personally to Sir Wm. Hamilton but to His Majesty's Minister at Naples, and he then desir'd that a Mr. Slade, a friend of his who was in the next room, might be present. Lord Maynard then very gravely ask'd me if I had receiv'd instructions from home that authorised the insult he had received at my door. Upon my desiring an explanation as I knew of no such insult, he mention'd the circumstances above related of Lady Maynard's intended visit, and the same time begg'd always to be understood that any insult or slight offered to Lady Maynard was the same as if offer'd to himself, as they were one and the same. I desired to call in a friend of mine, Mr. Mackenzie, who happened to be with Lady Hamilton, and in his presence Lord Maynard repeated what he had said before. I then assured his Lordship that his name had never appear'd in my instructions, nor did I believe that there ever had been an instance of any such personal instructions issued from any of our Secretary of States' offices. Mr. Mackenzie from his experience in these matters confirm'd the same. I added that certainly no affront had been intended either to Lord or Lady Maynard; that upon the chapter of visits every Lady was at liberty to receive or not, as she pleased, and that just before Lady Maynard had been at our door a Neapolitan Lady had been refused.

'He then asked me if I justified Lady Hamilton in continuing to refuse to meet Lady Maynard, and I answered that as Lady Hamilton had told me that "Consulting with her situation at Naples she thought that she could not act otherwise than she did", I on my part could not urge her to act contrary to her own feelings. Lord Maynard then press'd me to give reasons for Lady Hamilton's conduct, and I as often repeated the same words over again. His Lordship then flew out violently and said that the affair should not drop so, that the King should either give up his Minister at this Court or lose his friendship and support forever, with many other juvenile expressions which it is needless for me to report. I answered that tho' I was not conscious of having been wanting in respect to his Lordship, he was at liberty to refer the matter to my superiors to whom I was always accountable for my actions of a Public nature.

'A question Lord Maynard put to Mr. Mackenzie was singular enough: what Lady Betty Mackenzie would have done had the same thing happened to her? Why, said Mr. Mackenzie, she would have gone away and never return'd to the door again. The same evening Lord Maynard wrote me a note to desire me to present him to their Sicilian Majesties, which I did the next day.

'Had Lady Hamilton received Lady Maynard all the English Ladies here would have been much offended as not one of them have visited her, and Lady Maynard would certainly have desir'd to be introduced at the Neapolitan Court the next moment, which could not have been done, and must have brought on a more serious explanation which we have hitherto studiously avoided.'

Lord Maynard can hardly be blamed for leaping to the defence of the woman upon whom he had bestowed his name and title. Hamilton, who was tolerant and easy-going in his private capacity, felt that he must uphold the strong line taken by his wife, especially as the peace and quiet of the English community at Naples were at stake. As Minister Plenipotentiary he could not ignore this, and even as a private individual he probably considered that one irate Lord was easier to deal with than a cohort of scandalised and indignant matrons. Lady Hamilton, though quiet and retiring, could be firm when she thought it necessary, and with her unassailable position and strong religious feeling, she clearly thought this such an occasion. It was not the Viscountess Maynard but 'everybody's Mrs. Horton' to whom she took exception. In view of Sir William's later connection, however, a note of irony surrounds the whole episode. What would his thoughts have been had he known that his relation William Beckford would one day refer to Catherine Hamilton's successor almost in Walpole's very words as 'Lord Nelson's Lady Hamilton, or anybody else's Lady Hamilton'?[6] As to Lord Maynard's threatened protest, no more was heard of it, and Lady Maynard was denied the privilege of curtsying to Maria Carolina, whose enemies considered her to be quite the equal of any Mrs. Horton when it came to a question of amorous intrigues.

Whatever Beckford may have thought about the second Lady Hamilton (and he professed himself her ardent admirer while her husband lived) there is no doubt about his genuine devotion to Sir William's first wife. 'He revered Lady Hamilton as a superior being, and she showed for him all the fondness and solicitude of a mother', one of his biographers has written; 'she had an influence over him such as no other person ever had, elevating, purifying, and fortifying.'[7] His letters to her are full of passionate and romantic language which might make one think that his feelings for her were more than those of a young man for a sympathetic mother-figure, did we not know that during his visit to Naples he was emotionally attached to a youth of the distinguished Cornaro family whom he had met in Venice, and that before leaving England he had formed a similar attachment which was later to have unfortunate consequences.

Beckford reached Naples in November 1780. His arrival was sufficiently gloomy, as befitted a romantic author. 'Instead of entering Naples on a calm evening, and viewing its delightful shores by moonlight,' he wrote,[8] 'instead of finding the squares and terraces thronged with people and animated by music, we advanced with fear and terror through dark streets totally deserted, every creature being shut up in his house, and we heard nothing but driving rain, rushing torrents, and the fall of fragments beaten down by their violence.' Sir William Hamilton and Beckford's mother were cousins, so it was natural that he should be the guest of the British Minister during his stay. As much of Sir William's time was just then taken up in attending the King in the hunting field Beckford and Catherine Hamilton found themselves often in each other's company.

The sympathy between them was instantaneous and complete. Beckford appealed at once to the maternal side of Catherine's temperament, a side of her character which had so little chance to flower in Naples, and which had received so crushing a blow in the death of Cecilia. He, in his turn, found in this elder woman someone in whom he could confide with frankness. She was one of the few wholly good influences in his life and it was a tragedy for Beckford that they met at a time when her own life was nearing its close. She listened to his excitable outpourings without mockery; understood the real worth behind much of his romantic posturing; and had a calming and steadying influence on some of his wilder flights of fancy. Using the high-flown phrases which were second nature to him at this time, he wrote on 30 November from Caserta to his friend the artist Alexander Cozens: 'I still remain here, quiet and happy, with Lady Hamilton, who is perfectly in our way—we see nobody. Sir William hunts all day long with the King upon the Mountains, whilst we indulge our imaginations at home and play strange dreams upon the pianoforte and talk in a melancholy visionary style which would recall your ancient ideas and fill you with pleasing sadness.'

Beckford had early in life rebelled against the conventional pattern of a young Englishman of his class. 'To glory in Horses,' he wrote from Thun in Switzerland when only seventeen, 'to know how to knock up and how to cure them, to smell of the stable, swear, talk bawdy, eat roast beef, drink, speak bad French, go to Lyons and come back again with manly disorders, are qualifications not despicable in the Eyes of the English here. Such an Animal I am determined not to be!' He was certainly no such animal. Though only twenty at the time of his visit to Naples he was already something of a connoisseur, was a competent musician, and had written a satirical piece called *Memoirs of Extraordinary Painters*. He was also one of the richest men in England.

If Hamilton could not entirely approve of his exotic cousin's contempt for outdoor exercise, he found much in common with the young man's artistic and musical interests (always a strong bond as far as Sir William was concerned), and Beckford discovered in his relations in Naples a couple in whose company he could find genuine sympathy and relaxation. He talked art and literature with Sir William, played the harpsichord and pianoforte with Lady Hamilton, to whose skill he paid the highest tributes, and found in her a member of the older generation with whom he could confide his inmost secrets. 'Ten thousand times I have wished myself with you once more in peace and solitude,' he wrote to her from Rome when his visit came to an end in December. 'I can venture expressing to you all my wayward thoughts, can murmur—can even weep in your company. After my mother you are the person I love best in the universe. I could remain with you all my life listening to your music and your conversation. . . Give my love to Sir William and tell him how highly I value his affection. If I had the strength and spirits I would say a great deal more—and even then should fail of expressing half what I think—but both fail me at this moment. You can form no idea how melancholy and dejected I am. . . "[9]

Catherine Hamilton was to remain Beckford's good angel. He never forgot her. Seven years later, when she had been dead for five years, and when Beckford himself was living in Portugal in exile from English society whose conventions he had transgressed, he suddenly thought of her as he sat extemporising at the pianoforte. His mind went back to the calm and happy days they had spent together in Italy. 'I cannot help flattering myself that my compositions resembled those of my dear Lady Hamilton, those pastoral movements full of childish bewitching melody I have heard her so frequently compose during the autumn I passed at Caserta,' he confided in his Journal. 'The reflection of her being forever lost to me and the thought too that my lovely Margaret[10] was fled to the same dark cold regions from whence there is no return, and had left me desolate and abandoned, steeped my mind in profound melancholy.' The bitter attack he made on the character of

Emma Hamilton in his old age was motivated more by the veneration he had for the memory of Catherine than any real dislike he may have felt for her successor, whose vulgarities he seems to have noticed only after her death.

Letters continued to reach Lady Hamilton from her young admirer after he had left Naples. In January 1781, writing from Augsburg he told her: 'The gulf into which I was on the point of being precipitated has disappeared, and I am once more calm and happy,' a reference to those emotional entanglements he was able to confess to this understanding woman. 'It is chiefly to you I owe this enviable state,' he continues, 'your influence prevailed, your words never ceased to sound in my ears till the good work they had in view was accomplished. To express the transport I feel at my deliverance would be impossible.' In this mood of thankful liberation he tells her about the music he has been composing. 'Did you ever read in some Lapland history of certain gnomes who lurk in the mines and chasms of tremendous mountains? The music I have just now been composing was exactly such, I imagine, as elves and pigmies dance to—brisk and humming—moody and subterranean. Few mortals except ourselves have ears to catch the low whisperings which issue in dark hours from the rocks.'

From Strasburg she learns of his longing to return to Naples instead of proceeding to England: 'There I might hope to remain a few months in your company enjoying the spring on the coasts of your bay, and sharing with you my happy fantastic imagination.' By February he is in Paris where again he pictures himself transported to Caserta. 'I see the brown hills which environ it, and hear the winds talking to each other in the foliage—your voice seems mingled with their murmurs, and these, your visionary accents, breathe a certain pathetic tone which makes me often wake in tears.' Ten days later he tells her: 'You contribute more to my happiness than any human being, and if you were but sensible of the effect your letters have upon me you would wish the post went out every morning.' When letters did not come from her, he asks 'Why, my dear Lady Hamilton, have you forgotten that they were my greatest consolation?'[11]

The letters all contain affectionate references to Sir William, but it is to Catherine that Beckford pours our his high-flown phrases and it is for the light they throw upon her character that they are quoted. Hamilton's first wife still remains very much a shadowy and retiring figure; all that seems to come to us across the void of time is a distant cadence of music, the sound of a harpsichord quickly fading on the ear. Beckford's letters help to show us a woman of flesh and blood whose influence had a lasting effect on his wayward and self-indulgent nature. He was the only other man, apart from her husband, for whom she felt a romantic attachment, even though it was that of a mother for a son. The result of this was to make Beckford a somewhat better creature than he might otherwise have been, and though he was to remain always self-centred, such self-criticism as he managed to achieve can be traced back to the calm, quiet but lasting influence of Catherine Hamilton.

The Hamiltons were so settled in their life at Naples by the year of Beckford's visit that Sir William began, as he told Charles Greville, at the end of June 1780, to 'grow very in different to all ambitious views' as far as his professional career was concerned. 'It was 16 years last November that I first came to Naples,' he recalled,[12] 'and you know it is a bewitching place, I mean the local. I roll luxuriously in the sea every morning and we dine at our Casino at Pausilipo every day, where it is as cool as in England. Spring and autumn we inhabit our sweet house at Portici which you remember, and in winter I follow the King to Caserta and the Appenines after wild boars, etc., which amuses me in the day and the Queen's affability with musick, of which the King is now passionately fond, make the evening pass agreeably'. Life was indeed pleasant, the war in America seemed distant and was not yet disastrous, Etna was 'firing away' though Vesuvius was now calm after its eruption of the year before, and Lady Hamilton, he assured his nephew, was fonder of Naples than he was. Both Sir William and Catherine were completely under the spell of Parthenope, that Siren whose body was said to have been found on the shores of the dazzling bay where Naples now stands.

Visitors were constantly arriving and other events kept the Minister busy with the *trivia* of diplomatic life. His kinsman the Duke of Hamilton came with Dr. John Moore and Sir William took them to watch the ceremonies connected with the miraculous liquefaction of the blood of St. Januarius which they witnessed from a house directly opposite the portico of the Cathedral. Earlier in the year the Archduke Ferdinand of Milan came with his wife and attended a concert of music at the Palazzo Sessa. The Court and society were shocked when a member of the King's Swiss Guard tried to shoot the infant Prince Royal (brother to the child who had only recently died) when he was taken out for an airing with his sister Princess Louisa and their Governess. 'The Swiss soldier who fired off his piece', Hamilton reported with evident relief, 'has been proved to be out of his senses and is confined to a Mad House.' More agreeable was the rumour that the King of Spain had dismissed his confessor. 'This news seems to give great pleasure here as it is said to do in Spain,' Sir William informed Lord Hillsborough, the new Secretary of State, 'as that Monk, gained by French intrigue, is thought to have been the secret cause of Spain's having been so imprudent as to declare war against Great Britain.'[13]

In 1782 Sir William found himself acting as *cicerone* to a royal couple whose eccentric behaviour caused him both amusement and embarrassment. The Grand Duke Paul of Russia was then twenty-seven years old; he was the son of Catherine II, and his character, never very strong, was permanently warped by his mother's contemptuous neglect and by his own knowledge of that august matriarch's widely believed complicity in his father's murder, a fate which he would himself share within five years of his accession to the Russian throne. Like every visitor to Naples who could claim the privilege he insisted on being conducted up Vesuvius by the British Minister. Both he and his wife were soon defeated by the volcano when their attempted ascent was made; the Grand Duke was too weak in the lungs and his wife too corpulent of body to get very far. The Grand Duchess's feet came through her shoes in no time (though Hamilton had luckily warned her to take another pair) and the attempt had to be abandoned. 'However,' Sir William claimed, 'the novelty pleased them.'[14]

On another occasion Hamilton had to accompany the royal couple on a coach journey. The curious behaviour he was compelled to witness he later narrated to Sir Nathaniel Wraxall and can be told in his own words. 'The first time I was in the coach with them we had not proceeded far when Paul, as if unconscious that I was present, throwing his arms round the Grand Duchess, began to kiss her with as much warmth as he could have shown if they were alone and newly married. I was somewhat embarrassed at this unusual display of matrimonial attachment, hardly knowing which way to direct my view, for there was no other person with us in the carriage, and as I sat opposite his Imperial Highness, I could not easily avoid seeing all that passed, tho' I affected to look through the glass at the objects around me. At length the Grand Duke, addressing himself to me, said "*Monsieur le Chevalier, j'aime beaucoup ma femme!*" It was impossible not to credit the assertion, after the proofs which he had just exhibited. But we had not proceeded a mile further, when he recommenced the same demonstrations of attachment, which he repeated many times before we arrived at Portici, usually observing to me each time, "*Vous voyez que j'aime beaucoup ma femme!*" I could only express my satisfaction, concealing my astonishment at the testimonies of it which I had witnessed.'

Hamilton continued his archaeological expeditions with undiminished vigour for as he confessed to his nephew in February 1782 'tho' I am now 51 years old, and made pretty free with my constitution in my younger days, I bear fatigue much better than those who are much younger and fresher'. A year before this he had made an archaeological discovery which was greatly to amuse his friends. He had discovered a pagan fertility cult in full operation in the province of Abruzzo. The first announcement of this came in a letter to Joseph Banks in which the scientific and the bawdy were neatly intertwined. 'Greville will have told you that I have actually discovered the Cult of Priapus in as full vigour as in the days of the Greeks and Romans at Isernia in Abruzzo. I mean to send *Exvoti* and a faithful description of the annual fete of St. Cosmo's great Toe (for so the *Phallus* is now called, tho' it is precisely the same *thing*) to Solander to be placed near the ancient ones in the B. Museum.' He ends the letter: 'That your *Great Toe* and your purse may never fail you is the wish of, dear Sir, your most faithful humble Servant William Hamilton.'[15]

Sir William also sent an account of the cult to the Society of Dilettanti who resolved, in May 1784, to print his letter 'with such illustrations as they think proper'. As long as the disclosure of this thriving cult was confined to a narrow circle of friends little notice was taken of it. In 1786, however, Richard Payne

Knight, who had known Hamilton in Italy, brought out a book called *An Account of the Worship of Priapus lately existing in Isernia* which was based almost entirely on Sir William's discovery, though incorporated with it were some fantastic ideas culled from the mythological theories of D'Hancarville. The book caused great alarm among the prudish and was so bitterly attacked in a work called *The Pursuits of Literature* that the author tried to call in all copies.

In fact the publicity given to Sir William's discovery was to result in an ecclesiastical reform long before Payne Knight's book appeared. Replying to his friend in February 1782, Sir Joseph Banks noted: 'We are sadly disturbed here with the news Ch. Greville has given us that your observations on the Cult of Priapus have caused the Priests to enquire into and censure that curious remain of antiquity.'[16] The joke about Priapus was to crop up more than once in Hamilton's life, and a reference to it can even be found in James Gillray's famous caricature called *Dido in Despair* in which a vast blowzy Emma is seen bewailing the departure of Nelson's fleet.

It was in these pleasant pursuits that Sir William spent the first years of the decade that was to usher in the French Revolution. Only one event cast a cloud over his serene existence, and that was when the King of Naples showed him a letter from Paris which contained the news of Lord Cornwallis's surrender to the Americans at Yorktown on 19 October 1781. 'Tho' I was thunderstruck at this blow', he reported to Lord Hillsborough, 'I put on the best face I could and assured His Majesty that Great Britain, sensible of the justice of her cause, could not easily be cast down, and might make her enemies repent of having so unjustly attack'd her.' There was still a spirit of optimism in the air. Hamilton too, despite his fifty years, could also not yet easily be cast down.

1.   B.M. Egerton MSS 2636, f. 104.
2.   *Vide* Morrison: 42 (in French in the original).
3.   *Vide* Morrison: 46, 48 and 51 (originals in French).
4.   B.M. Egerton MSS 2636, f. 108, 110 and 124.
5.   B.M. Egerton MSS 2636, f. 100 *et seq.*
6.   L. Melville: *Life & Letters of William Beckford*, p. 231.
7.   J. W. Oliver: *The Life of William Beckford*, p. 48.
8.   W. Beckford: *Italy, Spain & Portugal*, p. 120.
9.   *Vide* L. Melville: *Life & Letters of William Beckford*, pp. 32, 97-8.
10. Beckford's wife. *Vide*: B. Alexander: *Journal of W. Beckford in Portugal and Spain*, p. 191.
11. *Vide* L. Melville, op. cit., pp. 99-105.
12. Morrison, 92.

13. B.M. Egerton MSS 2637, f. 166.
14. Morrison, 115.
15. B.M. Add. MSS 34048, f. 14.
16. B.M. Egerton MSS 2641, f. 135.

CHAPTER XII

A Cruel Loss

Hamilton's solemn thoughts, which he confessed to Greville in June 1780, that he had 'a presentiment that some thing or other will e'er long put an end to our residence here' were quite banished by the year 1782. So too were his hopes for another post. 'My utmost ambition now is to be left where I am,' he told his nephew in May of the latter year. His reasons for this change of attitude were now clearly set out: 'Upon the whole nothing at home, or even in a higher station abroad, would allow me to pass my time so much to my own satisfaction as I do at present, and I have already told my mind to my friends whom I believe to have weight in the present ministry. After 17 years service I do not think they would think of removing me, and all I ask of them is to let me alone. The present object seems to be peace; if that shou'd take place I wou'd endeavour to make a visit home, settle my affairs in Wales on another footing, and return here probably for the remainder of my days, for I find I grow old apace, and such a climate as this in old age is no inconsiderable object, and to Lady H's tatter'd constitution is become essential. As we have no children to place and provide for, we are to consult our own ease, and I protest I believe there is no place in the King's gift that cou'd suit me so well as this. To be sure I do regret the not being able to enjoy your society and that of another friend or two, but in this life nothing is compleat, however it may be in the next.'[1]

The British Minister was now so much a Neapolitan institution that it would indeed have been foolish of any Government to recall him or to transfer him elsewhere. His relations with the Royal Family remained as cordial as ever while in government circles he had found an ally of ever growing influence and power in the person of General Acton. This officer had come to Naples in 1778 when the Queen had asked her brother Leopold, Grand Duke of Tuscany, to send her an officer to reorganise the Neapolitan navy and marine, as she did not consider any of her own officers sufficiently experienced for the task. Acton was promoted from Captain to General Officer by order of the Grand Duke and dispatched to Naples in a frigate of the Tuscan navy. He was to remain in the service of the Neapolitan Royal Family for the remainder of his active career, rising from Minister of Marine to the position of supreme power as Chief Minister in the government.

John Francis Edward Acton was of English extraction, having been born at Besançon of an English father and French mother in the year 1736, descending on his father's side from an ancient family of Shropshire baronets to whose title he was ultimately destined to succeed. He began his service in the French navy but soon transferred to the fleet of the Tuscan Grand Duke (which was at that time commanded by his uncle, also named Acton) and was to gain distinction in the combined Spanish and Tuscan expedition against Algiers in 1775. Acton was ambitious, persevering, and direct in his dealings, which did not fail to disconcert the devious and circumlocutionary ministers he was soon to dominate. He was also a man of commanding presence and a bachelor, which did not fail to delight the Queen. Within four months of his arrival in Naples Hamilton was informing the Secretary of State in London that 'General Acton. . . comes frequently to my house and I flatter myself I have had the good fortune to gain his confidence and esteem. He is certainly a very sensible man and has the character of an excellent Sea Officer.'[2] By 1780 Acton had added the Ministry of War to that of Marine and was generally supposed to be the Queen's lover by Courtiers whose supply of gossip was based on conjecture rather than fact. There could, however, be little doubt that he was the man of the hour—and of the future.

In such a future, on intimate terms with the powerful Minister and in the full confidence of the Queen, Sir William could afford to contemplate his position with some complacency. Yet there is a note of resignation, almost of depression, in his letter to Greville with its plea that all he asks is to be left alone, the feeling that he grows old apace and the uncharacteristic reference to the incomplete nature of things in this world 'however it may be in the next'. It was only three months since he had been boasting to his nephew of how he could bear fatigue so much better than those who were younger and fresher than himself. This dark cloud was to prove only a passing one such as may overshadow any man who, in the middle of a full and vigorous life, is reminded of the inevitable passage of time. Hamilton, whose attitude to the world was one of frank hedonism, was no better equipped than the rest of mankind to repel the occasional chill which comes with the consciousness of life's briefness. His enduring fascination in art and nature would soon come to his rescue, but if any one sentence can be singled out from this letter to account for his attack of low spirits it is surely that which refers to his wife's 'tatter'd constitution', for in fact Catherine Hamilton's life was now rapidly drawing to its close.

Catherine was compelled to spend much time on her own in these last months. Her husband's official duties, his necessary attendance at Court, his place in the royal hunting expeditions, all kept him away from home, while her own growing feebleness now prevented her from sharing those social duties which previously had been their joint responsibility. A fleeting visit from William Beckford helped to cheer her, but many hours were spent in solitude at Portici, away from the noise and confusion of Naples, in calm preparation for the end she knew to be near. During this time the dying woman wrote three letters to her husband which reveal the depth of her devotion. However much a 'marriage of convenience' it may originally have been from Hamilton's point of view, these touching last letters of his wife's show her love for him to have been genuine and ever increasing.

Her one regret was that her husband did not share her religious belief. The first letter is in the form of a soliloquy. It is undated and was probably jotted down during the sad listless hours which the invalid was compelled to spend in the shaded rooms of her villa, a solitary prisoner of ill-health; it is not surprising that she found an outlet for her melancholy introspection by recording her thoughts in this manner. Unlike the other two it is not addressed directly to him, and it ends in the form of a prayer. Together with the other letters it was discovered in her work-box after her death.

'How tedious are the hours I pass in the absence of the beloved of my heart, and how tiresome is every scene to me,' Catherine wrote. 'There is the chair in which he used to sit. I find him not there and my heart feels a pang and my foolish eyes overflow with tears. The number of years we have been married instead of diminishing my love have increased it to that degree and wound it up with my existence in such a manner that it cannot alter. How strong are the efforts I have made to conquer my feelings, but in vain. How I have reasoned with myself, but to no purpose. No one but those who have felt it can know the miserable anxiety of an undivided love. When he is present every object has a different appearance, when he is absent how lonely, how isolated I feel. I seek peace in company and there I am still more uneasy. I return home, and there the very dog stares me in the face and seems to ask for its beloved master. Alas! I have but one pleasure, but one satisfaction, and that is all centred in him. Oh blessed Lord God and Saviour, be Thou mercifully pleas'd to guard and protect him in all dangers and in all situations. Have mercy upon us both, oh Lord, and turn our hearts to Thee. Give us that faith which is necessary to salvation. Preserve us, oh God, forgive us our numerous transgressions and grant us life and power to praise and bless Thee. O convert our hearts and draw them to Thee in spite of all temptations of the world. Oh Lord, bless and convert to thy faith my dear, dear husband, and grant that we may live to praise and bless Thee together.'

When Catherine Hamilton wrote these lines at some period early in 1782 she still felt a hope of recovery. Her prayer was that they might yet have a future together in this world. By April all such hope was gone. 'A few days, nay, a few hours, my dear Hamilton, may render me incapable of writing to you, I therefore will not delay it,' she wrote on the 7th of that month. 'But how shall I express my love and tenderness to you, dearest of earthly blessings! My only attachment to this world has been my love to you, and you are my only regret in leaving it. My heart has followed your footsteps where ever you went, and you have been the source of all my joys. I would have preferr'd beggary with you to kingdoms without you. But all this must have an end—forget and forgive my faults and remember me with kindness. I entreat you not to suffer me to be shut up after I am dead till it is absolutely necessary. Remember the promise you have made me that your bones should lie by mine when God shall please to call you, and give directions in your will about it. May every earthly and heavenly blessing attend you, my dear Hamilton, and may you be loved as I have loved you.'

The last line of this letter has a special poignancy with its hint of Catherine's awareness that her love for her husband was not returned with the same undivided devotion that she felt for him, for all the affection and respect in which he held her. The roles were to be reversed ironically in his subsequent adventure into matrimony. Catherine Hamilton was one of those people who have a profound reticence when it comes to expressing their deepest feelings. She had always been shy and reserved. Now, as life ebbed away, she felt able to put on paper those thoughts and feelings which she had never been able to put into words when face to face with the man she loved so wholeheartedly. To what extent these letters came as a revelation to Hamilton, whether he felt a tinge of conscience as he read them, we can only guess; but he preserved them all to the end of his life.

Catherine must have rallied somewhat after the crisis of April, for she lingered on until August. Her last letter to Sir William is undated; it was written during one of his absences and once again prays for his religious conversion: 'I feel my weak, tottering frame sinking and my spirits fail me; my only regret in leaving this world is in leaving you; was it not for that I should wish the struggle over. But my heart is so wrap'd up in you that you are like the soul that animates my body. You never have known half the tender affection I have borne you because it has never been in my power to prove it to you—forgive this effusion of my heart. I feel myself every day declining. You are absent from me, and God grant I may ever see you again. The dissipated life you lead, my dear Hamilton, prevents your attending those great truths in comparison of which all is folly—for God's sake do not reject those truths, nor despise the plain simplicity of a religion upon which our salvation depends, and which has been acknowledged and believ'd by the most sensible and greatest men after their having sustained the contrary; but they were convinced and were not ashamed to own it. God grant that you may imitate them and that we may meet in a better world than this. My lips, my heart, my soul blesses you and prays for you, dearest of earthly beings. Remember me with kindness and friendship, my dear Hamilton; remember your promise of being lay'd by me when God calls you away. . . And now, my dear Hamilton, my husband, my friend, my only attachment to this earth, farewell; forget my failings and cherish the memory of a wife who loved you beyond the love of women and dies yours most faithfully.'[3]

A tragedy occurred just before Lady Hamilton's death which cast an additional gloom over her last days on earth. Dr. Drummond, an old friend of the Hamiltons and Catherine's physician, was making the journey from Naples to Portici but instead of going by coach as was his custom, insisted on riding a high-spirited hunter. On the way the horse took fright and the doctor was thrown. His injuries were so bad that he died a few days later on 13 August. When the news reached

Catherine of her doctor's sudden and unexpected death the shock was thought to have hastened her end. She died less than a fortnight later on 25 August 1782, the cause of death being described as a bilious fever.

Lady Hamilton had always been shy and retiring, and the official side of her husband's life held no fascination for her. She never attempted to meddle in his political affairs or to influence his decisions. She preferred the quiet of their Villa at Portici to the splendours of the Palazzo Sessa or to what she described, without enthusiasm, as 'the gayest Court in Europe'. 'I am no Courtier', she admitted to a niece, 'and I know her Majesty's disposition too well to place any confidence in any encouragement she may be pleased to give me.' She was under no illusions about the character of Maria Carolina whom she saw with none of the idolising infatuation which so possessed her successor Emma. 'She is quick, clever, insinuating when she pleases, hates and loves violently, but her passions of both kinds pass like the Wind; she is *too* proud and *too* humble, there is no dependence on what she says as she is seldom of the same opinion two days. Her strongest and most durable passions are ambition and vanity, the latter of which gives her a strong disposition to Coquetry, but the former, which I think is her principle Object, makes her use every Art to please the King in order to get the Reins of Government into her hands in as great a measure as is possible.' To this perceptive catalogue Catherine added: 'With all this she is an excellent Mother and is very generous and charitable; did you ever know such a compound!'[4] How different is this from Emma's later rhapsodies about 'our dear much-loved Queen whom I adore'. If the first Lady Hamilton lacked the beauty and ambition of the second, she certainly excelled her in mind and judgement. Her death was a tragedy for her husband in more ways than one.

After so many years as an invalid Lady Hamilton's death came as no great surprise to her friends though Greville wrote a dutiful and rather sanctimonious letter in which he claimed that his uncle could have had no idea how shocked he was by the unexpected news of his loss. 'Yet when I consider the long period of her indisposition and the weakness of her frame, I ought to have been prepared to hear it,' he added.[5] 'I am glad that her last illness was not attended with extraordinary suffering and I know you so well, that I am sure you will think with affection and regret as often as the blank which must be felt after 25 years society shall call her to your memory, and it will not be a small consolation that to the last you shewed that kindness and attention to her which she deserved. I have often quoted you for that conduct, which few have the goodness of heart or principle to imitate.' Greville went on to assure his uncle that if he could have his own way he would come out to Naples 'without hesitation' to pass some months with the widower, but unfortunately he was much too involved in his brother's affairs to be able to leave England. Lady Hamilton's death was to give him much food for thought.

Horace Walpole was more matter-of-fact in his reaction to the news. 'Our papers say Lady Hamilton is dead in Naples,' he wrote to Mann on 25 September. 'I am very sorry for her; but I hope, as she was a good fortune in land, that Sir William loses nothing by her death. If you write to him, pray mention my concern.'[6]

Sir William in fact lost a good deal more than he expected in the death of his first wife, though not, as Walpole would have been glad to hear, on the material side. All that Catherine Hamilton had possessed was left to him. He had been easy going in his relations with her as he was in most human relationships. That he was not faithful to her we may guess from one or two references in letters to his friends. Many years before her death he told Greville of his attempts to console a girl whose parents had objected to her marriage to a young man in his employment: 'I endeavour to persuade her to forget him, but that will not do. The struggles between love and duty make her very interesting. I take her hand, the poor thing squeezes it when she thinks of Guido, and cries, and in the midst of all this distress the devil will have it that. . . and I grow confoundedly confused in all my councils.' Such episodes, however, were all that Catherine had had to complain of, and though this might be considered quite enough he never, in an age which acknowledged the existence of a mistress without a blush, put Catherine to any such humiliation, though many a monarch, minister, ambassador, or even bishop, would have thought nothing of doing so.

What Hamilton missed, and missed deeply, was the presence of a dear friend and companion in whose company his life had been spent for the past quarter of a century. He felt that his house was no longer a comfort to him and was grateful when the King and Queen asked him to their private gatherings, which they frequently did; and he looked forward to an opportunity to return to England as soon as it could conveniently be arranged. His true feelings he told only to his sister. 'In spite of all my Philosophy', he wrote to her two months after Catherine's death, 'I am quite unhinged by the cruel separation from an amiable and true friend with whom I have passed the last 26 years of my life, and my only comfort is that death has put a period to her sufferings which were becoming too frequent and severe.'[7]

If anything had been wanting to distract Hamilton from his melancholy thoughts it was provided in February 1783 when the southern portion of the Kingdom of Naples was convulsed by a violent earthquake. 'We have had here some shocks of an earthquake which, in Calabria Ultra, has swallowed up or destroyed almost every town, together with some towns in Sicily. . . ' he told Sir Joseph Banks on the 18th of the month, thirteen days after the first shock. 'Every hour brings in accounts of fresh disasters. Some thousands of people will perish with hunger before the provisions sent from hence can reach them. This, I believe, will prove to have been the greatest calamity that has happened this century. An end is put to the Carnival. The theatres are shut. I suppose Saint Januarius will be brought out.'[8]

Hamilton determined to visit the scenes of devastation himself both for reasons of scientific curiosity and as a distraction from his recent loss. It was no doubt for the latter cause that he decided to go alone on this expedition even turning down the offer of the Welsh artist Thomas Jones to go with him as draughtsman. Jones had asked for no payment, but his offer was rejected, much to his mortification. As a consolation Sir William allowed him to make use of the Palazzo Sessa during his absence, having the billiards-room set aside as a studio. He was not in the mood just then for any but the closest friend; to Greville he wrote: 'I wish you cou'd be of the party, but I chose rather to go alone than to have a companion that is not quite of my mind.' He set off on 2 May. The plan was to sail down the coast towards Sicily calling in at the various places where the earthquake had wrought its worst havoc. For this purpose Sir William had hired a couple of boats, a Maltese Speronara for himself and a Neapolitan Felucca for his servants from among whom, according to Jones, he took only two or three. 'I carry a tent with me and my trusty Cottier to take care of me', Greville was told, 'and I have 15 as fine Maltese sailors as you cou'd wish to see.'

Hamilton was to see many curious sights before he returned to Naples twenty days later. The account which he wrote of his experiences was sent to the Royal Society and was afterwards published in their *Philosophical Transactions*. The scenes he witnessed called for compassion as well as scientific investigation. He had known something of this beautiful countryside and of its inhabitants before it had been visited by disaster; now, as he wrote, 'to pass through so rich a country, and not see a single house standing on it, is most melancholy indeed; wherever a house stood, there you see a heap of ruins, and a poor barrack, with two or three miserable mourning figures sitting at the door, and here and there a maimed man, woman, or child, crawling on crutches. Instead of a town, you see a confused heap of ruins, and round about them numbers of poor huts or barracks, and a larger one to serve as a church, with the church bells hanging on a sort of low gibbet; every inhabitant with a doleful countenance, and wearing some token of having lost a parent.'

Another grim fact which Hamilton observed was the characteristic attitudes in which the dead were often discovered when they were unearthed from the rubble of fallen buildings: 'that the male dead were generally found under the ruins in the attitude of struggling against the danger; but that the female attitude was usually with hands clasped over their heads, as giving themselves up to despair, unless they had children near them; in which case they were always found clasping the children in their arms, or in some attitude which indicated their anxious care to protect them: a strong instance of the maternal tenderness of the sex.' Animals seemed more fortunate than humans in escaping the fatal consequences of the earthquake. Cows and horses appeared to have strange foreknowledge of a coming shock and to 'extend their legs wide asunder' to prevent themselves from being thrown down. According to observers with whom Hamilton talked the animals 'gave evident signs of being sensible of the approach of each shock'.

Sir William came across a good deal of confusion among the people he questioned, due more to ignorance than to the desire to exaggerate. 'They tell you that a town has been thrown a mile from the place where it stood without mentioning a word of a ravine, that woods and cornfields had been removed in the same manner', he noted, 'when in truth it is only on a large scale what we see every day on a smaller, when pieces of the sides of hollow ways, having been undermined by rain waters, are detached to the bottom by their own weight. Here, from the great depth of the ravine, and the violent motion of the earth, two huge portions of earth, on which a great part of the town stood, consisting of some hundreds of houses, were detached into the ravine and nearly across it, about half a mile from the place where they stood; and what is most extraordinary, several of the inhabitants of those houses, who had taken this singular leap in them were yet dug out alive, and some unhurt.' Of the victims of these disasters Hamilton recorded: 'It appears to me that the Calabresi have more firmness than the Neapolitans, and they really seem to bear their excessive present misfortune with a true philosophic patience.'

Many odd and bizarre incidents were brought to his notice. At one place the earth shook so violently that the heads of the largest trees almost touched the ground as they swayed from side to side; at Soriano two fattened hogs were buried under a heap of ruins and were dug out alive after forty-two days; in another place two mules were similarly trapped, one for twenty-two days, the other for twenty-three, and were rescued alive: 'They would not eat for some days but drank water plentifully, and were quite recovered.' A hen belonging to the British vice-consul at Messina also survived under the ruins of his house and was rescued alive on the twenty-second day. The Prince of Cariati showed Hamilton two girls, the elder aged about sixteen, who had been trapped for eleven days without food under a house at Oppido. 'The girl gave a clear account of her sufferings,' Sir William recorded, 'having light through a small opening she had kept an exact account of the number of days she had been buried. She did not seem to be in bad health, drank freely, but had yet a difficulty in swallowing anything solid. The other girl was about 11 years of age; she remained under the ruins six days only: but in so very confined and distressful a posture, that one of her hands, pressing against her cheek, had nearly worn a hole through it.'

The disaster, in terms of human suffering, was on a frightful scale. Hamilton reckoned that the number of lives lost must have reached a total of at least forty thousand. At one place over two thousand people, sheltering on the beach, were swept into the sea by a tidal wave and all perished. The toll from individual cities was great; above four thousand dead at Casal Nuovo, three thousand and seven at Bagnara, three thousand each at Radicina and Palmi. At Messina in Sicily, though great destruction was done in the city and port, only about seven hundred lives were lost out of a total population estimated at thirty thousand. Sir William visited Polistene where he was curious to talk with the survivors of a convent of nuns, but on arrival learnt that only one of the twenty-three sisters had been taken alive from the wreckage, and that she was eighty years of age. At

Terra Nuova, out of a population of sixteen hundred, only four hundred escaped with their lives.[9]

From these scenes of suffering and desolation Hamilton returned to Naples, reaching the city on 23 May. He wasted no time there. Permission for his leave of absence had come and the very next day he started on his journey to England. It was a sad journey, for Sir William was bringing back his wife's body to its final resting place in the churchyard at Selbeck on her Welsh estates. There, in accordance with the promise he had made, he would one day join her. Now in his fifty-third year and a widower, he must have been well aware that a chapter in his life had come to an end. But whatever the future might have in store for him he was firmly resolved upon one point; he would never leave Naples. 'I by no means think of exchanging the office I at present enjoy, not even for one that might be more brilliant and lucrative in appearance,' he had told his sister when he wrote to her about his wife's death: 'I have weigh'd well every circumstance and am sure that in the balance of my future happiness the Naples scale predominates.'

In reaching this conclusion Sir William was acknowledging the defeat of his political ambitions, which had never been strong. He was fully aware of the comparative unimportance of his post in the hierarchy of diplomatic appointments, and in the year 1783 he had no reason to suppose that the situation would change. He had no presentiment of the coming political earthquake of 1789 which was to throw all Europe into confusion. If he settled to remain in Naples it was because there was no other place where he could be better placed to continue his useful activities as an active patron of the arts, to indulge his passion for collecting, and pursue his scientific and antiquarian interests which now filled the main part of his life. Naples was too much his home to think of leaving it. When the German artist Wilhelm Tischbein visited the Palazzo Sessa he noticed an inscription on the wall of the staircase which read 'Where is my ease, there is my Fatherland'. It was in these terms that Sir William Hamilton envisaged his remaining years as British Minister to the Kingdom of the Two Sicilies. Reality was to present a very different picture.

1. Morrison, 118.
2. B.M. Egerton MSS 2636, f. 261.
3. *Vide* Morrison, 116, 117 and 120.
4. *Vide* Anson: *Mary Hamilton*, p. 146.
5. Morrison, 12.
6. Walpole, *Letters*, Vol. VIII, p. 284.
7. B.M.. Add. MSS 41198, f. 112.
8. *Vide*: E. Edwards *Founders of the British Museum*, Vol. 1, p. 355.
9. *Vide Philosophical Transactions of the Royal Society*, Vol. XV (1781—5), pp. 578-83.

PART TWO
1783—1803

CHAPTER XIII

A Leave of Absence

Sir William Hamilton's leave of absence lasted just over a year, from August 1783 until September 1784. Events resulting from this leave were to have momentous effects upon his subsequent life. In particular two young women were to occupy a good deal of his time and attention. One was his niece Mary Hamilton, daughter of his elder brother Charles, and then twenty-seven years of age; the other went by the name of Emma Hart, was the mistress of his nephew Charles Greville, and was in her nineteenth year. Their circumstances could hardly have been more different. Mary Hamilton sprang from a background of privilege, had held an appointment at Court and was a favourite of King George III and Queen Charlotte. She was intelligent, cultivated and lively, and devoted to her uncle the Minister at Naples who had taken an interest in her career since her father's death in 1771. Emma Hart was the daughter of a blacksmith, had lived by her wits since she was thirteen, and was already the mother of a child. She was perhaps the most beautiful woman of her generation. Though nine years younger than Mary Hamilton she was destined to become her aunt.

Hamilton had much to do during the year he was to pass in his native land. Attendance at Court, a visit to Wales to inspect the estates in Pembrokeshire which had come to him under his wife's Will, a journey to Scotland to call on his relations there as well as official business at the Secretary of State's office, all these activities were to take up a good deal of his time; the remainder he hoped to pass in the company of old friends like Horace Walpole, Joseph Banks, and his nephew Charles. Mary Hamilton was also eager to see her uncle and wrote to him as soon as he reached London. His reply was dashed off after making his bow at St. James's, 'tired to death and very hungry'. He told his niece he would meet her at his brother Frederick's (a rather worldly clergyman) as he was himself staying at an hotel in King Street. The note was signed 'your tired, hungry, but affectionate Uncle'. Soon after this he was able to meet Walpole who thought he looked much older and had 'the bronze of a patina'.[1]

Once again Sir William had brought a work of art back to London which he hoped to sell at a profit, but after the disappointing experience he had had with his 'Correggio' (which was still unsold) he now proposed to set about the business in a different way. The great publicity given to the picture was perhaps one of the reasons why prospective buyers had been frightened away; his plan this time was to make a private approach to someone he knew would be eager to possess this rare and valuable object, for the work of art in question was one of the most beautiful to be associated with his name. 'Except the Apollo Belvedere, the Niobes, and two or three others of the first-class marbles', he was later to write of it, 'I do not believe that there are any monuments of antiquity existing that were executed by so great an artist.' The contemporary artist John Flaxman considered it the apex of perfection. It was a vase of Roman cameo glass dating probably from the reign of Augustus and is now known as the Portland Vase.

This precious vase had previously belonged to the Barberini family where it was one of the most prized objects in their collection, occupying a place of honour in the library of their Roman palace. It was sold by Donna Cornelia Barberini Colonna, Princess of Palestrina, about the year 1780 (her extravagant losses at the card table being one of the reasons for the sale) and was bought by a Scotsman living in Rome called James Byres who was a mixture of architect, antiquarian, and art-dealer. Byres showed the vase to Sir William Hamilton during a visit to Rome some time between 1780 and 1783. Despite the fact that he was, as usual, short of cash at the time he found the temptation to buy it more than he could resist. The transaction, as Sir William later described it to Josiah Wedgwood, must have been one of the quickest on record. 'Is it yours, will you sell it?' Hamilton asked. Byres replied that it was his but he could not part with it for less than a thousand pounds. He knew his man; there was no haggling. 'I will give you a thousand pounds,' answered Hamilton and the vase was his.

Sir William's notion as to the origin of his vase was romantic rather than historical: 'I have no doubt of this being a work of the time of Alexander the Great, and was probably brought out of Asia by Alexander, whose ashes were deposited therein after his death', he assured Josiah Wedgwood, who was to spend many years in perfecting a copy of the vase.[2] A later opinion, equally determined to attach the vase to the name of some great historical character, considered it to be the cinerary urn of the Emperor Alexander Severus, an attribution based on the belief, since disproved, that it was discovered in the sarcophagus opened in 1582 at Monte del Grano and thought to have been the tomb of that emperor. In fact the origin of the vase is not known. It can, however, fairly be considered the most valuable work of art to have reached this country through the agency of Sir William Hamilton and it is still, in spite of the damage inflicted on it by a drunken vandal in the year 1845, one of the rare treasures of the British Museum.

The negotiations for the sale of the vase were conducted in an atmosphere of secrecy. Hamilton hoped to sell it to the dowager Duchess of Portland, an eccentric lady described by Horace Walpole as being 'a simple woman, but perfectly sober, and intoxicated only by *empty* vases'. She had formed a 'museum' at considerable expense in which specimens of coral, cases of butterflies, strange coloured sea-shells and fossils were found in odd juxtaposition with rare folios, fine heraldic bindings, antique medals and Etruscan vases. The general effect was considered as being 'very curious'. Arrangements were made for Sir William and Greville to visit her at Bulstrode but at the last moment Hamilton was prevented from going down there as he was given to understand that the King was about to ask him to Windsor and so had to remain in London in readiness for the royal command. This was early in December 1783. Between then and the following January the Duchess must have seen the vase and expressed her desire to possess it but Hamilton himself, instead of dealing directly with her, made use of his niece Mary as go-between. Why he did this is not made clear, but perhaps he thought it was better to make sure of a good sale privately rather than invite bids from other interested sources. Possibly also he wished to keep his part in the negotiations as secret as possible to avoid public curiosity. Certainly the publicity which had heralded the arrival of his 'Correggio' in England had quite failed to find a purchaser for it. The rather devious and secretive methods used to sell the Barberini Vase were to prove successful.

The Duchess of Portland must have shown her eagerness to add the vase to her collection as soon as she saw it, but Sir William felt a little shy at naming a price. As he explained to his niece, 'there is something in the act of selling that gives a disagreeable sensation, particularly when the value of the object for Sale can only be ascertained by what the French call *prix d'affection*, however as the first proposal did not come from me but from the Duchess I shall at once make what I think a reasonable offer to her Grace.' Perhaps his shyness was due to the fact that he hoped to persuade her to buy a good deal more than the vase. He suggested through Mary Hamilton that the Duchess should buy his Correggio for three thousand pounds, and if she accepted the picture at that price he would include the Barberini Vase for the sum he himself had paid for it. He also included in the offer a head of Hercules (or Jupiter—he refers to it as both in the same letter) and a 'little curious glass ring'. To encourage his prospective purchaser he added the information that his Correggio, which he had bought from the Duke of Lorenzano's family, had once been in the collection of Queen Christina of Sweden. 'I am convinced', he concluded, 'that if the Duchess does make this purchase Her Grace nor any of her Family will ever be the losers; for such very capital and well known Pieces must always bear their full value.'[3]

The thought of Venus disarming Cupid does not seem to have intoxicated the Duchess to the same extent as the prospect of owning the Barberini Vase. She did not buy Sir William's picture but he was able to sell her the vase with the other minor antiquities for the sum of eighteen hundred guineas, which represented quite a substantial profit. As Hamilton had arranged for Cipriani to make a drawing of the vase it remained in his care until the artist had finished his work. The Queen then expressed a wish to see it so that it was not until 8 June that Sir William was able to tell his niece that Cipriani would be delivering the precious vase to her for transmission to its new owner. 'Pray let me know when it is safely lodged', he wrote, 'as I am uneasy until I hear it is so.' Such was the secrecy observed that even Horace Walpole did not know what had become of the vase until a couple of months later. 'Sir William Hamilton's renowned Vase,' he told Lady Ossory in August,[4] 'which had disappeared with so much mystery, is again discovered; not in a tomb, but in the treasury of the Duchess of Portland, in which I fancy it had made ample room for itself. He told me it would never go out of England. I do not see how he could warrant that. The Duke and Lord Edward have both shown how little stability there is in the riches of that family; and *mine* has felt how insecure the permanency of heirlooms!'

Walpole's prediction on the instability of heirlooms almost came true in the case of the Portland Vase. Little more than a year after becoming its owner the Duchess died and the contents of her museum found their way into the sale-room. Fortunately the vase was bought by her son, the third Duke of Portland, who paid the sum of 980 guineas for it. It was he who lent the vase to Josiah Wedgwood, who was able to make a detailed examination of it before starting work on the copies he proposed to make. These copies, themselves exquisite works of art, were to tax his skill to the utmost. After his examination of the vase he wrote a long letter to Hamilton, by then returned to Naples, in which he explained his problems and asked advice on various points, in particular as to whether he should 'improve' certain faults in shape or design. Hamilton's reply was, as it appears Wedgwood expected and hoped it would be, that the vase should be reproduced as near as possible to its actual form. 'You are very right in there being some little defects in the drawing,' Sir William conceded, 'it would, however, be dangerous to touch that, but I should highly approve of your restoring in your copies what has been damaged by the hands of time.' The copies of the Portland Vase which were eventually issued by the firm of Wedgwood were a further tribute to Sir William Hamilton's influence upon the taste and artistic achievement of his day. Wedgwood was himself to acknowledge this three years later when he wrote in a letter thanking Sir William for the gift of some copies of antique busts: 'The whole nation, as well as I, have long spoken with gratitude of the patronage you have afforded, and the assistance you have given, to the arts in this country by the introduction of so many of the valuable relicts of antiquity.'[5]

The business of selling his vase, so satisfactorily concluded, helped to distract Hamilton's mind from the loss of his wife which he still felt keenly. He had described her to his niece Mary, in a letter from Naples, as 'the most amiable, the most gentle and virtuous companion, that ever man was blessed with'. Now, back in London, he gave her a memento of her aunt which, he said, he would place only in the hands of one whom he knew to have loved and respected her. It was a bracelet containing a lock of his hair which Catherine Hamilton had worn from the moment she was married. Before returning to his post he sent Mary another gift found among his wife's papers: 'I send you one book, copied by Lady H.— *Extracts of her Mother's Letters*, but when I looked over the other papers I cou'd not find it in my heart to part with them.'

Hamilton spent most of his leave in the company of Charles Greville. He had always had a great affection for this nephew which had grown originally from a similarity of tastes and a fellow-feeling for one who, like himself, was faced with the problems peculiar in that day and age to the position of a younger son. Now, as a widower, he found an added consolation in the company of one who was so intimately associated with all the details of his married life, for Greville had for many years looked after Catherine's interests in Wales which now, by her Will, devolved solely upon her husband. It was in Charles Greville's company that Sir William visited his property in Pembrokeshire, for its management would remain in Greville's hands after he had returned to Naples.

Before setting out on this expedition (which also included a visit to Scotland) Sir William had spent many agreeable hours in his nephew's house in Edgware Row in the parish of Paddington, which in those days still had a country air. Greville had moved to this new address from the more salubrious neighbourhood of Portman Square after taking under his roof an interesting young lady who had come under his protection some two years previously when she had appealed for his help upon finding herself in the unenviable position of being both pregnant and abandoned by the person who might, or might not, be the father of her child. Greville had offered her sound advice and practical help, for both of which she stood in great need, and, after the birth of a daughter, Emma Hart had been his acknowledged mistress since early in 1782.

Much legend has attached itself to the name of Emma Hart, some the tribute of a gullible public, not a little the invention of the lady herself. She was born, as far as can be established with any certainty, on or about 26 April 1765. Her father, Henry Lyon, was the village blacksmith at Neston in Cheshire; her mother, born Mary Kidd, came from Hawarden in Flintshire. She was christened in Neston parish church under the name of Amy, though from early years she seems to have been known as Emily until, under Greville's influence, this too was abandoned in favour of the more genteel Emma. Her father died while she was still an infant; her mother remained with her through all the vicissitudes of an adventurous career.

Emily Lyon started work at the age of thirteen when she was sent to train as a nursemaid in the household of a Dr. Thomas who lived in her mother's native village. Very soon, however, mother and daughter had migrated to London where Emily found similar employment in another medical household, acting as under-nursemaid to the family of Dr. Budd of Chatham Place, Blackfriars. She was not to remain long in charge of the doctor's nursery for she soon realised that there was little scope for an ambitious and determined young girl in a life of domestic service. Emily's sole capital consisted of a robust constitution and an exceptional beauty of face and figure; her only chance of breaking away from a life of drudgery which would rapidly have destroyed her beauty and undermined her health lay in exploiting these natural charms to the best of her ability. In seeking to do this she had the support and encouragement of her mother, a shrewd and imperturbable woman who about this time, for reasons which have never been made clear, adopted the name of Mrs. Cadogan.

So it was that Emily Lyon next appeared in surroundings very different from the innocent shelter of Dr. Budd's nursery in Chatham Place. The Temple of Health in Royal Terrace, Adelphi had little in common with her former places of employment except for a tenuous connection with the medical profession. Dr. James Graham, an ingenious quack, here dabbled in bogus medicine and 'magnetism', promising to restore vigour to his debilitated clients by means of electrical cures. The exact nature of the business carried on in Dr. Graham's Temple of Health has remained obscure. Whether in fact it was a rather superior sort of brothel is a matter for speculation. One of the sights to be seen there was a 'Celestial Bed' which was guaranteed to cure sterility. That this piece of furniture was for the use (at £50 a night) as well as for the contemplation of his clients suggests that Dr. Graham's establishment was not exclusively dedicated to abstract science. When lecturing to the public on his therapeutic methods the doctor would be surrounded by scantily clad young ladies in graceful tableaux representing the goddesses of Health, Wisdom, and Beauty. It was here that the future 'Nymph of the Attitudes' (as Horace Walpole would later call her) first learnt to pose.

While working at the Temple of Health Emily's beauty was on show to anyone who could afford the sum of five shillings charged for admission. It was almost certainly here that she was first seen by Sir Harry Fetherstonehaugh, a young baronet of considerable wealth and of a convivial temperament. Emily, who had now started to call herself by the name of Hart, was very soon his mistress. The move from Dr. Graham's decidedly unholy Temple to the neighbourhood of Sir Harry's beautiful house on the South Downs must have been a welcome change, and in the classical setting of Up Park the young girl threw herself wholeheartedly into the uninhibited roysterings of the young squire and his friends. The story that Emily entertained her lover's guests by dancing naked on the dining-room table belongs to this period. The story is almost certainly untrue but that such a story could be invented and believed gives some indication of the background against which Emily's life was lived at this time, a life which she herself later described as 'wild and thoughtless'.

It is difficult to imagine the careful and cultivated Charles Greville against such a background, yet he was certainly an occasional visitor at Up Park. His serious nature and rather melancholy good looks set him apart from the others, suggesting more dependable qualities, and it was to him that Emily turned for help when Sir Harry finally sent her packing. After just less than a year as his mistress she found herself pregnant, and her protector must have had good reason to think the child was not his or he would hardly have turned her loose with no more than enough money to get her back home to Cheshire. Her plight was indeed desperate. She wrote seven letters to the obdurate Sir Harry but received no reply. It was then that she sent the illiterate but heartfelt scrawl to Greville that was to change her whole life: 'O G., that I was in your posesion or was in Sir H. What a happy girl I would have been!—girl indead, what else am I but a girl in distres? For God's sake G, write the minet you get this, and only tell me what I am to dow. . . I am allmos mad. O, for God's sake, tell me what is to become on me. O dear Grevell, write to me. Write to me. . . '[6]

Greville received this letter on 10 January 1782 and answered it the same day. He urged Emily to make it up with Sir Harry if she could, but that if she felt unable to do this the time had come to think a little seriously about her future. 'If you love Sir Harry', he told her frankly, 'you should not give him up, and if you continue with him it would be ridiculous in me to take care of his girl, who is better able to maintain her. But besides this, my Emily, I would not be troubled with your connexions (excepting your mother) and with Sir H. friends, for the universe.' If, on the other hand, she wished to leave Sir Harry and place herself under Greville's own protection he made it quite plain that he must first know from her that she was clear of every other entanglement and would never take them up again without his consent. If that was the case, he assured her, 'I shall then be free to dry up the tears of my lovely Emily and to give her comfort'. As to her child: 'its mother shall obtain it kindness from me, and it shall never want.' He enclosed some money in the letter telling her not to throw it away, for he was already aware of the extravagance which neither he nor anyone else would ever be able to curb.'[7]

At no point did Greville hold out to Emily Hart the possibility of marriage. Such a thought would not have occurred to either of them. She knew as well as he did that this was quite out of the question, that if he married it would be with an eye to a substantial dowry. She also knew that he hoped to make a 'good' marriage of this sort as soon as he could do so, so that at the best her life as his mistress could not be indefinitely prolonged. As it was, his post at the Admiralty brought in little enough and as a result of taking Emily under his roof he had to move to more economical quarters.

Very soon Charles Greville, Emma (as she now became) and Mrs. Cadogan had established an agreeable *ménage* in Paddington. Emma became an almost ideal mistress. She was to grow deeply attached to the man who had rescued her at the crisis of her career and who now undertook the direction of her education. She quickly learnt to preside quietly and efficiently over his household, to behave decorously, and to engage in polite conversation with his serious-minded friends whose interest in *objets d'art* and classical antiquities was in such contrast to the loutish companions of Sir Harry Fetherstonehaugh. Outbursts of girlish high spirits occurred from time to time but for the most part Emma was content to pass her days in the acquisition of more ladylike qualities, in having music and singing lessons, and in sitting for her portrait so that her beautiful features could be recorded for posterity. George Romney, to whom she sat on many occasions, was certainly more than a little in love with her, but Emma's own conduct was never to give Greville any cause for complaint.

It was in this happy and peaceful setting that Hamilton first set eyes on his nephew's mistress when he returned to England in 1783. The situation that presented itself to him was one of which he highly approved. He did not expect Greville to live the life of a hermit while waiting for a suitable match to come his way, and he applauded his nephew's choice of this girl who welcomed the opportunity for self-improvement which her situation offered, and who hoped (in her own phrase) to transform the 'wild unthinking Emma' into a 'grave thoughtful philosopher'. He was also enchanted by the presence of such charm of person; the urbane ageing connoisseur, who had for so long admired youth and beauty, could not fail to be captivated by so arresting a combination of both. Emma became to him 'the Fair Tea-Maker of Edgware Row' and he rejoiced in his nephew's good fortune in securing so bright a prize. His affection for her was that of an uncle for some fresh and ingenuous niece; Emma responded to this harmless devotion and quickly lost any awe she may have felt for her protector's distinguished relation with his red riband and star. Very soon she was calling him 'Pliny' and accepting an avuncular kiss.

In June 1784 Hamilton and Greville set off on their tour of inspection of the Pembrokeshire property which was now Sir William's and which Greville was to manage for him. While they were away from London Emma was sent up to Cheshire to be with her child. From Chester, and later from Parkgate, she sent a series of letters to Greville full of protestations of love and gratitude. Her style had become more fluent since the day she wrote to him before the child was born, but her spelling retained its characteristic originality. The letters abound in affectionate references to Sir William. 'My love to Sir W., and say everything you can', from Chester; from Parkgate: 'Tell Sir William everything you can, and tell him I am sorry our sittuation prevented [me] from giving him a kiss. . . ask him how I looked, and lett him say something kind to me when you write.' This message must have been passed on for about a fortnight later she writes: 'Tell Sir William I am much oblidged to him for saying I looked well. I hope he will allways think so, for I am proud of [his] good word and I hope I shall never forfeit it.' A week later the message is warmer: 'Give my kind, kind love to him. Tell him next to you I love him above any body, and that I wish I was with him to give him a kiss.' She loved him as a kindly elderly friend who took a fatherly interest in her affairs, for she begs Greville not to be affronted at this affectionate message: 'If I was with you I would give you a thousand, and you might take as many as you plesed,' her lover is assured, for she longed to see him again.'[8] As to Sir William, he was sufficiently interested in the young lady, or at least in her beauty, to buy a portrait of her as Bacchante which Romney had just painted. It was shipped out to Naples where it would serve to remind him of his nephew's 'fair tea-maker' and the agreeable evenings passed at Edgware Row.

It was in the setting of this comfortable *ménage* that Sir William was to spend the most pleasant hours of this otherwise rather sad leave, the first he had passed without the companionship of his wife. His solitary plight and recent bereavement, however, did not prevent speculation in Court circles about his future, for though now over fifty he was still considered a good match and many a maiden lady would gladly have exchanged her spinsterhood for the chance of being an ambassadress. King George and Queen Charlotte were both to show their curiosity on this point, for when Hamilton went to pay them his respects before returning to his post the King told his consort to 'fish out' whether his envoy at Naples was going to marry again or not.

The Queen's attempt to discover the answer to this interesting question was not exactly subtle. 'I believe you have a bad opinion of our sex', she asked, to which Sir William replied that this was not so but that after so many happy years with his late wife he was fearful that he might not again meet with the same good fortune. At this point the King joined in the conversation and added even more to the confusion felt by his former foster-brother. He asked Hamilton whom he intended to make his heir, adding, 'I suppose your nephew Mr. Greville.' The question was all the more embarrassing as Greville was standing next to his uncle while the King was talking to him. Long residence at the Court of Naples had at least taught Sir William how to cope with royal tactlessness and he replied respectfully that this was a question he would certainly keep to himself. Lord Stormont, who was present at this interview, later related it to Mary Hamilton who was astonished at what she considered the very improper remarks of the King and Queen.

Shortly after this Sir William returned to what his friend Walpole called 'the kingdom of cinders' leaving Greville no wiser than his sovereign on the question of what would be found in his Will. Meanwhile calamity had overtaken the unfortunate William Beckford who was no longer able to avail himself of the wise counsel and sympathetic advice of Catherine Hamilton. A public scandal had resulted from the untimely discovery of his relationship, too intimate to be considered wholesome, with William, the young son of Viscount Courtenay. Though no positive charges were brought against Beckford his peerage, which was about to be gazetted, was cancelled and he thought it prudent to retire abroad. Greville sent Sir William an account of the unhappy affair, not omitting the details of what the tutor had seen when he clapped his eye to the keyhole, and concluded that Beckford would not be able to brave it out as it was all too public to pass as a mere slur. He would probably retire to Italy, unless, Greville added as a facetious afterthought, he aspired to the office of Great Chamberlain to the King of Prussia.[9]

Hamilton reacted with his usual tolerance to the news of his young relative's fall from grace. Perhaps he thought that had Catherine lived to accompany him on his last leave the tragedy might have been averted. At least he saw no reason to turn against the man who had been his wife's dear friend and who was his own close relation. He advised him to take outdoor exercise and avoid introspection, and continued to remain on good terms with him until the end of his life.

Fortunately not all Greville's letters contained bad news. 'Emma remembers you with affection and gratitude,' he had written after his uncle's departure from Naples; 'I have every reason to do so too. I wish I could be free from the various shackles which confine me to this cold spot. I should be near you. Do you believe, we have had a whole morning's snow this day.' If this letter revived thoughts of the happy domestic scene at Edgware Row in Sir William's mind, it gave rise to other considerations in his nephew's. For all the comfort of Emma's company he had not forgotten the necessity for a rich marriage. Very soon he would begin to consider her as among his shackles, though it would be his lover rather than himself whom he would plan to send to Italy to be near his affectionate uncle.

1. Walpole, *Letters*, Vol. VIII, p. 408
2. W. Mankowitz: *The Portland Vase & the Wedgwood Copies*, p. 29
3. *Vide* E. and F. Anson: *Mary Hamilton*, pp. 155-7
4. Walpole: *Letters*, Vol. IX, p. 3
5. *Vide* Finer and Savage: *Selected Letters of Josiah Wedgwood*, p. 307
6. Morrison, 113
7. Morrison, 114
8. *Vide* Morrison, 124-6, 128
9. Morrison, 133: The King of Prussia was said to share Beckford's proclivity for young men.

CHAPTER XIV

The Problem of Emma

By the time Sir William Hamilton had returned to Naples he had shed a good deal of the melancholy which had surrounded him at the period of his departure. From Parma he had written to his nephew of his satisfaction at basking once again on the south side of the Alps far from the fogs and contentions of Great Britain. He was even able to indulge in a little flirtation. At Turin he had met Lady Clarges, a widow who greatly took his fancy. They met again at Rome where the friendship prospered, and a shared taste in music added to their pleasure in one another's company; but when the lady also turned up in Naples Hamilton began to grow apprehensive. 'I like her much,' he confessed to Greville in February 1785 when back at his post: 'In one of my moments of admiration I sayd to her that I wished she would take possession of my empty apartments. She gravely answered that she was much flattered but had resolved never to marry again. The Devil take me if I meant to propose tho' I own I often have thought she wou'd suit me well. Her musical talents you may imagine weight greatly with me, and she is gentle.'[1] It was a close shave. Perhaps Sir William would not have been so put out as he pretended had Lady Clarges accepted. The incident at least shows his frame of mind when he returned to the familiar setting of the Palazzo Sessa; he was as susceptible as ever to feminine charm but, as he had confessed to Queen Charlotte, afraid to risk a situation which might bring him less happiness than he had enjoyed in the company of his first wife.

Fortunately he had other things to occupy his mind. Almost as soon as he arrived back he launched out in a scheme to interest the Queen of Naples in establishing an English Garden in the grounds of the palace of Caserta. Maria Carolina took up his idea with enthusiasm and Hamilton was soon writing to Sir Joseph Banks to enlist the help of this distinguished botanist in their plans. 'The Queen of Naples has adopted my project and has given me the commission to send for a British Gardener and Nursery-man', he informed Banks on 20 February.[2] 'I told her you had been so good as to promise to assist me in procuring one. Will you then be so good as to set about that business directly but to avoid all difficulties I should wish to know his terms before he sets out for Naples. A man of sense and judgement and high in his profession must certainly be tempted to quit his country and establish himself in a distant foreign one. He shou'd therefore be liberally paid, and I am sure the Queen will agree to any terms that you should think reasonable. *Entre nous*, she told me she wou'd allow out of her privy purse about £100 sterling a month for her garden. All this is to be done without the King's interference and she rejoices in the thought of surprising the King some day with a plate of fruit out of her garden much superior to his. . . As the Queen does me the honor to give me the Superintendence of her Garden, the Gardener will have less difficulty than if he was under the direction of a foreigner.'

The idea of creating a garden appealed to the philosophical side of Hamilton's nature, and he assured Banks that he promised himself great pleasure from this new occupation. 'As one passion begins to fail', he observed, 'it is necessary to form another; for the whole art of going through life tolerably in my opinion is to keep oneself eager about any thing. The moment one is indifferent *on s'ennuye*, and that is a misery to which I perceive even Kings are often subject.' Perhaps the image of Lady Clarges was not far from his mind as he wrote these lines. Any thoughts, however, of gardens, of eligible widows, or even of failing passions, were soon to be banished. As the year 1785 progressed he began to receive a series of letters from Charles Greville on a subject which, to begin with at least, he almost certainly, would rather had never been raised. Twelve months were to pass before he would be persuaded to accept his nephew's strange and astonishing proposal, for what Greville was in fact suggesting was that his uncle should relieve him of the 'fair tea-maker of Edgware Row' and take the fascinating Emma Hart under his own protection in Naples.

Greville's plan to dispose of Emma by placing her in his uncle's bed has often been attributed to calculated and cold-hearted self-interest on his part. In fact it was not so much self-interest as a sort of desperation. It has been said that his object was to prevent his uncle from remarrying so that he could be assured of securing the inheritance which a second marriage by Sir William might jeopardise. In fact Greville had no certainty at that time that he was Hamilton's heir. All he knew (for he had been present when George III had raised this embarrassing issue) was that his uncle considered himself free to leave his money where he chose. Of course he knew that he was the most likely candidate but his uncle was hale and hearty and in all probability had many years to live. Greville was also man of the world enough to know that the possession of a young mistress was no guarantee against a man remarrying. In his present circumstances he did not feel that he could wait perhaps twenty years for an inheritance that was by no means certain; he must lose no time in making a rich marriage himself. The only obstacle to this was the presence of Emma and so (however fond he might be of her) Emma must go.

The dilemma in which Greville found himself had been explained to Hamilton in a letter written in January 1785 before the idea of sending Emma to Naples had occurred to him. At this particular moment all he was sending to his uncle was Romney's picture of her in the character of Bacchante. In the letter he explained how much she had improved in character since she had come to live with him; the bad habits and giddiness were all things of the past; she had elegance and fitted herself easily into any situation, having both quickness and sensibility. 'I am sure she is attached to me,' Greville continued,[3] 'or she would not have refused the offers which I know have been great; and such is her spirit that, on the least slight or expression of my being tired or burthened by her, I am sure she would not only give up the connexion but would not even accept a farthing for future assistance. This is another part of my situation. If I was independent I should think so little of any other connexion that I never would marry. I have not an idea of it at present, but if any proper opportunity offer'd I should be much harassed, not know [how] to manage or how to fix Emma to her satisfaction, and to forego the reasonable plan which you and my friends have advised, is not right. I am not quite of an age to retire from bustle, and to retire to distress and poverty is worse. . . '

The need to rid himself of Emma became more acute as time passed. He had been cultivating the acquaintance of Lord Middleton who had been his neighbour in Portman Square and who still had an unmarried daughter on his hands whose fortune, it was understood, was in the neighbourhood of thirty thousand pounds. The discovery that her elder sister's dot had been no more than twenty thousand came as something of a shock, but Greville was determined not to be discouraged. There were other heiresses. But first his own impediment must be removed. Had he turned Emma onto the street, as Sir Harry had done, contemporary society would have viewed his act with indifference, but Greville had a much better plan which took account of everything except Emma's feelings for him. He had noticed, indeed been a little jealous of, the attentions his uncle had paid her. What better plan than to send her to Naples? In this way the uncle would be gratified, Emma provided for, and his own hands freed of an encumbrance at which even the most broad-minded or elderly heiress would have drawn the line. But if the plan was simple the problem of persuading his uncle to agree to it would be a more difficult one. Greville set himself to the task with resolution.

He opened his attack with a letter written on 10 March. The first part was concerned with political gossip such as Hamilton loved to hear, but half-way through the theme is suddenly changed:

'They say here that you are in love. I know you love variety and are a general flirt, and of the 60 English, what with widows and young married ladies, an amateur may be caught. Some have said you have had the gout. I say I neither know whether your head or feet are lightest, but that I believe them both sound. . . '

After this mixture of banter and flattery Greville moved nearer to the point of his letter. 'I am from frequent experience convinced that I can judge for you and you for me; at least suppose cases in which we should think alike, and on those cases in which comfort may arise you are more than myself able to realise suppositions by experiment; for the limited experiment I make I know to succeed, altho' from poverty it cannot last. If you did not chuse a wife, I wish the tea-maker of Edgware Row was yours, if I could without banishing myself from a visit to Naples.'

To soften the impact of this sudden suggestion (which must have made Sir William sit up with a start when he read it) Greville added that he did not know how he could part with something he was not yet grown tired of; only his unfortunate financial situation made him contemplate such a step—and even so he was determined that Emma should never want. Of course, he assured his uncle, if he could manage to carry on he would never dream of making such an arrangement, 'but to be reduced to a standstill and involve myself in distress further than I could extricate myself, and then to be unable to provide for her at all, would make me miserable from thinking myself very unjust to her'. She was, he pointed out, too young and handsome to retire into a convent or to bury herself in the country. It was a situation well calculated to move his uncle's heart, and all the more so as the solution lay in his hands. 'Judge then,' the letter ends, 'as you know my satisfaction on looking at a modern piece of *virtù* if I do not think you a second self in thinking that by placing her within your reach I render a necessity, which would otherwise be heartbreaking, tolerable and even comforting.'[4]

The comparison between Emma and a piece of *virtù* was not perhaps the most tactful way of presenting her to an ageing connoisseur. It was a comparison which others would be quick to observe. Sir William's reply to this letter has not survived but something of its tenor can be deduced from the opening paragraph of Greville's next instalment. He considered that he still had a great deal of persuading to do and certain misunderstandings to resolve. 'I received your letter,' he wrote on 5 May, 'I have no doubt of your kind wishes towards me, therefore the interest you take in my situation is by me very sensibly felt. If I could have thought that no line could be taken but that of making E. do the honors of your house, I confess I never should have dreamt of it; this is a line so different from what I have practised that I should be amongst the first to lament that you adopted an unwise plan. I tell you fairly that your expressions of kindness to E., and the comfort you promised her in case anything happened to me, made such an impression on her that she regards you as her protector and friend, and in moments of her thinking [of] your goodness she related to me your last conversation, and I concluded that your regard to me had been the only reason for your not making present offers.'

Greville, however, was out for more than mere promises for the future. He continued his letter with a long catalogue of Emma's perfections, not failing to point out how much she had improved in looks since Hamilton's departure, and concluded with frank and worldly advice which lost nothing by its directness even though it might not have been wholly relished by its recipient. 'At your age a clean and comfortable woman is not superfluous, but I should rather purchase it than acquire it, unless in every respect a proper party offer'd.' So much for Lady Clarges! 'Would your friends have thought Lady C. a more prudent connexion than E.?' Greville asks, driving his point home. 'I know the sentiments of all your friends, and my delicacy prevented my writing on that subject, but I can assure you they feel very happy at the departure of Lady C.'[5] Hamilton's family, as well as his friends, were, it seems, of the same opinion. 'Your brother spoke openly to me', the letter continues, 'that he thought the wisest thing you could do would be to buy Love ready made, and that it was not from any interested wish, as he was perfectly satisfied with the fortune he had, that it was enough for his family, and that he should be very glad to hear you declare openly your successor, and particularly so if you named me; I write without affectation or disguise.' As Sir William's eldest brother had been dead for more than ten years it can only be supposed that this advice came from his clergyman brother Archdeacon Frederic, a somewhat un conventional ornament of the Established Church. 'If you find me either reserved or artful you may despise me;' Greville goes on, 'but in opening my heart and thoughts do no impute conceal'd designs. I wish you every happiness in this world and long life to enjoy it. I protest, I do not think the odds in our lives are proportioned to the difference of our years. You have spoken kindly of your intentions towards me, and you have shewn readiness to assist me in every thing that I could in reason expect; I am very sensible and very grateful.'

The letter ends with a further analysis of his financial situation and of his need to marry a lady of considerable fortune. If Hamilton's goodness were to assure him of 'an estate which would come hereafter' then, in Greville's opinion, 'there is no doubt but a lady with such a fortune might not reject me.' This being the case he confesses that the only reason he has in wishing to know his uncle's intentions towards him is that such certainty would be 'the means of my being married to a lady of at least £30,000'. Returning finally to the question of Emma he finishes with the remark: 'I shall only add to this long letter that taking E. is no part of the request, tho' it is not impossible I should soon put the question to a lady now totally inaccessible whose fortune is what I mention; therefore I do not write idly.'[6]

Hamilton replied to his nephew's letter on the first of June. He began by putting Greville's mind at rest on the question of his inheritance: 'Was I to die this moment my Will, which I made in England and left with Hamilton of Lincoln's Inn and brought a Copy here, would show that you are the person I esteem most—but I never meant to tell you so as the changes in this life are so various that no one can answer for himself from one moment to another. For example, had I married Lady C., which might have happened, it must have been a cruel disappointment to you, after having declared you my heir. I only made my Will, as every one ought to do, in case of accident, but as I have struggled through many difficulties in life and am now by Lady Hamilton's goodness secured from want, nay, have enough to live comfortably shou'd I be dismissed from His Majesty's Service, I shou'd not chuse to put anything out of my power. To be sure, so far I am selfish and I have lived long enough to experience that most people are so, but was it not for the thought of your profiting on my death (which according to the course of nature must happen before your moment arrives many years) I should not hesitate in selling the Welsh Estate and purchasing an annuity for my life. Being a younger Brother myself and having made my own fortune and being at liberty to dispose of it as I please at my death when I can no longer enjoy it, I shall have a satisfaction in its going to a younger Brother whom I love and esteem more than any man on Earth. . . '

On the question of Emma Sir William's answer was less to Greville's way of thinking, and displayed a humanity and concern for the young girl's feelings which were absent from his nephew's anxious calculations: 'As to E., was I in England and you was to bring your present plan to bear and she wou'd consent to put herself under my protection, I wou'd take her most readily for I really love her and think better of her than of any one in her situation. But, my dear Charles, there is a great difference between her being with you or me, for she really loves you when she cou'd only esteem and suffer me. I see so many difficulties in her coming here, should you be under the necessity of parting with her, that I can never advise it. Tho' a great City, Naples has every defect of a Province and nothing you do is secret. It would be fine fun for the young English Travellers to endeavour to cuckold the old Gentleman their Ambassador, and whether they succeeded or not would surely give me uneasiness. My regard for E. is such that if she leaves you and retires in the country, which I suppose she would do was you to marry, I wou'd willingly make her an allowance of £50 a year till your circumstances enable you to provide better for her. I do assure you when I was in England tho' her exquisite beauty had frequently its effects on me, it would never have come into my head to have proposed a freedom beyond an innocent kiss whilst she belong to my friend; and I do assure you I should like better to live with you both here and see you happy than to have her all to myself, for I am sensible that I am not a match for so much youth and beauty.'[7]

It is to be noticed that in this letter Sir William made Emma's consent a condition of her coming under his protection. It is a matter for sadness that he was ultimately prevailed upon to forgo this condition. In fact the second part of this letter with its gentle insistence on the practical and human aspects of the case as opposed to the strictly financial problems was as unsatisfactory from Greville's point of view as the first part was gratifying to his ambitions. 'I will not tell you what I think of your letter, but I shall, if possible, respect and love you more than I have hitherto done. . . ' he replied with reference to the assurance of his being Hamilton's heir. 'I should be ungrateful indeed if I did not feel your goodness to me. I am doubly so that you did not withdraw it when I risqued appearing, as I might have done to a less partial friend, mean and interested.' He agreed entirely with what his uncle had to say about Naples, but countered it with the strange suggestion that Emma should be confined in some secluded spot as though she were the heroine of a comic opera: 'Give her one of your villas, or rather take a small retired house on the Hill at Naples, very small; she will not want to go about, and going to dine, or at any other hours, to your villa or house, when it may be convenient, will make a party of what by another plan would be a daily habit.'[8] Fortunately Hamilton had more sense than to accept this proposal; he had already indicated that he had no wish to be cast in the role of Dr. Bartholo. As far as Greville was concerned there was no question of his uncle being made a cuckold: 'as to Englishmen, there is nothing to fear; left to herself she would conform to your ideas.'

This letter was written, probably in June 1785, soon after Sir William's had been received. It failed in its purpose of changing the ambassador's mind, for in November Greville was urging his scheme once more, but by then there were clear indications that his uncle was beginning to weaken, if he had not already fallen for the plan. 'You may suppose that I did not increase Emma's uneasiness by any hint of the subject of our last correspondence,' Greville wrote, 'at any rate, it cannot take place before the spring, and she goes on so well and is so much more considerate and amiable than she was when you saw her and also improv'd in looks, that I own it is less agreeable to part; yet I have no other alternative but to marry or remain a pauper; I shall persist in my resolution not to lose an opportunity if I can find it, and do not think that my idea of sending her to Naples on such an event arises from my consulting my convenience only. I can assure you that she would not have a scarcity of offers, she has refused great ones; but I am sure she would prefer a foreign country with you to any other connexion at home, and I would not expose you to any risque.'[9] By now Greville seems to be eager to convince himself as much as his uncle as to the wisdom of the plan about which the un fortunate Emma still knew nothing.

Between July and November Hamilton was reluctantly won over to accepting Greville's plan; but he remained nervous and half-hearted even after the details had been arranged, for in every letter his nephew continued to expatiate on the subject of Emma's charms, as though he dreaded that Sir William would suddenly withdraw his consent. 'She may be trusted by you anywhere,' he wrote at the end of the year, all suggestions of her being confined to some remote villa being now forgotten. 'She likes admiration, but merely that she may be valued, and not to profit by raising her price. I am sure there is not a more disinterested woman in the world, if she has a new gown or hat, etc., it is easy to make a little novelty go far. . . You will be able to have an experiment without any risque. If it should not turn out as I expect she will have profited by seeing a little of foreign parts; she will have improved herself and may come home.' He added: 'I know you are above acting unkindly to any woman, but particularly to a pretty woman,'[10] which was certainly true of Hamilton, but it never seems to have occurred to Greville how unkindly he was himself acting to a young woman who by then loved him deeply.

It is unfortunate that in these unique negotiations we have virtually only one side of the correspondence. We do not know in what terms Sir William finally submitted to Greville's determined and persistent onslaught. His single surviving letter of 1 June shows him in a good light in this extraordinary interchange between uncle and nephew. He does not completely ignore the rights of Emma as though she were no more than an article in an agreement or a commodity in a business transaction to be bargained over like a sack of coal. Even when all was settled and Emma was on her way Hamilton was still full of apprehension. 'The prospect of possessing so delightful an object under my roof soon certainly causes in me some pleasing sensations,' he confessed to Greville in April 1786,[11] 'but they are accompanied with some anxious thoughts as to the prudent management of this business; however, I will do as well as I can and hobble in and out of this pleasant scrape as decently as I can. You may be assured that I will comfort her for the loss of you as well as I am able, but I know, from the small specimen during your absence from London, that I shall have at times many tears to wipe from those charming eyes, and which, if shed for any other but yourself, must give me jealousy.' The day after this letter was written Emma arrived in Naples.

The final plan for her departure from England had been settled between Greville and his uncle at the end of the year, following a suggestion which the latter had first proposed in June, before Sir William had been quite prepared for it. 'If you could form a plan by which you could have a trial', he had then written, 'and could invite her and tell her that I ought not to leave England, and that I cannot afford to go on, and state it as a kindness to me if she would accept your invitation, she would go with pleasure.' Emma was now told that Greville would have to spend much of the summer of 1786 visiting places where she could not prudently accompany him, and that while he was thus engaged she could go to Naples as the guest of Sir William, to be joined there later on by her lover. When this plan was proposed to her she seems to have accepted it readily, little supposing that her dearest Greville had no intention of leaving England at all. Hamilton only agreed to this deception after his nephew had convinced him that this was the kindest way to accomplish their end.

In attempting to soothe Sir William's uneasy conscience over the whole business Greville put as much emphasis as he could upon Emma's devotion to 'Pliny', exaggerating what was little more than gratitude and mild affection on her part until it seemed to Hamilton that next to Greville he was the person she loved most. 'If there was in the world a person she loved so well as yourself after me I could not arrange so much *sang froid*,' he had told his uncle when the question of her coming to Naples was first mooted, and now, when she was ready to leave, Hamilton was assured that she could only tolerate being separated from his nephew because 'there was not a person in the world whom she could be happy with, if I was dead, but yourself'. Greville represented Emma's frame of mind on her departure in a way which could only mislead Sir William: 'I told her that she would be so happy that I should be cut out, and she said that if I did not come for her or neglected her, she would certainly be grateful to you; but that neither interest nor affection should ever induce her to change, unless my interest or wish required it, and that you could comfort her, altho' she made all the distinction of the difference of age, but that she had seen enough to value a real friend whenever she could find one, and that you had shown more real kindness to her than any person in the world beside myself, and therefore you was, after me, the nearest to her heart.'[12]

This statement was hardly calculated to prepare Sir William for the reception of a young girl so deeply in love with Greville as to be almost hysterical at the thought of being parted from him, or of being capable of thinking in this calm manner of accepting either Hamilton or anyone else as his successor. By the time Greville wrote this letter Sir William was almost as much deceived as to the truth of the situation as was Emma herself, and yet, in their own curious way, both Greville and Sir William thought they were doing what was for the best, both in their own interests and in Emma's. They were, after all, living in an age when the most respectable women submitted willingly to a marriage system in which they were quite simply bought and sold; when a father thought nothing of advertising the extent of his daughter's dowry to attract a suitable husband; and when no one would have thought Charles Greville at all odd in disposing of his mistress in order to make himself more eligible for the purpose of securing 'a lady of £30,000'. In such matters Sir William Hamilton was neither a pioneer nor a reactionary; he accepted the standards of his day. Most of his contemporaries and friends would agree that he was doing an act of kindness, if perhaps being a trifle quixotic, in offering his protection to the beautiful Emma Hart.

Emma herself, prompted by Greville, wrote to Sir William on 30 December asking if she could come and stay with him while her lover was away: her letter spoke of the hope she looked forward to of his joining her there later on. Meanwhile, she promised Hamilton: 'I shall always keep my own room when you are better engaged or go out, and at other times I hope to have the pleasure of your company and conversation, which will be more agreeable to me than anything in Italy.'[13] Hamilton's reply reached London on 18 January. Two days later Greville wrote to say that Emma was preparing to leave on 1 March. Once again he implies that she is more than half-ready to take Hamilton as her 'protector' in the fullest sense. 'She has always said that if ever she was to part she might be weaned by degrees; she talks of the chances of our not meeting again, and that on the least neglect she will accept your offers, and that she will by her conduct merit your kindness. She must have in her mind a stronger impression of the chances than she expresses, but she says that she would not put herself in the reach of chances with any person but yourself, and she does not say this from compliment, but from her heart.'[14] Emma's conduct on her arrival in Naples, her bewilderment and despair when she discovered that Greville had no intention of joining her there or of asking her to return, make one wonder whether she ever made the remarks he attributed to her in this letter. At the best it may be said that he read into her words a meaning which they never contained.

Sir William Hamilton, no less than Emma, was to find himself placed in a false and very embarrassing position by Greville's exaggerated assertions on the subject of his mistress's readiness, sooner or later, to submit calmly to the plan for her future which had been so elaborately concocted behind her back. Greville's exclusive preoccupation with his own self-interest had blinded him to the fact that Emma was in love with him. He was a cold man; love was an emotion which did not enter into his neat calculations. Perhaps this was why, despite the sacrifice of a mistress and acquisition of an inheritance, he was never to find his lady of thirty thousand pounds. Fate had decreed that Charles Greville would die a bachelor.

The transportation of the attractive 'Mrs. Hart' from Paddington to Naples did not pass unnoticed in the larger world of fashion, nor did interest grow less when it was discovered that she had left the arms of a nephew for those of his uncle. It was not unknown for a mistress to console two generations of the same family but when such rare events had occurred the progress from one generation to another had usually been in the other direction, from elder to younger. Even Hamilton himself was a little abashed and wrote to Sir Joseph Banks: 'It is a bad job to come from the Nephew to the Uncle, but one must make the best of it, and I long to see poor Charles out of his difficulties.' For the gossips and scandalmongers of the age the story presented a splendid opportunity for some sustained flights of fancy, and for the next few years many tales of Emma's origins, and numerous accounts of her adventures, would be exchanged, which would lack nothing in invention but contain little enough of the truth.

Five years later when Emma Hart was on the verge of becoming Lady Hamilton, one of Sir William's colleagues, Sir James Bland Burges, an under-secretary of state in the Foreign Department, noted down an account of the events just recorded which by then was generally believed: 'This Mrs. Hart,' he wrote,[15] 'on her first coming from the country, set out as a common Prostitute in Hedge Lane. Being very handsome, she was engaged by the Committee of the Royal Academy to exhibit herself naked as a model for the young Designers. Having continued for some time in this situation, she rose in the Scale of Debauchery, till at length she was taken into keeping by Mr. Charles Greville, who, growing poor, and being desirous of preventing his uncle William Hamilton (from whom he had expectations) from marrying, took her with him to Naples, where Sir William was Minister, and introduced her to him. Sir William grew fond of her, and Mr. Greville was easily prevailed upon to transfer her to him.' The inaccuracies about Emma's early years might well have been due to natural ignorance, but Sir James Burges should at least have known that Greville never visited Naples in 1786. The legend was already beginning to grow, and the story of Emma having exhibited herself as a model was to persist, though it had no foundation in fact. A generation later, writing about Naples, Stendhal himself would make his contribution with the addition of exact but equally false details: 'Miss Hart, later destined to be known as Lady Hamilton, was renowned for her rare beauty, and had lived for many years in Rome, exercising the profession of *model*, in which capacity her services might be enjoyed by art-students for the sum of six francs precisely.'

The Countess de Boigne, on the other hand, who was to know Emma as Lady Hamilton in her days of glory, gave a version of her first encounter with Greville which was reminiscent of a scene from *Cinderella*. Writing in her *Memoirs* the Countess declared that Greville had first seen her in the kitchen of his house, sitting in a corner of the fireplace with one leg bare because she was mending one of her stockings. 'When she lifted her face', Madame de Boigne continued, 'she revealed features of divine beauty. He found she was the sister of his groom.' Sir William, in this account, himself took Emma back with him to Naples, and only managed to do so in the nick of time for, the Countess assures her readers, 'he came to fetch her at the moment she was being expelled from Mr. Greville's house by the bailiff.'[16]

Other writers of letters or reminiscences preferred wisely to confine themselves to matters of fact and did not speculate on the obscure origins of the interesting young lady. Thus James Byres, writing to the Bishop of Killaloe, simply commented: 'Our friend Sir William Hamilton is well. He has lately got a piece modernity from England which I am afraid will fatigue and exhaust him more than all the volcanoes and antiquities in the Kingdom of Naples'; while the *World* newspaper, recalling 'any of the dozen portraits' which Romney had done of Mrs. Hart, concluded that 'of these any might have gone abroad with Sir W. Hamilton and answered all his purposes full as well as the piece he had taken with him, a piece more cumbrous and changeable than any of the foregoing'.

The arrival of Emma Hart in Naples under such unusual circumstances could hardly be expected to pass without notice. It was to be the subject of a good deal of misrepresentation. A legend would grow around her name which her subsequent career would do nothing to diminish. Once the shock of separation was over and she had settled down in her new life, no one was to contribute more enthusiastically to the growth of this legend than the lady herself.

1. B.M. Add. MSS 42071, f. 2.
2. B.M. Add. MSS 34048, f. 22.
3. Morrison, 134.
4. Morrison, 136.
5. The identity of 'Lady C' has sometimes been taken as referring to Lady Craven, but Lady Clarges is the only one mentioned by Hamilton himself as engaging his affections at this time.
6. Morrison, 137.
7. B.M. Add. MSS 42071, f. 4.

8. Morrison, 138.
9. Morrison, 139.
10. Morrison, 142.
11. Morrison, 149.
12. Morrison, 142.
13. Morrison, 143.
14. Morrison, 145.
15. Fitzwilliam Museum, Percival Bequest MSS.
16. *Memoirs of the Countess de Boigne*, p. 55.

CHAPTER XV

Artists and Antiquities

Emma Hart arrived in Naples on the 26th April 1786, the day on which she celebrated her twenty-first birthday. Her mother, Mrs. Cadogan, was with her. They had set out from England in the company of Gavin Hamilton, the artist, who then was living in Rome, and who travelled with them as far as Geneva. Greville had led Sir William to believe that he would find a young woman more than half ready to forget the past and settle down to a new life in which she would, without much trouble, adapt herself to becoming his mistress. In fact Emma had by no means forgotten her old life or her old love, and for a time remained obstinately attached to the belief that Greville's heart would be moved by her distress, and that he would either come out to Naples or recall her to England where their former relationship could be resumed. Greville, of course, had no intention of doing either the one or the other, and Emma was soon to discover that he had abandoned her.

Emma was at best a rather silly woman, though generous and warm-hearted in an impulsive way. It is her misfortune that she has been taken too seriously by some of her later defenders, not a few of whom have been tempted to take her at her own valuation. She is perhaps better understood if regarded as one of the comic characters of English history. Behind the beautiful mask, beneath the histrionic skill, lay a rather shallow personality, often dazzling on the surface but never in any sense profound. The quality she possessed in superabundance was tremendous animal vitality which, coupled with unique physical beauty, had an overwhelming effect. She was quick in picking up languages and was soon fluent in Italian and French (though not losing her provincial accent when speaking English), but she never managed to acquire more than the most superficial knowledge of art or politics, though most of her time would now be passed in circles where such interests predominated. The 'attitudes' which she would soon be performing with such grace and charm were to have an ironic relevancy, for most of her life would be spent in adopting attitudes of one sort or another in which she would herself be the first person to be convinced of the veracity of the pose. She would become a brisk, busy, self-satisfied woman with the easy confidence of those blessed with great beauty. Like many people of only limited intelligence she would be made to imagine that she was controlling great events when in fact she was merely being used by other people more clever than herself.

But if during much of her existence she was consciously or unconsciously acting a part there were two occasions at least when all artifice was cast aside; the second of these still lay in the future and would take place on a stormy voyage from Naples to Palermo; the first was when she discovered that Charles Greville had let her down. There can be no doubt that on this occasion she loved without self-interest or self-deception. To begin with she had only felt gratitude for the man who had saved her from destitution at the time of the birth of her child, but this had turned into a love which Greville could neither understand nor return. Youth and vitality came quickly to her rescue when the truth of her situation in Naples dawned on her, but she would never be able to love in this way again.

Her first letter is dated only four days after her arrival. 'I love you to that degree', she tells Greville, 'that at this time there is not a hardship upon hearth, either of poverty, hunger, cold, death, or even to walk barefooted to Scotland to see you, but that I would undergo. Therefore my dear, dear Greville if you do love me, for my sake try all you can to come hear as soon as possible. You have a true friend in Sir William, and he will be happy to see you, and do all he can to make you happy; and for me, I will be everything you can wish for.' Hamilton, faced with the tearful and distraught Emma, had perhaps told her, as he had already told Greville, that he would as soon see them both in Naples than have Emma there alone. Certainly he was doing all he could to make her happy. 'You do not know how good Sir William is to me,' the letter continues, 'he is doing everything he can to make me happy. He as never dined out since I came hear; and endead, to speake the truth, he is never out of my sight. He breakfasts, dines, supes, and is constantly by me, looking in my face. . . ' She was under no illusion that Sir William would be content to gaze in her face for ever—'he loves me now', she confesses—but at the memory of Greville she found the thought of anything else insupportable: 'Endead, I am sorry, for I cannot make him happy. I can be civil, oblidging, and I do try to make myself as agreable as I can to him. But I belong to you, Greville, and to you only I will belong, and nobody shall be your heir-apearant.'

Despite her tears and protestations Emma was able to give an account of the social events that Sir William had already arranged for her; a little concert the night before, as well as a dinner party with some English visitors; and could describe the presents he had given her, a camel hair shawl, a beautiful gown that had cost twenty-five guineas, and 'several little things of Lady Hamilton's'. But it is Greville she thinks of, though it is clear that her excitement at the gifts and the new experiences had not been utterly obliterated by grief: 'You are everything that is dear to me on hearth, and I hope happier times will soon restore you to me, for endead I would rather be with you starving then from you in the greatest splender in the world.' As to living as Hamilton's mistress, this is something she cannot even bring herself to think of: 'I have had a conversation this morning with Sir William, that has made me mad,' the letter ends. 'He speaks—no, I do not know what to make of it. But Greville, my dear Greville, write some comfort to me.'

The letter, which in full covers five pages, shows the confused state in which Emma found herself. One moment she is weeping for Greville, the next describing some new gift; she gossips about Hamilton's visitors and their family affairs, and then bewails her lover's absence; she repeats with evident satisfaction the compliments Sir William has made her but recoils at the thought of what he might ask next; she declares that she can never make him happy and then proclaims how good and kind a friend he is to her. Her plight was one to arouse pity. The days of 'the wild unthinking Emma' were long past; she had grown used to being treated with consideration. The years she had spent with Greville had taught her the value of security. The removal of his protection, upon which she had relied with such confidence, now made her feel helpless and lost. For some time she could think of no one else to turn to. She wrote him (so she claimed) as many as fourteen letters in the next three months. His only reply was one brief enclosure in a letter addressed to his uncle.

Presented with this difficult and delicate situation Sir William acted with wisdom and restraint; he did not press matters but quickly realised that Emma must first get used to her new surroundings and rediscover her sense of security. He kept her constantly occupied and amused. He placed four pleasant rooms at her disposal in the Palazzo Sessa where she could admire the splendid view of the bay of Naples and pass the time quietly in her own company or that of her mother without fear of interruption. He arranged for her to have lessons in languages, singing and music, in all of which she was to prove herself an apt pupil. Two artists were engaged to paint portraits of her for one of which she sat wearing a Turkish dress and turban, and for the other a black Rubens hat with feathers and a gown of blue silk; and he promised that Angelica Kauffmann should paint her when next she came to Naples.[2] Far from hiding her in some remote or secluded villa he gave her one of his carriages in which to take the air and allowed her to go for walks, chaperoned by the redoubtable Mrs. Cadogan, in the Villa Reale, while he himself took her on expeditions to Pompeii and Sorrento or on sailing trips to Capri and Ischia. Between sighs at the thought of Greville and sobs at the memory of Edgware Row, life for Emma was becoming a very interesting affair. It was not for nothing that Hamilton had spent a lifetime in diplomacy, and he stood in very little need of the constant flow of hints, suggestions and advice on the subject of Emma which continued to reach him from his nephew's anxious pen.

Emma's spirits quickly revived as a result of this treatment, but Greville's hold on her affections was strong and she could not abandon him without a struggle, even after the truth had dawned upon her that she had herself been heartlessly abandoned by her beloved Charles. Her letters alternated between pleas for him 'for God's sake to send me one letter', and cries of 'Oh, my heart is intirely broke', to boastful and tantalising references to her success in Naples, written partly as a result of her returning exuberance and partly from a forlorn hope of arousing his jealousy.

She has, she tells Greville, a *cicisbeo* in the person of a certain nobleman whom she calls 'Prince Draydrixton', a designation unknown to the Almanach de Gotha but possibly meant to indicate Prince Dietrichstein. The Prince is a friend of the Queen of Naples who asks him to walk Emma near her so that she can get a sight of the beautiful stranger from England. He speaks English himself, and declares her to be 'a dymond of the first watter and the finest creature on hearth', and attends her on all occasions. The King himself is not insensible to her charms: 'the King as eyes, he as a heart and I have made an impression on it.' Ferdinand in fact had sailed in his royal barge close to the Hamilton's boat at Posillipo with his band of music playing in Emma's honour. When they went to land he made her a gallant bow, saying that it was a sin that he could not speak English. It was not often that Ferdinand was known to deplore his ignorance of anything, let alone the English language. His confession was indeed a tribute to the power of Emma's charm. But these were innocent conquests, the obliging Prince Dietrichstein telling everyone that she was Hamilton's friend 'and she belongs to his nephew'.

Though these pleasures and distractions were rapidly reconciling Emma to her new life, and the descriptions of them began to take pride of place in her letters to the reproaches she flung at Greville, she was still unable to look upon Hamilton as more than a friend. When in the following July it was suggested to her, presumably by the down-to-earth Mrs. Cadogan, that she should live 'you know how' with Sir William, she felt that she could not do so. Memories of Greville, and also of the way he had treated her, stood in the way. 'No, I respect him, but no never', she told her former lover, 'shall he peraps live with me for a little wile like you, and send me to England. Then what am I to do? What is to become of me? But excuse me, my heart is ful. I tell you, give me one guiney a week for everything, and live with me, and I will be contented.' In August her opinion was still the same: 'Sir William is ever friend', Greville was informed, 'but we are lovers.'[3] To this letter she added a postscript which must have given him some food for thought: 'If you affront me, I will make him marry me.' It was a threat, but just how serious a threat Greville could only guess.

Greville was, in fact, getting decidedly alarmed at Emma's intransigence, nor had Hamilton, in his exposed position as ambassador, any wish to make himself look foolish by the young lady's continued residence under his roof in so very undefined a capacity. To be known to keep a charming young mistress would cause little comment or surprise in Naples, though it might be the occasion for envy. But to be known to be providing for someone else's mistress, albeit abandoned by her lover, would merely make him look ridiculous, and the Neapolitans had a keen eye for such *opera buffa* situations. By October Hamilton and Greville were seriously discussing the possibility of Emma's return to England in the following spring, by which time she would have spent a full year in Naples. There was, however, no question on Greville's part of her resuming her place in his life; this he made quite clear: 'If she will put me on the footing of a friend, which she says

I always have assumed. . . her future comfort shall be my serious concern; but she must not think that I can resume that close connexion and live as I did with her.' Hamilton, for his part, was prepared to settle some money on her if she went back, and Greville suggested that George Romney, whose disinterested devotion to Emma was well known, should be appointed her trustee. But he concluded very firmly that 'it will be much better that the plan is generally discussed and approved before it is executed', having no wish to be compromised a second time.[4] A month later the situation was no better and Greville concluded gloomily: 'Without any other plan she must wait events, and the difficulty will be to reject improper offers; and, if a journey homewards should give a favourable one, it should not be lost. But, at any rate, she will have the good sense not to expose herself with any boy of family; she must look to from 25 to 35, and one who is his own master.'[5] It looked as though the great plan to settle Emma in Naples with Sir William had failed.

This was the situation in the autumn of 1786: by Christmas all had changed. At some point late in November or early in December Emma Hart became Sir William Hamilton's mistress. It is difficult to decide what exactly was the cause of this sudden change of heart, for sudden it must have been. She had already realised that Greville would never take her back; perhaps she had discovered the plan for her own return to England and the thought of having to face her faithless lover had proved too much for her and she had settled to remain in Naples, which could lead to but one consequence. She may have concluded that the role of *abbandonata* was not one that could be sustained in definitely. No doubt Mrs. Cadogan, who was a practical woman, had lost no opportunity in pointing out where Emma's interest now lay, and her own letters, even when they are at their most violent against Greville, make it very clear that she found life in Naples extremely agreeable. Greville himself had remarked to Hamilton that he never expected from a woman the power to withstand favourable opportunity and a long siege, and Emma, it seems, had proved no exception to this cynical rule. Hamilton's tact, kindness, and gentle coaxing had at last succeeded in melting her resistance. Emma, who herself was full of impulsive generosity, could not hold out any longer against so generous and kindly a friend. She was affectionate by nature; she had nursed her grief long enough; she was young and full of life; Sir William's care and attention for her now had its reward.

Having once made the decision to accept Hamilton as her lover she did not repine. Emma could not divide her affections. All the endearments which had previously been reserved for Greville were now laid at the feet of his uncle. Her first letter to him that has survived after becoming his mistress was written from Caserta on the 26th of December 1786, and speaks for itself: 'Pray don't scold me for writing to you, for endead I can't help it, and I should have been ashamed to have wrote to you without an excuse for doing it, therefore Smith as returned the letter I sent to town, and I told Cottier that I would send it you, or else he might think I was so much in love I could not be 3 days without sending to you. But lett them think if he will; certain it is I love you and sincerely, and endead I am appreensive two much for my own quiet, but lett it be. Love as its pleasures and its pains; for instance, yesterday when you went a whey from me, I thought all my heart and soul was torn from me, and my grief was excessive I assure you; today I am better *perche*? The day after to moro is friday and then I shall have you with me to make up for the past pain. I shall have much pleasure and comfort, and my mind tells me you will have much pleasure to come home to me again, and I will setle you and comfort you. . . *Adio*, my dear Sir William; laying jokes aside, there is nothing I assure you can give me the least comfort tell you come home. I shall receive you with smiles, affection and good humer, and think had I the offer of crowns I would refuse them and except you, and I don't care if all the world knows it. If some times I am out of humer, forgive me, tell me, put me in a whey to be grateful to you for your kindness to me, and believe me I will never abuse your kindness to me, and in a little time all faults will be corrected. I am a pretty whoman and one can't be every thing at once; but now I have my wisdom teeth I will try to be ansome and reasonable. . .'[6]

A certain tranquillity now settled on Hamilton's private life which was not to be disturbed for a number of years. Emma was to be a good and faithful mistress to him though the dark threat she had made to Greville, in a moment of anger and despair, that she would marry Sir William was never entirely lost sight of, at least by Emma, though it would be five years yet before the chance would come to put it into effect. But if the future promised domestic happiness the events of the past seven months had left Sir William's affairs in a state of some confusion, and while Emma's fate was still undecided Greville had occasion to remind his uncle rather sharply of his official duties. 'I wrote to you several letters on the subject of some reeds for hautboys and clarinets, which you told me you would not forget, tho' you thought it an useless commission, being as good in London,' Hamilton was told;[7] 'But the King has repeatedly mentioned your forgetfulness, and has asked Fisher, who you was civil to, and he said you had sent them. I think it very likely you forgot them, but you must write me a few lines expressing your sorrow that those you sent had not reached me, and that you should send another parcel, and desire me to present them, and add some proper civilities to the giver of the commission; and my brother will be in waiting, and I shall send the letter to him, by which you will get out of the scrape. These little fiddle faddle things are mountains at our Court.'

While King George was being kept waiting for his clarinet reeds the Queen of Naples was no nearer the fulfilment of her ambition of surprising her royal spouse with a plate of fruit from her English garden, though on this occasion the delays were not due to any forgetfulness on Hamilton's part. In fact Sir Joseph Banks had sent out a skilled gardener in answer to Sir William's appeal and this man, whose name was Graffer, had reached Naples just after Emma but, like her, had taken his time in settling down. He did not speak Italian; no proper quarters had been provided for him; his wife and children could not easily accustom themselves to their strange new surroundings, and his ignorance of the language was exploited by those people who are ever ready to cheat unwary foreigners. It was not a very propitious beginning.

By September, however, nearly four months after Graffer's arrival, the situation was slightly improved. 'I have done wonders to get matters as forward as they are,' Hamilton told Banks. 'That Graffer might be quite detached from the King's Gardeners and Gardens I have got his Majesty to purchase a charming piece of ground adjoining the wall of the Royal Caserta Garden, which is laid out in the most detestable taste. Our piece of Ground is upwards of 50 acres and has every capability—the richest soil imaginable and command of the purest water—so that I have no doubt we shall have (except in the dog days) as fine a Verdure and as good a turf as in England.'

The King took very little interest in the project to begin with, and beyond providing the ground and having it walled in, left everything to Hamilton and the Queen. In April 1787 Banks was informed that Graffer hoped to have it all finished in about a year and a half. Maria Carolina was eager to get on with it as fast as possible and was spending as much as fifty pounds a week on the garden. This caused a good deal of jealousy and ill-feeling among her ladies, as Sir William explained to Banks:

'As the Queen used always to give her savings to her bed- chamber women and servants about her you may well imagine what an uproar this new expence occasions.' Graffer had an excellent foreman, but unfortunately he was 'a Drunken Dog'. Hamilton declared that unless he could prevail upon the fore man to give up spirits and content, himself with wine he 'will soon burn himself up in this warm climate'.

Ferdinand's indifference to the English garden did not last very long. Sooner or later he had to interfere, much to the annoyance of the English Minister who took the greatest pride in the garden's progress. Two and a half years after reporting on their initial success in getting the work going Hamilton was complaining to Banks of being 'discharged' with Graffer from the Queen's service in the planning of the garden, and of being no longer consulted. The Queen, in fact, was beginning to tire of her horticultural experiment. Ferdinand had then stepped in and upset everyone. First he had announced that he would have the whole area ploughed up and sown with Indian corn. Now, it seemed, the King wanted to make a maze or labyrinth so that he could 'have the fun of bewildering his courtiers'. Graffer was appealed to for a plan but was soon at a loss over it; Hamilton, characteristically, could only help him by 'showing him one on an antique medal'. Banks' assistance was required once more. 'All I know', Sir William wrote in a petulant tone, 'is that Graffer must obey, for His Sicilian Majesty has no other idea of being a King but the doing just what comes into his head.'[8] Ferdinand himself thought this an excellent way of being a king and in a moment of royal confidence told Graffer, with whom he had formed the democratic habit of walking about arm in arm, that the English monarch was but 'a King of straw and cannot do what he likes'. Hamilton does not record the gardener's reply to this piece of royal indiscretion.

The garden managed to survive in spite of its changes of patronage, and became a favourite place of royal relaxation. Some few years later (2 June 1793) Emma would record the pleasure that she and Sir William took in it: 'The English garden is going on very fast. The King and Queen go there every day. Sir William and me are there every morning at seven o'clock, sometimes dine there, and allways drink tea there. In short, it is Sir William's favourite child, and booth him and me are now studying botany, but not to make ourselves pedantical prigs and to shew our learning like some of our travelling neighbours, but for our own pleasure.' Graffer, she adds, is 'as happy as a prince'.[9] The story of the English garden was destined to have a happy ending; the remains of it can still be seen at Caserta today.

The Palazzo Sessa in these last years before the outbreak of the French Revolution was still a place of pilgrimage for scholars, artists, and men of letters. Whether he was engaged in planning a garden, arranging his vases, negotiating a commercial treaty or making arrangements for the visit of a Royal Duke, Sir William Hamilton was always ready to welcome a wandering artist, help him to find commissions, and introduce him to suitable patrons. He continued to add to his own collection of pictures and began to gather a second collection of Greek vases which, in the opinion of Adolf Michaelis, was 'larger and more important than the first'. Of the many strangers who came to see him (other than the travelling British visitors and young men making their Grand Tour) some were quite obscure artists with nothing to recommend them but their work, others were men of great reputation who came presenting impressive letters of introduction. All were equally welcome. In the spring of 1787 Sir William was to receive in his house one of its most distinguished visitors. Johann Wolfgang von Goethe was thirty-seven years old and already a poet of European renown when he arrived in Naples in the course of his famous Italian journey. For the German poet this visit to the south represented the fulfilment of a long felt desire. He shared the English ambassador's enthusiasm for antiquity being, like him, a disciple of Winckelmann, whose *History of Ancient Art* had been published in the year in which Hamilton began his long residence in Naples.[10] The Italian journey was to be one of the greatest experiences in Goethe's long life; he was at the height of his powers yet still eager for new impressions and inspiration. He was delighted with Naples from the moment he arrived there: 'Naples at first sight leaves a free, cheerful, and lively impression; numberless beings are passing and repassing each other. The King is gone hunting, the queen *promising*; and so things could not be better.'

Goethe had as companion the painter Wilhelm Tischbein who had travelled with him from Rome where he had acted as guide to the poet in his study of the art treasures of the eternal city. Tischbein was to become so attached to Naples that he remained there, becoming an intimate member of Hamilton's circle (he was to describe Sir William as 'a good, an excellent, a rare man') and was eventually to be known in his native Germany as 'Neapolitan' Tischbein to distinguish him from the many other members of his family who achieved fame in the arts. He was later to help Hamilton in the illustration of his second collection of vases and to paint a portrait of Emma in the character of Iphigenia. His devotion to Naples would in time be rewarded by the King and Queen with the appointment of director of the Neapolitan Academy of Painting.

The two travellers first met Hamilton at Caserta. They were introduced to him by Philip Hackert the topographical view-painter, a fellow German and a great favourite of Ferdinand and Maria Carolina who had made him their official Court painter and had lodged him in a wing of the Francavilla palace where Goethe examined his studio. The poet found him a 'very precise and prudent personage who, with untiring industry, manages nevertheless to enjoy life'. Examples of his work hung in Sir William's collection, including a view of the English garden.

At the British Minister's house at Caserta, on 16 March, Goethe and Tischbein not only met Sir William but were also among the first to see Emma perform her *tableau-vivant*, that series of classical poses which later achieved much celebrity as the 'Attitudes'. Goethe was clearly charmed by the exhibition, which was not to everybody's taste, and left a vivid description of what he saw in the *Italienische Reise*. Emma at this time had only been living as Hamilton's mistress for little more than three months, but the Attitudes were already a finished production capable of fascinating one of the most fastidious men in Europe, the great apostle of culture. They must, therefore, have had their origin in the very earliest stages of Emma's and Sir William's relationship, if not, indeed, even before it reached the stage of complete intimacy. Perhaps these dramatic poses had started as an attempt to amuse and distract Emma when she was still disconsolate; the earliest form they had taken, as Goethe later discovered, had already been abandoned. Sir William, too, may well have devised the Attitudes as a palliative for his own feelings at a time when it seemed that Emma herself would remain for ever beyond his reach. The instinct of the collector with a beautiful object to display no doubt also had some part in their original conception.

'Sir William Hamilton', Goethe wrote,[11] 'who still lives here as ambassador from England, has at length, after his long love of art, and long study, discovered the height of these delights of nature and art in a beautiful young woman. She lives with him; an English girl of about twenty years of age. She is very handsome with a beautiful figure. The old knight has made a Greek costume for her which becomes her extremely. Dressed in this, letting her hair fall loose, and making use of a couple of shawls, she exhibits every possible variety of pose, expression, and aspect, so that in the end the spectator almost imagines himself in a dream. Here one sees in perfection, in ravishing variety, in movement, all that the greatest artists have loved to express. Standing, kneeling, sitting, reclining, grave or sad, playful, triumphant, repentant, alluring, menacing, anxious, all states of mind flow rapidly one after another. She suits the folding of her veil to each expression with wonderful taste, even adapting it into every type of head-dress. The old knight holds the light for her and enters into the exhibition with his whole soul. He thinks he can see in her a likeness to all the most famous antiques, to the beautiful profiles on Sicilian coins—yes, to the Apollo Belvedere itself! This much at any rate is certain, as an entertainment it is quite unique. We saw it on two evenings with complete enjoyment.'

A week later Sir William received Goethe at the Palazzo Sessa. The old palace and its splendid position were to receive the poet's flattering approval. 'No doubt one who has abundance of time, tact, and means, might remain here for a long time with profit to himself,' he wrote after his visit; 'Thus Sir William Hamilton has contrived greatly to enjoy a long residence in this city and now, in the evening of his life, is reaping the fruits of it. The rooms, which he has had furnished in the English style, are most delightful, and the view from the corner room perhaps without equal. Below you is the sea, with a view of Capri, Posillipo on the right, with the promenade of the Villa Reale between you and the grotto; on the left an ancient building belonging to the Jesuits, and beyond it the Coast stretching from Sorrento to Cape Minerva. Another view equal to this is scarcely to be found in Europe; at least, not in the centre of a great and populous city.' Tischbein was no less enthusiastic, noting that the house was a meeting place for all people of taste. The staircase, he noticed, was adorned with the heads of two philosophers 'one who deplored, the other who laughed at the follies of this world'. Of the ambassador himself Goethe wrote: 'Hamilton is a person of universal taste, and after having wandered through the whole realm of creation has found rest at last in a most beautiful companion, a masterpiece of that great artist—Nature.'

Shortly after this Goethe left for Sicily, but in May he was back in Naples again. It was on this second visit that he was taken into the cellars of the Palazzo Sessa, into what Hamilton called his 'secret lumber-vault of art', and shown an extraordinary collection of miscellaneous treasures heaped up in every sort of confusion. There were busts, torsos, vases, bronzes, antique household implements in Sicilian agate, pictures, and even a small carved and painted chapel. Where ever the eye turned there were curiosities of one sort or another, some works of art, others mere junk. It was through Philip Hackert's influence with Sir William that Goethe was allowed to see this hoard, for it was not on view to everyone—and not without reason, perhaps, to judge by a little incident which Goethe recorded with amusement. 'Seeing a long box lying on the ground with the lid partly open, I had the curiosity to push it back, and behold! two splendid bronze candelabra. With a sign I drew Hackert's attention to this treasure and in a whisper asked him if they did not look exactly like those at the Portici museum. In reply he signalled to me to hold my tongue; it was not impossible that they might have strayed here from the cellars of Pompeii. Perhaps because of these and other fortunate acquisitions the knight might have very good reason for only showing these hidden treasures to his most trustworthy friends.'[12]

The visit to the lumber-vault was to reveal another secret. 'I was next struck by a chest standing upright, open in front, painted black inside and the whole surrounded by a splendid gold frame,' Goethe's account continues. 'There was sufficient room inside for a human figure to stand, and it was from this fact that we discovered the use to which it had been put. Not content merely with seeing the beautiful creature he possessed as a moving statue, this connoisseur of art and women wished also to have the pleasure of seeing her as a brilliant, inimitable picture, and had on various occasions set her within this golden frame, her bright dress showing to advantage against its black background. This had been done in the style of the antique paintings of Pompeii and sometimes of more modern works of art.' It seemed that these displays were now discontinued; the box was too heavy to move about and was difficult to illuminate properly. 'We were not, therefore, to be indulged with so pretty a spectacle,' Goethe sadly concludes.

If Goethe found 'the old knight' a sympathetic character (Hamilton was in fact now in his fifty-seventh year), he was a little more severe in his judgement of Emma, whose Attitudes had caused him so much delight. Undoubtedly she was very beautiful, but he considered her 'by no means richly endowed in respect of mind' and her expression of voice and language did not, in his estimation, live up to the 'wealth of soul' betokened by her fair figure. Viewing her with the eye of a philosopher he had hoped to find more than a mere surface beauty, and he had been disappointed. Tischbein, on the other hand, saw her with the eye of a painter, and was content with what he saw.

When Goethe left for Rome on his journey home Tischbein remained in Naples. He soon became very friendly with 'Ritter Hamilton' as he called him in his letters to Goethe. He was to witness at Posillipo a display of another sort with which Hamilton used to amuse himself during his leisure hours in this pleasant retreat. 'After dinner we saw a dozen boys swimming in the sea,' he told Goethe. 'A beautiful sight it was with their many varied groupings and postures in the water. He pays them for swimming so that he can enjoy this pleasure every afternoon.' Of the villa itself Tischbein declared: 'Anything more glorious is not to be seen on this globe.' He was the type of younger man with whom Sir William could establish that easy relationship in which the offices of mentor and friend were happily combined. It was a relationship which gave Sir William himself great pleasure and from which his younger friends derived considerable profit. Tischbein certainly responded warmly. 'I like Hamilton uncommonly,' he confided in Goethe: 'I had a great deal of conversation with him in his house here and while we were driving by the sea. I heard much from his lips which gave me the highest pleasure and I hope many good things of this man.'

Much of Hamilton's time during the next few years would be spent in preparing his second collection of vases for publication, and the plates which illustrated these volumes, of an exquisite simplicity of line and a much higher quality than those illustrating the first collection, would be prepared under

Tischbein's direction. When the volumes were eventually published in 1791 Hamilton explained: 'The magnificent Edition of my first Collection of Vases . . . became too expensive a work to answer the purpose which I first intended when I encouraged that Publication, for young Artists are not often in a situation of making such a purchase; to obviate that material objection I have now confined this new Publication to the simple outline of the figures on the vases, which is essential, and no unnecessary Ornaments or colouring have been introduced; by these means the purchase becoming easy it will be in the power of Lovers of Antiquity and Artists to reap the desired profit from such excellent models as are now offered.'

Following contemporary taste at the time he made his first collection Sir William had imagined his vases to be largely Etruscan. He was now convinced of their Greek origin. In 1790 he wrote to Greville, emphasising the words by underlining, that 'a treasure of *Greek*, commonly called *Etruscan*, Vases have been discovered within these 12 months, the choice of which are in my possession, tho' at considerable expence. I do not mean to be such a fool as to give or leave them to the British Museum, but I will contrive to have them published without any expence to myself and artists and antiquarians will have the greatest obligation to me; the drawings on these vases are most excellent and many of the subjects from Homer.'[13] Hamilton does not explain how he intended to publish his collection without expense to himself. He certainly had little enough money to spare just then; preparing new apartments for Emma had set him back three thousand pounds and he admitted to spending as much again on Antiquities since his last leave in England, though it was 'a most extraordinary collection' and he was sure that he could not lose by the purchases he had made. In self-justification he admits disarmingly to his nephew: 'You know that it is impossible for me to be without an object whilst I can command a farthing.'[14]

Hamilton's argument that the vases were of Greek rather than Etruscan origin was set out in the first volume of his *Collection of Engravings from Ancient Vases*, which was published by Tischbein in 1791. The text on this occasion was his own work. 'Much has been written upon the subject of these sort of Vases,' Sir William declared, 'but the most rational account of them is to be found in the works of Mr. d'Hancarville and the Abbé Winckelmann. Most of the authors that wrote before them attributed such monuments of Antiquity solely to the Etruscans. Buonaroti and Gori being themselves Tuscans meant to do honor to their native Country by attributing such Elegant Works of Art to the Etruscans, and subsequent Authors adopted their opinion. When I began to form my first Collection, which is now in the British Museum, I had the same idea, but the famous Vase in that Collection on which Antephates King of the Lestrigons is represented at the Hunting of a wild Boar, and his name wrote over him, as are the names of his companions, in most ancient Greek Characters, and in the manner called Bustrophedon (and which manner of writing was disused in Greece more than five hundred years before the Christian Era) being dug out of a Sepulchre near the ancient city of Capua, gave the first idea of these Vases being of a Grecian, and not of an Etruscan Origin. The stile of the figures, independent of the letters, wou'd have certainly decided that very curious Vase to have been Etruscan. Most of the Vases of this sort in the different Museums of Europe I am confident were found in the Kingdom of the Two Sicilies. There is no certainty of the Vases, with figures on them, in the Collection of the Great Duke of Tuscany having been found in Tuscany. The Collection of Vases in the Vatican at Rome was purchased from Joseph of Valetta, a Lawyer of Naples, but the strongest proof against the Tuscan writers are the very fine Vases of this sort that have been found, and are preserved in Sicily, and which are exactly similar to the finest of those that are found in the neighbourhood of Naples, and when they have inscriptions on them, the letters are Greek, and not Etruscan, besides there is not any account of Etruscan Settlements in Sicily.'

The edition of Hamilton's second collection comprised four volumes, issued between 1791 and 1795. The volumes, as he had hoped, were to have considerable influence not only with crafts men like Josiah Wedgwood who already owed a debt to his taste, but also among younger men like Henry Fuseli and John Flaxman, the latter one of the greatest artists of the English Neoclassical school. His illustrations to the Odyssey, which brought him international fame, show clearly the influence of Tischbein's plates. Flaxman himself, in a letter written to Sir William in March 1792, paid tribute to 'that regard and attention which genius and talents always meet with from you liberality'.[15] Thanks to Hamilton's recommendation Flaxman received the commission for a monument to Lord Mansfield. The designs, at the request of Mansfield's son, were sent to Naples for Sir William's approbation, and represented the departed Earl 'on an exalted seat between Wisdom and Justice, his attention earnestly fixed on the equal balance of the scales of Justice'. In sending his design Flaxman once again makes his grateful acknowledgements to the ambassador for the trouble taken on his behalf.[16] It was tributes such as this that made Hamilton feel that his activities as a collector and patron of the arts were justified.

Shortly after publishing the volumes on his second collection Sir William had made an attempt at influencing taste in an altogether different quarter. He had sent 'a colossal head of Augustus of the first rate Grecian sculpture'[17] as a gift to the Prince of Wales. In a letter announcing this gift, written on 12 November 1788, Hamilton explained to the Prince: 'I will tell your Royal Highness fairly what induced me to think of taking this great liberty. When I was last in England I perceived with pleasure that your Royal Highness had a great love for the Arts and a desire of acquiring a knowledge of them. The only method is to examine with attention such works as are accountedly of the first class and compare them with others that pretend to be so. I am convinced that when this bust of Augustus is placed at a proper hight and your Royal Highness is accustomed to look upon it you will never bear the sight of a bust of indifferent sculpture.' To this excellent aesthetic advice Sir William added a few words of criticism on the subject of the Prince's father. 'His Majesty, who is certainly a great lover of the Arts and has given them great encouragement, for want of forming his taste early on works of the first class has never been sensible to what is properly called the Sublime in the Arts.' Thinking this criticism of his royal master a little bold, even for a privileged foster-brother, he ends: 'This favourite subject of mine has, I fear, already carried me too far.'[18] He was prepared none the less, to stick to his aesthetic theories at the risk of royal displeasure, though such criticism of his father would be unlikely to disturb the unfilial Prince of Wales.

This head of Augustus was almost certainly the one referred to by James Irvine in a letter to George Cumberland written from Rome in April 1783. 'Sir William Hamilton has lately got a head of Augustus without the neck and half the chin which he values at an enormous price. . . He sent it to Mr. Byres to get it restored, only to show *how little* was wanting and in such a manner that the Modern part might be separated from the Antique at pleasure.'[19] It is interesting to note that Sir William's ideas on the subject of the proper restoration of ancient works of art were no less enlightened than the aesthetic theories he derived from their study, and it is only to be regretted that his ideas were not always followed by others.

Though Hamilton allowed himself to criticise his sovereign's deficient sense of the sublime he was genuinely upset when news of his former foster-brother's serious illness reached Naples late in 1788. His distress at the King's disorder, and at the regency crisis to which it gave rise, caused him 'most cruel uncertainty and anxiety'. This was not just an official phrase suitable for inclusion in a dispatch but came in a letter to his old friend Joseph Banks with whom he was used to discuss his affairs with complete frankness. In the same letter Hamilton gave vent to his indignation at the form of prayer used for King George's recovery which he considered to be a piece of thoroughly unsound theology. 'I must own I was shocked at the Capuchine's Prayer you are offering up in England for his Majesty's recovery,' he wrote, 'and where it seems as if the Almighty for our Sins had visited this virtuous Prince so severely knowing He would afflict us in the most sensible part. What an Idea of a Supreme Being; it is of a piece with calling the Earthquake of Calabria *Flagello di Dio*.' This was the authentic voice of the eighteenth-century Enlightenment.

Hamilton wrote this letter in December; by June 1789 the news was better. 'The account you give me of the King's present state of health is indeed most pleasing to me,' Banks was told. 'What a train of evils and confusion have we escaped by this happy recovery. The day after Tomorrow there shall be such a sirloin of Beef on my table as I am sure never appear'd before at Naples. I have invited all the English, factory and all, to partake of it and they shall drink His Majesty's health in the best wines I have, which I can assure you are not despicable and are rare in this country where nobody seems to give themselves any trouble to be well served.'[20]

Both these letters to Banks contained references to Emma. In the first Sir William wrote: 'The lovely Emma, who improves daily and is universally loved and admired, sends her kind love to you. The very first composers allow she sings wonderfully and will be really Capital in another year when I hope to be able to let you judge if I have exaggerated.' In the second he refers to a journey they had both just made to Puglia. 'Emma says she will write you an account of her journey in Magna Grecia, for she has taken notes—she is as clever as she is Beautiful.' Emma, in fact, was now having the time of her life. A long letter to Greville of twelve folio pages, started on August 1787, but not finished until four months later, had kept her former lover informed of her adventures. He was now quite forgiven, 'for you will ever be dear to me,' Emma tells him, 'and tho' we cannot be together, lett ous corespond as friends.'

Her catalogue of events, to judge by her report, was certainly a full one. She has been to Sorrento as the guest of a duke, from whose house they had seen the lava flow down the slopes of Vesuvius. 'I have made some drawings from it, for I am so used to draw now, it is as easy as A.B.C.' She has singing lessons from one of the best masters in Italy and certainly gives Sir William a good return for employing him, for Greville is told 'the last night I sang fifteen songs'. The good people of Sorrento have theirs heads turned by this display: 'I left some dying, some crying, and some in despair.' Sir William is very fond of her and their house is full of painters painting her. After the duke at Sorrento she and Sir William visit a countess at Ischia. 'The countess makes me set by her and seemed to have pleasure to distinguish me by every mark of attention, and the (*sic*) all allowed the[y] never seen such a *belissima creatura* in all their life.' Once more she is persuaded to sing and gets such applause 'that for ten minutes you could not hear a word'. A priest is so overcome by her that Sir William is 'oblidged' to give him her picture on a snuff-box which the priest then carries in his breast—'This is a priest, mind you!'

She has had offers to be 'first whoman' in the Italian Opera at Madrid at six thousand pounds for three years, but refuses 'as I should not like to go into Spain without I knew people their.' However, Sir William may give her leave to sing in London; he has taken her master into the house so that he cannot give lessons to any one else. Her voice, as perhaps Greville was surprised to read, 'is the finest *soprano* you ever heard, so that Sir William shuts his eyes and thinks one of the *Castratos* is singing'. Sir William gives a diplomatic party and after dinner Emma sings to his guests. The great Banti, *prima donna* of the San Carlo Opera House, is invited to sing with her. Emma was nervous to begin with—but when I begun all fear whent awhay and I sung so well that she cried out, "Just God, what a voice!"'

So the giddy catalogue goes on. She visits the opera on a gala night in honour of the King of Spain's birthday and 'had the finest dress made up on purpose' as she had a box near the King and Queen. Her gown was 'purple sattin, wite sattin peticoat trim'd with crape and spangles'. Her cap 'lovely, from Paris, all wite fethers'. The poor, no less than rich and great, flock to see her. They have got it into their heads, she assures Greville, that she is the Virgin, and come to beg favours of her. It is all very different from Edgware Row! 'But Sir William allready is distractedly in love, and indeed I love him tenderly.' And, as though she was indeed a goddess, she adds graciously: 'He deserves it.'[21]

Life seemed to be following an unchanging but agreeable pattern for Hamilton as he neared his sixtieth birthday. It is true that Catherine was no longer with him (for the pretty creature who had taken her place could hardly claim to come in the same category) and the hope he had once had of heading a great embassy was long since abandoned, but he could still take part with undiminished vigour in all his other pursuits which made his life so full of interest and value. He was still sought out by all people of consequence who visited Naples, where he remained a figure of the first importance. He could feel that he was helping to spread useful knowledge through the volumes he had published in the past and planned for the future; that art and industry had benefited from his studies.

If he had any regrets it was that his post still afforded him so little opportunity to take part in that great activity which Pope Julius II had called the *Jocho del Mondo*, the great political game that seemed always to pass by the Kingdom of the Two Sicilies where he had represented this country for so long. It must, therefore, have seemed little more than a formality for him when he noted in a dispatch to the Duke of Leeds, dated the 4th of August 1789, that 'the news of the late extraordinary Revolution in France has cast a visible gloom upon the face of this Court'. The calm of life in Naples, he must have felt, would remain undisturbed, whatever might happen in the world elsewhere.

1. Morrison, 150.
2. Angelica's portrait of her as the Comic Muse was to become Emma's favourite picture of herself.
3. *Vide*: Morrison, 152, 153.
4. Morrison, 154.
5. Morrison, 156.
6. Morrison, 157.
7. Morrison, 156.
8. B.M. Add. MSS 34048, ff 31, 34 and 57.
9. Morrison, 221.
10. Geschichte der Kunst des Alterthums, published in 1764. Winckelmann died in 1768.
11. *Vide* Goethe's *Travels in Italy*, p. 199 et seq.
12. Op. cit., p. 880.
13. Morrison, 180.
14. Morrison, 182.

15. Morrison, 207.
16. Morrison, 224.
17. Hamilton presumably meant in the Grecian style as a head of Augustus could not be Greek.
18. B.M. Dept. of Greek and Roman Antiquities, Hamilton Papers, 1-3.
19. B.M. Cumberland Papers, IV. (Add. MSS 36494, f. 9) [F].
20. B.M. Add. MSS 34048, ff. 48 and 50.
21. Morrison, 168.

CHAPTER XVI

Hamilton's Second Marriage

When the news of the storming of the Bastille reached Naples Sir William Hamilton had completed almost a quarter of a century as British Minister at the Court of Ferdinand IV. They had been years of diplomatic tranquillity. During this peaceful period he had more than once wished himself in a post of greater importance. It was ironical that now, when he was in his sixtieth year and happily reconciled to the thought of finishing his career in this quiet post, the Court of Naples should become a place of great diplomatic activity. With the advance of the revolutionary armies into Italy, the development of the British naval campaign in the Mediterranean, the vital necessity of keeping the port of Naples open to the British fleet and the Neapolitan government safe from the grasp of the French, Sir William found himself, at a time of life when many men would begin to think of retirement, placed in a position which would have taxed the strength and tested the skill of a man many years younger.

The change, however, did not come immediately. The news which reached Naples in August 1789 sent a chill through the Court where the monarchs were sister and brother-in-law to the Queen of France. It left Maria Carolina bewildered and angry but hardly kept Ferdinand from his hunting. The full consequences of the happenings in Paris were not immediately apparent even to the French. In Naples life went on very much as usual. The more liberal among the nobles took heart, but at this time they were unorganised, few in number, and not very practical, more wedded to the mumbo-jumbo of Freemasonry than to the real business of social reform. They had even enjoyed the mild encouragement of Maria Carolina herself. As for the common people, the *lazzaroni*, they remained utterly indifferent to the call of liberty.

For Hamilton life went on in much the same way until France declared war on Great Britain in February 1793. Until that date he continued to occupy himself with the preparation of the volumes illustrating his second collection, with his pictures, the English garden, the behaviour of Vesuvius and the enjoyment and education of Emma. In November 1790 he wrote to the Duke of Leeds asking for leave in the following spring. It was seven years since he had last been in England and his affairs in Wales required his presence. He also hoped 'as a very old and truly attached servant to the King' to have 'infinite satisfaction in being able to have the honor of kissing His Majesty's hand and congratulating His Majesty in person on his most happy and perfect recovery.'[1] The upheaval in France was considered as no impediment to the granting of this request.

Emma, meanwhile, had firmly established herself in Hamilton's affections. He allowed her two hundred pounds a year to keep herself and her mother in clothes, and as she 'long'd for diamonds' he made her a present of five hundred pounds worth of 'single stones of a good water and tolerable size'. She continued her singing and music lessons and Sir William, at least, was satisfied with the result. Others, though generally applauding the Attitudes, were not so unanimous in praising her voice; Lady Palmerston[2] even going so far as to wish that she had never learnt to sing; 'for certainly her talents do not lie that way'. Her progress in French and Italian, on the other hand, was excellent, Hamilton even declaring that she spoke the latter language more correctly than he did. The same, alas, could not be said of her English, but Sir William, like his friend the Earl-Bishop of Derry, was quite enchanted by 'dearest Emma's Dorick dialect'.

The role of mentor, as we have seen, was one that Hamilton delighted in; he was never happier than when forming some young person's mind or guiding their taste and appreciation of the arts. If Emma lacked the intelligence of some of his other pupils he was compensated by the gratitude she showed him and the affection he felt for her. But Emma herself had set her hopes on something more than either diamonds or pearls of wisdom; she had no intention of remaining for ever what Horace Walpole was to describe as 'Sir William Hamilton's Pantomime Mistress'. Time was very soon to show that the threat she had once made to Greville that she would make his uncle marry her had indeed been no idle one. If her gratitude and affection were genuine and sincere so, too, was her ambition; she intended to become Lady Hamilton.

Sir William was certainly aware of this by the spring of 1789. He had just returned from his visit to Puglia which had taken up thirty-two days, twenty of which 'were employ'd in travelling slowly from morning to night thro' a charming country, but the most execrable roads, and without any other accommodation but what we carried with us; for a single man who might sleep every night in a convent the journey would not be so inconvenient, but Emma would be of the party, and she is so good there is no refusing her.' Emma had used this opportunity, while Sir William was away from the distractions of the Court and his official duties, to make some hints in the direction of marriage, for it is in his letter to Greville after their return, written on 26 May, that he first refers to her 'hopes'—hopes which at that time he did not see his way to fulfilling.

'Emma often asks me, do you love me? Ay, but as well as your new appartment?' he wrote. 'Her conduct is such as to gain universal esteem, and she profits daily in musick and language. I endeavour to lose no time in forming her, and certainly she would be welcome to share with me, *on our present footing*, all I have during my life, but I fear her views are beyond what I can bring myself to execute; and that when her hopes on that point are over, that she will make herself and me unhappy; but all this *entre nous*. If ever a separation should be necessary for our mutual happiness, I would settle £150 a year on her and £50 on her mother, who is a very worthy woman. But all this is only thinking aloud to you, and foreseeing that the difference between 57 and 22 may produce events; but, indeed, hitherto her behaviour is irreproachable, but her temper, as you must know unequal.'[3]

His attitude to Emma's hope of marriage was, as one would expect, both reasonable and enlightened considering the general ideas on such matters of the age in which he lived. He was neither angry nor outraged as many of his contemporaries might have been; none the less he had his public position to consider and he did not think that marriage with Emma was compatible with this. He could not act with the freedom of a man in a purely private situation. But he was sympathetic to Emma's point of view as well, and if her disappointment should make them both unhappy then it would be best to part, in which case he would make what financial provision he could for her. But he clearly did not want this to happen; he very sincerely hoped that they would be able to continue on their present footing, and to emphasise this hope he underlined the phrase in his letter to Greville.

Meanwhile rumours began to spread that Sir William and Emma were secretly married. These rumours were certainly current in 1790, if not earlier, for in March 1791 Heneage Legge, then on a visit to Naples with his ailing wife, in a letter to Greville declared that 'last Year' he had met Lord and Lady Elcho in Switzerland who had spent the preceding winter at Naples and had assured him that 'altho' Sir W. H.'s public situation would not permit him to declare it, there was no doubt of his being married to Mrs. H.' Sir Joseph Banks was certainly aware of such rumours early in 1790 and wrote to his old friend to discover whether or not they were true. Hamilton replied on 6 April. Eleven months had passed since he had written to Greville on the same subject but his opinion had not changed. 'To answer your question fairly,' he told Banks, 'was I in a private station I should have no objection that Emma should share with me *le petit bout de vie qui me reste* under the solemn covenant you allude to, as her behaviour in my house has been such for four years as to gain her universal esteem and approbation, but as I have no thoughts of relinquishing my Employment and whilst I am in a public character, I do not look upon myself at liberty to act as I please, and such a step I think wou'd be imprudent and might be attended with disagreeable circumstances—besides, as amidst other branches of natural History I have not neglected the study of the animal called Woman, I have found them subject to great changes according to circumstances and I do not like to try experiments at my time of life. In the way we live we give no Scandal, she with her Mother and I in my apartment, and we have a good Society. What is to be gained on my side? It is very natural for her to wish it, and to try to make people believe the business done, which I suppose has caused the report in England. I assure you that I approve of her so much that if I had been the person that made her first go astray, I wou'd glory in giving her a public reparation, and I would do it openly, for indeed she has infinite merit and no Princess cou'd do the honors of her Palace with more care and dignity than she does those of my house; in short she is worthy of anything, and I have and will take care of her in proportion as I feel myself obliged to her. But as to the Solemn League, *Amplius Considerandum Est.* Now, my Dear Sir, I have more fairly delivered you my Confession than is usually done in this country, of which you may make any discreet use you please. Those who ask out of mere curiosity I shou'd wish to remain in the dark.'[4]

Whether Emma started these rumours of a secret marriage herself it is impossible to say; what is clear from this letter is that she made no effort to deny them. The situation in the Palazzo Sessa was now the reverse of what it had been when she first arrived there. Then the question had been whether or not Emma would become Sir William's mistress; now it was a question of whether Hamilton's genuine desire to do justice to Emma's hopes would triumph over his sense of what was due to his position as the representative of his sovereign at a foreign Court. Emma scored a decided point when in January 1791 she persuaded him to allow her to do the honours at a concert and ball attended by all the foreign ambassadors and their wives. She appeared dressed in white satin, and afterwards wrote in triumph to Greville: 'As it was the first great assembly we had given publickly all the ladies strove to out-do one another in dress and jewels, but Sir William said I was the finest jewel amongst them.' Hamilton may well have looked upon this occasion as a sort of trial run. What Emma did not tell Greville was that her lover had chosen the moment for this experiment at a time when the King and Queen of Naples were absent on a visit to Austria.

Emma passed the test of this public appearance to Hamilton's satisfaction, though Heneage Legge, who observed her with more critical eyes, considered that though she did the honours of the house 'with great attention and desire to please' she none the less lacked refinement of manners, and he wondered that she had not made more progress in this direction in the years she had spent in Naples.

Legge had, in fact, been shocked by what he had seen during the course of his visit, and two months after the diplomatic reception at which Emma had presided he recorded his opinion of her in a letter to Greville which must have given Sir William's nephew some gloomy thoughts. 'Her influence over him exceeds all belief,' he wrote, 'his attachment exceeds admiration, it is perfect dotage. She gives everybody to understand that he is now going to England to sollicit the King's consent to marry her, and that on her return she shall appear as Lady H. She says it is impossible to continue in her present dubious state, which exposes her to frequent slights and mortifications; and his whole thought, happiness and comfort seems so centr'd in her presence, that if she should refuse to return on other terms, I am confident she will gain her point, against which it is the duty of every friend to strengthen his mind as much as possible. . . '

Clearly Emma was bringing all the pressure she could to bear upon Sir William in the hope of influencing his decision. Legge's attempts to dissuade her met with no avail. 'I have all along told her she could never change her situation for the

Sir William Hamilton.
By William Thomas Fry.
National Portrait Gallery, London.

Sir William Hamilton and his First Wife.
By David Allan. Blair Castle, Perthshire.

Dedicatory Plate from Hamilton's 'Greek and Roman Antiquities'.
By courtesy of the Trustees of Sir John Soane's Museum.

Naples from Posillipo.

Plate by Pietro Fabris from Hamilton's 'Campi Phlegraei'. By permission of the British Library.

Venus disarming Cupid, attributed by Hamilton to Correggio.
Reproduced by permission of the late Earl of Radnoor, K.G.

View of Lake Avernus.

Plate by Pietro Fabris from Hamilton's 'Campi Phlegraei'. By permission of the Britsh Library.

Sir William Hamilton in the robes of a Knight of the Bath.
By David Allan.
National Portrait Gallery, London.

Vesuvius in Eruption.
Plate by Pietro Fabris from Hamilton's 'Campi Phlegraei'.
By permission of the British Library.

Sir William Hamilton in 1777.
By Sir Joshua Reynolds.
National Portrait Gallery London.

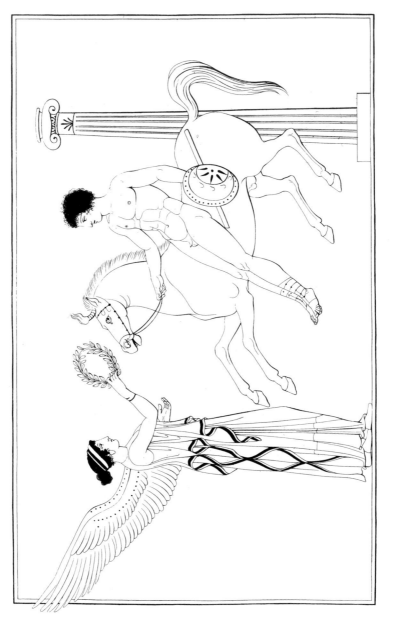

Plate from Hamilton's 'Collection of Engravings from Ancient Vases'.
Photograph by Raymond Earles. By courtesy of the Trustees of Sir John Soane's Museum.

Emma Hart, later Lady Hamilton.
By George Romney.
National Portrait Gallery, London.

Excavation of the Temple of Isis at Pompeii.

Plate by Pietro Fabris from Hamilton's 'Campi Phlegraei'. By permission of the British Library.

Vice-Admiral Viscount Nelson.
By Sir William Beechey.
National Portrait Gallery, London.

The 'Hamilton Vase' from the Hamilton Collection
By permission of the British Museum

better,' he continues in his letter to Greville, 'and that she was a happier woman as Mrs. H[art] than she would be as Lady H., when, more reserved behaviour being necessary, she would be depriv'd of half her amusements, and must no longer sing those comic parts which tend so much to the entertainment of herself and her friends. She does not accede to that doctrine, and unless great care is taken to prevent it I am clear she will in some unguarded hour work upon his empassion'd mind and effect her design of becoming your aunt.'[5] The use of the word 'aunt' in this context must have given Greville a start when he read it. It was not at all what he had bargained for when he had first planned to send Emma out to Naples; least of all an aunt who might at any moment burst into a comic song.

Such arguments as Heneage Legge used had little effect upon Emma for by the time he wrote his letter to Greville she knew that her point was gained. Hamilton, who five years before had confessed 'I am sensible I am not a match for so much youth and beauty' had now, in his turn, been unable to withstand a prolonged siege. Only the King's positive refusal of consent, which was required so long as Sir William remained in the royal service, could now prevent her hopes from being fulfilled. When she hinted that he would seek this royal permission during his forthcoming leave, she spoke no more than the truth.

There can be little doubt that Hamilton would rather have left things as they were. There was no reason on his side to make him wish to alter the sensible arrangement he had outlined in his letter to Sir Joseph Banks, but Emma's pride and ambition made her no longer content with any other position than that of wife. The education which Charles Greville had started and Sir William had continued gave her a new assurance, but also a keener sense of her dubious state; while the doting devotion which surrounded her shielded her from criticism. She really thought that she could pass muster in a fault-finding world as Lady Hamilton. It would have surprised her to hear the view of Frederick Hervey who counted himself as one of her partisans. 'Take her as anything but Mrs. Hart, and she is a superior being,' the Earl-Bishop had said, 'as herself, she is always vulgar.'

What had really won Emma her point was Sir William's innate sense of justice. She had been a good mistress to him; she had striven hard to improve herself; and she had never given him cause for jealousy despite 'the difference between 57 and 22'. Hamilton was very sensitive on this point, for one of his very earliest fears had been that he might be exposed to ridicule should the young English travellers 'endeavour to cuckold the old gentleman their ambassador'. On this delicate score Emma had never given him a moment's uneasiness. If she could show her gratitude, so too could he. He would certainly rather they continued on their present footing but he felt that Emma had earned some right to what she asked. He came to his decision with some reluctance, much as he had come to his original decision to ask Emma to join him in Naples, and his consent had one condition upon which he insisted: the King must agree. Hamilton neither wished, nor could he afford, to abandon his profession.

The month of April 1791 saw Hamilton, Emma, and Mrs. Cadogan on their way to England. They travelled overland across Europe. In Florence a letter was waiting from William Beckford; he was in Paris and wrote, somewhat prematurely as events would soon show, 'The reign of grim Gothic prejudices is nearly over, and people begin to serve God and themselves in the manner they like best.' Here also they met the King and Queen of Naples who were returning from Vienna, and it was in Florence that Sir William took formal leave of them. He was also presented to Maria Carolina's brother Leopold whom he had previously known as Grand Duke of Tuscany, but who had succeeded to the Imperial throne the year before. Leopold's succession had been due to the death, in his forty-ninth year, of Joseph II, who had once hoped to see Sir William as British ambassador at his Court. Later on in their journey they were to have another strange encounter, a reminder of the still unresolved state of the royal house of France. The Count d'Artois, brother of Louis XVI, one of the first princes to emigrate, was in Venice when Hamilton and his party arrived there. The future Charles X passed an evening with Sir William who found him 'very easy, polite, and agreeable'.

The party reached London at the end of May, and the first part of the leave was taken up by Hamilton in attending to his business affairs. This took him to Wales to visit his property there, which Greville had been managing in his absence. The journey was broken at Fonthill where Sir William stayed as the guest of his kinsman William Beckford, now back from France. It was also on this leave that he was to receive his last public honour when he was sworn a member of the Privy Council. It was a recognition of twenty-five years' faithful service in his post at Naples.

If Emma's departure for Naples five years previously had caused some little interest, her arrival now in Sir William's company caused a good deal more. Rumours that they would marry had been whispered for long enough for there to be considerable curiosity about the young woman who had previously been known, if at all, as Greville's mistress or Romney's model, and by a few with longer memories as a former priestess of the Temple of Health. Society ladies were no less eager than their husbands to see the Attitudes, and as Sir William knew that their effect seldom failed to please, it was in the character of the 'Nymph of Attitudes' that he generally and wisely chose to introduce Emma into the critical and not necessarily charitable circles in which he hoped to win her acceptance.

In August they were in Bath where Emma met the Duchess of Devonshire. Lady Elizabeth Foster was present and noted her impressions of 'the celebrated Mrs. Hart' in her diary. She began by quoting Lord Charlemont who had declared that Emma's Attitudes had 'found out a new source of pleasure to mankind'. With regard to the Attitudes Lady Elizabeth agreed; 'every one was perfect—everything she did was just and beautiful,' but her singing was dismissed as 'a secondary talent and performance'. Though the comic songs (the thought of which had so alarmed Heneage Legge) were 'inimitable from expressions and vivacity' Lady

Elizabeth's general verdict was not favourable: 'Her serious singing appeared to me not good—her voice is strong, she is well taught, yet has a forced expressions and vivacity', Lady Elizabeth's general verdict: 'wants flexibility.' As to Emma when not either singing or attitudising, 'her conversation, though perfectly good-natured and unaffected, was uninteresting, and her pronunciation very vulgar.' Could this be, Lady Elizabeth asked herself, because until the age of nineteen the unfortunate young woman had lived in the lowest situation, and since then in 'no higher one than the mistress of Sir W. Hamilton'?

Against Lady Elizabeth Foster's criticism of Emma's singing can be set the opinion of Horace Walpole. He did not very much approve of his friend Hamilton's behaviour in exhibiting his mistress's talents in the houses of their various friends, but curiosity compelled him to see for himself what the 'pantomime' was like, and he went to hear her sing and perform her Attitudes at the Duke of Queensberry's. He was completely won over. 'Oh! but she sings admirably,' he wrote to Mary Berry, 'has a very fine strong voice; is an excellent buffa, and an astonishing tragedian; and then her Attitudes are a whole theatre of grace and various expressions.'[6]

Not everyone, however, was charmed by the Attitudes. Among those who wrote asking for the privilege of witnessing this display was Sir James Bland Burges, the Foreign Under-Secretary of State. Hamilton replied on 20 September to his colleague's request, and asked him to be present in Romney's studio the following Sunday. Sir James appeared not to be edified by what he saw. In a few lines written on the back of Hamilton's letter he noted how, in the five years she had lived in Naples, Emma had become accomplished in music and languages 'while at the same time she improved her skill in attitudes by the study of antique figures, from which she learned a variety of the most voluptuous and indecent postures'. Sir James Burges is the only witness who ever suggested that there was anything even mildly indecent in the Attitudes. Perhaps he was very easily shocked, or perhaps he had not quite recovered from the shock of disapproval at what happened almost immediately after his visit to Romney's studio, for the Under-Secretary ends his note: 'two days after he invited me to see her, he married her and took her back with him to the Court of Naples as Lady Hamilton, the wife of His Majesty's Envoy Extraordinary and Minister Plenipotentiary.'[7]

The wedding, which shocked Sir James Burges almost as much as the Attitudes, took place on 6 September, but before the ceremony could be solemnised Hamilton had to obtain the King's permission. George III had no objection to his old foster-brother marrying again, but in view of the lady's past he did not think that he could ask the Queen to receive her at Court. This meant that Emma could have no official position at Naples. She would be the wife of Sir William Hamilton, but she would not hold the rank of Ambassadress of Great Britain. She was never to enjoy this position though she often gave herself ambassadorial airs, and even once, in a letter to Greville, was to refer to her mother, the worthy Mrs. Cadogan, as *La Signora Madre dell'Ambasciatrice*, as though she could not confine her magnificence to herself. But this was mere *folie de grandeur* on Emma's part; an affliction to which she would become increasingly subject as time passed.

At the moment, however, no one was taking Emma very seriously. If Queen Charlotte shuddered at the thought of her past, the King found the situation more diverting and chaffed Hamilton on the subject of his pretty young friend, making a pleasant joke of the whole thing. Emma herself was with Sir William's favourite niece while he was away at Windsor. Mary Hamilton had now become Mrs. Dickenson, and on 29 August she wrote to her husband on the subject of her guest: 'She read me a very affect. letter of his [Sir William's] from Windsor. The King joked him about Em. at a distance and gave a hint that he thought he was not quite so religious as when he married the late Lady H.'[8] In this cheerful atmosphere the royal consent was given. It was the last occasion upon which Sir William Hamilton and George III would meet in this warm and friendly spirit.

Sir William and Emma were married very quietly at Marylebone Parish Church on the morning of 6 September 1791. The witnesses were Lord Abercorn, a kinsman of Sir William's, and Mr. L. Dutens, secretary to the British Ministry at Turin. Emma was married in her true name of Amy Lyon and the ceremony was performed by the Rector of Elsdon in Northumberland. Neither Mrs. Cadogan nor Charles Greville took any official part in the ceremony and there is no record of their having been present.

The marriage caused no great stir. Sir William had very wisely postponed the ceremony until the end of his leave so that Emma was spared any of the unpleasantnesses she might have had to face from the more strait-laced and disapproving members of society. Horace Walpole's comment was typical of the mixture of amusement and indifference with which the news was received: 'Sir William Hamilton', he told Miss Berry on 11 September, 'has actually married his Gallery of Statues, and they are set out on their return to Naples.' Letters from old friends followed them on their journey; Lord Pembroke referred to 'your lovely Lady H', and his old school fellow the Earl-Bishop of Derry wrote to congratulate Hamilton 'upon the fortitude you have shown and the manly part you have taken in braving the world and securing your own happiness and elegant enjoyment in defiance of them'.

Even the press found very little to say that was disagreeable, though earlier in their leave the *Morning Herald* had felt itself obliged to inform its readers that 'Mrs. Hart, the celebrated *élève* of Sir William Hamilton K.B., of whose feminine graces and musical accomplishments all Europe resounds, was but a few years back the inferior housemaid of Mrs. Linley of Norfolk Street, in the Strand.' The only really unkind comment came from the pen of Dr. John Wolcot who, as 'Peter Pindar', had previously cast poetic doubts on the genuine antiquity of Sir William's 'mugs and gods' when these had been purchased for the British Museum. His *Lyric Epistle to Sir William Hamilton*, written at the time of the marriage, was even less complimentary:

O Knight of Naples, is it come to pass
That thou has left the gods of *stone* and *brass*,
To wed a Deity of *flesh* and *blood*?
O lock the temple with thy strongest key,
For fear thy Deity, a *comely* She,
Should one day ramble in a frolic mood—

For since the Idols of a *youthful* King,
So very volatile indeed, take wing;
If *his* to wicked wanderings can incline,
Lord! who would answer, poor old Knight, for *thine*?
Yet should thy Grecian Goddess fly thy fane,
I think that we should catch her in Hedge-Lane.

The sting of these verses was undoubtedly in the tail, for Hedge Lane, it must be pointed out, was then a well-known haunt of prostitutes.

More annoying to Emma than these attacks, however, was the blow to her pride when she learnt that she would not be received at Court, for if the forbidding Queen Charlotte refused to receive her in England it would be contrary to etiquette for the more easy going Maria Carolina to receive her officially in Naples. This was, for Emma, the one unsatisfactory note in her triumph, and she even tried to persuade people (as Lady Elizabeth Foster recorded) that she had never lived with Sir William a his mistress. 'I was under the protection of his roof,' Lady Elizabeth reported her as saying, 'my mother was with me, and we were married in private two years before he married me openly in England.' Emma's desire for respectability was understandable, but she could hardly expect people to believe such stories as this.

For the most part, however, she had nothing to complain about. Whatever might be lacking in her official status no one could deny that she was now Lady Hamilton. There were moments when she could hardly believe it herself. 'Ah, Madam,' she wrote to her husband's niece Mary three weeks after the wedding, 'how much do I owe to your dear Uncle. I feel every moment my obligation to him and am always afraid I can never do enough for him. . . I say to myself, Am I his Wife, and I can never separate more. Am I Emma Hamilton? It seems impossible I can be so happy. Surely no person was ever so happy as I am.'[9] One person certainly was not, and that was the other Emma, the child born nearly ten years ago and now living in north Wales. Her mother had not bothered to visit her. Only Greville, who had looked after the child's welfare, and Mrs. Cadogan, her grandmother, made the journey north to visit this lonely reminder of the days of 'the wild unthinking Emma'.

If Hamilton himself had agreed somewhat reluctantly to make Emma his wife he was now prepared to make the best of being her husband, and determined, with true eighteenth-century optimism, to see only the bright side of the picture. She is really an extraordinary being', he wrote to Walpole after his return to Naples, 'and most grateful to me for having saved her from the precipice into which she had good sense enough to see she must without me have inevitably fallen, and she sees that nothing but a constant good conduct can maintain the respect that is now shown her by everybody. It has often been remarked that a reformed rake makes a good husband. *Why not vice versa?*'[10] This was at least frank, and refreshingly free from romantic self-deception.

Sir William and his bride passed through Paris on their way back to Naples. Though France had officially become a constitutional monarchy earlier in the month (the new constitution was passed by the National Assembly on 3 September) the days of the royal family were in fact numbered. News of the Hamiltons in this capital of revolution came to England in a letter from Sir William's old friend Lord Palmerston, written to his wife on 14 September. 'Sir William and Lady Hamilton are arrived at this hotel and are to stay here a few days. I have been introduced to her and had the good luck to be the means, by speaking to Monsr. Noailles, of getting them placed yesterday in the Assembly. She is very handsome but not elegant, her face is very much like what I have seen in a fine old portrait and she wears her hair something in that style. She seems very good humoured, very happy and very attentive to him. . . '[11]

Emma scored a minor triumph in Paris when Marie Antoinette received her. Very possibly the Queen of France, who had other things to think about, was unaware that Sir William's wife had not been presented to the Queen of England. More probably she decided that times were past when a mere matter of etiquette could be allowed to let her miss the chance of getting a message through to her sister in Naples. No difficulties were made over Emma's presentation and she was entrusted by the Queen with a letter to Maria Carolina, an unconscious kindness on the part of Marie Antoinette for it opened the door to Emma's own reception at the Neapolitan Court.

Maria Carolina, as things turned out, put up no more than a token resistance to receiving the wife of the British Minister. Sir Charles Blagden[12] passed on a rumour to Lord Palmerston that Sir William had resolved not to attend the Court at Caserta when no notice was taken there of Emma after her return from England as Lady Hamilton, and that on account of this a report went about London that he had been recalled. 'However,' Sir Charles explained, 'some days after, a messenger was sent importing that the Queen would be glad to see Lady Hamilton, in consequence of which, a time was settled for her presentation and they are both to spend the holiday at Caserta with the Royal Family.'

It is most unlikely that Sir William would have risked his political career in this way. He knew perfectly well that his wife could only be received by the Queen in a private capacity, and was quite agreeable to this condition as Emma's obvious unsuitability to act as ambassadress had been his own chief objection when she had first wished to marry him. As he assured Sir James Burges after his return: 'She is totally indipendant of the Diplomatic line.' He made no attempt to have her received at Court except as the wife of a private individual. This is clear enough from a letter to Mary Dickens on written on 15 January 1792. Hamilton had nothing to hide from this favourite niece: 'The Queen of Naples,' he told her, 'informed of all my proceedings, told me she wou'd see my Wife, tho' she could not acknowledge her as the Wife of the English Minister, and she received her most kindly. Emma very naturally told her whole story and that all her desire was by her future conduct to shew her gratitude to me, and to prove to the world that a young, beautiful Woman, tho' of obscure birth, cou'd have noble sentiments and act properly in the great World. In short the Queen of N. is quite fond of her and has taken her under her protection.'[13]

Shortly after returning to Naples Emma wrote to Romney that she was now 'the happiest woman in the World'. She had been an excellent mistress to Sir William and for some years she would be a good wife; but marriage did not have a good effect on her character. Gradually she began to give herself airs of grandeur; she developed an exaggerated notion of the importance of her position; she became intolerant and passionate in her views and managed to persuade herself, as she attempted to persuade others, that she had an important political role to play. She brought little dignity to her husband's career, and ended by becoming rather ridiculous. Hamilton remained touchingly loyal to her. He had married her out of kindness; he would have been wiser to have left matters as they were.

1. B.M. Add. MSS 41199, f. 74.
2. Wife of the second Viscount Palmerston.
3. Morrison, 177.
4. B.M. Add. MSS 34048 f. 61.
5. Morrison, 190.
6. Walpole: Letters, Vol. IX, p. 340.
7. Fitzwilliam Museum: Percival Bequest MSS.
8. E. and F. Anson: *Mary Hamilton*, p. 312.
9. E. and F. Anson: *Mary Hamilton*, p. 315.
10. Morrison, 208.
11. B. Connell: *Portrait of a Whig Peer*, p. 248.
12. Blagden had been Secretary of the Royal Society since 1784.
13. E. and F. Anson: *Mary Hamilton*, p. 317.

CHAPTER XVII

The Struggle Against France

Though some observors considered that Hamilton doted a little too much on Emma or, as Lady Palmerston put it, that 'she and Sir William are rather too fond', he was under no romantic illusions about his marriage when he discussed it with an old friend like Sir Joseph Banks. 'Lady Hamilton has nothing to do with my public character but Their Sicilian Majesties are so good as to receive and treat her as any other Travelling Lady of distinction,' he wrote to Banks in March 1792. 'She has gained the hearts of all, even of the Ladies, by her humility and proper behaviour, and we shall I dare say go on well. I will allow with you that 99 times in a hundred such a step as I took would be very imprudent, but I know my way here, and here I mean to pass the most of the days that I can have a chance of living. Without a Woman you can have no society at home and I am sure you will hear from every quarter of the Comforts of my house.'[1]

This matter-of-fact viewpoint was very much in line with Sir William's philosophy of life as he outlined it at this time to Emma: 'My study of antiquities has kept me in constant thought of the perpetual fluctuation of everything. The whole art is, really, to live all the *days* of our life; and not, with anxious care, disturb the sweetest hour that life affords—which is, the present. Admire the Creator and all his works, to us incomprehensible; and do all the good you can upon earth; and take the chance of eternity without dismay.'[2] His outlook remained hedonistic; he lived for the moment, and the passing pleasure of the hour, but he believed in equipping himself to enjoy that pleasure to the full. For the rest he relied on a simple Deism and an enlightened sense of duty to see him through.

One way Emma fitted into this scheme was to keep her husband amused as well as to preside over the comforts of his house. While he always encouraged her in the now rather perfunctory efforts she still made at improving her mind he also derived considerable pleasure from the frivolity and naïveté of her nature; and what many people dismissed in her as shallowness or vulgarity he clearly found highly entertaining. Lady Palmerston, an acute observer, noted this when she met the Hamiltons again in March 1793. 'Lady H. is to me very surprising', she wrote, 'for considering the situation she was in she behaves wonderfully well. Now and then to be sure a little vulgarness pops out, but I think it's more Sir William's fault, who loves a good joke and leads her to enter into his stories, which are not of the best kind. She is vastly desirous to please and is very civil and good humoured to all her friends and her attention to Sir William is infinitely amiable.'[3]

Almost the moment that Hamilton returned from leave he found himself, in December 1791, entertaining one of the sons of his Sovereign. Prince Augustus, later Duke of Sussex, the sixth son of George III, was then on a visit to Italy. The Prince was eighteen years old and like all the children of King George and Queen Charlotte was highly susceptible. This fact alone made the visit something of a liability to the Minister responsible for his safety, and Sir William was required to send back a confidential report on the Prince's behaviour. The recipient of these letters was, by an odd chance, the same Sir James Burges who had professed to be so scandalised by the 'indecent postures' of the young woman who was now Lady Hamilton.

The reason for these confidential reports can easily be guessed from the first, which was dated 7 December, and went straight to the point: 'As I write to you without reserve and trust to your prudence to communicate as much or as little as you think fit', Hamilton wrote, 'I must tell you that if it is true, as I have been inform'd, that an inclination which Prince Augustus shew'd some time ago for Lady Anne Hatton at Florence had not been approved of at Home, Lord Hervey has not acted prudently or wisely in having brought this lady herself as far as the Gates of Rome and having sent her forward to Naples where she arrived two days before H.R.H. She lives with her sister Lady Eliz. Monk and the Prince is often at their house. As Lady Anne Hatton has been living publickly with Lord Hervey at Florence, most of the English Ladies at Naples have not returned her visit and decline all connection with her.'[4]

The English ladies in Naples formed themselves into a solid phalanx against Lady Anne when they learnt of her unconventional conduct in Tuscany, though it had been very little different (except for the fact that she made no attempt to conceal it and had no complacent parent to pose as a chaperon) from the position of Emma Hamilton only a few months previously in Naples, for Lord Hervey occupied the post of British Minister at Florence. Lady Anne had, however, thrown discretion to the winds; and though the fact that she had lived 'publickly' with Lord Hervey might have been overlooked, setting her cap at Prince Augustus was quite another thing. The other ladies decided on a boycott. 'Many of the English Ladies. . . ' Sir William duly reported on 24 January, 'have not returned the visit of Lady A. Hatton on account of their not having approved of her conduct in Tuscany. She endeavour'd to persuade the Prince on that account to take no notice of these ladies but on the contrary I see with pleasure that H.R.H. is much more in company with these ladies than in her Ladyship's.'

It looked as though the danger had been averted. The Prince, meanwhile, was certainly a success in Naples. At his own request he lived quite independently of the Court, observed 'a most regular life', and, in Hamilton's opinion, 'his goodness and affability gains the hearts of all who have the honour of approaching him.' By

27 February, Sir William was able to report, with a sigh of relief, that 'Lady A.H. has continued her attacks on the Prince but He has very wisely kept clear of her and lives with the English Ladies Malmesbury, Plymouth, and Mrs. Legge, where Lady Anne has not access. In short, it is not possible for a young man to conduct himself with more propriety than the Prince has done here.'

Sir William's troubles were not yet over, however; the Prince's malady had simply moved from his heart to his stomach. In the same confidential report Hamilton noted: 'On Sunday last at my house I observed that H.R.H. was paler than usual and remarkably chilly. He went home early in the evening and took an Emetick which he likewise repeated yesterday, and finds himself greatly releaved today, which shews that his slight indisposition proceeded from the Stomach not from any return of his former complaint. I have mentioned nothing of H.R.H.'s indisposition in my dispatch, nor do I believe that the Prince wishes it should be mention'd at home, but to fulfill my promise to you I tell you exactly what I know.'

The Prince's condition did not improve as quickly as had been hoped, and by early March his illness was described as being 'a Rheumatic Fever'. From this he in due course made a complete recovery; his doctor, on the other hand, was less fortunate. This young man, who though a German, was called Murray, grew alarmed at the disorder and, on the advice of Baron Hanstein, the Prince's chief attendant, called in the aid of Dr. Cutunio, one of the Court Physicians. The Italian doctor confirmed his diagnosis, but Murray grew jealous, thinking that the Prince had more confidence in Cutunio than in himself and, in Hamilton's phrase, 'worked himself up into a sort of despair, tho' Cutunio had approved of all he had done'.

The tragic sequel was described by Sir William in a letter to Burges dated 6 March. Baron Hanstein and one of his companions imagined that they had calmed Murray's mind 'but unfortunately it proved otherwise, for not coming down to breakfast at the usual hour on Sunday morning, and their finding his door locked and no answer returned when called, a ladder was placed to the window and the unfortunate young man was found dead having cut his throat with a razor from ear to ear. In this cruel dilemma Baron Hanstein (whose calm prudence I cannot sufficiently praise) took every precaution that this unhappy accident should be kept a secret from the Prince until H.R.H. shou'd be perfectly recover'd. Cutunio sent one of his aides to attend the Prince constantly, the Prince having been told that Mr. Murray was ill in bed, and Baron Hanstein and I agreed to ask Their Sicilian Majesties' friendly assistance that the body of Mr. Murray might be got out of the House and every precaution taken to avoid the Prince's being alarmed. Every assistance was given by the Court and yesterday the body was removed. Thank God in the midst of all this confusion Prince Augustus's fever is taking a very favourable turn and Cutunio does not doubt that H.R.H. will be perfectly recovered in a few days.'

A week later Hamilton completed his account of this sad business. 'I have only to assure you,' he told Burges, 'as in my Dispatch, that I think Prince Augustus perfectly recovered. He is told Mr. Murray is removed from Portici to Naples on account of his fever being putrid, but will not be acquainted with the shocking accident until the last moment. The poor man was certainly mad—he had cut the arteries of his thighs, wrists, and his throat at the same moment and left his intention in writing, so that there was no room for doubt. This government lent every friendly assistance that the Prince might not be alarmed during his illness, but the necessary process has prevented this being a secret at Naples, and I believe Prince Augustus is the only person that does not know it.'

What with the Prince's amorous proclivities, his illness, and his doctor's suicide, Sir William must have been glad when Prince Augustus finally left Naples. Later that year, in September 1792, he remarked, in a further letter to Sir James Burges, that the Prince had talked of spending the winter in Naples, but Hamilton showed no great enthusiasm at the prospect; indeed there is a note of relief rather than resignation in his comment that 'as I have not heard from H.R.H. I suppose he will not come so far'.

While the British Minister had been entertaining the young son of George III the Neapolitan government, now dominated by General Acton, had been trying to make up its mind whether to receive the envoy of France, who had been cooling his heels in Naples for some time. The plight of the French royal family, so closely related to the Neapolitan sovereigns, had caused Ferdinand and Maria Carolina alternating bouts of fury and alarm. In July the Duke of Brunswick had issued his threatening declaration that he would destroy Paris if the royal family were harmed, but the old hero of the Seven Years War was unable to back his threats with force. Sir William, a veteran of that war, wrote hopefully to Burges: 'What horrid news we receive by every post from Paris! What a contrast between the present situation of Great Britain and France! I am fully acquainted with the Duke of Brunswick and have a thorough confidence in his consummate ability and military experience.'

Only a month, later, however, the Court of Naples had to receive the man who, though still officially representing Louis XVI, in fact represented his jailors. 'Yesterday', Hamilton wrote in a dispatch to Lord Grenville dated 24 August, 'Monsieur Mackau presented his credential letters to His Sicilian Majesty as *Ministre Plenipotentiaire du Roi des français*. He was, I have been informed, received very cooly, and he will probably pass his time very ill at Naples, as the nobility in general are determined not to take any notice of him, having the character of being a violent democrate (*sic*), and the unprincipled proceedings of that party in France has caused them to be very justly abhorred here.'[5]

The presence of a French Minister made for a good deal of confusion in Neapolitan society, especially among the undeclared sympathisers with the revolution. In the months before and after the battle of Valmy their hopes rose and fell with the fortunes of France, which on 22 September had thrown aside the pretence of a constitutional monarchy and proclaimed itself a republic, as a result of which the position of Monsieur Mackau once again became a highly equivocal one. For Sir William, who had for many years been Doyen of the Diplomatic Corps, the situation was far from easy. Mackau himself did nothing to help. He appeared at the San Carlo opera house wearing the uniform of the national guard 'to defy the Queen in public', an act which he could hardly hope would endear him to his diplomatic colleagues; and he had the Bourbon lilies cast down from his official residence and the cap of liberty put up in their place. Towards the end of the year illness removed Hamilton from these embarrassing scenes. If it had been a 'diplomatic illness' no one would have been surprised, but in fact it was the first serious illness of his life.

Hamilton had been very fortunate in the excellent health he had enjoyed for so many years, but he was now sixty-two years old and had made few concessions to advancing age. Emma, who nursed him through this illness, declared that it had been long gathering and was a liver complaint. Fortunately they were at Caserta, away from the bustle of the capital, when he was finally compelled to take to his bed where he remained for fifteen days in a bilious fever. In reporting the news to 'my dear Mr. Greville' as she now, with the air of a *grande dame*, called her former lover, Emma said that for eight days she watched him 'without undressing, eating, or sleeping'. She certainly nursed Sir William with devotion but her letter to Greville shows that even in the crisis of her husband's illness she could not resist adding a note of drama to the situation: 'the King and Queen sent constantly morning and evening the most flattering messages, but all was nothing to me. What could console me for the loss of such a husband, friend and protector? For surely no happiness is like ours. We live but for one another. But I was too happy. I had imagined I was never more to be unhappy. . . '6 As he read these lines Greville had to remind himself that the letter was to inform him of his uncle's convalescence and not of his death.

It was a dangerous illness, causing alarm to his friends, but with Emma to care for him (her histrionics were reserved for others) he soon began to improve. In the early months of 1793 he was able to tell his nephew that he felt better and more alive than for some years past. This was just as well, for in the next few years he would need all his strength. The political situation was getting rapidly worse. While Sir William was convalescing at Caserta the Neapolitan government had been publicly humiliated when a French naval squadron had sailed into the bay and remained at anchor for twenty-eight hours, very menacing and unwelcome guests. The fleet had scarcely gone before a storm had driven them back again. While the battered ships were being repaired the French admiral gave encouragement and open support to the revolutionary elements in the city who, emerging from their obscurity, enjoyed a brief and intoxicating hour of triumph. As a final insult to his hosts the admiral chose King Ferdinand's birthday, 12 January, to give a banquet on board his flagship at which toasts were drunk to the French republic, odes to liberty chanted, and the extermination of tyrants proclaimed.

The French fleet had hardly sailed before word reached Naples of the execution of Louis XVI. The news was received with horror and widespread grief, which did not confine itself to the circles near the Court. There was general gloom and despondency, the representative of the French republic alone making himself conspicuous by refusing to wear mourning. Eleven days later, on 1 February 1793, France declared war on Great Britain to the unconcealed delight of Maria Carolina whose fury against the French, and anxiety for the safety of her sister Marie Antoinette, knew no bounds.

A few days after the declaration of war, but before the news of it could have reached him, Hamilton sent a secret and confidential report to Lord Grenville on the state of the Kingdom of the Two Sicilies. This dispatch, which was dated 4 February, is important for the light it throws on Sir William's view of the Neapolitan sovereigns and government, which was by no means one of uncritical approval. He was personally attached to Ferdinand and Maria Carolina but by no means blind to their faults, and he was still as conscious as he ever had been of the need for a reform of almost every part of the royal government.

After the war had started all Hamilton's energy would be centred in keeping Naples in the struggle against France or in ensuring its benevolent neutrality. This duty took priority over all others; it was no longer a time to criticise but rather one to conciliate, to flatter and to encourage. For this reason it has often been thought that Sir William Hamilton approved of all he saw in Naples and exercised his ambassadorial mission with the blind zeal of a sycophantic courtier. Though allowances must be made for his increasing hostility to the ideas of the French revolution, his eyes were as open now as they had been in the past to the many imperfections of the *régime* under which the subjects of Ferdinand IV were compelled to live.

He began his dispatch by repeating his now familiar opinion of the King, for whom he had grown to have a rather grudging respect, and went on to discuss the position of the Queen, still all powerful in matters of government, and the Chief Minister, who had recently, rather surprisingly, succeeded to an English title: 'To best of my judgement His Sicilian Majesty, accustomed to a life of continued dissipation, gives but little attention to the affairs of State, which are transacted chiefly by the Queen and General Acton. His Majesty by the goodness of his heart and great affability has certainly gained the love of all his subjects but they regret his not trusting more to his own judgement, as whenever he does take upon himself to decide, it is always on the right side, as His Majesty is certainly not deficient in understanding and is thoroughly inclined to do justice on all occasions.

'The Queen is by no means popular, but as her power is evident, is greatly fear'd. No one doubts of the capacity or the integrity of General Acton but they complain, and I fear with some reason, that having taken upon himself almost every department of the State, he has not time (Tho' a perfect Slave to business) to transact the half of that which he has undertaken, and which being left to the corrupt clerks in his office causes much clamour and discontent. His uncle, a British Baronet, died last year and left him his house and a part of his estate, and being the immediate heir to the title he is now Sir John Acton, of which he is not a little proud, and I have reason to think that he is meditating his retreat from an elevated but perilous situation to his quiet family seat in Shropshire.'

Acton's English title was to cause a good deal of confusion in Italy; the republicans and 'patriots' were later to claim that it had been bestowed on him for secretly promoting British interests in Naples. After dealing with this interesting topic Sir William concluded his dispatch with an account of the political situation which was hardly complimentary to Acton's administration, despite the good opinion in which he held Sir John Acton as a man. It showed that Hamilton was well aware of the discontent that lay beneath the calm surface of Neapolitan society, and feared the dangers that could result from a too complacent or a too repressive attitude of government.

'The Neapolitans', the dispatch ends, 'have certainly an utter aversion to the French, but the late transactions in France have opened their eyes. They are now sensible that in this country justice does not exist, that the Government of it is very defective, and that the people have a right not to be trampled on. So that if this Government does not speedily and seriously set about a reform in all its branches, the general discontent now silently brooding will probably, sooner or later, break out into open violence. Nature has certainly done more for the Kingdom of the Two Sicilies than for any kingdom in Europe, and yet I have been witness myself of more misery and poverty among the inhabitants of some of its richest Provinces than I ever saw in the whole course of my travels.[7]

This was the last time that Hamilton would be able to make an appraisal of affairs in Naples that was not conditioned by the necessities of war. As an indictment of the civil administration of the country it could hardly have gone further with its plain acknowledgement that justice was non-existent, government defective, and the people trampled underfoot. It may be asked why, knowing this sorry state of affairs, Sir William reacted so violently against the rebels who wanted to see all these things changed. One reason, as has been pointed out, was because they were identified with the enemies of his country, but the main reason was one of temperament. Hamilton was a disciple of the Enlightenment, but like many of the people who supported the ideas of the *Philosophes*, when it came to a question of practical application he was deeply conservative. He also combined with an inherent belief in legitimacy an aristocratic abhorrence of the mob. He believed that revolution (and nothing that had happened in France had made him change his mind) merely substituted one form of tyranny for another, and that of these two forms of tyranny the mob was the worse, for while a despot might show benevolence the mob was always predatory. He still believed that it was the business of the government to reform itself and not of other people to reform the government.

From now on, however, all questions of reform were swept aside. With the opening of hostilities against France the Mediterranean became a main theatre of war so far as Great Britain was concerned, and Sir William suddenly found himself in a post of importance.

In April he began preliminary negotiations with Acton for a treaty of alliance between their two countries. For the first time in the twenty-eight years that he had been Envoy at Naples dispatches were brought to him by King's Messenger, and the event caused such interest that he had to pretend that the Messenger was carrying letters for Prince Augustus (who was then in Rome) in order to allay curiosity. In June Sir William received a dispatch announcing that the Secretary of State had the King's command to transmit to him 'a Full Power under the Great Seal' to negotiate a treaty with the King of the Two Sicilies, and the treaty was duly signed on 12 July. By the terms negotiated between Hamilton and Acton the Neapolitan merchant fleet was to receive the protection of the British Navy and all trade with France was forbidden. Naples was not to conclude a separate peace without the consent of Great Britain, but if this consent was given and Britain continued fighting then Naples was to observe a strict neutrality. As to the actual hostilities, Britain promised to keep a fleet in the Mediterranean during the period of emergency, and the King of Naples agreed to supply six thousand troops, four ships of the line, four frigates and four lesser vessels for action in the Mediterranean.

The day after the treaty was signed Hamilton wrote to Sir James Burges at the Foreign Office: 'I flatter myself that the next three months will be rich in events and that by our carrying On the war with such vigour a speedy end will be put to it. Our admiral will surely be pleased with the little additional force this Court will give him, for General Acton has really done wonders in the Marine, but their frigates are better than their Line of Battle Ships. All that I can assure you is that this Court is highly sensible of the general manner in which our Government has acted and I am convinced will be happy to show its gratitude on all occasions.' The time for optimism was not yet over.

After the treaty was signed the traditional exchange of presents took place. Hamilton was told that a snuff-box with the King's portrait 'enriched with diamonds' was being ordered for each of the three Neapolitan plenipotentiaries who had signed the treaty with him, and that he was to present these to them in the name of King George. He was also informed that the King had been pleased to direct 'the usual present of £500' for the Neapolitan Department of Foreign Affairs.[8] He had to wait until November for his own present from King Ferdinand. It consisted of that far from handsome monarch's features on a tortoise-shell box set with three rows of diamonds which the Court jeweller assured him had cost the King three thousand ducats, a sum Hamilton computed as being between five and six hundred pounds. He was also shown the box intended for the British Foreign Secretary which was nearly twice as rich. It was the first time in all his long years in the Foreign Service that Sir William had been able to share in the spoils of diplomacy.

As a result of the treaty signed by Hamilton and Acton the bay of Naples was to receive another naval visit, not, on this occasion, from a hostile fleet, but from a single friendly ship. On the evening of 11 September 1793, Captain Horatio Nelson, commanding His Britannic Majesty's ship *Agamemnon*, reported his first sight of Mount Vesuvius, and the next day was rowed ashore with dispatches for Sir William from Lord Hood, commander-in-chief of the Mediterranean fleet. After the humiliations of the visit of the French squadron the sight of a friendly flag was doubly welcome and the English sea-officer was greeted with unusual cordiality. Because of this, and because the *Agamemnon* was the first British man-of-war to enter the port of Naples since the two countries had entered into an alliance, Hamilton decided to break with his usual custom and offered Nelson the hospitality of the Palazzo Sessa. He was given the room which had been prepared for Prince Augustus.

Two weeks before Nelson appeared in the bay Admiral Hood had occupied Toulon and was now urgently in need of the troops and ships promised by the Neapolitans under the terms of the treaty. The purpose of Nelson's visit was to arrange for the dispatch of these reinforcements with all possible speed. With Hamilton he called on General Acton and matters were quickly settled between them though Nelson seems to have had less faith in the promises of his new allies than in the business-like qualities of the British Minister. 'I should be wanting', he noted in his private journal, 'did I not say how active Sir William Hamilton has been in getting these troops sent off, for left to themselves I am sure they would not have sailed these three weeks. . . ' Acton was insistent that the Neapolitan forces should serve only under Lord Hood, and not under a Spanish or Sardinian commander.

During the course of the four days he spent in Naples Nelson was received very flatteringly by the King, who insisted that the English captain should sit at his right hand at a dinner given in his honour at the Palazzo Reale. Ferdinand declared that the British Fleet were the saviours of Italy and of his own kingdom in particular, which was certainly very gratifying though not what Nelson had come to hear. He was not presented to the Queen as Maria Carolina was in the last stages of one of her innumerable pregnancies and was not appearing in public. Nelson hoped to return the royal hospitality by entertaining the King on board his ship. Preparations to receive him were well under way when news came in that a French corvette had been sighted off the south coast of Sardinia with a small English vessel in tow as her prize. Nelson decided to give immediate chase and had to forgo the honour of entertaining his royal host. As he sailed out of the bay in search of the enemy the seven Neapolitan men-of-war and one Spanish frigate he had noticed in the harbour all remained safely at anchor. He was not impressed.

Sir William's ability to inspire the confidence of men much younger than himself never stood him in better stead than at this first meeting with Nelson. He was then in his sixty-third year; Nelson was a few weeks short of his thirty-fifth birthday. The two men took to each other at once. Hamilton shrewdly guessed the great qualities of leadership which the younger man was soon to show, though whether, at this early stage, he actually prophesied to Emma that Nelson would become 'the greatest man that England ever produced' (as Emma later claimed) must remain open to doubt. Nelson, for his part, considered Sir William a man after his own heart—'You do business in my own way'. Though they were not to meet again for another five years he kept up a regular correspondence with the British Minister at Naples, and when they did meet again it was as old friends.

So much official activity was crowded into the four days spent ashore that Nelson could only have passed a few short hours in the company of Lady Hamilton. She herself took his young mid-shipman stepson Josiah Nisbet under her wing and showed him the sights of the city. No doubt her celebrated figure which was beginning to take on a voluptuous outline, made its impression on Nelson but there is nothing to suggest that he took more than a polite interest in his host's beautiful young wife. To his own wife he wrote: 'Lady Hamilton has been wonderfully kind and good to Josiah. She is a young woman of amiable manners, and who does honour to the station to which she is raised.' The excitement of being Lady Hamilton was still enough of a novelty to Emma for her to have thoughts for much else, and Nelson had not yet become a hero. There is no evidence to suggest that at this time he made any special impression on her or that she paid him any more attention than the demands of good manners required. It was entirely as Sir William's friend and protégé that Nelson first entered the doors of the Palazzo Sessa.

The visit of the *Agamemnon* and its energetic commanding officer had had an excellent effect on the morale of the Neapolitan Court. A month later came the news of the execution of Marie Antoinette and gloom descended once more.[9] The tidings of her sister's death had a terrible effect on Maria Carolina whose nerves had been shattered by months of helpless anxiety. She remained for a long time in a morbid and depressed state with occasional hysterical outbursts which alarmed and terrified her courtiers. The situation was not helped by the fact that she was in the last month of her pregnancy when the news was broken to her, and her health suffered seriously in consequence of the violence of her grief. At first she refused to speak French, vowing that she could not bear to hear 'that murderous language', and a thirst for vengeance now dominated her thoughts and actions. Under a picture of her sister which hung in her room she inscribed the legend: *Je poursuiverai ma vengeance jusqu'au tombeau*. This was to be her policy from now on.

Meanwhile Neapolitan troops were engaged in warfare for the first time in half a century. The forces which had been sent in accordance with the terms of the treaty of alliance were soon taking part in the desperate attempt to hold Toulon against increasing republican pressure from the land. They formed part of a mixed force composed of British, Spanish and Sardinian elements as well as a contingent of French royalists. Acton had insisted that the troops he had sent should serve under the command of Lord Hood alone. This request sprang from his wish to emphasise the independence of Naples from Spanish control and his distrust of commanders from other Italian states; Hamilton welcomed it as being more likely to contribute to the unity of the allied forces.

This hoped for unity was not achieved. Soon Sir William was receiving letters of complaint from General Acton about the 'coolness' and misunderstandings which had broken out between the British and Neapolitan commands. They had for some time been in the habit of corresponding in English, a language which Acton wrote with great fluency but no very secure grasp of idiom. It was a valuable precaution in a country where even the most official letters were likely to be opened and read, and it was in English that the Chief Minister now addressed his grievances to the British envoy.

The first letter is undated, but is endorsed by Hamilton: 'Genl. Acton, Oct 28th., 1793.' 'The papers of Marshal Forteguerri have been returned to me after the perusall of them by their Majesties,' Acton began.[10] 'The content seems directed to explain the circumstances of the most disagreeable coolness between Mylord Hood and Our Marshall. I think that we must endeavour, by employing all the means in our power, to put an end to them in the best manner possible. There is certainly some misunderstanding, of which I do not conceive the Cause at present, nor from whence derived the influence. The ships and troops of His Sicilian Majesty are in want and require necessarily help and friendly as well as regular assistance in promoting and securing their discipline after a Peace of 50 years. Their martial conduct and courage want experience, and for this a direction; Lord Hood in his letter to you agrees on this article particularly. They do require in consequence the constant and vigiliant attention of their Superiors. We cannot leave them intirely alone under a foreign dipendency without the check of their own Commander. Our small Navy wants especially the direction of her chiefs. I am perfectly convinced that no explanation has been properly given from Forteguerri on this subject, otherwise My Lord Hood had certainly considered this article under a different aspect. These complaints from our General are not only disagreeable but might produce evil of many kinds which we must avoid certainly, and destroy the foundation of such a disposition as much as we can.'

On 4 November came another letter on the subject of 'the bad humour and coolness' that continued between the two admirals, which the two civilians were doing their best to resolve and settle. 'I wish most earnestly', Acton concluded, 'that our papers forwarded to the Navy may bring the things to bear on a better footing for the good of the Common Cause and Service.'

Problems of stores and provisions as well as of military discipline lay at the heart of the difference. Acton, indeed, had suggested to Nelson that it might be better for the Neapolitan forces to delay a week or two before sailing in order to collect more provisions, for he knew Lord Hood to be in short supply. These thoughts, no doubt, were in his mind when he wrote again to Sir William on 26 November: 'I apply, dear Sir, to your discretion and friendship. I do not complain openly, and do not mean to do it, but I see with a true concern and great uneasiness that the business does not go properly: the coolness with our chief, the want of provisions in a short time as our troops are consuming the victuals of our ships, and are all at a short allowance, as I find by letters of the common soldiers. I fear that these disagreeable inconveniences may destroy the good effect of all the disposition we took so much pain in making, and with so much expense. You know that the articles of Transport and of Victualing the troops out of this Kingdom were not at our charge. I hope that you will excuse my lamentations on this motive. . . '[11]

The Neapolitan forces, inexperienced in war, suffered heavy casualties, while the growing crisis of the siege of Toulon did not create the most helpful atmosphere in which to smooth out differences of opinion between hard-pressed commanders jealous for the honour of their troops. Nelson was later to describe Admiral Forteguerri as 'the most of all men unlikely to conciliate the esteem of the English'. The problem over which Acton and Hamilton had striven to find a solution ceased to exist when Toulon was recaptured by the French on 19 December; it was blown away, with a good deal else, by a few well aimed cannon shots fired under the direction of a certain young Colonel Bonaparte, a name which Europe was now hearing for the first time. That friction and discord were not confined to the Neapolitans was confirmed by Sir Sidney Smith in a letter to Hamilton written on Christmas eve, 1793, from on board the *Victory*. In the course of his long account of the fall of Toulon he remarked that 'Discord, the natural consequence of the assemblage of so many nations, showed itself on every occasion, extending from *the chiefs* to the *private sentinels*, so that nothing went on with spirit. There was no Commander-in-Chief acknowledged as such by all.'[12]

While Sir William was occupied with the increasing official business resulting from the war Emma was enjoying the social round at Naples and Caserta, and basking in the sunshine of royal approval. In June she wrote to Greville complaining of having to return to her house at two or three in the morning 'after the fatige of a dinner of fifty, and a ball and supper of hundred'. She rattles off the names of the distinguished English travellers who visit them. In spite of her unofficial position she introduces the ladies to the Queen as though she were indeed an ambassadress. She is on the most friendly terms with Maria Carolina who allows her to come to the palace very often in private. 'In the evening I go to her and we are *tête-à-tête* 2 or 3 hours,' she tells Greville. 'Sometimes we sing. Yesterday the King and me sang duetts for 3 hours. It was but bad, *as he sings like a King.*' The flattering attentions of royalty had not yet gone to her head to the extent of making her lose her sense of humour. Though she spends the evenings merrily enough with the Queen, when they meet next day at the drawing-room she keeps her distance and pays the Queen great respect, 'which pleased her much'. Maria Carolina, in return, shows Emma 'great distinction' and tells her many times how much she admires her good conduct. 'I onely tell you this', Emma adds ingenuously, 'to shew and convince you I shall never change but allways be simple and natural.'[13]

She was certainly simple and natural in that she accepted the flattery of the Queen of Naples at its face value. No doubt the Queen found amusement and relaxation in the company of this artless, down-to-earth young woman with her gushing and uncritical devotion; it was at least a pleasant change after her own ladies who never stopped whispering and intriguing. But Maria Carolina did very little without a purpose. As the British alliance became more and more the corner-stone of her policy it became increasingly necessary for her to have a line of approach to the British Minister that could, if necessary, by-pass her husband the King. This was the real reason why Emma was to find herself, in the months ahead, on ever more cordial and intimate terms with the 'adorable Queen' for whom she professed such an ecstatic admiration.

1. B.M. Add. MSS 34048 f. 66.
2. *Lord Nelson's Letters to Lady Hamilton* (1814), Vol. II p. 173.
3. B. Connell: *Portrait of a Whig Peer*, pp. 208 ff.
4. This and the following letters to Sir James Burges are in the Fitzwilliam Museum, Cambridge, Percival Bequest MSS.
5. B.M. Add. MSS 41199, f. 99.
6. Morrison, 215.
7. B.M. Add. MSS 41199, f. 110.
8. B.M. Add. MSS 41199, f. 143.
9. The Queen of France was guillotined on 16 October 1793.
10. B.M. Egerton MSS 2639, f. 101. Rear-Admiral Forteguerri was commander of the Neapolitan forces united with the British.
11. B.M. Egerton MSS 2639, f. 122.
12. Morrison, 231.
13. Ibid, 221.

CHAPTER XVIII

Eruption and Espionage

The year 1794 opened dismally with the return of the wounded survivors from the siege of Toulon and the report of those two hundred who would never return again. With the fleet came nearly four hundred indigent royalist refugees. A month later the news broke of the discovery of a terrorist plot to capture the forts which dominated the city, burn the arsenal and docks, and massacre the royal family and leading members of the government. It was a grim beginning for a new year.

As though these depressing events were not enough, in the early summer Mount Vesuvius, that turbulent but familiar neighbour, showed signs of the approach of another climax of violence. Between June and August an earthquake and eruption of terrific force shook the whole region, destroying the towns of Resina and Torre del Greco, and changing the contour of the mountain so that the surrounding ridge of Mount Somma was seen to rise higher than the crater of Vesuvius. According to Hamilton, who could now speak with an authority none dare challenge, except for the terrible eruptions of the years 79 and 1631 this was the most violent recorded by history.

The volcano had been remarkably quiet for seven months before the eruption. The first strange sign occurred when the water in the well at Torre del Greco began to dry up and a thick vapour was seen to gather on the mountain at about a quarter of a mile below the crater. It was also observed that the sun and moon had an unusual reddish cast. Shortly after this, and eight days before the eruption itself began, a man and two boys working in a vineyard above Torre del Greco were alarmed by the noise of a slight explosion followed by a sudden puff of smoke coming out of the ground close to where they were working. This was, in fact, the very spot where later one of the mouths would open in the side of the volcano from which a torrent of lava would flow down to destroy the town.

The first indication of danger was felt in Naples on 12 June. 'About 11 o'clock at night. . . ' Sir William wrote in the account he sent to the Royal Society,[1] 'we were all sensible of a violent shock of an earthquake; the undulatory motion was evidently from east to west, and appeared to have lasted near half a minute. The sky, which had been quite clear, was soon after covered with black clouds. The inhabitants of the towns and villages which are very numerous at the foot of Vesuvius felt this earthquake still more sensibly and say that the shock at first was from the bottom upwards, after which followed the undulation from east to west.

This earthquake extended all over the Campagna Felice; and the royal palace at Caserta, which is 15 miles from this city and one of the most magnificent and solid buildings in Europe, the walls being 18 feet thick, was shook in such a manner as to cause great alarm, and all the chamber bells rang. It was likewise much felt at Beneventum, about 30 miles from Naples; and at Ariano in Puglia, at a much greater distance; both which towns have been often afflicted with earthquakes.'

A somewhat milder shock was felt three days later, at the same moment 'a fountain of bright fire' shot up from about the middle of the cone of Vesuvius. Almost at once other jets of lava were seen to break out at many points but all took the same line of flow towards the fated towns of Resina and Torre del Greco. Hamilton counted fifteen separate torrents and believed many others were obscured by the smoke. 'It is impossible', he wrote, 'that any description can give an idea of this fiery scene or of the horrid noises that attended this great operation of nature. It was a mixture of the loudest thunder with incessant reports, like those from a numerous heavy artillery, accompanied by a continued hollow murmur, like that of the roaring of the ocean during a violent storm; and added to these was another blowing noise, like that of the going up of a large flight of sky-rockets, and which brought to my mind also that noise which is produced by the action of the enormous bellows on the furnace of the Carron iron foundry in Scotland, and which it perfectly resembled.' A curious feature of this eruption was that though many vents appeared in the side of the mountain neither fire nor smoke was seen to escape from the crater at the summit.

Very soon immense clouds of black smoke and ash hid the mountain from view. This enormous and dense body of cloud began, according to Sir William, 'to give signs of being replete with the electric fluid by exhibiting flashes of that sort of zig-zag lightning which in the volcanic language of this country is called *ferilli* and which is the constant attendant on the most violent eruptions.' It was the most vivid display of this sort he had seen during the thirty years he had spent in Naples, and unlike previous occasions the discharge of 'electrical matter' caused explosions like those of the loudest thunder.

Though the crater remained hidden in clouds for several days, early on the morning of the 16th the lava which had rushed from the new fissures was seen to have reached the sea, and, more ominously, to have 'overwhelmed, burnt, and destroyed' the greater part of Torre del Greco, the irresistible river of destruction having ploughed its way through the very centre of the town. When the wind cleared the pall of smoke from the summit of Vesuvius for a short time two days later, 'we discovered', Sir William wrote, 'that a great part of its crater, particularly on the west side opposite Naples, had fallen in, which it probably did about 4 o'clock in the morning of this day, as a violent shock of an earthquake was felt at that moment at Resina and other parts situated at the foot of the volcano.' The summit of the mountain in the part where the crater had fallen away was lowered by about a ninth of its whole height above sea-level. It was now that the ridge of Mount Somma stood higher than the cone of Vesuvius.

The darkness which covered Naples during these terrifying days was so profound that night was indistinguishable from day. The weight of ashes caused buildings to crash in ruins. Panic swept the city, giving way to religious fear. Processions were formed and columns of people, some barefooted, others in penitential dress, made their way towards the Maddalena bridge chanting hymns and prayers. Surrounded by his clergy the Cardinal-Archbishop carried the phial containing the blood of St. Januarius through the streets while the golden statue of the saint followed. The relic was turned towards the turbulent volcano and the saint invoked for the protection of the city. While the pious prayed and criminals looted the ruined buildings those of a more practical bent followed the advice of the magistrates and cleared the roofs and terraces from fallen ashes.

The lava that destroyed Torre del Greco and was seen to continue on towards the sea formed itself into a new promontory which extended for more than a thousand feet. On the morning of 17 June, though the danger was still considerable, Hamilton was unable to suppress his impatience any longer and set out in his boat to inspect the damage. As he approached the stricken coast he had a narrow escape from catastrophe. 'I observed that the sea-water was boiling as in a cauldron where it washed the foot of this new formed promontory', he wrote in his report to the Royal Society, 'and though I was at least a hundred yards from it observing that the sea smoked near my boat I put my hand into the water, which was literally scalded; and by this time my boatman observed that the pitch from the bottom of the boat was melting fast and floating on the surface of the sea, and that the boat began to leak. We therefore retired hastily from this spot and landed at some distance from the hot lava.'

Hamilton learnt with relief that out of a population of about eighteen hundred no more than fifteen individuals had perished in the town. The scene that presented itself was one of complete desolation. The cathedral was covered by forty feet of lava and the average depth appeared to be about twelve feet. 'I walked in the few remaining streets of the town', Sir William wrote, 'and went on the top of one of the highest houses that was still standing, though surrounded by the lava. I saw from thence distinctly the whole course of the lava that covered the best part of the town; the tops of the houses were just visible here and there in some parts, and the timbers within still burning caused a bright flame to issue out of the surface. In other parts the sulphur and salts exhaled in a white smoke from the lava, forming a white or yellow crust on the scoriae round the spots where it issued with the most force. Often I heard little explosions and saw they blew up, like little mines, fragments of the scoriae and ashes into the air. I supposed them to have been occasioned either by rarefied air in confined cellars or perhaps by small portions of gunpowder taking fire, as few in this country are without a gun and some little portion of gunpowder in their houses.'

It was not until the end of the month that he thought it prudent to attempt an ascent of Vesuvius itself. The volcano was still active, the scene calling to mind some passage from the *Inferno*: 'The crater of Vesuvius, except at short intervals, had been continually obscured by the volcanic clouds ever since the 16th, and was so this day, with frequent flashes of lightning playing in those clouds and attended as usual with a noise like thunder.' It was an intrepid climb for a man in his mid-sixties but Hamilton took it calmly enough, merely remarking that it was the sixty-eighth time that he and his old companion Bartolomeo Puma had been together on the highest point of Vesuvius. As they climbed higher the surface of ash became extremely fine, leaving tracks like newly fallen snow. From this they were able to observe that a fox had been up before them 'that appeared to have been quite bewildered to judge from the many turns he had made'. They could even distinguish the tracks of lizards, insects, and other little animals. They were unable to reach the main crater, but climbed many new ones, some of which rose to a height of two hundred feet. It was an exhausting day, Sir William noting that the pair of boots he wore, to which he had added a thick new sole especially for the expedition, were burnt through at the end of the climb.

The eruption continued throughout July, one of the many new craters throwing up fire and smoke as late as the 22nd of the month. When the lava at last began to cool it often cracked, causing loud explosions. Following the peril of molten lava great torrents of mud swept down the mountain causing untold damage to vineyards and other property. It was not until the beginning of August that the period of danger could be said to have passed. Hamilton was struck, as before, by the way people returned to the ruined sites of their homes and began to build again, oblivious of the possibilities of future havoc. He recorded how the citizens of Torre del Greco were soon 'obstinately employed' in rebuilding their town on the still smoking lava despite the fact that Ferdinand IV had offered them a more secure situation elsewhere. It had been the same after the earthquake in Calabria; only the authority of government, Sir William observed, could oblige the inhabitants of those ruined towns to change their situation for a much better one.

Sir William had taken no account of his years as he followed the progress of this devastating eruption. His exertions would have exhausted a much younger man and it is no surprise to learn that in September he fell victim to a disorder which afflicted many Neapolitans following the earthquake. Emma herself did not escape the ailment; her husband, meanwhile, was reduced to so low an ebb that once again she began to fear that she might lose him. The Queen of Naples placed the royal villa at Castellammare at the disposal of the two invalids for their convalescence and here, in Emma's phrase, they were soon 'as happy as possible in the Queen's Palace, enjoying every comfort and happiness that good health, royall favour and domestick happiness can give us. In these agreeable surroundings they celebrated the third anniversary of their wedding. 'Sir William told me he loved me better than ever, and had never for one moment repented,' Emma recorded;

'Think of my feelings in that moment, when I could with truth say the same to him.' This confession was sent in a letter to the man she now addressed as 'my dear Mr. Greville'.[2]

At the end of the year the Hamiltons' existence was enlivened by a visit from Sir William's old school-fellow Frederick Hervey, Earl of Bristol and Bishop of Derry. The Earl-Bishop was not likely to pass unobserved in Naples as it was his habit to appear dressed in a white hat edged with purple, a coat of crimson or puce velvet, a black sash spangled with silver, and purple stockings. The simple Neapolitans, accustomed only to Cardinals, were left to imagine that this was the usual dress of a protestant prelate. On this occasion his costume, which combined so many of the more colourful accoutrements of the papal court, was enhanced by a miniature which the bishop wore round his neck where custom more usually decreed a pectoral cross. Those who expected to see the image of a saint would have found, had they examined the miniature more closely, that it contained the features of the Countess of Lichtenau, who was generally supposed to be the bishop's mistress. In fact their relationship was certainly a more innocent one, for the Countess (who soon followed him to Naples) was still the acknowledged mistress of King Frederick-William II of Prussia, but the Earl-Bishop did little to discourage the rumours that surrounded them when he insisted always upon addressing her as *chère adorable amie or chère comtesse et adorable amie* and never failed to use the familiar *tu*.

The bishop's letters were no less surprising than his dress. To say that they were lacking in an episcopal spirit would not be to exaggerate. When writing to 'Ever dearest Emma' to propose himself as a guest at Caserta (having failed to meet her at the Opera) he added by way of general comment: 'You say nothing of the adorable Queen; I hope she has not forgotten me, but as Shakespeare says, "who doats must doubt", and I verily deem her the very best edition of a woman I ever saw—I mean, of such as are not in *folio*, and are to be *had* in *sheets*. . . ' The letter was signed 'ever and invariably, dearest dear Emma most affectionately yours'.[3] Had Hamilton not known his old friend so well he might have imagined he had cause for jealousy, but the bishop dealt in superlatives and 'adorable' and 'dearest' were his favourite adjectives. Emma herself described him admirably to Greville when she wrote, 'He is very entertaining and dashes at everything.'

The bishop had arrived full of schemes. He was trying to negotiate a marriage between his grandson and a daughter of the Countess of Lichtenau and also hoped to persuade Sir William to exchange his embassy at Naples for the post at Florence where his son Lord Hervey had been Minister since the death of Sir Horace Mann. Both plans came to nothing; indeed there was small hope now for anyone who attempted to make Hamilton think of leaving Naples.

As a guest Lord Bristol could be embarrassing. Prince Augustus was once more in Naples and the Hamiltons arranged a concert in his honour at which Mrs. Billington, the greatest English singer of her day, was engaged to entertain the company. The Prince, no less eccentric in his way than the bishop, showed his appreciation by adding his own voice to that of the singer's, which might have been a happy compliment had he been able to sing. Unfortunately nature had not endowed him with this gift. The resulting cacophony was endured with stoicism by all but the Earl-Bishop who turned to the Prince and said: 'Pray cease, you have the ears of an ass.' Fortunately the remark was taken in good part but the Prince looked upon it as a challenge, for he continued to sing even louder and volunteered one or two solos of his own. This the bishop regarded as 'very fine braying but intolerable singing'.

In spite of his odd behaviour the Earl-Bishop was a welcome visitor at Naples and at the 'little cabin at Caserta' as he somewhat romantically described the Hamiltons' house in the neighbourhood of the palace where the royal family spent the winter months. To the Queen he was 'ce cher bon et bien faisant évêque' and his disregard for the nicer points of etiquette caused her no offence. As a life-long collector, at that time busily assembling works of art for the vast house he was building at Ickworth, he had much to discuss with Sir William on matters of taste, and after he left he continued to send his old friend letters full of the political gossip which he picked up in the course of his restless wanderings about Europe. Emma also received letters from him, gallantly expressed, and containing many flattering references to her beauty.

This famous beauty of figure was past its best, though her face retained its radiant good looks. She was now very stout. Sir Gilbert Elliot (afterwards Lord Minto) visited Naples from Corsica, where he was acting as Viceroy, a year after the Bishop of Derry and left a frank account of the appearance of the British Minister's wife. 'She is the most extraordinary compound I ever beheld,'[4] he wrote. 'Her person is nothing short of monstrous for its enormity, and is growing every day. She tries hard to think size advantageous to her beauty, but is not easy about it. Her face is beautiful; she is all Nature and yet all Art; that is to say, her manners are perfectly unpolished, of course very easy, though not with the ease of good breeding, but of a barmaid. . . ' He found her 'excessively good humoured and wishing to please and be admired' and, unlike Goethe, found something to admire in her 'considerable natural understanding'. He considered her conversation with men 'exaggerations of anything I ever heard anywhere' and was 'wonderfully struck with these inveterate remains of her origin— though the impression was very much weakened by seeing the other ladies of Naples'. Sir Gilbert later met Maria Carolina, recalling that the last time he had been at a royal function was at Versailles where he had seen her unfortunate sister still in all her glory and lustre. 'The Queen', he noted, 'has a strong powerful mind, and is full of courage, vigour, and firmness.'

Elliot's opinion of Emma 'wishing to please and be admired' and his impression of Maria Carolina's masterful personality are of special interest at this time, for it was between the visits of the Earl-Bishop and Sir Gilbert Elliot that the Queen of Naples began to make use of Lady Hamilton as an instrument in her political designs. Though Ferdinand IV reigned in Naples it was still Maria Carolina who ruled, assisted by her able and powerful minister General Acton. As a bitter enemy of France she considered the alliance with Great Britain as of vital importance to her policy, and she began to pass on to Sir William any piece of political information that might be of value to the British cabinet. In order to do this, however, she had to make use of devious means. The King was jealous of his power, though too lazy to exercise it, and the Queen was compelled to go behind his back, for left to his own devices Ferdinand would almost certainly have favoured a policy of neutrality. Etiquette forbade Maria Carolina as Queen Consort to receive the British Minister in audience; if she wished to have a political correspondence with him a go-between was essential. It was thus that she began to make use of Emma, whose devotion was unquestioning, as a means of communication with Sir William, and what Emma imagined to be her own political career was launched.

The Queen had an expert eye for discovering the weak point in a person's character and exploiting it for her own ends. A French *émigré* officer, Count de Damas, observed a curious example of this in connection with the King. 'His brain', the Count wrote in his *Memoires*, 'becomes exalted when he sees a glove well stretched over a beautifully shaped arm. It is a mania he has always had and which has never varied. How many affairs of the greatest importance have I seen settled by the Queen's care to pull her gloves over her pretty arms while discussing the question which engrossed her. I have seen the king take notice of this, smile, and grant her wish.' With Emma the Queen had no need to go to such ends. Flattery was enough. The former inmate of Dr. Graham's Temple of Health had no defences against the blandishments of a daughter of Maria Theresa; she became the Queen's utterly devoted slave. The many letters addressed to '*Ma bien chère Miledy*' were endorsed by the recipient with such adulatory phrases as: 'From my dear, dear Queen. . . ', 'From my ever dear Queen at Caserta', or, in a climax of devotion, 'From my ever dear respectable and adorable Queen of Naples. . . Oh! that everyone could know her as I do! They would love and esteem her as I do from my soul! May every good attend *her and hers*!'

In April 1795 Sir William had another attack of bilious fever and was in bed for eight days. The Hamiltons were at their house at Caserta, and Emma once again acted as nurse to her ailing husband. The Queen wrote constantly to enquire after the health of '*le digne Chevalier*', not missing the opportunity to praise Emma at the same time: 'I am very uneasy and eager for intelligence of your husband's health, how he has passed the night, and how you feel yourself in the midst of such troubles and anxieties. I am in pain from my sincere friendship for you. But trust in God who never abandons anyone who commends himself to him, and rely on the sincere friendship and concern of your attached friend.' Later the same day (17 April) the Queen sent some quinine for the invalid with more unction for the nurse: 'I send you the Quinine and I will do willingly everything in my power to be useful to you and soothe the worthy Chevalier. . . I would fain keep you company; my friendship might comfort you. . . '[5]

No wonder Emma was carried away by these intimate attentions! She now began to see herself in a new role as someone of influence in political affairs. 'Send me some news, political and private', she wrote to Greville on 19 April, 'for, against my will, *owing to my situation here*, I am got into politicks, and I wish to have news for our dear much-loved Queen, whom I adore. Nor can I live without her, for she is to me a mother, friend, and everything. If you cou'd know her as I do you would adore her! For she is the first woman in the world; her talents are superior to every woman's in the world, and her heart is most excellent and strictly good and upright. But you'l say it is because we are such friends, that I am partial; but ask everybody that knows her. She loves England and is attached to our Ministry, and wishes the continuation of the war as the only means to ruin that abominable French council.[6] From now on Emma would give herself the airs of an ambassadress whatever her official status might be.

Some ten or twelve days after the gift of quinine (about the 28th or 29th of April) Emma received another letter from the Queen. 'I send you a letter in cypher from Spain, from Galatone,' Maria Carolina wrote,[7] 'which you must return to me before twenty-four hours so that the King may find it again. There are some very interesting facts for the English government which I am delighted to communicate to them, to show my attachment to them and my confidence in the worthy Chevalier, whom I only beg not to compromise me. . . ' Spain, ruled by Ferdinand's elder brother Charles IV and his vain chief-minister Manuel Godoy, at best an unreliable ally, was now putting out feelers of peace towards the French republic. The fact that the Queen could send this letter still in cypher to the British Minister suggests that Hamilton had for some time been in possession of the Spanish code. No doubt this, too, had been supplied by the Queen, who clearly needed no encouragement in sending secret information to her friend the 'worthy Chevalier'.

The information was sent sometimes by letter, more often by word of mouth, for the Queen constantly came in contact with Lady Hamilton and it was safer to communicate with Sir William on these dangerous topics by means of verbal messages. Later in the year she was able to show Hamilton a letter to Ferdinand from Charles IV himself which made the King of Spain's intentions clear. 'In my letter of April 2nd', that monarch began, 'I wrote to you that I was thinking of doing what would be possible for me to hasten on a solid and permanent peace which might enable mankind to pause from the horrors of a war so cruel and devastating as the present.'[8] After confessing his inability to continue fighting after three fruitless campaigns and referring, somewhat unconvincingly, to 'the moderate system of actual government' now operating in France, the King came to the point of his letter: 'I have begun to treat with the French for peace, which, though not yet concluded will I hope not delay long in being settled to the full satisfaction of the two nations, and above all to the advantage of my own so far as can be hoped from the circumstances, critical enough, in which we find ourselves. . . ' In conclusion he assured his brother that he would never be forgetful of Italy—'and far less of your own states'—and declared that he was ready to obtain for Naples the same benefits of peace which he hoped to obtain for his own country—'as to which object, I have already made some proposals in your behalf, which I apprehend will be well received. God send that it may be for us a means more to the purpose for sparing the blood of the rest of our ill-fated family than war has hitherto been.'

A copy of this letter was at once sent to London for the information of the Foreign Secretary, Lord Grenville. Hamilton himself kept a transcription in Emma's handwriting of the letter in its original Italian which he endorsed 'Copy of the King of Spain's Letter to the K. of Naples Aug. 11th, 1795, having made Peace with the F. Rep.' As Spain had made peace with France on 27 July the date in August presumably refers to the day upon which the letter came into Sir William's hands, or upon which it reached Naples. By the time a copy reached London the news of Spain's defection must have been known, but the Spanish King's declared intention to persuade Naples to follow his example in making peace with France gave Hamilton sufficient food for thought. He must have been thankful that he had so fervent and willing a collaborator in the person of the Queen and that that royal lady had still so powerful an influence over her weak and indolent husband.

At least one other letter from Charles IV to his brother, as well as documents of less distinguished origin, was to find its way to Sir William's desk before Spain declared war on Great Britain in October 1796. In every case Maria Carolina was (as she herself expressed it) 'delighted to communicate' such valuable documents and information to her ally. Many years later, when widowed and almost destitute, Emma was to take credit for it all, trying to persuade a Government deaf to her appeals that it was she who had 'discovered' that a letter had come from the King of Spain, and that through her influence with the Queen she had 'prevailed' upon her to take it from the King's pocket and show it to Sir William. As Maria Carolina's own letters show, she needed no prevailing upon; it was entirely her own idea to pass on information to the British Minister. Had it not been necessary for her to find a suitable go-between Emma would have played no part in the business at all.

The year 1796 had not begun auspiciously. Hamilton and Mrs. Cadogan were both ill with colds and fever. On 2 January Maria Carolina had written to Emma urging her to 'Salute the Chevalier; tell him that he must be patient and docile and think only of getting well again, and that I hope to see him again soon to comfort me with his restored health.' The Queen's anxiety was genuine. She dreaded the possibility of Sir William's retirement. All her hopes now rested on the power of Great Britain whose navy protected her coasts and whose implacable enmity towards France was in accord with her own vow of vengeance against the murderers of her sister. If Sir William left Naples and a stranger took his place her schemes to keep her kingdom in the struggle against the common enemy might well fail.

The months that followed were to witness a rapid deterioration of affairs in Italy from the point of view of the countries allied against France. In April General Bonaparte took command of the Army of Italy promising his soldiers that he would lead them to the most fertile plains in the world where fruitful provinces and large cities would lie at their mercy. It was no idle promise. By 15

May he had entered, Milan in triumph, having defeated the armies of Austria and Sardinia in a series of rapid and brilliant victories. Neapolitan troops had fought bravely with units of the Austrian army but the news from north Italy contained little else to comfort the Queen or to encourage a martial spirit in the breast of her timid husband, who thought it prudent to come to terms with the enemy while he still had an army left. In London Lord Grenville advised the Neapolitan ambassador that if his government hoped for an honourable peace they should lose no time about it; a neutral Naples was of more value to Great Britain than one occupied by the French. Only one voice, seemed to be raised against the idea of an accommodation with the enemy: 'I am satisfied Piedmont has been lost by treachery, and not by the force of the French. . . ' Captain Nelson wrote to Hamilton on 20 May. 'I hope the Court of Naples has not caught the Genoese panic, for it is owing to that alone that the French have done what they have.'[9]

The Prince di Belmonte was sent to negotiate with General Bonaparte. It took him some time to find the victorious general whose rapid movements from place to place completely mystified those who were more accustomed to the leisurely pace of pre-revolution diplomacy. Bonaparte was eventually discovered at Brescia. The Prince proved an able negotiator and an armistice was signed on 5 June as a result of which Ferdinand recalled his soldiers from Lombardy and withdrew his ships which were serving with the British Fleet. Belmonte then proceeded to Paris where a treaty of peace was signed on 10 October. Naples was to remain neutral; she was to allow no more than four ships to enter her ports from countries still engaged in hostilities against France; and all Frenchmen imprisoned within her dominions on charges of treason were to be liberated. By a secret clause the Neapolitan government was required to pay within a year an indemnity of eight million francs. Five days before the treaty was signed Spain declared war on Great Britain, having agreed to an alliance with France in the previous August.

During these anxious and depressing months General Acton was fearful lest the British fleet should quit the Mediterranean and thus leave Naples completely exposed to French attack. On 28 October he wrote to Hamilton to say how the King and Queen had been 'charmed with the comfortable resolution' of Admiral Jervis not to leave the Mediterranean '*as yet*', adding in his curious English: 'God forbid that we should be deprived of this Protection under every prospect and a change even of circumstances.'

Hamilton replied the next day. 'Allow me, my dear Sir,' he told Acton, 'to speak out freely, and I do not do so as the Minister of Great Britain at this Court, but as an impartial Englishman who from very particular circumstances during a Residence of 32 years in this Country, is nearly as much attached to it as to his native one, and feels equally for the Prosperity, Honor, and Glory of both.' What followed was a statement of the policy for the success of which both he and the Queen had been plotting and struggling, and which was to be set aside (at least for the time being) by the treaty just concluded in Paris. The terms of this treaty were not yet officially released in Naples and Sir William refers to the negotiations in his letter as though still taking place. In fact he already knew the terms, and had on his desk a copy, in Emma's handwriting, of the secret and additional articles, dated the same day as Acton's letter.

'After the compliance of Sir John Jervis and Sir Gilbert Elliot to the wishes of their Sicilian Majesties and of their Government by which I verily believe they have saved the Two Sicilies and all Italy from the most imminent danger of absolute ruin and subversion', Sir William's letter continued, 'it must be expected that this Government will as soon as possible (with propriety) exert itself to the utmost and join Great Britain with all its powers to distress the Enemy. It is plain that Naples will never have reasonable offers of Peace from the French Directory by following half-measures; the French will continue to delay and give hopes, but will not conclude. In my humble opinion then, the Armistice should be broken as soon as possible (and indeed I have reason to think that your Excellency is of the same opinion) and as many of his Sicilian Majesty's ships, frigates, galliots, gun boats, etc., etc., as can be spared consistently with the immediate safety of these kingdoms should be directly prepared and sent to Sir John Jervis. In short, knowing, as we do, how very ill, not to say wickedly, inclined the Court of Spain is at this moment towards that of Naples, the latter should not I think hesitate on the first favourable moment to put itself entirely under the protection of Great Britain and join issue with it against every enemy. . . '

Sir William was hoping to show Acton the value he put on the treaty just negotiated and which he knew to be signed by the plenipotentiaries of France and Naples. He considered that it was quite worthless and that the French would themselves cast it aside whenever it suited them to do so. He ended his letter on the note that 'violent disorders require violent remedies; half-measures seldom or ever turn to good account', and characteristically referred Acton to an inscription in a church dedicated to the Virgin Mary at a place in Naples called *La Pietra Santa* which he considered admirably summed-up his point of view. He had written a letter of which his friend Captain Nelson would have highly approved.

Acton answered at once; his letter has the same date as Hamilton's. 'You are much in the right,' he admitted with more truth than command of syntax, 'this Government without loss of time should act with energy and employ all the most efficacious measures which at present [are] in its hands, and fortunately after many and hard works, ready and well disposed. No Peace, dear Sir, with the French will, nor can, assure the rest and tranquillity of the Two Sicilies: I shall go further, War with all its anxieties and consequences is even preferable to a Peace with people without faith and resolved to follow for any rule whatsoever his own ambition, rapacity, and ferocious overpowering every Nation, every Government, every Order. *Timidity*, as you very conveniently observe, ruins the Governments, when Boldness, Audacity, and activity make Empires prosperate. . . ' You have not seen yourself our

Camps, which I was wishing, as you would have seen what sort of Operations have been wanted to produce such effects in men, furnitures, *prodigious* artillery and ammunitions in a country without war since 63 years and certainly averse, by its natural dispositions and contrary habit, to any warlike measures. . . ' He went on to tell Hamilton that the Austrian General Mack 'is given to us for the direction of our Army' and to embroider on the various diplomatic activities which he hoped would improve the general situation and result in a proper peace.[10]

This exchange of letters between the diplomat and the statesman, both fully aware that the other knew of the signing of the peace treaty with France, shows the spirit in which Naples entered on her period of uneasy neutrality: 'Nominally neutral but never in our feelings' as the impulsive Maria Carolina wrote to Lady Hamilton. At the end of the year Sir William had a letter on this same subject of the Neapolitan peace treaty from his friend Nelson, now acting as commodore. 'I wish', he wrote, 'any mode could be adopted that individually as an officer (I may, I hope, without vanity say of some merit) I could serve the King of Naples; it is the French fleet that I dread appearing before Naples, but a vigorous and some may think desperate attempt might be made for their destruction. . . '[11] It was a strange letter to come from a man who had visited Naples but once, and then only fleetingly, and had expressed no very high opinion of Ferdinand IV. Time would soon make his wish to serve the King of Naples come true.

1. *Philosophical Transactions of the Royal Society*, Vol. XVII (1791-6), pp. 492-506.
2. Morrison, 246.
3. Child-Pemberton: *The Earl-Bishop*, Vol. II, p. 493.
4. *Life and Letters of Lord Minto*, Vol. II, p. 364.
5. J. C. Jeaffreson: *The Queen of Naples & Lord Nelson*, Vol. I, p. 285-6.
6. Morrison, 263.
7. Jeaffreson: op. cit., Vol. I, p. 289-90. Galatone was Neapolitan Ambassador to Spain.
8. Jeaffreson: op. cit., pp. 294-6.
9. Morrison, 280.
10. B.M. Egerton MSS 2639, ff. 329, 333 and 337.
11. Morrison, 290.

CHAPTER XIX

Hamilton's Second Collection

Though Hamilton's political and diplomatic duties continued to increase he did not abandon his other interests and studies. His letters to the Royal Society on the great eruption of Vesuvius had been received with avid interest in London where they were read at two sittings of the Society. 'You may suppose that so interesting a narrative of such an event has not lain in the President's drawer during the recess of the Society,' Greville told him.[1] 'Your friends have been favoured with a sight of it, and I can assure you the labour you must have had in collecting it is thankfully acknowledged.' The letters were later published in the *Philosophical Translations* illustrated with maps and engravings of the mountain in eruption.

The second collection of vases had now surpassed the first, but his perennial financial difficulties decided Hamilton to attempt another sale. It was his ambition, if possible, to sell the collection complete rather than see it broken up into lots, and with this end in view he wrote in May 1796, to the Earl-Bishop of Derry's 'adorable friend' the Countess of Lichtenau in the hope that he might be able through her influence to sell the entire collection to the King of Prussia. The attempt did not prove successful, but Hamilton's letter to the Countess is worth quoting for the description it gives of the collection, for showing the value he placed on it and the hopes he expressed of the influence it might have on the other arts.

'I think my object [of keeping the collection complete] will be attained, he wrote, by placing my Collection, with my name attached to it, at Berlin. And I am persuaded that, in a very few years, the profits which the arts will derive from such models will greatly exceed the price of the Collection. The King's [porcelain] manufactory would do well to profit by it. . . For a long time past I have had an unlimited commission from the Grand Duke of Russia; whilst at Berlin it would be in the midst of men of learning and literary academies.

'There are more than a thousand vases, and one half of them figured. If the King listens too your proposals, he may be assured of having the whole Collection, and I would further undertake to go, at the end of the war, to Berlin to arrange them. On reckoning up my accounts—I must speak frankly—I find that I shall be a loser unless I receive Seven thousand pounds sterling for this collection. That is the exact sum I received from the English Parliament for my first collection. . . As respects the Vases, the second is far more beautiful and complete than the series in London, but the latter included also bronzes, gems, and medals.'[2]

Hamilton remained true to the theory he had expressed thirty years ago when he had issued the volumes illustrating his first collection, that works of art surviving from antiquity should not be 'merely the objects of fruitless admiration' but should serve a useful purpose, that 'good models give birth to ideas by exciting the imagination' and that the example of the past can instruct and inspire the artist of the present day. It is a great pity that Sir William's letter to the Countess of Lichtenau had no effect. The King of Prussia did not buy the collection. It remained unsold and was destined, though not completely destroyed, to become a casualty of war, much to the distress of the man who had spent so much care, time and money in bringing it together.

While Sir William was endeavouring to sell his collection and cope with the increasing demands of his office which grew in volume and importance as the political situation in Italy worsened, Emma was becoming ever more self-satisfied with the position she had established for herself in Naples. Much of her time was now spent in helping her husband who had virtually no staff to assist him in the clerical side of his work. With her fluency in French and Italian, both of which she spoke well, she was able to assist in copying out letters and documents while Hamilton was busy with his dispatches. The Queen continued to make use of her as a means of communication with the British embassy. She received attention and flattery from the Neapolitan ministers and courtiers and vied with the most outspoken in her contempt and criticism of the 'rebels' upon whom she poured scorn in the most abusive terms, declaring that they all deserved to be hanged. In her attempts to impress her former lover she only succeeded in making herself appear rather absurd. 'We have not time to write to you', she told him in Septembers 1796, 'as we have been 3 days and nights writing to send by this courrier letters of *consequence* for our government. They ought to be grateful to Sir William and *myself in particular*, as my situation at this Court is very *extraordinary*, and what no person as yet arrived at; but one has no thanks, and I am allmost sick of grandeur.'[3] This effusion was followed by the now habitual reference to 'my adorable Queen' and a request that Greville would undertake some commissions for her; the latter request being followed by an imperious 'we desire it', which must have caused Greville a wry smile. The sense of humour that had once softened her little outbursts of vanity was no longer apparent.

Hamilton himself was in poor health. In the spring of 1797 he told his old friend Sir Joseph Banks: 'The constant agitation and fatigue of mind which I have undergone for six years past has injured my health very much, and my stomach and bilious complaints are more severel and frequent.'[4] It probably did not occur to him as he wrote these lines that it would be six years the coming autumn since he had married Emma. In this year Banks became a Privy Councillor and Sir William was able to remind him that they were now 'Brother Privys, Brother Red Ribbons, besides Brothers of the Royal Society, Antiquaries, Dilettanti Society etc.' Whatever his own troubles of the moment he could still take pleasure in his friend's successful career.

He certainly had no lack of troubles in that grim year. It began with Bonaparte's crushing defeat of Austria at Rivoli on 4 January. The next month brought more cheering news with Sir John Jervis's victory over the Spanish fleet off Cape St. Vincent, an action in which Nelson had taken a conspicuous part. This was some consolation for the loss of Corsica, which Britain had occupied since 1793 but had abandoned in the previous November when the British fleet had left the Mediterranean. This victory, however, was quickly followed by further reverses on land. Only a few days after the battle at which the Spaniards had paid so dearly for abandoning their former allies the Pope was compelled at Tolentino to sign away Romagna, Bologna and Ferrara to France and was forced to pay a huge indemnity. In July another blow was struck at the remaining Italian thrones when the Cisalpine Republic was proclaimed in north Italy and the former Papal territories were incorporated into it. In October Austria was compelled to make peace, ceding Belgium and Lombardy to France and receiving in return parts of the former territory of the Republic of Venice. The map of Italy was being re-drawn to the advantage of republican France.

All these events weighed heavily on Hamilton's spirits. He was at last beginning to feel his age and to look forward (especially when the news was bad and his health indifferent) to his eventual retirement. These thoughts were in his mind when, on 28 March of this dismal year, he wrote a long letter to Greville from Caserta. 'Its an age since I heard from you', he began, 'and indeed I have not wrote often to any of my most intimate friends for these last two years that every moment of my time has been taken up with the King's business and often of the most serious nature particularly at the time of the Evacuation of Corsica. As you are in Council and in high office at Court perhaps you will have known what I was about. I have, now that this Court has thought proper to sign a Peace with the French Republic, but little business to do with it, but Sir Gilbert Elliot has left me a numerous Colony of French and Corsican Emigres that give me sufficient employment and, to tell you the truth, teaze my heart out always wanting something and never satisfied with the generous protection and support they receive from the King's bounty. However, as the Peace is made I think I may soon without impropriety ask the King's leave to go home and give a look to my own affairs, and take some arrangement as to my continuing here which I certainly can not do on my present income as every expence is increased, and from every Foreigner coming well recommended to my house which is well known all over Europe, I am at double expence of any Foreign Minister here and, *entre nous*, the Princes of our own Blood Royal that have visited Naples, and H.R.H. who is with us now[5] and has been here many months, is an additional expence. I will dwell no longer on this disagreeable subject but I am determined not to be any way distressed in my latter days—and indeed I begin to find repose necessary and I shall seek it, but

I will not give up what I have until I see clearly what I may expect for my long Service and in which I certainly have spent more than all I have ever received from Government, and my own money too.'[6]

Hamilton had good reason to feel depressed. The treaty of Campo Formio between France and Austria brought a momentary lull in hostilities, but no one had much faith in France's pacific intentions. The Directory's ill-concealed dislike of Acton resulted in this minister's temporary eclipse. Though he remained in office there was a decided coolness noticed in his relations with the Queen which Sir William attributed to that lady's 'sudden and violent impressions', a weakness shared, in his opinion, by all the daughters of Maria Theresa. The Marquis di Gallo, who had long been Neapolitan ambassador at Vienna, was recalled and made Foreign Minister with a seat in the Council of State. Gallo had managed to keep on good terms with the French without sacrificing the patronage of Maria Carolina with whom, during his tenure of the Vienna embassy, he had carried on a regular correspondence. During the negotiations at Campo Formio he had represented Austria, though still in the Neapolitan service. Gallo did not share Acton's enthusiasm for England. Hamilton, and later on Nelson, distrusted him for his francophile leanings. Emma went even further; in her estimation the new Minister of Foreign Affairs was 'a frivolous, ignorant, self-conceited coxcomb, that thinks of nothing but his fine embroidered coat, ring, and snuff-box'.

At the end of the year a further disaster added to Sir William's anxieties and despondency. A critical situation had developed in Rome. Four days after Christmas, in a fracas outside the French embassy, a young officer on the staff of the ambassador was accidentally shot. The episode was exaggerated by the ambassador (who was General Bonaparte's elder brother Joseph) to suggest that the officer had died as a result of a deliberate plot, and refusing to listen to explanations he took himself off to Florence. This gave the French Directory the opportunity for a punitive expedition. General Berthier marched on Rome, entering the city on 10 February 1798. Pius VI, who had once hoped to restore to Rome the glories it had known under Leo X, was treated with coarse brutality when he refused to abdicate at the dictation of a French republican commissioner, and on 15 February the Roman Republic was proclaimed on the site of the ancient Forum while the eighty-year-old Pope was banished into exile. The revolution had now reached the very frontiers of the Kingdom of the Two Sicilies.

These developments made Hamilton postpone any hopes of leave. He was now in his late sixties, no longer robust in health, and faced with more arduous duties than he had known in all the thirty-four years he had lived in Naples. Though he was quite able to cope with the additional burdens of his office there were moments when he became a little querulous. The world he had known all his life was beginning to crumble as the forces of revolution drew ever nearer. The old certainties no longer held and Sir William was too old and too set in his ways to seek a *modus vivendi* with the new ideas; in the circumstances of war it was, to him, anyway, no longer a question of ideas but of loyalties. Meanwhile disturbing rumours filtered through from England of mutiny in the fleet, of a financial scare and the banks refusing payment. From Milan, in April 1798, came the news that his old school-fellow the Earl-Bishop had been imprisoned by the French. (This exuberant prelate was to remain incarcerated until February 1799.) In Naples itself there was an atmosphere of conspiracy and distrust; it was no longer the city which Goethe had so recently extolled as a place where everyone could live after his own manner in intoxicated self-forgetfulness.

The rather petulant and disenchanted note which characterised Sir William's letter to Greville was to remain until Nelson reappeared in the bay of Naples bringing a revival of enthusiasm and a new sense of purpose with him. Meanwhile Hamilton turned again for comfort to the all-embracing interest of his life, his collection. On 14 July 1798, he took a pen, and passing from room to room of the Palazzo Sessa, drew up a catalogue of his pictures.[7] He began in the water-closet in which hung a sketch of St. Gaetano by Luca Giordano and a moonlight view of the lake of Geneva. In the library, which came next on his list, was a sketch in oils of 'an official family' by Paul Veronese, a drawing of a shoemaker by Titian, an unidentified sketch by Rubens, Raphael Mengs' sketch for the head of Christ, Flaxman's self-portrait in terra cotta, three drawings of Emma illustrating the story of Orestes by Tischbein, and various copies of old masters.

From the library Sir William passed on to what he simply describes as 'Next Room', but as it contained fifty-three pictures it must have been a room of some size. Here were to be seen a portrait of the artist's mother by Rembrandt, an old man and a girl by Moroni, two sea pieces by Vernet, a 'sketch of the head of one of Rubens' wives' by Rubens, two holy families by Schidone, a battle piece by Wouvermans, two views of Venice by Canaletto, David with the head of Goliath by Guido, a Dutch scene by Chardin, a holy family sketch in oil on paper by Rubens, the laughing boy by Leonardo da Vinci referred to by many visitors to the Palazzo Sessa,[8] a miniature portrait of Oliver Cromwell by Cooper, a Virgin and child in the clouds by Paul Veronese, a marriage scene by Van der Velde, a sketch of the miracle of the True Cross by Andrea Sacchi and various pictures without attribution. There were also two more pictures of Emma, both by Gavin Hamilton, ten pictures by Sir William's protégé Pietro Fabris, two water-colour landscapes and 'portraits of my first wife's dogs' by Hackert's brother 'who died in England'.

Hamilton must have walked round the rooms pen in hand as he made his list, going every now and then to dip the quill in the inkstand as the ink ran dry, for the writing keeps fading and is often difficult to decipher despite his clear hand. His tour took him next to the First Antechamber which contained a portrait of the Duke of Brunswick by Pompeo Battoni, two more Canalettos, a Guido, a sketch of Christ on the Cross by Van Dyck, a Nativity by Taddeo Zucchero, a collection of views of Vesuvius in eruption by Fabris and Hackert, and one of an eruption of Stromboli by 'Vernet's brother'.

The staircase and closet contained a further eleven pictures including another view of Venice and a portrait of Mengs both by unnamed artists, another eruption of Vesuvius, and a sketch of the coronation of Charlemagne by Raphael. The closet led into a series of three rooms with another sixty-four pictures beginning with eleven views of Venice by Canaletto. Here also hung a Tintoretto sketch (Christ dragged to execution) a view of Antwerp by Teniers, an infant Jesus by Luca Giordano, two landscapes by Salvator Rosa, 'Stripping the dead after a battle' by Michelangelo delle Battaglie, a dancing satyr by Polenburg, a Zuccarelli, a Cuyp, a St. Sebastian by Van Dyck, and many more volcanic and view paintings of Naples by Fabris and Hackert, including the latter's view of the English garden at Caserta.

Next came the Gallery, an almost superfluous name to give to a room in a house so full of pictures. Here were another thirty-six, including a 'fine portrait of a man from Basaniello's collection and called there a Leonardo da Vinci'. There was also a portrait by Franz Hals, a 'Philosopher meditating on the effects of Time' by Salvator Rosa, a Virgin and Child by Parmeggiano, two studies of Emma by Romney and another by Vigée Le Brun, a portrait of a Moresco slave by Velasquez, another portrait of Emma by Angelica Kauffmann, a *Pietà* by Tintoretto, a Christ before Pilate by the same artist and a portrait of a man of the Barbarini family by Titian.

The bedroom contained very appropriately a sleeping Venus and a Cupid by Gavin Hamilton as well as two more portraits of Emma and one of Prince Rupert by Sir Godfrey Kneller. This was presumably a state bedroom on the *piano nobile*, for Sir William lists it between the Gallery and the Green Drawing-room. The latter, very properly for an embassy, contained a portrait of King George III and another of Prince Augustus. There was also a Holy Family by Nicholas Poussin, a Bacchus on an ass by Luca Giordano, and two works by the same artist described as 'Virgin Mary watering the Carmelites with her milk' and its companion 'a Pope delivering the souls from Purgatory by his intercession with the Virgin Mary'. With these were 'two upright pictures, subjects relative to the Carmelites by Simonelli, scholar of Giordano'. Of the pictures forming this group Sir William noted: 'The 4 pictures out of a Church in Naples where I left copies by Candido in their place.' There were altogether forty pictures in the Green Drawing-room including a St. John by Andrea del Sarto, three pastels by Rosalba, the portrait of an unidentified poet and a view of the Elysian Fields. The Long Gallery, which came next, contained four large pictures of saints and miracles by Simonelli, another Luca Giordano (a St. Francis), a boy's head in pastel by Rosalba, a portrait of Catherine Hamilton, another Nicholas Poussin, more Neapolitan views by Fabris and a 'Beggar by a young English Painter'.

A further Closet and bed-chamber remained and another forty-seven pictures. To many of these Hamilton gave no name, merely jotting down 'Fruit Piece' or 'Rising sun by ——' leaving the name of the artist blank. Here were to be found, in the same room, a portrait of the august Emperor Joseph II of Austria and the homely Mrs. Cadogan, Emma's mother. There was also a 'Housemaid washing by old Moreland', Emma's portrait by a nameless young Frenchman, and still more views of Vesuvius in eruption. Two canvasses in the last room are dismissed by Hamilton as '2 bad landscapes'.[9] He had recorded a total of 347 pictures in all the rooms he had visited as he made his catalogue. Even allowing for the fact that some of his attributions were at fault it was a considerable collection for a man who had never enjoyed great wealth.

Scattered through the rooms of the Palazzo Sessa there were altogether fourteen different portraits of Emma; three by Romney, three by Tischbein, two by Gavin Hamilton and Vigée Le Brun, and one each by Angelica Kauffmann, Sir Joshua Reynolds, a Mr. Head and the unknown young Frenchman. These showed her in various poses; on a couch, in a hat holding a book, as Bacchante dancing, 'en Sybille', as Bacchante resting, with a dog, with a lamb, and in other voluptuous or classical attitudes. Sir William never tired of admiring the beauty of his wife as interpreted by the various artists who portrayed her, just as he continued to rejoice in the presence of the original even though the sylph-like figure that Romney had loved to paint in London had now assumed more generous proportions. The 'piece of modernity' which his nephew had sent him from England was still the gem of his collection in spite of the fact that the acid and vituperative Lady Holland considered that it was 'impossible to go beyond her in vulgarity'.

Hamilton very clearly did not share the opinion of Lady Holland, who was herself hardly the *nonpareil* of meekness and gentleness having, in 1797, been divorced from her former husband for adultery. After seven years of marriage and twelve years living under the same roof as Emma Sir William had no complaints to lay at her door; he was still devoted to her. The exact nature of their relationship must remain a matter for speculation, but it is probable that he was not a very ardent or demanding husband. The fact that he had no children by either of his marriages (if we assume that the daughter who died in 1776 was an adopted child) might well suggest that he was either impotent or sterile. Emma, as we know, had a child long before he met her and was later to present Nelson with a daughter and possibly another child who was still-born. Hamilton's amorous adventures during his first wife's lifetime have a note of comic opera about them and consisted in little more than mild philandering; there is no evidence that he ever had any illegitimate children. His lifelong love of beauty, the 'Attitudes' that featured so early in his life with Emma, his whole manner of treating her like a wonderful *objet d'art* which so often amused his friends, the swimming boys who performed for his entertainment at Posillipo (as Tischbein witnessed) are all indications that in matters of sex Sir William was possibly one of those men for whom a feast for the eyes is banquet enough.

If this was so there is nothing to suggest that Emma was dissatisfied with her lot. She had given him no cause for jealousy nor had she ever exposed him to the ridicule he feared. Her boundless energy found an outlet in her busy social round and especially in the intrigues she carried on with the Queen which flattered her vanity and compensated for her lack of any official status in Naples. The suggestion, which has been made, that Lady Hamilton and the Queen had a lesbian relationship need not be considered seriously. Not only was Maria Carolina, who gave birth to eighteen children, almost always in some stage of pregnancy during the time she was closest to Emma, but nothing in the character of either woman could give support to the charge. The Queen was notorious for her flirtations with the handsome young men of her court. Emma herself had very few women friends; it can be said, in fact, that most women tended to dislike her. The charge was made, among others, by Napoleon, who had every political reason for wishing to defame the Queen. There was no truth in the accusation, any more than there was anything consciously homosexual in the *rapport* that Hamilton was always able to establish with intelligent men younger than himself.

At the time of Nelson's return to the bay of Naples Emma was completely settled in her life there, sure of herself, arrogant rather than informed in her opinions, and violent in her denunciations of those who disagreed with her. Sir William's long period of indifferent health seemed to have given a new strength to his wife, just as her exploitation by the Queen had given her an inflated notion of her political influence. Her intelligence, unfortunately, had not widened in proportion to the power she imagined she could wield, and upon the whole her character had not improved. Like her friend the Earl-Bishop of Derry who 'dashes at everything' she was beginning to show signs of impetuosity and an almost total lack of self-criticism, while her tendency to self-dramatisation continued to grow. When she wrote to Greville that she was 'allmost sick of grandeur' (something she would never be), perhaps unconsciously she was beginning to feel that she needed a larger stage on which to perform her public attitudes than was provided by an embassy where she had no official position and a husband who was approaching his seventieth year.

The news that a British naval force was returning to the Mediterranean had reached Naples in May 1798 when Lord St. Vincent, the commander-in-chief, wrote to inform Hamilton officially of the fact. Rarely had news been more welcome after the dismal and depressing months just passed when all news had been bad news, when nerves had been at full stretch and spirits low. Nelson, now Rear-Admiral of the Blue Squadron and a Knight of the Bath, had in fact left England in March to reinforce St. Vincent's fleet and serve under his command. 'Nothing in the world can exceed the pleasure I shall have in returning to you', was the last message he sent to his wife before hoisting his flag.

Though the Hamiltons as well as the Neapolitan Court were braced by the tonic effect of the good news of the British fleet's reappearance (for to Maria Carolina it was still a case of the 'brave, honest, loyal English' and 'those rogues of Frenchmen' in spite of her official neutrality) they were soon to hear very alarming reports from another quarter. On 19 May, a fleet sailed out of Toulon consisting of thirteen line-of-battle ships and four hundred transports carrying an army of thirty-five thousand troops. General Bonaparte himself was in command of this formidable force whose destination was unknown. In fact he was sailing for Egypt, but when intelligence first reached Naples that this great fleet had put to sea it could only be assumed that the Kingdom of the Two Sicilies was about to suffer invasion. Almost the whole of northern Italy was now in the hands of the French; it was logical to suppose that the turn of the south had come at last.

On 12 June Sir William heard from his old friend who was searching for the enemy with orders to 'take, sink, burn or destroy' their fleet if it fell into his hands. 'If the *Transfer* sloop of war has arrived at Naples', Nelson wrote from on board the *Vanguard* cruising off Elba, 'you will know that the British fleet is in the Mediterranean, and that I have the honour of commanding it. . . I beg you will assure the King and Queen of Naples that I will not lose one moment in fighting the French fleet, and that no person can have a more ardent desire of serving them and of fulfilling the orders of the good and great King our Master.' Nelson was anxious for information: 'Are the ports of Naples and Sicily open to his Majesty's fleet? Have the Governors orders for our free admission, and for us to be supplied with whatever we may want?' He was in need of frigates, those fast-sailing vessels which were the eyes of the fleet, and enquired after good pilots for the coasts of Sicily, the Adriatic, or 'what ever place the Enemy's fleet may be at—for I mean to follow them if they go to the Black Sea'.[10] The letter was very official, referring to Sir William as 'Your Excellency', so that it could, if necessary, be shown to General Acton.

This letter had scarcely reached the Palazzo Sessa before the sails of Nelson's squadron were observed on the horizon. The Admiral did not himself come ashore; he hove-to outside territorial waters, sending Captain Thomas Troubridge there to represent him. The need was still for frigates and the use of Sicilian ports. 'If the enemy have Malta', he wrote in the note Troubridge brought for Sir William, 'it is only as a safe harbour for their fleet, and Sicily will fall the moment the King's fleet withdraws from the coasts of Sicily; therefore we must have free use of Sicily to enable us to starve the French in Malta.'[11] Nelson was using the language of war which took little account of any treaty of peace between Naples and the French Republic. It was Hamilton's business to translate it into the language of diplomacy.

While Sir William and Troubridge were engaged on this task two letters were sent to the Admiral on board his flag-ship from Emma. The first was a mere note of welcome: 'God bless you, my dear Sir, I will not say how glad I shall be to see you. Indeed, I cannot describe to you my feelings on your being so near us. Ever, ever dear Sir, your affte. and grateful Emma Hamilton.' The second letter was more enigmatical. Enclosed with it was another, written in the ungrammatical French of Maria Carolina. 'I send you a letter I have this moment received from the Queen,' Emma's accompanying note explained, '*Kiss it*, and send it back by Bowen, as I am bound not to give any of her letters, Ever yours, Emma.'[12] As

Nelson could neither read nor speak the French language he could do little more than kiss the letter sent to him under such unusual circumstances.

Precisely why Emma should send Nelson a letter he was unable to read without explaining to him what it contained is a question only she could answer. She may have wished to impress upon him the close intimacy she shared with the Queen. The simple signature 'Emma' was no doubt an impulsive rather than a calculated indiscretion to a man who as yet had never addressed her as anything other than 'My dear Lady Hamilton'. In fact Emma was merely indulging her passion for the dramatic. To many people the gesture would have seemed silly as well as pointless, but the man who liked to talk symbolically of laurel and cypress found no difficulty in responding to histrionics of this order. He kissed the letter and returned it with the gallant assurance that he hoped soon to have the honour of kissing the Queen's hand 'when no fears intervene'. Two great actors had just played their first scene together; many more scenes were to follow.

Hamilton and Troubridge, meanwhile, had been trying to persuade the Neapolitan Ministers to meet some of Nelson's urgent requirements. The situation was not easy. Not only was the Kingdom of the Two Sicilies still technically at peace with France but Acton could not ignore the possibility of the French fleet appearing in the bay at any moment, even as Nelson sailed away. The British Admiral's own last intelligence of the enemy was that their sails had been sighted off the north coast of Sicily steering a course eastwards; news that held little comfort for the Neapolitans. As far as Acton himself was concerned he was eager to give what help he could, but the Marquis di Gallo was also present and this Minister was not prepared to compromise the extremely delicate relations with France. In the circumstances they could not agree to supplying Nelson with frigates. The most that Hamilton could extract was an informal order to the governors of all ports in Sicily to furnish the British Admiral with such supplies as he required. Even this, however, must be done *sub rosa*, for at least the appearance must be kept up of not admitting more than four belligerent ships into any Neapolitan port.

Sir William was aware that Acton and Gallo dared not offend the French; he knew also that they dreaded the thought of the British having again to withdraw from the Mediterranean while Naples was still menaced by Bonaparte's sea-borne army. If Nelson was forced to retire to Gibraltar for supplies the port of Naples would be left wide open to the French fleet which was already frighteningly near. It was this thought more than anything else which prompted Acton to give his 'informal' orders. That these orders were in fact given was confirmed in a note from Acton sent to Hamilton eight days after their meeting. 'Every proper order', he wrote,[13] 'has been given in Sicily for the British Squadron in the way mentioned here with the brave Captain Troubridge.'

The meeting between the ambassador and the Neapolitan ministers had of necessity to be brief for Nelson was anxious to weigh anchor and continue his search for the enemy. His guess was now confirmed that Malta had been one of their objectives. Troubridge took back with him a letter from Hamilton giving Nelson all the news he had been able to collect, which included the information that the Maltese were all under arms preparing for a vigorous defence. 'God send you, my dear Nelson', Sir William added, 'the success that may be expected from your well-known bravery and experienced conduct, and with such a chosen band under your command.' Nelson's ships had hardly gone before it was learnt that Malta had fallen on 12 June and that the French had left a garrison on the island and sailed on. The ancient rule of the Knights of St. John was over.

The news that Hamilton sent to Nelson had reached the Palazzo Sessa in a note from the Queen to Emma. Following her usual custom of passing on valuable information to the British Minister in this way Maria Carolina reported that the Republican fleet was before Malta and had also sent a ship to the island of Pantelleria to enquire whether it belonged to Malta or to Sicily. 'Having learnt the latter', her note continued, 'they quitted it; that proves their hostility is directed against Malta, the capture of which would be a great misfortune to us as it is a stronghold with a port, directly opposite to us, from whence no one would be able to dislodge the rogues. . . Perhaps it would be useful to communicate this news to Nelson, our friend and preserver, but it would be well for the Chevalier to go to the good honest General [Acton] who will inform him more fully.' It should again be emphasised that the Queen forwarded this information entirely on her own initiative. She needed no encouragement either from Lady Hamilton or from anyone else. A few days later (the Queen rarely dated her letters) she reported the fall of the island. It was, she declared, 'an incalculable misfortune for our peace'.[14]

The news of the fall of Malta might have come as a final blow to Hamilton's spirits, which had been depressed enough at the beginning of the year. In fact it had exactly the opposite effect as was shown in the vigorous letter he addressed to Nelson on the subject of the measures he considered should be taken as a result of this hostile act directed by France against the Neapolitan Kingdom. 'You know how much I am the enemy to half measures', he wrote on 26 June, 'and your actions have long proved your determined character. Malta itself, as you know, belongs to the Crown of Sicily; the opinion I ventured to give here upon the arrival of the news of its having been given up to the French was that His Sicilian Majesty shou'd send away Mr. Garat, the Ambassador of the French Republic, and march on directly to Rome, sending an express to the Emperor to acquaint him that His Majesty had thought it absolutely necessary to draw his sword again and throw away the scabbard, and that he flattered himself that His Imperial Majesty wou'd not suffer him to be sacrificed by a faithless enemy. The Emperor must then have come forward, and, by our Government's sending you the frigates, galeots, gunboats and small vessels, of which you are in want of, directly, there would be the best chance of counteracting and frustrating all the diabolical plans of the

French Directory. But, alas! I see plainly there is not energy and resolution enough in this Government to come to such a decision and, I think, salutary measure. All our present dependance is in you, my dear Nelson, and I am convinced that what is in the power of mortal man to do you will do.'[15]

The Queen alone in Naples had the spirit to respond favourably to Hamilton's suggestions. The King was too lazy and too timid to act: the French were out of sight and as far as he was concerned they were out of mind. Why worry? It might interfere with his hunting. Acton and Gallo were now engaged in discussion with Austria and any peremptory move might upset their delicate negotiations; furthermore it had always been their policy that Austria must move first. As to Gallo, he was very far from committing himself to so irretrievably anti-French a position; he was the sort of minister who liked to know which way the wind was blowing and at present the weather-vane gave no clear indication. Only a crushing defeat of the French and the invigorating presence of Nelson himself would stir up King Ferdinand to attempt the execution of a plan very similar to what Sir William now proposed. By then it would be too late.

Having missed the French at Malta Nelson rightly divined that they were heading for Egypt. His lack of frigates prevented him from exploring the alternative possibility that they might have made for Corfu and he sailed directly for Alexandria. In fact he outstripped the enemy fleet with its slow-sailing transports and arrived at Alexandria to find the port empty save for one Turkish warship, some frigates, and an assorted collection of merchant vessels. His supply situation was now becoming desperate and reluctantly he returned to Sicily to benefit from Acton's promise of provisions. On 20 July he dropped anchor before the port of Syracuse.

What precisely happened at Syracuse is difficult to say. Nelson got his supplies but the letters he wrote from the port present a confused picture. Perhaps they simply mirror the perplexity of the Governor who had publicly to uphold the treaty of peace with France and privately provide the British fleet with the supplies and provisions they required, while Nelson himself had no wish to compromise his friends should his letters fall into the hands of the enemy. First, on 22 July, he complained to Emma that he was 'so much distressed at not having had any account of the French fleet, and so much hurt at the treatment we receive from the power we came to assist and fight for, that I am hardly in a situation to write a letter to an elegant body. . . I wish to know your and Sir Wm.'s plans for going down the Mediterranean, for, if we are to be kicked in every port of the Sicilian dominions, the sooner we are gone the better. Good God! how sensibly I feel our treatment. I have only to pray I find the French and throw all my vengeance on them.'

Between writing this letter and sitting down on the following day to address Sir William the Governor of Syracuse must have had a change of heart. Perhaps he felt it incumbent on him to put up a token show of resistance; all we can be sure of is that on 23 July Nelson found his requirements met, though his irritation had not completely subsided. 'The fleet is unmoored,' he told Hamilton, 'and the moment the wind comes off the land I shall go out of this delightful harbour, where our present wants have been most amply supplied, and where every attention has been paid to us; but I have been tormented by no private orders being given to the Governor for our admission.' Nelson had other reasons to feed his feelings of frustration as well as equivocal behaviour by a port Governor; to these he gave vent in the last sentence of his letter: '*No frigates*—to which has been, and may again, be attributed the loss of the French fleet.'[16] Lord St. Vincent was also sent an account of the 'shameful' treatment they had received: 'Acton promised to send orders. *None has been sent*. What do you think of this?'

Hamilton took Nelson's letter of protest to Acton where he read it to the Minister 'abuse and all'. Acton gave further assurances but by then Nelson was already at sea. The main point was that he had got his supplies and the fresh water his ships so badly needed. By the time Sir William had heard that the Admiral had left Syracuse fully satisfied and had again shown his letter to the Neapolitan Minister the battle of the Nile had been fought and won, though the news of the victory had not yet reached Naples. 'I saw with great satisfaction yesterday', Acton wrote, 'what you was so kind to show me of Adml. Nelson's letter, wherein he had left Syracuse, as he says, fully satisfied with the reception, assistance and provisions of all kind which he met with in that Port. As by his first letter the Admiral mentioned his provisions on board for only 7 or 8 weeks, I think, my dear Sir, that no time should be lost in preparing what is wanting for victualing his Squadron without going to Gibraltar, which would be for the Two Sicilies the worst of Evils.'[17] This letter was written on 15 August. Unknown either to Acton or to Sir William Hamilton the British Admiral had at last caught up with the enemy he had been chasing for so many weeks. On 1 August he defeated the French fleet in a decisive victory in Aboukir Bay. The news did not reach Naples until the beginning of September.

1. Morrison, 252.
2. *Vide* E. Edwards: *Lives of the Founders of the British Museum*, Vol. 1, p. 357. Hamilton actually got £8,400 for his first collection.
3. Morrison, 287.
4. B.M. Add. MSS. 34048, f. 87.
5. Prince Augustus.
6. B.M. Add. MSS 42071, f. 11.
7. B.M. Add, MSS 41200, ff. 121-6.
8. This picture is now attributed to Luini.

9. For a complete list of Hamilton's pictures see Appendix.
10. Morrison, 315.
11. Ibid., 319.
12. B.M. Add. MSS 34989.
13. B.M. Egerton, MSS 2640, f. 75.
14. *Vide* Jeaffreson: *The Queen of Naples & Lord Nelson*, Vol. I.,
    pp. 333 and 335.
15. Morrison, 322.
16. Morrison, 325 and 326.
17. Egerton MSS 2640, f. 89.

CHAPTER XX

Victory and Defeat

News of the Battle of the Nile reached Naples on 3 September when the *Mutine* brig sailed into the bay carrying Nelson's dispatches. In a letter addressed to Sir William the victorious Admiral declared: 'Almighty God has made me the happy instrument in destroying the Enemy's fleet, which I hope will be a blessing to Europe. You will have the goodness to communicate this happy event to all the Courts in Italy, for my head is so indifferent that I can scarcely scrawl this letter. Captain Capel, who is charged with my despatches for England, will give you every information. Pray put him in the quickest mode of getting home. . . ' He would soon be bringing his battered fleet to Naples for refitting. As for Bonaparte, his army, stranded on land, was 'in a scrape, and will not get out of it'.[1] People had become so accustomed to news of defeat, to the anxious knowledge that the Neapolitan kingdom lay ever more openly at the mercy of the advancing armies of France, that they could hardly believe their ears when the facts of the victory became known. The thought that the invincible Bonaparte was cut off from Europe without means of retreat seemed too good to be true. A sort of hysteria broke out in Naples. Sir William announced that he felt ten years younger; when the news reached the palace the Queen kissed her husband and rushed about the room embracing all the people present while she proclaimed Nelson the saviour of Italy; and Emma, on being told of the victory, promptly fell into a faint. She was, it must be admitted, so much of an actress that it is difficult to believe that the swoon was genuine, but she performed it with such abandon that she could still feel the bruises over a fortnight later.

The joy which Sir William felt was all the greater because he could claim the victor as his friend. 'History, either ancient or modern,' he wrote to Nelson on 8 September, 'does not record an action that does more honor to the heroes that gained the victory than the late one of the first of August. You have now completely made yourself, my dear Nelson, immortal. God be praised, and may you live long to enjoy the sweet satisfaction of having added such glory to our country, and most probably put an end to the confusion and misery in which all Europe wou'd soon have been involved. This country feels its immediate good effects, and their Sicilian Majesties, their ministry, and the nation at large, are truly sensible of it, and loudly acknowledge eternal obligation to your undaunted courage and steady perseverance. You may well conceive, my dear sir, how happy Emma and I are in the reflection that it is you, Nelson, our bosom friend, that has done such wonderous good in having humbl'd these proud robbers and vain boasters.'[2]

Acton wrote to Hamilton conveying the good wishes of the King and Queen: 'I have their Sicilian Majesties' orders to beg of you to say how grateful has been to them the news and the service so bravely performed and resulting from the brave action,' while Maria Carolina let her feelings go in an ecstatic letter to Emma: 'Ah! if they take a portrait of the great Nelson, I will have it in my chamber. My gratitude is engraven on my heart. Live! Long live this brave nation and her honoured navy! It is a glory in which I participate, as much for our gain, which is very great, as for the glory of the first flag in the whole world. Hip! Hip! my dear Miledy; I am wild with joy!'[3] For the first time since the death of her sister Marie Antoinette she felt that the vengeance she had sworn in her moment of bitterness and anguish was beginning to have effect.

Among those who each day scanned the horizon for the first sign of the victorious fleet was an English woman just turned forty and her aged mother. Both ladies had recently arrived from Rome, where they had lived for many years, and had made themselves known to Sir William and Lady Hamilton. Lady Knight, the mother, was a rather silly woman, the widow of an admiral. The traveller Henry Swinburne had known them twenty years before and had been amused by the elder Lady's eccentrically mistaken observations, as when she had talked of the romantic groves where Tasso had composed his Ariosto or, on visiting the basilica of St. John Lateran, had wondered at the extraordinary circumstance of a church having been named in honour of St. John's latter end. It was surprising that such a woman should have produced so intelligent a daughter. Swinburne described the latter as '*a bel esprit*, clever and learned',[4] and she had lost nothing of her sharpness with the passage of years.

Cornelia Knight, who had literary tastes and had published a 'classic novel' in two volumes, was possessed of an acute sense of observation. Very little escaped her keen eyes. She had not been long in Naples before she was able to record a curious fact about Maria Carolina. The Queen, she noticed, was subject to fits of religious devotion 'at which times she stuck short prayers and pious ejaculations inside of her stays, and occasionally swallowed them'. This quaint trick of the Queen's had been observed on a previous visit; Miss Knight and her mother were now in Naples as refugees from Rome, and as victims of the republican régime in that city were especially anxious to witness the arrival in the bay of the victor of the Nile.

'Two ships of the line at length appeared in sight', she afterwards wrote in her *Autobiography*. 'The weather was particularly calm and a great number of boats went out to meet them, conveying not only English residents but many of the natives likewise. The King himself went in his barge, followed by a part of his band of music in another, and several of the foreign ministers and others joined in the glad procession. I was with Sir William and Lady Hamilton in their barge, which also was followed by another with a band of musicians on board. The shore was lined with spectators who rent the air with joyous acclamations, while the bands played 'God save the King' and 'Rule Britannia'. As we approached the two ships we made them out to be the *Culloden*, Commodore Troubridge, and the *Alexander*, Captain Ball. . .

'The King of Naples did not go on board either of the ships, but from his barge saluted the officers on deck. His Majesty had expressed his desire to be *incognito*, so as not to give the trouble of paying him the usual honours. Sir William Hamilton, observing some of the seamen looking earnestly out of the port holes, said to them, "My lads! that is the King, whom you have saved, with his family and Kingdom". Several of the men answered, "Very glad of it, sir—very glad of it".'[5]

Nelson's flag-ship was at last seen approaching on the evening of 22 September. The *Vanguard* was so scarred and battered that she arrived in tow. Sir William and Emma sailed out to meet her and boarded the ship about a league out at sea. On deck the Admiral stood ready to receive them, still pale from his heroic exertions, his head 'ready to split' from the wound he had suffered. But neither his wound nor his manifest exhaustion could rob Emma of an affecting scene: with a cry of 'Oh God! Is it possible?' she flung herself at his one remaining arm 'more dead than alive'. Her little scene was hardly played out before the King arrived and for a while she had to abandon the centre of the stage. Ferdinand grasped Nelson by the hand and called him his deliverer and preserver 'with every other expression of kindness'.[6]

It was five years since Nelson had set eyes on either Sir William or his wife. In that period time had left its mark on all three of them. Nelson's uniform now displayed an empty sleeve as well as the red riband and star which also decorated Sir William's coat. Cornelia Knight, seeing him for the first time, noted that 'Admiral Nelson is little, and not remarkable in his person either way; but he has great animation of countenance, and activity in his appearance: his manners are unaffectedly simple and modest.' The British Minister, his features gaunt but still handsome, had aged. As his old friend the Earl-Bishop put it, he now looked 'old, shrivelled. . . a piece of walking *verd antique*'. Emma had coarsened, her figure had become huge, only the face still showed traces of a once fabulous beauty. Nelson was within a few days of his fortieth birthday; Emma was thirty-three; Sir William would be entering his sixty-ninth year in December.

Before this re-encounter took place on the quarter-deck of the *Vanguard* Nelson had written suggesting that when he reached Naples he should find rooms elsewhere than at the Palazzo Sessa, where he knew a room would be placed at his disposal. He was answering Hamilton's congratulatory letter and the request that he would 'repose the few wearied limbs you have left' on the soft pillows that Emma had prepared for him. 'With your permission and good Lady Hamilton's', he replied, 'I had better be at a hotel; it will not deprive me of being with you long enough to teaze you, and, as I must have much business with every officer it may be more convenient. I am truly sensible of your and her Ladyship's goodness, and leave this matter to your determination; if you agree with me, pray order your servant to get me some apartments.'[7]

His insistence was not very strong nor his reason very cogent, but he felt obliged to make the suggestion, knowing well that it would be thrust aside by his hospitable friend, proud and eager to welcome the hero under his roof. Did Nelson have some qualms about living at such close proximity to the voluptuous Emma whose impulsive conduct he had already sampled when she had sent him the Queen's letter to kiss? It is true that she had taken no special notice of him when he had stayed at the Palazzo Sessa five years before, but the letter she had written to him after his victory had been of an enthusiasm quite beyond the limits of usual correspondence between ordinary acquaintances. Nor was there any reason to suppose that Emma's indifference of five years ago had been reciprocated on Nelson's part; few men could remain indifferent to her powerful attraction. Now she wrote to say that she would rather have been 'an English powder-monkey or a swab' in his victory 'than an Emperor out of it'. This, and the eagerness she expressed to embrace him, were enough to cause him alarm. It was not at all what one expected in a letter from an ambassador's wife.

There is nothing to suggest that Nelson was in any way unsatisfied with his married life at the time when he returned to Naples in September 1798. When Lady Knight told him that she supposed the day of his victory would now be accounted the happiest in his life he answered: 'No, the happiest was that on which I married Lady Nelson.'[8] Before leaving for his present command he had told Lady Spencer, wife of the First Lord of the Admiralty, that Lady Nelson was beautiful, accomplished, and 'an angel'. When Lord Lansdowne offered him the use of his box at the theatre, adding that some very handsome ladies also made use of it, Nelson replied that he might have been tempted were he a bachelor, but as he was possessed of 'everything which is valuable in a wife' he had no occasion to think beyond a pretty face. When he was wounded in the head during the battle of the Nile his first thought had been of her. Imagining the wound to be fatal he had exclaimed: 'I am killed: remember me to my wife.' His eagerness to return to her has already been recorded. Lady Nelson had neither great beauty nor great fascination; she was retiring and a little too timid for the position of wife to a man so often exposed to danger; but he had found nothing to complain of in eleven years of married life. 'My love is founded on esteem,' Nelson had once told his wife, 'the only foundation that can make the passion last.'[9] It was not to last very much longer.

As far as Sir William and Emma were concerned there was no question of Nelson staying anywhere but at their house. When they saw his pale, weary face and his scarred brow they realised that any thought of an hotel was quite out of the question. He needed rest and care and this, they were determined, should be provided by no one but themselves. He entered the Palazzo Sessa and was soon installed in a room which commanded a splendid view of the bay, where he could see his ships riding at anchor. 'I am in their house', he wrote to his wife in London, 'and I may tell you it required all the kindness of my friends to set me up.' It was seven weeks since his victory over the French; it was also the day of Lady Nelson's defeat, though it would be some time yet before any of them would be aware of the fact. But Nelson was certainly conscious of the risk he ran; a fortnight after reaching Naples he ended a letter to Lord St. Vincent with the sentence: 'I am writing opposite Lady Hamilton, therefore you will not be surprised at the glorious jumble of this letter. Were your Lordship in my place, I much doubt if you could write so well; our hearts and our hands must be all in a flutter: Naples is a dangerous place, and we must keep clear of it.'[10]

The enthusiasm which had greeted the news of Nelson's victory broke out afresh when the hero himself arrived in the city. Naples blazed with illumination, the Palazzo Sessa shone with the glare of three thousand lamps, the name of Nelson was on every lip, his exploits the subject of song and sonnet. Lady Hamilton elected herself high-priestess of his shrine and quickly discovered that the hero's appetite for praise was as unassuageable as his hunger for glory. Enrolling Cornelia Knight as an attendant spirit she prepared her first set-piece in honour of Nelson's birthday which was celebrated on 29 September. The eight hundred guests who were invited to the embassy were all presented with ribbons and buttons decorated with the heroic name and at an appropriate moment Emma stepped forward and with a splendid gesture unveiled a rostral column engraved with the legend *Veni, vidi, vici*, and the names of all the captains in the battle of the Nile. The column would never be removed, she declared, so long as she and Sir William remained in possession of the house. Then, in her lusty soprano voice (which the unkind Lady Holland had referred to as 'vile discordant screaming') she led the assembly in a new verse to the National Anthem which Miss Knight had composed specially for the occasion:

> Join we great Nelson's name,
> First on the roll of fame,
> Him let us sing;
> Spread we his fame around,
> Honour of British ground,
> Who made Nile's shores resound—
> God save our King!

The Admiral was enchanted and sent a copy of the verse home to his wife with the remark; 'I know you will sing it with pleasure.' When the celebrations were all over, however, and Emma's vaunting praises momentarily silent, he felt a sudden longing to escape to his ship. 'I trust, my Lord, in a week we shall be at sea', he wrote to St. Vincent on 30 September. 'I am very unwell, and the miserable conduct of this Court is not likely to cool my irritable temper. It is a country of fiddlers and poets, whores and scoundrels.'[11] It was not only the conduct of the Court that irritated him. His stepson Josiah Nisbet, now a Captain and old enough to know better, had been very drunk during the birthday celebrations of the previous night. He had been removed from the room by some of his brother officers whose names adorned the rostral column, but not before he had expressed the opinion that his hostess was receiving attentions that by rights belonged to his mother. Gossip would soon be spreading the story around Naples—and beyond.

Nelson was eager to continue the war against the French and was anxious to follow up his resounding sea victory by driving them from the Italian peninsula. The plan he had in mind was the very one Sir William had proposed after the fall of Malta and had first suggested to Acton as long ago as 1796, when the treaty of peace with France had been signed; an advance on Rome which would provoke similar action from Austria in the north, leaving the French at the mercy of both armies. The Austrian General, Baron Karl von Mack, who had long been promised to command the Neapolitan Army, was expected at any minute, and on the principle that 'the boldest measures are the safest' Nelson urged immediate action.

The Queen, whom he considered 'truly a daughter of Maria Theresa', was with him, and so was Acton, but Gallo procrastinated and with the King and other ministers kept putting off what Nelson described as 'the evil day'. They wanted to be sure of Austrian co-operation. The man of action was irritated by the caution and circumlocution of the diplomatists and politicians. The Marquis di Gallo, in particular, he detested, feeling that the minister, with his fine court manners, looked down upon someone like himself bred in the 'rough element' of the sea. Nelson lacked Hamilton's patience, born of long experience of the diplomatic trade, and his understanding of the Italian mind; he thought the British Minister was too good to them; they required, in his estimation, 'the strong language of an English Admiral telling them plain truths . . .' Sir William, alas, could not enjoy this freedom. Lord Grenville, the British Foreign Minister, had warned him of the danger which would attend any plan undertaken without the fullest support of the Court of Vienna. Hamilton was fully committed to Nelson's point of view; the plan, after all, was his own; but he had to tread warily, knowing that nothing could be accomplished without the approval of the vacillating King and the ministers who followed Ferdinand's example rather than the Queen's.

He had other problems to cope with. At the conferences with Gallo and Acton and in audiences with Ferdinand and Maria Carolina he had to act as interpreter for Nelson, who was unable to converse in either French or Italian. The fact that Sir John Acton could speak some English was not always as helpful as it might seem, and occasionally caused considerable confusion, as was shown by a letter which the Minister sent to Sir William after a meeting on 3 October.

'I have a scruple, my dear Sir,' Acton wrote,[12] 'my expressions in English might have produced a different idea from my meaning. I expressed to Admiral Nelson the probability of our troops marching towards Bologna and Tuscany, and the thought of sending the *Van of our army* to Leghorn by sea, before the French entrance to that town by land. In mentioning the *Van* of the army or *l'avant-garde* I said in English the *Vanguard*—the ship now mounted by the brave Admiral Nelson, meaning as to myself only that we should send our *van* by sea, and were in hopes for protection and help from the English squadron. I had no other meaning; but on recollection of an answer of the Admiral which I did not consider at first, I should be very sorry that he had thought that I could present him a proposal of transporting troops in any part. You are acquainted with my odd English as I am out of use of speaking it since many years. I felt some pains, in consequence, of a mistake if my meaning had been misunderstood.'

After meeting General Mack (who had reached Caserta on 9 October, travelling with a cavalcade of five carriages) Nelson sailed for Malta. During his absence Sir William continued to press for military action. Emma, in a performance in which (as she told the Admiral) she put out her left arm, 'like you', continued to hector the Queen in 'the language of truth' though Maria Carolina was perhaps the only member of the Court, of whose warlike temper Nelson so much despaired, who did not require this dramatic exhortation. On 26 October, in a long letter to Nelson, Hamilton announced that a message had come from Vienna advising the King of Naples 'to act openly against the French at Malta as His Imperial Majesty would certainly support him', and added his own comment that 'this takes off all difficulties'. No doubt he had Grenville's warning in mind as well as the doubts and reservations of Gallo and the King. He was going too far, however, in imagining that the Emperor of Austria's support for an attack on Malta would also apply to a more adventurous expedition against the French army in central Italy. General Mack, meanwhile, had been visiting troops on the frontiers of the Kingdom, and Acton had shown Sir William a list of the Neapolitan army 'in three columns which, on paper, makes an astonishing appearance, more than 60 battalions of infantry and thirty squadrons of cavalry'. The Court and Ministry, he assured Nelson, were in high spirits, 'and they say the army is the same'.[13]

By November Nelson was back in Naples, in time to hear of the honours that had been conferred upon him by his grateful sovereign. He was created a baron, with the title of Lord Nelson of the Nile, though many people, including Hamilton, considered that he should have been made a Viscount. For Emma no rank in the peerage was high enough; she wanted to hail him as 'Prince Victory'. His own chief worry on his return was a growing distrust in the abilities of Mack. The Neapolitan army was now encamped at San Germano. The Hamiltons took Nelson there to witness the manoeuvres which Mack had planned and were highly disconcerted when the troops playing the part of the 'enemy' won the day, surrounding the Austrian general whose strategy, so ignominiously defeated, had intended exactly the opposite conclusion. It was not a very encouraging *dénouement* and helped to confirm Nelson's distrust for a General who could never travel without his five carriages. 'I have formed my opinion,' he observed dubiously; 'I heartily hope I may be mistaken.'

In spite of ominous indications of the military commander-in-chief's incompetence a gala atmosphere prevailed at San Germano. 'The King had taken up his quarters in this camp', wrote the historian Colletta, 'prepared to march with the army; the queen, attired in a riding-habit, constantly drove along the lines in a chariot and four, accompanied by the ambassadors from friendly sovereigns, and other foreigners of distinction, the barons of the Kingdom, and Lady Hamilton, who, under pretence of escorting her Majesty, displayed her own beauty in all its magnificence to the camp, and paraded her conquest over the victor of Aboukir who, seated beside her in the same carriage, appeared fascinated and submissive to her charms.'[14] Whatever might be the worries of Nelson or of her husband, Emma had rarely enjoyed so public a triumph, or one that appealed so flatteringly to her self-esteem. She was to be seen everywhere in the company of the hero of the Nile. Always an actress, she had at last discovered a rôle which satisfied her vanity no less than her ambition. Sir William watched the scene with complacency. He had indulged Emma's whims for far too long to wish to deny her the pleasure of appearing in public on a hero's arm, nor did he entertain a moment's anxiety over her motives, which at this time were innocent enough. As for Nelson, he was his greatest friend; he looked upon him as a son. He had complete trust in his honour and integrity.

Though malicious tongues were already beginning to wag and inquisitive minds to speculate about the exact nature of the tie which bound this interesting trio together, there were in fact at this time no grounds for gossip. All the same Emma's lack of restraint and Nelson's obvious infatuation with her, though still innocent, coupled with the fact that Hamilton was a generation older than either of them, were all facts little calculated to silence rumour, however inaccurate or misinformed. Before the year was out Lady Nelson had been made sufficiently uneasy by the things that were being whispered to threaten to 'join the standard at Naples' unless her husband returned in the next few months.[14] She was easily dissuaded, but Nelson's ardent references to Sir

William and Emma in the letters he sent her were not such as might calm her fears, though his very open enthusiasm was sufficient indication of a still untroubled conscience. 'What can I say of her and Sir William's goodness to me?' he wrote to her of his host and hostess after three months at Naples; 'They are in fact with the exception of you and my dear father the dearest friends I have in this world. I live as Sir William's son in the house and my glory is as dear to them as their own. In short I am under such obligations that I can never repay but with my eternal gratitude.' Lady Nelson did not come out to Naples, but she remained uneasy.

All three were far too much involved in the preparations for the invasion of the Roman Republic to have thoughts for much else. It was better, both Hamilton and Nelson urged, to march before the French launched an attack which was in any event inevitable. Emma saw her rôle as the inspiration of the expedition, a sort of royalist version of the republican goddess of Liberty, urging them all to acts of heroism. The final plans were drawn up in November and it was decided that Nelson's ships should transport and land troops at Leghorn in the enemy's rear while Mack invaded the former Papal territory from the south across the Neapolitan frontier. The Austrians, it was hoped, would then march in from the north and the French would be caught in a three-pronged attack.

Then, at the last moment, dispatches bringing disturbing news arrived from Vienna. Francis II, who had succeeded the Emperor Leopold in 1792, did not share the sanguine outlook of Maria Carolina, who was both his mother-in-law and aunt. His minister Baron Thugut refused to commit his country to any rash adventure; he promised no help unless the French could be made to appear as aggressors. Ferdinand showed signs of hesitation; Gallo's prudence seemed to be justified. The plan which Hamilton and Nelson had so eagerly pressed was on the point of being scrapped when the English Admiral's impatience got the better of his sense of etiquette. To him Gallo and the Austrian Minister were little better than traitors. Turning on the flustered and uncertain Ferdinand he told the King that he must either advance, trusting in God for his blessing on a just cause and prepare to die sword in hand, or remain quiet and be kicked out of his kingdom. The astounded monarch decided to march.

The rebuff from Austria was embarrassing for Hamilton. The British Foreign Secretary had already warned both Sir William and the Neapolitan ambassador in London of the dangers involved in an attack on the French without 'the fullest assurances of support' from the Imperial government in Vienna. He believed, in fact, that French power on land was such that there was no safety for Naples but submission. It was now quite clear that no assurances could be expected from the Imperial government, but Hamilton did not change the advice he had given the Court to which he was accredited. He was far too deeply committed to the support of the plan which he had himself first proposed when he had proclaimed his distaste for half measures and had told

Acton that 'violent disorders require violent remedies'. Since then Nelson's presence and his insistence upon the necessity of attack, as well as his violent dislike of Gallo, had added a partisan atmosphere to the councils of war, and there was no doubt upon which side Sir William stood. On this issue he could no longer offer detached or impartial advice. Emma's vehement behaviour had compromised her husband even further so that he could hardly offer to withdraw his support from the plan without exposing himself to ridicule. In any event, carried away by the enthusiasm of Nelson and upheld in his decision by the victorious Admiral's immense prestige, he undoubtedly believed firmly in the rectitude of their counsel from both a military and a political viewpoint. Whatever his duty should have been, his advice remained unchanged: attack.

On 22 November the army marched from San Germano with the King and General Mack at its head, and Nelson's fleet sailed for Leghorn. Sir William and Emma remained in Naples where Maria Carolina assumed the duties of Regent. The feeling of anti-climax which followed upon the army's departure was emphasised by the empty walls of the Palazzo Sessa. For the past month workmen had been busily engaged in dismantling Hamilton's great collection, the pictures and works of art being boarded up in packing cases. All the best canvasses and drawings were packed up between 26 October and the end of the year; it required fourteen packing cases to accommodate nearly two hundred canvasses, while a further five cases contained his marbles and bronzes. A careful inventory had been made of the contents of each case with a description of the subject of every picture and its measurements in Neapolitan *palme* and *once*. This catalogue,[16] the most complete one of the collection, was drawn up by James Clark, a picture-restorer and minor painter, but the pages show various corrections in Hamilton's hand. The collection represented almost the whole of Sir William's capital and he had no wish to see it fall into the hands of the French should the military expedition fail. His collection of vases, which he had tried without success to sell to the King of Prussia, had been packed separately and, thanks to Nelson's help, was already on its way home to England in the hold of the store-ship *Colossus* which had sailed out of Naples in October.

The Hamiltons waited anxiously for news. On 29 November Ferdinand entered Rome in triumph, the castle of St. Angelo alone remaining in the hands of the enemy. The French, however, had not been defeated; they had merely withdrawn before the advancing Neapolitans in order to re-deploy themselves for attack. Mack's military leadership showed extraordinary ineptitude in allowing the enemy to withdraw and reform themselves without attempting any preventive action. He seemed to think that his presence in Rome was in itself sufficient to frighten them into submission. The King was quite oblivious of any danger. He installed himself in the Farnese Palace and sent a grandiloquent letter to the Pope inviting him to leave his place of exile and 'borne on the wings of the cherubim descend into the Vatican and purify it with your holy presence'. Nelson, meanwhile, had reached Leghorn and disembarked his troops. He wrote at once to Hamilton. saying that he would return to Naples the moment the weather moderated, and added that he had captured the *whole* Ligurian navy—which consisted of two twenty-gun ships.

The *Vanguard* sailed into the bay of Naples on 5 December and Nelson went at once to the Palazzo Sessa. He had already sent an unsatisfactory report to Hamilton of the behaviour of the Neapolitan commanding officer at Leghorn who had refused to seize the French ships there on the 'pretence' that the King of Naples was not at war with the French (which was in fact quite true, for Ferdinand had advanced on Rome without making any formal declaration). This was to prove typical of the behaviour of many Neapolitan officers whose loyalty was at the most half-hearted, while others secretly sympathised with the republican cause. Many of the officers in Mack's army would soon be acting in the same way when face to face with the enemy. Their example quickly undermined the morale of their troops, whose loyalty to the King was strong but whose discipline gave way to panic when they saw themselves betrayed by their officers. The few who had loyal commanders put up a brave fight.

Ferdinand's rôle as liberator of Rome came to a sudden end. Having wasted a week there during which time nothing had been done to consolidate his position, his army was driven ignominiously from the city by General Championnet, who had been able to concentrate his forces and deliver a shattering counter-attack. The Neapolitans were soon in full retreat. On 7 December the King hurriedly left the city to avoid capture while the army upon whose military exploits he had placed such high hopes was scattered. The retreat quickly became a rout.

The day after his return to Naples Nelson had written to Lord St. Vincent: 'If Mack is defeated, this country in fourteen days is lost, for the Emperor has not yet moved his army, and if the Emperor will not march this country has not the power of resisting the French.'[17] It was all very well to blame the Emperor, but Nelson had known perfectly well before the march began that there was little or no chance of Austrian help. It was he himself who had urged the King in the frankest of terms to attack the French, and it was Hamilton who had failed to make clear to the King the dangers that would result if Austria refused her co-operation. If Mack's incompetence was the immediate cause of the Neapolitan military collapse, neither Nelson nor Sir William could escape their share of the blame.

As Ferdinand rushed back towards his capital the Queen wrote in despair to her 'dear Miledy'. Maria Carolina, like Nelson and Hamilton, had been among the most vociferous supporters of the plan to march against the French, and she now realised that its failure would wreck all her political ambitions. The fate of her sister was never far from her thoughts; she knew that she could expect little mercy at the hands of the French, and she looked upon Nelson's presence and protection as her only hope. 'We will do everything if these rascals should come *en masse,*' she told Emma, 'we will sacrifice life, everything. But if the people continue to fly like rabbits we shall be lost. Thus the stay of the brave Admiral, to whom I should in case of calamity be able to confide my children, will be a great blessing. We will do everything but debase ourselves. But my spirit is darkened.' At the beginning of the letter she had spoken of her anxiety for the King 'living in the midst of heart-breaking troubles and vexations of every kind', and added 'Mack is in despair, and not without reason.'[18] The letter brought little comfort to the Palazzo Sessa where every message that arrived contained more alarming and discomforting news from the front. Naples was in a state of growing apprehension; only the republicans and Jacobins welcomed the thought of a French invasion.

That the French would be in Naples quickly enough had been clear to both Hamilton and Nelson as soon as they heard that Mack was in retreat from Rome. Sir William's first duty was to arrange for the evacuation of the British residents for whose safety he was responsible. He was fully prepared for this; it had been settled some time before that in the event of such an emergency they should be transported to the comparative safety of Sicily, where they could be better protected by the British fleet. Indeed as early as 3 October, before the disastrous campaign had started, Nelson had told Emma that it might become his duty at very short notice to evacuate not only his fellow-countrymen living in Naples but also the King and Queen and their family. He was now able to place three transports at Sir William's disposal for the personal effects of the British residents, at the same time informing the ambassador that his entire squadron was ready to embark the residents themselves should the need arise, but he added the necessary warning that the operation should be carried out with as much secrecy as possible so as not to attract any unwelcome attention from hostile elements in the city. Hamilton, meanwhile, had chartered two Greek vessels to take the French *émigrés* who looked to him for protection.

Ferdinand returned on the evening of 13 December. It was just three weeks since he had marched from San Germano to drive the French out of Rome and restore the Pope to his throne. His first impulse on reaching Naples was to gather his loyal subjects round him and hurl defiance at the enemy. His poorer subjects were loyal enough but the experience of the brief campaign had taught him that their leaders could not be trusted. Many of the nobility sympathised with the revolutionary doctrines and were anxiously waiting for what they hoped would be the dawn of liberty; others considered the monarchy lost and were ready to change their allegiance as soon as the French appeared. The *lazzaroni* showed a frenzied loyalty to Ferdinand. To demonstrate the extent of their devotion they dragged a wretched man, whom they imagined to be a French spy, below the windows of the palace and murdered him before the eyes of the King. Ferdinand realised with horror that the innocent victim of their brutality was one of his own royal messengers. The day before he had witnessed this frightful sight General Mack had written urging him to fly before the French arrived in his capital. The fury of his supporters no less than the thought of the vengeance of his enemies made the King decide to accept the protection of Nelson's fleet and escape to his second capital at Palermo. It was a decision for which Hamilton, Nelson, and the Queen had long been prepared.

While the plans for the flight of the Royal Family were being discussed between Hamilton and Acton, Lord Nelson wisely withdrew his ships beyond the range of the cannon in the Neapolitan forts. The Queen, realising the necessity for secrecy, once again made use of the British embassy as a screen to cover her activities, for her friendship with Emma was sufficiently well known not to attract notice. As Nelson later pointed out to Lord St. Vincent, it would have been 'highly imprudent' for either himself or Sir William to have gone to Court at this time as all their movements were watched and there was danger of their being taken by the Jacobins as hostages. Rumours that the Royal Family might be leaving brought angry crowds into the streets. On one occasion the mob was only pacified after the King and Queen had appeared at a window of the palace and spoken to them. Wise people remained within their houses behind locked doors.

In the days immediately before the embarkation the Queen sent endless consignments of boxes, trunks, jewel-cases and valuables of every description to Lady Hamilton at the Palazzo Sessa to be carried from there to the waiting ships by Nelson's sailors. So as not to attract attention everything was done at dead of night, while with each delivery came a succession of letters and instructions from the Queen to her devoted friend. 'I venture to send you this evening all our Spanish money, both the King's and my own,' Emma read on 17 December, 'they are sixty thousand gold ducats. It is all we have, for we have never hoarded. The diamonds of the whole family, both men and women, will arrive tomorrow evening. . . ' Next day: 'Behold three more portmanteaus and a little box. In the first three is a little linen for all my children and in the box some little petticoats. I trust I am not imprudent in sending them to you.' On the nineteenth: 'I abuse your goodness and our brave Admiral's. Let the great boxes be thrown in the hold and the little ones be near at hand. It is so, because I have unfortunately an immense family. I am in the despair of desolation and my tears flow incessantly. The blow, its suddenness has bewildered me, and I do not think I shall recover from it. All my gratitude is devoted to you.' Emma, according to her practice, endorsed these letters with eulogistic notes: 'My adorable unfortunate Queen! God bless and protect her and her august family! *Dear, Dear, Dear Queen!*' or more simply just: 'Unfortunate Queen!'

Lady Hamilton, it must be pointed out, was only at the receiving end of this avalanche of royal baggage. It was Maria Carolina who organised the packing and dispatching of the various crates and boxes, handing them over to trusted servants for delivery at the Palazzo Sessa. On the nineteenth a second request came from the Queen: 'This evening I will send some other boxes and clothes for my numerous family and myself, for it is for life. Tell me frankly whether I may send our trunks this evening to the dock by a trusty man. . . or whether a transport should be able to convey them or whether it will cause trouble. In that case I will take other measures.'[19] This letter, which is signed 'The most wretched of women, mothers, queens, but your sincere friend', presents a very different picture from the claims made by Emma in *Lady Hamilton's Statement* twelve years later, when she wrote: 'I, however, began work myself and gradually removed all the jewels and more than thirty-six barrels of gold to our house.' As in the case of messages which the Queen had earlier sent to Sir William through his wife's agency, Emma could not resist the temptation to exaggerate the part she played in the business of the escape of the Royal Family. Her help was valuable but no more than ancillary; this is what she could later never bring herself to admit.

On 19 August Acton wrote to Hamilton: 'It seems after many debates that the Royal Family with a small retinue (not less, however, than 13 or 15 Persons) will embark *tomorrow night* with the greatest Secrecy. It will however be fixed tomorrow morning and then I am to send you for Lord Nelson the notes [of people embarking]. If it is postponed, it shall not go later than the Day after tomorrow, 21st. This is what I have been told, as all the answers which Lord Nelson has been so good as to give Prince Belmonte have been extremely approved of. . . ' Next day came notice of further delay: 'The embarkation is put out for tomorrow night', Acton told Sir William, 'as the money ready for going on board is not yet secured on board of the ships. Every delay certainly is dangerous, but we are in hopes that these few hours will not exasperate more than at present our position.' The Minister had good reason to wish to be sure that the money was secure before sailing, for Hamilton calculated that the treasure in jewels and money carried on board the *Vanguard* and other ships amounted to two and a half million sterling.[20]

Later the same day Acton sent definite word that the Royal Family would embark on the twenty-first, though his letter suggested that things were still in some confusion at the palace. 'I receive just now the enclosed letter from the King,' Sir William read, 'with three notes of his own hand for the embarkation, as His Majesty approves entirely what Lord Nelson has proposed in his written answers to Belmonte's questions. The embarkation ought to succeed in this very night, but as the money could not be put on board of the *Alcmene* in the night, for many reasons depending on the Bulk, bad chests, etc, etc, it is likely it shall be postponed for tomorrow night. Count Thurn shall open the little rooms at the Mole, and there receive Lord Nelson or what officers his Lordship pleases to send, with the word *All goes Right and well*, or in case of the contrary *All is wrong you may go back*, as Lord Nelson has expressed himself to Belmonte.'[21] As he read this third letter Hamilton must have been in some doubt as to which of the two phrases Lord Nelson was most likely to hear.

He was now able to make final plans for his own and Emma's escape. It was essential for people to believe that everything was going on in a normal fashion, for in the excited state which prevailed among the population any unusual act might set off a riot or bring angry crowds round their door. The fate of the murdered royal messenger was still a vivid memory as well as a grim warning of what could happen. On the evening of the twenty-first, trying to appear as calm and untroubled as possible, Sir William, Emma, and Mrs. Cadogan announced that they were to visit some friends nearby and sent their servants away, but told them to return in two hours, send the coach, and prepare supper in readiness for the family's return. As soon as the servants had gone the party walked hurriedly to the shore, an anxious journey for three such well-known people, and there a boat was waiting for them. It took the boat two hours to reach the *Vanguard*, moored far out in the bay. Nelson, meanwhile, had made his way to the quay opposite the royal palace. This was connected by a secret passage to the Queen's room. Here were assembled Ferdinand, Maria Carolina and their family, ten in all. Nelson escorted them back down the airless staircase to armed boats. In these he took them across the dark stretch of sea to where his fleet lay at anchor. By midnight all were safely on board. According to the *Vanguard's* Journal, as well as the Royal Family and the British Minister's party, Nelson had on board his ship the Imperial Ambassador and his suite, several Neapolitan nobles with their servants, and most of the English residents who were in Naples. Some two thousand of other refugees, including Lady Knight and her daughter, were dispersed among the other ships under his command.

When the morning of 22 December dawned the weather was so rough that the ships were unable to sail; it was too stormy even for there to be any communication between the various ships of the squadron. The next day was calmer and brought boat-loads of people out from the city begging the King not to leave them. Many Neapolitans were sincerely distressed to see him go. Carlo de Nicola expressed what was in many minds when he wrote in his diary on the day the *Vanguard* eventually weighed anchor: 'Who knows, who has prejudiced him so deeply against a people most attached to him? . . . Who knows whether those in whom our good Master most confides are worthy of such complete trust? . . . He is betrayed by those nearest him, the English have sacrificed him, and the desire for vengeance that animates his wife has ruined her and us. If these memoirs of mine were to be read now I should be ruined, yet it is affection for my Sovereign that speaks, and the sorrow I feel at my heart. He was adored, and now the hearts of the Neapolitans are already alienated from him. . . .'[22] Those who thought like de Nicola, and there were many of them, considered the British ambassador and his wife much to blame for the loss of their King and the horrors that followed on his departure.

The King gave a last audience to Baron von Mack the day he sailed. It was a pitiful scene when he came on board the *Vanguard*. The General, who had nothing to report but the defeat of his army, was completely exhausted. Even Nelson, who had never cared for him and had a poor opinion of him as a soldier, was moved to compassion. 'My heart bled for him,' he recorded, 'he is worn to a shadow.' He was told that if his army was unable to hold Naples he should fall back towards Sicily, and with this gloomy information he took his leave. The same day, 23 December, at seven in the evening, the fleet made sail. With the *Vanguard* were the *Sannite* and the *Archimedes*, and about twenty other vessels, merchantmen and transports.

As a student of human nature Sir William must have looked upon the King of Naples with some interest as the ship in which they both sailed slipped past Capri and made for the open sea. He was at the crisis of his reign with half his kingdom in enemy hands, his capital abandoned, and the future of his dynasty in the balance. As the distant lights of the most beautiful city in the world, over which he had ruled since childhood, disappeared below the horizon, what thoughts occupied the mind of this son of the House of Bourbon? It was a speculation calculated to intrigue the curiosity of a philosopher. If Hamilton had expected to hear any lofty sentiment or melancholy reflection he was in for a disappointment. As he drew near to where the King was standing on deck Ferdinand was wrinkling his immense nose as he sniffed the breeze. 'We shall have plenty of woodcocks, *Cavaliere*,' said the King, 'this wind will bring them—it is just the season, we shall have rare sport. You must get your *cannone* ready!' He then turned away from the ambassador and fell into a long discussion with his game-keeper.[23]

What the wind in fact brought was the worst gale that Nelson had known in all his years at sea. The next day—Christmas eve—was one which many people on board thought they would never survive. The *Vanguard* split her three topsails and many of the passengers gave way to panic or despair. Sir William, having done what he could for the comfort of his fellow passengers, was lost from sight. He was later discovered, at the height of the storm, sitting with a loaded pistol in each hand. When Emma expressed her surprise he replied that he had no intention of hearing the 'guggle-guggle-guggle' of water in his throat, but would rather shoot himself the moment he felt that the ship was sinking. The Imperial Ambassador, Count Esterhazy, also imagining himself on the threshold of eternity, thought it prudent to commit his snuff-box to the waves as it was decorated with the portrait of his mistress in the nude.

This day of tempest was perhaps the greatest in Emma's life. She spent the whole time nursing and encouraging the prostrate and stricken Royal Family without any thought for her own comfort or safety. In the face of the grim reality and terror of the storm there was no question of attitudinising or self-dramatisation; she worked with courage and calmness, never once abandoning her post even for a moment's rest. On Christmas morning the youngest of Maria Carolina's children, the six-year-old Prince Carlo Alberto, was taken ill with convulsions. All through the day Emma nursed him but at seven in the evening he died of exhaustion in her arms. On reaching Palermo Nelson recorded her services with pride in his report to Lord St. Vincent: 'here it is my duty to tell your Lordship the obligations which the whole Royal Family as well as myself are under on this trying occasion to her Ladyship. They necessarily came on board without a bed, nor could the least preparation be made for their reception. Lady Hamilton provided her own beds, linen, etc, and became their *slave* for, except one man, no person belonging to Royalty assisted the Royal Family nor did her Ladyship enter a bed the whole time they were on board.' Of her husband he added: 'Good Sir William also made every sacrifice for the comfort of the august Family embarked with him'.[24]

The battered fleet reached Palermo in the early hours of the morning of the twenty-sixth. The grief-stricken Queen went ashore at once, 'being so much affected by the death of Prince Albert' as Nelson recorded, 'that she could not bear to go on shore in a public manner'. For some days she was seriously ill; the first words she wrote when she began to recover are sufficient testimony to the state of her feeling: 'I have lived long enough—even two or three years too long.' The King remained on board Nelson's ship until he could enter his Sicilian capital in style. His royal standard floated at the main-top-gallant-mast head of the *Vanguard* and was not lowered until he stepped into the admiral's barge to be rowed ashore, while every proper honour was paid to him by the ship's company. At nine o'clock in the morning he came ashore to be received with 'the loudest acclamations and apparent joy' by the citizens of Palermo.

When Sir William and Emma landed they were utterly exhausted by the experience of the voyage. Both were ill and overwrought. The city of Palermo, a rival in beauty of position to Naples itself, looked bleak and unwelcoming on this December morning. The first house they occupied was built for summer use and was totally unsuited to the winter season. In this cold and dispirited state they sat down to take stock of the new situation. So far only one thing was settled; as soon as he could leave his ship Nelson would continue to make his home under their roof.

1. Morrison, 329.
2. Morrison, 334.
3. Jeaffreson: *The Queen of Naples & Lord Nelson*, Vol. II, p. 7.
4. H. Swinburne: *Courts of Europe at the Close of the Last Century*, p. 217.
5. C. Knight: *Autobiography* Vol. I, p. 113-15.
6. Nelson to Lady Nelson: 25 September 1798.

7. Morrison, 337.
8. C. Knight: op. cit., Vol. I, p. 139.
9. *Vide* C. Oman: *Nelson*, p.90.
10. G. Rawson: *Nelson's Letters*, p. 207.
11. G. Rawson: op. cit., p. 206.
12. B.M. Egerton MSS 2640, f. 126.
13. Morrison, 349.
14. P. Colletta: *History of Naples*, pp. 250-1.
15. Alexander Davison to Lord Nelson, 7 December 1798.
    Nelson was at Palermo before this letter reached him.
16. Now in the Fitzwilliam Museum, Cambridge. See Appendix.
17. Jeaffreson: op. cit., Vol. II, p. 27.
18. *Vide* Jeaffreson, op. cit., Vol. II, pp. 24-5.
19. Jeaffreson: op. cit., pp. 32-6.
20. *Vide* Morrison, 369.
21. B.M. Egerton MSS 2640, ff 155, 157 and 159.
22. *Vide* Giglioli: *Naples in 1799*, pp. 93-4.
23. *Vide* P. Lockhart Gordon: *Personal Memoirs*, Vol. I, p. 205.
24. G. Rawson: *Nelson's Letters*, p. 216.

CHAPTER XXI

Reflections on Misfortune

As soon as the Hamiltons had settled into their draughty and unsuitable house 'without chimneys and calculated only for summer' (it was called the Villa Bastioni and was close to the gardens known as the Flora Reale) Sir William retired to his bed suffering from a severe cold and a return of his bilious complaint. The two weeks he spent in his room gave him time to reflect on the disasters of the past two months, both personal and political. To Charles Greville, the recipient of so many of his comments, both good and ill, on the comedy of human existence, he now sent his sombre reflections on the recent events in which he had been so closely involved.

'My former dispatches to Lord Greville', he wrote, 'will have prevented his Lordship from being too much surprised at receiving one dated from Palermo. I must own, however, that I never could have imagined that a fine army of near fifty thousand effective men, commanded by Mack, allowed to be one of the best generals in Europe, cou'd moulder away and be reduced to less than 20 thousand in 22 days without ever having had anything like what cou'd be called an action, and nothing but treachery and stinking cowardice cou'd have caused such a cruel reverse, for the French were never more than seven or eight thousand effective men, and in all Italy there were never more than 27 thousand French when the Neapolitan army march'd to Rome in confidence of the Emperor's army marching forward at the same time; we yet knew nothing of that army. Naples pretends to be much disgusted at the departure of the Court, but you will see that it will end in their fraternising with the French. This kingdom is certainly loyal but it must put itself into a true state of defence, and the French must be kept out of Calabria if possible, for you know that it is but 3 miles over from that coast to Messina. The French were at Fondi and in Puglia by the last accounts, and said to be reinforced, but that is all the same, as not a man of the Neapolitan army will fight, and the officers are the first to run away.'[1]

Hamilton continued to blame the Austrians for failing to invade Italy from the north and continued to ignore the fact that the government in Vienna had made no promise to come to the rescue, of the Neapolitans unless it could be shown that the French had acted as aggressors. He refused to accept any responsibility on his own part or on Nelson's for the miscalculations that had led to so complete a rout. It was more than he could do to suggest that the victor of the Nile had been at fault; all blame must be laid at the door of Mack and the Austrians. As for himself, all he would do was to admit to his nephew that he was at last beginning to feel his age and the need for rest and recuperation: 'I am really in want of repose, having had for these six years past the whole load of business on my hands, and since the arrival of the British fleet in the Mediterranean my labours have been doubled, and I feel age creeping upon me, but I will bear up as long and as well as I can, and not give up as my father did twenty years before he died, calling himself a dying man—and so we all are.'

Both he and Emma looked forward to coming home on leave as soon as possible, perhaps in the spring. 'Lord Nelson,' Hamilton had written, 'whose health is not robust, may like to go home about that time; if so, his Lordship would certainly take us.' In fact events would prevent this from happening until Sir William was finally recalled in June 1800. In a letter to Greville dated the day after her husband's (7 January 1799) Emma gave some indication of what the flight to Palermo had cost them: 'We have left everything at Naples but the vases and best pictures; 3 houses elegantly furnished, all our horses, and 6 or 7 carriages I think is enough for the vile French, for we cou'd not get our things off not to betray the Royal Family, and as we were in councel we were sworn to secrecy, so we are the worst off, all the other ministers have saved all by staying some days after us. Nothing can equal the manner we have been received here; but *dear, dear, Naples* we now dare not show our love for that place, for this country is jealous of the other.' She also mentioned their hope of coming home in the spring; meanwhile she was busily comforting her 'dear adorable queen'. '*We weep together*', she told Greville, 'and now this is our only comfort. Sir William and the King are philosophers; nothing affects them, thank God, and *we* are scolded even for shewing proper sensibility.'[2]

Sir William was to need all his philosophy in the next few months, not least in respect of Emma. In the sultry, semi-African climate of Sicily she was to lose all restraint and parade her conquest of Nelson in a manner which caused the greatest embarrassment to his friends, though the hero himself seemed oblivious of the notoriety they caused. The strident, vulgar side of Emma's character which Sir William's tutelage had hidden but not destroyed was to burst forth with all the frenzy of a half-tamed animal which had been trapped too long in an elegant but restricting cage. The citizens of Palermo, accustomed to the institution of the *cicisbeo*, saw nothing unusual in the situation which quickly developed, and some of the English residents preferred not to notice. Cornelia Knight, who went to live with the Hamiltons after her mother's death, declared that 'there was certainly at that time no impropriety in living under Lady Hamilton's roof', but many of the officers who had fought with Nelson at the Nile were humiliated to see their heroic leader caught in the apron-strings of the ambassador's wife. As to Sir William, his absolute trust in Nelson's integrity and his long familiarity with Emma's habit of self-dramatisation made him blind to what was happening in his own house.

An unfriendly eye was turned on Emma when Lord Montgomery and Pryse Lockhart Gordon called on the British Minister in the early months of 1799. 'We entered the Mole without coming to anchor and proceeded with Captain Hope to our minister's house, and were presented to Sir W. Hamilton and Lord Nelson, who lived with him,' Lockhart Gordon wrote in his *Personal Memoirs*. 'Our introduction to the fascinating Emma Lady Hamilton was an affair of more ceremony, and got up with considerable stage effect. When we had sat a few minutes, and had given all our details of Naples, which we thought were received with great *sang-froid*, the Cavaliere retired, but shortly returned by a *porte battante*, and on his arm or rather on his shoulder was leaning the interesting Melpomene, her raven tresses floating round her expansive form and full bosom. What a model for a Roman matron! but alas! poor Emma was indisposed, 'dying', she said, 'of chagrin for the loss of her beloved Naples'. Yet the roses on her cheek prevailed over the lilies, and gave hopes that her grief would not prove mortal. The ceremony of introduction being over, she rehearsed in a subdued tone a *mélange* of Lancashire and Italian, detailing the catalogue of her miseries, her hopes and her fears, with lamentation about her dear queen, the loss of her own charming Palazzo and its precious contents, which had fallen into the hands of the vile republicans. But here we offered some consolation, by assuring her Ladyship that every article of the ambassador's property had been safely embarked in an English transport, and would be dispatched in a few days. All this we afterwards learned she knew, as the vessel had actually arrived. During this interesting conversation the Lady discovered that she was Lord Montgomery's *cousin*, and appealing to her husband said, "A'nt us, Sir William?" His Lordship made his bows and acknowledgements, and we were invited to dinner, her Ladyship regretting "that her small house could not accommodate him"—it was a palace of fifty rooms at least.'

Pryse Lockhart Gordon was later to witness a scene which, even allowing for his obvious hostility, gives a distressing picture of the way Emma's character was beginning to deteriorate. The Emperor Paul of Russia had sent dispatches to Nelson by a Turkish messenger, and Lockhart Gordon was present at a dinner given in honour of this imperial messenger, 'a coarse savage monster', by Sir William Hamilton, at which both Emma and Lord Nelson were present, as well as a Greek who was able to interpret the language of their guest of honour.

'The only memorable event which occurred at the minister's entertainment', he wrote, 'was this warrior getting drunk with rum, which does not come under the prohibition of the prophet. The monster, who had the post of honour at her Ladyship's side, entertained her through the interpretation of the Greek with an account of his exploits; among others, that of his having lately fallen in with a French transport, conveying invalids and wounded soldiers from Egypt, whom he had brought on board his frigate; but provisions and water having run short he found it necessary to get rid of his prisoners, and amused himself by putting them to death. 'With this weapon', said he in his vile jargon, and drawing his shabola, 'I cut off the heads of twenty French prisoners in one day! Look, there is their blood remaining on it!' The speech being translated, her Ladyship's eye beamed with delight, and she said, 'Oh, let me see the sword that did the glorious deed!' It was presented to her; she took it into her fair hand covered with rings, and looking at the encrusted Jacobin blood, kissed it and handed it to the hero of the Nile! Had I not been an eyewitness to this disgraceful act, I would not have ventured to relate it.

> 'Mrs. Charles Lock, the beautiful and amiable wife of our consul-general, was sitting *vis-à-vis* to the Turk, and was so horrified at the scene (being near her accouchment) that she fainted and was taken out of the room. Her Ladyship said it was a piece of affectation, and made no efforts to assist her guest. . . The toad-eaters applauded, but many groaned and cried 'shame' loud enough to reach the ears of the Admiral, who turned pale, hung his head, and seemed ashamed. Lord Montgomery got up, and left the room, and I speedily followed.'

The same visitor was no more friendly in his assessment of Sir William, whom he considered to have become a perfect Neapolitan both in mind and manners. But he very much over-estimated Emma's influence when he wrote of Hamilton that 'the little consequence he retained as ambassador was derived from his wife's intrigues; but as long as he could keep his situation, draw his salary, and collect vases, he cared little about politics; he left the management of them to her Ladyship.' In reality Emma only had influence with the Queen, and Maria Carolina's power was now greatly curtailed as the King continued to blame her for the loss of Naples and the disasters of Mack's campaign.

Acton retained his power (and, indeed, increased it, for his rival Gallo had been sent on a mission to Vienna) but he had no need to make use of Emma's good offices in order to approach the British Minister. Ferdinand at this time had no great love for her either, not least because she was a friend of his wife's. At one, time he actually threatened to have her thrown out of a window.[3]

The ageing ambassador and his heavily theatrical wife struck Lockhart Gordon as a grotesque pair. He was unable to appreciate any of Hamilton's finer qualities as scholar and arbiter of taste, he saw him only as the complacent husband of Nelson's Emma; it was a foretaste of posterity's careless judgement on a long and distinguished career. Even the Attitudes failed to thrill him. 'I have more than once witnessed these exhibitions,' he wrote. 'On one occasion, being desirous to astonish a gentleman who had just arrived and had not heard of her Ladyship's attitudinal celebrity, she dropped from her chair on the carpet, when sitting at table after dinner. The comb which fastened her superabundant locks had been removed (like Caesar she had fallen gracefully) and nothing could have been more 'classical or imposing than this prostrate position. Sir William started up to open a little of the curtain in order to admit the proper light, while the stranger flew to the sideboard for water, with which he plentifully sprinkled the fainting dame, before he discovered that it was a *scena* (and not a fit as he thought) which had been got up. "You have spoiled, my good good friend," said the Knight, "one of the most perfect attitudes that Emma ever executed—how unlucky!"[4]

The ambassador had had much to try him since he reached Palermo. Now, on top of ill-health, Emma's indiscreet behaviour, and distressing bulletins from Naples (where Ferdinand's viceroy surrendered to the French on 11 January), came the shattering news that the *Colossus* with his collection of vases in its hold, had foundered off the islands of Scilly and gone to the bottom of the sea. Sir Gilbert Elliot, when he heard of the disaster, wrote to his wife: 'It will go far, I think, to break his heart, and I am really most heartily grieved at his loss.' Sir Gilbert's verdict came very near to the truth.

The task of breaking the news fell to Greville. He discovered his uncle's loss when Lord Spencer told him that some boxes belonging to Hamilton had been on board the ship. 'What they were I know not,' Greville wrote on 9 January, 'but I dread the result of enquiry lest some of your invaluable collections may have been in those cases.'

The next day he had more information, and wrote again. His letter contained no comfort. As well as Sir William's collection the ship had brought home the body of Admiral Lord Shouldham and this, so far, was all that had been salvaged. 'I find that she sank in deep water near the shore,' he now wrote, 'and it is probable when fine weather comes some things may come ashore, at least, I augur well from this circumstance.' After describing how the body of Lord Shouldham had been freed from the wreckage and brought to the surface, he continued: 'I find your boxes were deep in the hold; therefore, till the ship is to pieces, they will remain there, and, even if they withstand the shocks of a ship whose timbers, etc., give way to their force, it is a hope but a forlorne one.'[5]

Greville's letters took a long time to reach Palermo, for his uncle's reply is dated 22 March. 'I have received only your letters of the 9th and 10th of January,' it began. 'You do me justice in thinking and knowing me to be a philosopher, but my Philosophy has been put to the Trial by the loss of the *Colossus*. You give me but little hopes, but I have heard that the body *insolvent* of Adml. Shouldham has been saved from the Wreck of which you do not seem to have had any intelligence. Damn his body, it can be of no use but to the Worms, but my Collection wou'd have given information to the most learned and have convinced every intelligent Being that there is but one Truth, and that God Almighty has never made himself known to the miserable Atoms that inhabit this globe otherwise than bidding them to increase and multiply and to leave the rest to Him—so thought the Wise Ancients when the mysteries of Bacchus and Eleusis were established. Never will there be collected such a number of clear monuments to prove the truth of what I say again. Yet I hope some of the eight cases on board the *Colossus* may be saved. But come to the worst I have had the precaution of publishing the best that are supposed to be lost, and I have many living witnesses that the originals existed.'[6]

Hamilton was not just distressed at the thought of the destruction of irreplaceable works of art or of the waste of all the time, knowledge and expense that had gone into the formation of the collection; his grief was all the more bitter as he hoped that this collection which, even if sold, would be known by his name, would be a monument to himself as well as to his aesthetic theories. He had stipulated this as a condition when attempting to sell it to the King of Prussia and no doubt still cherished the hope that his name might go down to posterity in this way. Fortunately the loss was not total. 'I have the rest of my vases here on board of a transport, and most of my best pictures,' his letter continues, 'and I hope they may get home safe, but if insurance is not too high I shall take that method of saving something at least from the general wreck that has attended my fortune of late. As to myself I care not one farthing for I am sure of every necessary of life and even what I esteem the greatest luxury, which is everything that is simple and good of its kind for the few years I have to live, and I shall be able after all to leave sufficient to Emma and something for my best Friend and those I love best.'

He felt the loss deeply in spite of his determination to be 'philosophical' and put a brave face on it. He returned to the subject again on 8 April in the course of a long letter to Greville; the thought of the destruction of so unique a collection continued to distress him and he hoped against hope that some vases at least might be salvaged. 'As to my 8 cases,' he wrote, 'all of the best vases in my collection that were on board the *Colossus*, I fear none will be recovered, and it is a pity, for never in this world will such a collection be made again. The cases are so well made and vases so well packed that I dare say they may float when the ship goes to pieces. . . ' The vision of his priceless vases on the bottom of the sea brought other losses to mind; for though most of his pictures and 'some few vases' were on board a transport at Palermo, he told Greville that nearly all his furniture at Naples, Caserta and Posillipo, which he had had no time to carry off, had fallen into the hands of the French. His troubles and losses reminded him that time was passing: 'God knows I have little time to lose, for I feel old age coming on fast.'[7]

On 8 June Greville was able to report the recovery of about ten vases 'of which one only is of consequence'. This was a drinking cup decorated with the design of a boar and sheep's head. He was hopeful that more might be thrown up from the wrecked ship, and Sir William had to content himself with this small grain of comfort. The wreck of his collection of vases meant very much more to him than the loss of mere worldly possessions, it represented the fruits of a lifetime's study, and Sir William could not easily shrug off the feeling of deprivation, almost of bereavement, which the loss caused him. The news had come like a cruel finishing stroke to all the evils he had suffered since the revolution had burst upon his ordered life sweeping away so much that seemed familiar and secure. It left him feeling stunned and for a time unresponsive to what was happening around him.[8]

Life became a little easier for Sir William, at least in so far as his physical comforts were concerned, when he removed to the Palazzo Palagonia, which was situated near the Mole and was altogether more suitable for service as an embassy. Here he could keep warm in the winter months, but his health was never really good for the whole time he was in Palermo. 'This thick air and *sirocco* of Palermo do not agree with any of us,' he told Sir Joseph Banks towards the end of the year, 'Lord Nelson, Emma and myself having been frequently attacked with bilious complaints, but from these attacks, owing to my age, I do not recover as soon as they do.'

Nelson made their new house his home, and shared the expenses with the ambassador. Here Emma was able to resume entertaining on the same lavish scale as she had been accustomed to do in Naples. Her temperament was not one that rejoiced in the consolations of a retired life and she was quite unable to economise. She liked to be the centre of an admiring circle. At Palermo she discovered a passion for cards and would sit gambling until late at night while Nelson sat dozing beside her, a docile captive. Sir William himself had never much cared for cards, and as a young man had only played for low stakes and even then largely from a sense of duty to keep an eye on the English 'milords' who came to Naples to gamble and were likely to get into scrapes. Emma's new craze added another burden to their expenses. She helped herself liberally to Nelson's money as well as her husband's, sometimes staking as much as five hundred pounds a night. 'Her rage is play,' Mr. Rushout, Lord Northwick's son, told Sir Gilbert Elliot, 'and Sir William says when he is dead she will be a beggar.' He spoke more prophetically than he thought.

While Ferdinand and Maria Carolina and such members of the diplomatic corps as had accompanied them on their flight were establishing themselves at Palermo the situation at Naples had gone from bad to worse. Seeing the inevitability of a French occupation a Portuguese naval officer had, on 8 January, set fire to the remaining ships of the Neapolitan navy to prevent them from falling into enemy hands. The destruction of these fine ships, which had been carried out on Nelson's orders, was a bitter blow to the Queen and Acton, who had together been responsible for the creation of this fleet, but it was a necessary and unavoidable precaution for the French were at the gates of the city, and only three days later the regent Prince Pignatelli agreed to humiliating terms of armistice dictated by General Championnet.

Following the armistice anarchy broke out in Naples. General von Mack, who was at Casoria, promptly surrendered and was sent to Paris as a prisoner of war. In the streets of Naples the *lazzaroni* took over, seizing weapons from the demoralised regular troops and attacking the garrisons in the forts. A period of pandemonium followed, but when it was learnt that the French were advancing, the *lazzaroni* alone were prepared to defend the capital. Such nobles as remained in the city were already in league with the French and only awaited their arrival to proclaim a republic. It was a situation which hardly accorded with the accepted revolutionary pattern, for the common people were passionately determined to resist the 'liberators' in the name of their king while a handful of egalitarian noblemen stood waiting to hoist the republican flag. Only Naples could present so bizarre a spectacle which found its epitome in the answer of a certain Michele il Pazzo (Mad Michael) when asked the meaning of the word 'Citizen': 'I don't know, but it must be something worth having, since all the big-wigs have taken it for themselves.'

The *lazzaroni* fought with great frenzy against the French. For three days the city was given over to hand-to-hand fighting and the invaders were compelled to take it street by street. Hamilton's friend Tischbein was one of those who had remained in Naples and witnessed what soon developed into a miniature civil war when the more prudent citizens began to side with the French and turned against the patriotic rabble. The fighting was conducted with savage brutality on both sides. Tischbein's own life was only spared by convincing the invaders of his German nationality when the house in which he lived was captured and its inhabitants threatened with death. Eventually the resistance of the *lazzaroni* was overcome and on 23 January 1799 the republic was proclaimed. With a respect for antiquity which Hamilton might have applauded had he not held all republicans in contempt it called itself the Parthenopean Republic. It was to survive for five months.

The news that a republic had been established in Naples caused no surprise in Palermo, only a fierce feeling of resentment and a desire on the part of the Queen to 'save Naples or perish'. Ferdinand alone seemed indifferent to what happened in his former capital. 'Your dear Father,' the Queen wrote to her daughter the Empress in January, 'whether from religion or resignation, keeps well and is content. He has taken a pretty little country house, builds and gardens, in the evenings goes to the theatre or the masquerade, is cheerful, and I admire him. Naples, as far as he is concerned, might be the land of the Hottentots; he does not give it another thought.'[9] Republicans or no republicans, this extraordinary monarch was determined to continue his life as though nothing had happened.

This carefree attitude could not be the policy of his government if Naples was to be recovered. The Queen was still in disgrace with Ferdinand but he could not overcome the habit of a lifetime, and his laziness and indifference soon gave her the chance to assert herself once again, though her old imperious spirit had been broken and she lacked the firm hand with which she had once guided affairs in Naples. Acton remained the chief Minister and adviser of the King, but his relations with the Queen were no longer happy. She now relied for a sense of security upon the presence of her 'Saviour', as she called Nelson, the 'dear virtuous brave Admiral', and upon her friends Sir William and Lady Hamilton, who for the next few months became more like ministers of this Bourbon Court than representatives of the King of Great Britain.

The state of affairs in Calabria, where the population was loyal, could still be turned to the advantage of the King if quick action were to be taken. Ferdinand had no army with which to invade the mainland, but with the right leader a popular rising could be planned which, if properly and vigorously conducted, might save the southern half of the kingdom and even—if events elsewhere prevented Championnet from being reinforced—succeed in driving the French from Naples. A leader presented himself from a walk of life where military virtues are not usually held to predominate. Fabrizio Ruffo was himself a Calabrian of noble family now in his mid-fifties; he had previously been treasurer and war minister in the government of Pope Pius VI, and for the past five years (though only in minor orders) had been a Cardinal of the Holy Roman Church. It was into his unlikely hands that the campaign was now committed. On 25 January the King signed a commission declaring the Cardinal his vicar-general with 'the unrestricted quality of *alter ego*',[10] and on 7 February he landed at Punta del Pezzo with eight companions. He was to prove a very much more successful general than Baron Karl von Mack.

As soon as he landed Cardinal Ruffo issued a proclamation calling upon his fellow-countrymen to rise in defence of their religion, their fatherland, and their King. This appeal to throne and altar brought an immediate response and soon he was in command of a force numbering seventeen thousand men. As an army this mixed mob, which contained every kind of volunteer from priests and landowners to artisans, peasants and brigands, would have astounded a professional soldier and the Cardinal himself often had only a tenuous hold over its wilder elements, but it was filled with a violent fanaticism which carried it forward in a victorious advance towards Naples.

This frightening and blood-thirsty force showed neither mercy nor quarter to its opponents and fought with a zeal that terrorised the areas through which it passed and brought little credit to the proud title under which it fought: the Christian Army of the Holy Faith. Horrible indeed was the dilemma of any unfortunate creature who found himself caught between the White Terror of this wild and undisciplined horde and the Red Terror of the desperate Jacobins. The latter, whose power was upheld by the military presence of General Championnet's army, realized that the crisis was at hand when Austria declared war on France in March, and it became clear that their French allies, having enriched themselves to the extent of sixty million francs at the expense of their fellow republicans, would soon be leaving the Parthenopean Republic to its fate.

The Austrian declaration of war (which Hamilton and Nelson had looked for in vain the previous autumn) greatly helped Ruffo's advance. A vast Austrian and Russian army under Marshal Suvarov marched into north Italy, while a joint Russian and Turkish squadron captured Corfu and promised to send help to the Cardinal's forces. To the south General Sir Charles Stuart, having captured Minorca from the Spaniards, was able to send two British regiments to assist in the defence of Sicily. On 7 May, General Macdonald, who had succeeded Championnet, began the withdrawal of his army of occupation from Naples. It was no comfort to the Parthenopean leaders to be told that he did this out of a tender regard for the freedom and independence of the new republic: they knew that it meant their ruin. The Army of the Holy Faith, carrying the royal standard of Ferdinand IV, would soon be surrounding the city. Already, since the beginning of April, the port had been blockaded by a British naval squadron under Captain Troubridge; Salerno and Castellammare were in royalist hands.

When the news of Ruffo's successful advance reached Palermo Sir William decided to postpone his opportunity for taking leave (he had decided to take a passage in the next ship sailing for Gibraltar) as he now saw the probability of the King being seated once more on his throne of Naples. Describing this new state of affairs in a letter to Greville of 28 April, he wrote: 'I knew well that if some negotiation was to be necessary between His Majesty, his nobles, and people, no one cou'd go between them with such a probability of success as myself, and they all knew it. Besides, Lord Nelson, for want of languages and experience of this court and country, without Emma and me, wou'd be at the greatest loss every moment. Considering all this, altho' I have rheumatism in my hip, and am tired and worn out almost, I will not abandon their Sicilian Majesties in so very interesting a moment. It will be a glorious circumstance if we can recover Naples without any further aid than that of Great Britain. At this moment there are not two thousand French in Naples, and they seem to be on the wing, having called in their outposts.'[11]

This letter shows the extent to which Hamilton now identified himself with the cause of Ferdinand and Maria Carolina and how he took it as a matter of course that Nelson would be sent to Naples as their envoy. Lord Nelson himself found his loyalties sharply divided between the requirements of his commander-in-chief and his promise to protect the Court of Palermo. Not the least attractive of the reasons for favouring the latter alternative was what he described as Emma's 'affectionate care' and 'good Sir William's wit and inexhaustible pleasantry', both of which he found beguiling reasons for remaining where he was. Early in May, however, news came that a French fleet had escaped from Brest and hoped to join forces with the fleet of Spain and make for the Mediterranean. Nelson lost no time in putting to sea. When he discovered that the enemy had made for Toulon without joining the Spaniards he returned to Palermo which he looked upon as a suitable base from where he could defend Sicily and at the same time continue the blockade of Naples. It also meant that he was not separated from Lady Hamilton. It was becoming clear that the Admiral could hardly bear to be out of her sight; when he was away he wrote to her every day, and in this month he added a codicil to his will leaving her a gold box set with diamonds as a token of his respect for her 'very eminent virtue'.

On 5 June Nelson was reinforced by the arrival of a small squadron which included the newly-built *Foudroyant* of eighty guns and to this ship he now transferred his flag. Ruffo's victories and the surrender of the islands blockaded by Troubridge, and, after his recall, by Captain E. J. Foote, encouraged the King and Queen to persuade Nelson to embark a Neapolitan force under the command of their eldest son the Hereditary Prince Francis and escort them to Naples. The arrival of this force would, the Queen hoped, result in the collapse of the republican régime. 'I hope that the imposing force by sea', she wrote to Nelson on 11 June, 'and their being surrounded on all sides, will be sufficient, without shedding blood, to induce them to return to their allegiance, for I would spare even my enemies.' As Hamilton had said to Greville, it was expected that he would accompany Nelson on this expedition. 'As to what relates to yourself. . . ' Acton had written to him on the same day that the Queen had sent her letter to Nelson, 'His Majesty will be glad, as it is desired by Lord Nelson, and likewise as a convenient means for the proper Intelligence and notions of this Country that you would be with him in the Expedition, as your own attachment to this Country and their Sicilian Majesties has been, and is from a long time, known to them and all the nation. . . The King with this answer did not tell me that he required that you would embark, but if you do not dislike it and have no objection, His Majesty will see it with pleasure and satisfaction.'[12]

Sir William does not, as things turned out, appear to have embarked with Nelson on this occasion. Perhaps he intended to follow later when it was known that the troops were landed safely. In fact neither the troops nor the Prince nor the Admiral were to get anywhere near Naples; the fleet had hardly left port before they were met by two ships with news from Lord Keith, the new Commander-in-Chief, that another French fleet was at large and thought to be heading for Naples. Nelson put about and returned to Palermo where he disembarked the Prince and his army and put to sea again as soon as he could in search of the enemy. The disappointed Court had to be content for the time being with the Admiral's view of the situation: 'I consider the best defence for his Sicilian Majesty's dominions is to place myself alongside the French.'[13]

While Nelson was away conflicting reports began to reach Palermo about events in Naples. On 18 June the Queen wrote to Emma with the good news that the forts had been 'partly taken', but the next day had to revise this view in the light of more recent information: 'Our news from Naples is still confused. The two Castles are still in the power of the rebels. May God grant that all may end well and that we may have true tranquillity.'[14] The forts in question were those called the Castel dell'Uovo and the Castello Nuovo, the one jutting out into the sea at the point of Santa Lucia and the other flanking the royal palace and looking out in one direction over the harbour and in the other over the main piazza which contained the government buildings. Both commanded the lower part of the city and were held by the troops of the Parthenopean Republic. A third fort, the Castel di Sant' Elmo, dominated the entire city from the crest of the hill behind the convent of San Martino and was held by the remnant of the French army of occupation.

News that these strong and strategically well-placed fortresses had surrendered would mean that Naples had fallen to the Cardinal's army.

On 16 June Acton told Sir William that he had received letters from Count Thurn, the officer serving in the Neapolitan navy who had helped in the escape of the Royal Family, containing a report that royalist troops had entered Naples two days previously: 'The people has (*sic.*) helped the royalists and are attacking Castel Nuovo and Castel dell'Uovo. St. Elmo does not fire yet, but has the French colours. . . The same letter advises that the French fleet is at Genoa.' Hamilton immediately sent a copy of Acton's letter to Lord Nelson adding comments of his own which show that both he and Nelson (and presumably Ferdinand and the Queen also) were already apprehensive lest the Cardinal should treat the King's rebellious subjects too leniently. 'Your Lordship sees that what we suspected of Cardinal Ruffo has proved true,' Sir William wrote, 'and I dare say when the capitulation of Naples comes to this court their Sicilian Majesties' dignity will be mortified. You see the business was done on the 14th, and had we arrived on the 15th, the soonest we could, we could only have modified the Cardinal's terms. *His Eminency was resolved to conquer Naples himself,* no matter, as long as the business is done.'[15]

Hamilton's reaction to the news seems carping and ungrateful, for when all was said and done Ruffo appeared to have achieved what everyone most desired, the reconquest of Naples. The distrust in which the Cardinal was now held by the Court had grown with his success and came from a general fear which had festered in the hearts of the King and Queen ever since they had fled to Palermo; a fear which made them doubt the loyalty of any but those who were the most narrow and unquestioning in their allegiance. Ruffo was a humane man. 'In winning back Naples', he had written, 'I foresee that our greatest obstacle will lie in the fear of deserved punishment. Now, if we show that we mean to try, and punish; if we do not make them believe that we are completely persuaded that it was necessity, error, the force of the enemy, and not treason, that occasioned the rebellion, we play into the hands of the enemy and cut off our own way to reconciliation.'[16] This wise council, which might have saved Naples from the White Terror which followed the fall of the republic, was now an anathema to the King and Queen, whose feelings of magnaminity to their enemies did not long survive the news of victory. They now took their line of conduct from Lord Nelson who had proclaimed: 'I ever preach that rewards and punishments are the foundation of all good government.' The thought that Ruffo was about to offer terms to the rebels filled them with horror; they begged Sir William to urge Nelson once again to turn his fleet in the direction of Naples.

Everything in Hamilton's past life should have made him side with the Cardinal against the rigid, unimaginative, and politically *naïve* advice of Nelson who regarded rebellious subjects in the same light as mutinous seamen and saw a complex political situation as a simple problem in black and white. Always sublime at sea, Nelson's touch was less sure in purely civilian matters; his ideas were circumscribed and conditioned by his consuming hatred of the French. Sir William was altogether more liberal in his outlook, but his respect for Nelson and gratitude to the victor of the Nile had made him blind in his admiration; and if he did at times entertain doubts on the subject of some of the admiral's crisp quarter-deck decisions his doubts were quickly put to flight by Emma's shrill and persistent echo of her hero's opinions. Sir William was feeling old, his health was far from good, he still mourned the loss of his prized collection of Greek vases; he was no longer a match against the combined forces of Nelson, Emma, and Maria Carolina.

Sir William's letter, with its implied rebuke for not being already at Naples, made Nelson reconsider his plans. If the French fleet were heading for Naples and the relief of the Parthenopean Republic, he was more likely to meet with them in the bay than cruising off Ustica where Hamilton's letter found him. The Queen had told Emma: 'All we want is a second 1st of August, an Aboukir by our brave admiral.' Sicily could come to no harm and would still be covered by his fleet. On 20 June he sent a note to Sir William: 'I am agitated, but my resolution is fixed. . . I am full of grief and anxiety. I must go. It will finish the war. It will give a sprig of laurel to your affectionate friend.'[17] This *staccato* note bespoke a man whose nerves were at full stretch. The thought of an enemy fleet at large, the thought of restoring a king to his throne, the thought of being with Emma again were all to contribute to the disturbed state of his emotions. The next day he was in Palermo, his squadron arriving almost as soon as the swift sailing-ship that carried his message. A quick conference was held at the palace; no time was lost; Sir William and Lady Hamilton were hurried on board the *Foudroyant* and by noon next day the fleet was under way and heading towards the bay of Naples.

1. Morrison, 369.
2. Morrison, 370.
3. *Vide* Acton: *The Bourbons of Naples*, p. 428.
4. *Vide* P. Lockhart Gordon: *Personal Memoirs*, Vol. I, pp. 201-11, Vol. II, pp. 385-6.
5. Morrison, 371, 372.
6. B.M. Add. MSS 42071, f. 14.
7. Morrison, 381.
8. It is difficult to discover the exact extent of Hamilton's loss. Mr. O. E. Deutch (*Sir William Hamilton's Picture Gallery*, Burlington Magazine, Vol. LXXXII, pp. 36-7) claims that two-thirds of the collection was ultimately salvaged.
9. Giglioli: *Naples in 1799*, p. 282.

10. *Vide* Gutteridge: *Nelson & the Neapolitan Jacobins*, p. 24.

11. Morrison, 384.

12. B.M. Egerton MSS 2640, f. 251.

13. N. H. Nicolas: *Letters and Dispatches of Lord Nelson*, Vol. III, p. 380.

14. Jeaffreson: *Lord Nelson & the Queen of Naples*, Vol. II, pp. 66—7.

15. Gutteridge: op. cit., pp. 94 and 98.

16. *Vide* C. Oman: Nelson, p. 350.

17. Gutteridge: op. cit., p. 144.

CHAPTER XXII

In the Bay of Naples

The *Foudroyant* made towards Naples at the head of a fleet of eighteen sail-of-the-line. Part of the wardroom had been set aside as an 'apartment' for Sir William and Lady Hamilton; Nelson, in Emma's phrase, was 'here, there, and everywhere'.[1] The narrow confines of an eighteenth-century man-of-war did not allow for much privacy. For the last few months Nelson, Emma, and Sir William had been sharing the same house, but it has been described as a palace of at least fifty rooms. Now all three were thrown together in such a way as to make the closest physical proximity a necessary condition of their existence. It was the first time that Nelson and Emma had been at sea together since the frightful voyage to Palermo the previous December when the Admiral's whole attention had been directed to the safety of his ship and Emma's to the plight of the terrified passengers. Now they were sailing through summer seas, 'stealing on with light winds'. There was an atmosphere of tension aboard.

All three were in a state of mental strain. Nelson was in an irascible temper. It must be remembered that he had hardly known a moment's respite since his engagement with the French nearly a year before from which he had emerged victorious but wounded and exhausted. Barely a month ago he had written to Hamilton: 'I have not been free from head-ache, sickness and with want of rest, for I know not what sleep is since I left Palermo.'[2] The decision to sail to Naples had only been made after a struggle with his conscience, for though it in no way went against his general orders to prevent the Franco-Spanish fleet from attacking Sicily or attempting to relieve the Army of Egypt, he knew that his commander-in-chief did not share his personal concern for the Neapolitan Sovereigns (whom he had pledged himself to protect) and might very much wish him elsewhere than in the bay of Naples. To these physical and professional strains were added his growing passion for Emma and the bitter conflict which this emotion kindled in his soul, for Nelson had not yet reached the point where he could forget that he was a married man or that Emma was herself wedded to his best friend 'good Sir William'. Her close and alluring presence made his infatuation no easier to bear. The result was that he was short-tempered, overbearing, and uncooperative for the whole time they were anchored off Naples.

Hamilton was in hardly a better state. Two months ago he had written to Greville: 'We have all suffer'd in our health, but as I wax old it has been hard upon me having had both bilious and rheumatic complaints.' He continued to complain of illness and suffered from lassitude and irritability which would increase after his return. The loss of his collection of vases still rankled; even in the middle of his negotiations with Cardinal Ruffo it was never far from his thoughts. Just before leaving Palermo he had heard that some cargo and cannon had been salvaged from the wreckage of the *Colossus* and hope for his eight cases rose again. 'Spare no expence, my dear Charles, to recover them if you can, as the like were never seen or ever will be', he wrote to his nephew from on board the *Foudroyant*.[3] He blamed the Neapolitan Jacobins for the disaster and was in no mood for forgiveness. Emma's boisterousness was no anodyne for his tattered nerves; all her attention was focused impetuously upon her hero. She was quite unable to understand the nature of her husband's loss or the feeling of emptiness that haunted him. Sir William was beginning to have a vague consciousness of neglect.

It may be wondered what Lady Hamilton was doing on board the *Foudroyant* at all. Nelson and Sir William could at least claim that they were forwarding the interests of their own country in an undertaking in which they both appeared very much more like agents of the King of the Two Sicilies than servants of King George III. Naples had joined Pitt's Second Coalition against France on 1 June and it was therefore in the general interest of the allies to see Ferdinand IV restored to his throne and the French occupation of Naples finally ended. There was, however, no precedent for the presence of an ambassador's wife on such an expedition, and Emma did not even have that status to justify her interference. Hamilton considered her presence necessary to help him in the business of translating, and Nelson was unlikely to question a decision which corresponded so happily with his own desires. Emma herself considered that she was there as the representative of the Queen. 'She sent me as her Deputy,' she told Greville grandly,[4] though why the Queen should require a deputy when her husband was already so fully represented is a question which Emma clearly did not consider as needing an answer. Maria Carolina remained in Palermo but she was avid to hear of everything that went on in Naples and to have someone who could bring her own views to bear on Nelson and Hamilton, and Emma was the only possible candidate for this meddlesome task, to which she did full justice. Unlike the others she suffered neither from nerves nor ill-health; she was in a state of euphoria. As 'Deputy' of her adored Queen and Nelson's enthusiastic votaress she saw herself on a dizzy pinnacle of power.

While Nelson's fleet was still at sea the articles of the treaty between Ruffo and the defenders of the castles were agreed and signed. The signatures included those of the Russian and Turkish representatives and Captain Foote (who had taken over command of Troubridge's blockading fleet) as well as the commanders of the castles, the French Colonel Mejean, who held Sant' Elmo, and Cardinal Ruffo. Foote, when he signed the treaty, added the cautious note that he did so 'saving the honour and rights of his sovereign and the British nation'.[5]

The treaty made no distinction between the French and the Neapolitan troops of the now defunct republic. They were to hand over the forts to the Cardinal's forces but would be allowed to march out with all the honours of war, 'drums beating, colours flying, matches lighted and each with two pieces of artillery'. They were then to lay down their arms on the beach. Their persons and property were to be protected and guaranteed and they were to have the choice of embarking for Toulon or of remaining in Naples without being molested. A similar protection was to cover their families. Furthermore they could all remain in the forts until the vessels destined to convey such as wished to go to Toulon were ready to sail.[6] The treaty was generous to the defeated republicans but was in accord with Ruffo's known humanitarian principles. He had pressed anxiously for its completion in order to prevent further bloodshed and to forestall a period of anarchy if his wild followers got out of hand or the *lazzaroni* initiated another Terror. He had a further reason for wishing for a speedy conclusion; he was eager to get the treaty signed before a French fleet appeared in the bay.

News that a treaty was being negotiated caused alarm in Palermo. Two days after Nelson had sailed General Acton sent a letter to Sir William which, allowing for his quaint use of English, managed to convey the disquiet which prevailed at Ferdinand's Court: 'We hear that a Capitulation or Treaty is at present on foot for the addition of St. Elmo, Capria and Gaeta, and the French are to carry with them a number of patriots, but this Treaty having no time determined, Lord knows with what an intention it is carrying on. If time and a prolongation allows it, Lord Nelson will be there, and we hope in him for a relief of what is against His Majesty's dignity and interests. The Cardinal *alone* ought to send the Treaty to the King for his Majesty's approbation.'[7] It did not seem to occur to Acton that the Cardinal could not afford to wait while messages passed backwards and forwards between Naples and Palermo; he had to act before the French arrived. Delay would simply play into the enemy's hands, for the longer the negotiations lasted the more chance there was of the French fleet coming to their rescue.

Both sides were scanning the horizon with a mixture of hope and fear when Nelson's fleet appeared before Naples on June. The Admiral and Lady Hamilton saw with indignation that flags of truce were flying on the castles and from the masthead of Foote's ship the *Sea-horse*. Foote himself, who was quite unaware of the fact that Ruffo no longer enjoyed the King's confidence, came aboard the *Foudroyant* bringing with him a copy of the treaty which he had signed in good faith, only to be told by an irate Nelson that he had been imposed upon by the Cardinal who was attempting to form a party hostile to the interests of his Sovereign. The remark was a cruel slander on Ruffo who had been winning the King's battles for the past four and a half months. The same evening Sir William sent a formal letter to the Cardinal saying that Lord Nelson had examined a copy of the capitulation which his Eminence had 'seen fit to conclude' with the commanders of the castles, and that 'he disapproves entirely of these capitulations, and that he is firmly resolved on no account to remain neutral with the respectable force which he has the honour to command'. Captains Troubridge and Ball were sent ashore early next morning with the letter to explain the admiral's point of view which was 'to conquer the common foe and to submit his rebellious subjects to the clemency of his Sicilian Majesty'.[8] Nelson then signalled the annulment of the armistice and drew up his fleet in line of battle before the city.

Cardinal Ruffo, who had been waging war for months past and had taken Naples without help from anyone save his Russian and Turkish allies together with cover from Foote's squadron (all of whom had signed the treaty), was in no humour to receive the admiral's envoys calmly. He resented the interference of a British naval officer who had taken no part in the reconquest of Naples and who had not, so far, shown any commission from the King of Naples that superseded the one he held himself as vicar-general and *alter ego*. He considered Nelson's conduct as high-handed and discourteous, and rejected the 'Observations' on the treaty which the two captains brought with them. In this document[9] Nelson proposed to Ruffo that the French and the Rebels should be told 'in their joint names . . . that the arrival of the British fleet has completely destroyed the compact, as would that of the French if they had had the power (which, thank God, they have not) to come to Naples'. He insisted upon a distinction being made between the French and the 'rebels', as he called the forces of the defeated republic, and that 'as to Rebels and Traitors, no power on earth has a right to stand between their gracious King and them: they must instantly throw themselves on the clemency of their Sovereign, for no other terms will be allowed them; nor will the French be allowed even to name them in any capitulation'. Nelson's observations were contrary to the whole spirit of Ruffo's negotiations; if the Cardinal had accepted them at that moment he would have considered himself guilty of the grossest breach of faith. He could not fail to reject them out of hand.

The Cardinal decided to visit Nelson in person. He came aboard the *Foudroyant* during the afternoon and was given a salute of thirteen guns. The meeting was a total failure. Hamilton described Ruffo as being 'the very quintessence of Italian finesse' and told Greville that 'nothing but my phlegm cou'd have prevented an open rupture on the first meeting between Cardinal Ruffo and Lord Nelson'.[10] The Cardinal explained that he had made the treaty in order to save Naples from destruction and repeated his view that only a policy of forgiveness (with a few possible exceptions) could ensure the peaceful restoration of the monarchy. Nelson, on the other hand, continued to hold stubbornly to the proposition that kings do not capitulate with their rebel subjects. Hamilton acted as interpreter during this exchange but seems to have made no attempt to bridge the gap between the two men; it was as though, in the presence of Nelson, he had forgotten his trade of diplomacy. He left everything in the hands of the admiral and ended his account of the day's events in a letter to Acton with the words: 'As Lord Nelson is now telling Lady Hamilton what he wishes to say to the queen, you will probably know from the queen more than I do of Lord Nelson's intentions.'[11]

The meeting on board the *Foudroyant* had ended in deadlock. The Cardinal withdrew in order to discuss the situation with his Russian and Turkish allies, both of whom upheld the treaty as it had ended civil strife and would result in the expulsion of the common enemy. Nelson meanwhile sent Ruffo a declaration calling on the castles to surrender: the cardinal refused to accept it. If Nelson declined to acknowledge his treaty Ruffo declared that he would withdraw the army of the Holy Faith and leave the British to reconquer Naples themselves. Once again he went on board the flagship but no progress was made. Nelson decided that an admiral was no match in talking with a cardinal and the discussions came to an end. He presented Ruffo with his written decision that the treaty could not be put into execution without the approbation of the King of the Two Sicilies and the British commander-in-chief, Lord Keith. Ruffo retired a second time and sent a warning to the forces inside the castles that he could not answer for Lord Nelson allowing the truce to con tinue. A night of terror and panic ensued in the capital.

The panic might have been less but for the irresponsible behaviour of Emma Hamilton. Among the many people who rowed out to the British fleet when it sailed into the bay was Egidio Pallio, the chief of the *lazzaroni*. This ruffian (whom Emma recognised and called aboard) promised the help of his followers but complained that only twenty of them were armed. Lady Hamilton translated his remarks to Nelson who promptly handed over 'a large supply of arms' to Pallio for the rest of his people—he claimed that they numbered ninety thousand—while Emma told him that all they required of him was that he should keep the city quiet for ten days. Nelson may well have had no notion of the ferocity of the *lazzaroni* but Emma must have known that to arm Pallio's followers was like handing over police duties to professional criminals. In no time they were fighting Ruffo's troops, ignoring his appeals for order, paying off old scores in blood, and arresting and terrorizing innocent citizens. Emma imagined that by this act of folly she had 'made' the Queen's party and contributed to that unfortunate woman's popularity.[12] She was quite oblivious of the suffering she had caused.

The breakdown of talks between Ruffo and Nelson caused the greatest confusion in Naples. The population, fearing the possibility of being caught in cross fire between the castles and the fleet, attempted to escape from the city. On 26 June the Cardinal was preparing for a further day of frustration when a letter was delivered to him signed by Sir William Hamilton. 'Lord Nelson begs me to assure your Eminence', he read, 'that he is resolved to do nothing which might break the armistice which your Eminence has granted to the castles of Naples.'[13] This note, which must have been prompted by the fact that no precise orders had yet reached the *Foudroyant* from Palermo, resulted in the rapid evacuation of the castles of Nuovo and Uovo. Those of the 'rebels' who had elected to go to Toulon were permitted to embark in the ships which had been assembled for them but they were not allowed to sail. The operation was conducted with speed; there was not time for the 'honours of war' to be observed.

The day before Nelson agreed to recognise (or at least not to oppose) the Cardinal's treaty General Acton was busy at his desk in Palermo. He did not yet have the full details of the capitulation but he knew that a truce had been arranged. 'The King,' he now wrote to Sir William, 'far from admitting a Capitulation with Rebels nor any dishonourable capitulation and articles with the French, and amongst these dishonourable ones is to be reckoned a Truce of 20 days, so much prejudiciables (*sic*) to His Majesty's interests, security, honour, and dignity, disapproves entirely such a condition, and writes to the Cardinal that no Capitulation is to [be] made with Rebels who are to confide and rest only on His Majesty's mercy and clemency; that no Capitulation is to be admitted without His Majesty's ratification in regard to the French. But as his Majesty's good Ally's Forces the British Squadron under Lord Nelson's command is to appear, and act in support of the King's interest and his good people in Naples, what ever intimation Lord Nelson shall think proper to make the Cardinal is to abide by it and every precedent is to be void and without effect. . . I beg of you, my dear Sir, to present Lord Nelson with these declarations of His Sicilian Majesty, who puts and confides his authority as to every military operation and his own dignity into the Excellent and Brave Lord Nelson's hands.'[14] Lest there should be any doubt as to his meaning Acton followed his letter with two more to the same effect, all written on the same day.

The King wrote as well as his Prime Minister and two days later a further letter from Acton enclosed orders for seizing the Cardinal in the event of his disobeying the royal commands.[15] Fortunately for his reputation Nelson did not have to go to this extreme. It can be argued that Ruffo acted beyond his powers (which were never clearly defined) when he negotiated the terms of capitulation with the defenders of Naples; and he may have failed, in the heat and confusion of his campaign, to keep the King and Acton regularly informed of all his doings; but he had succeeded in capturing Naples for Ferdinand and it was he, rather than Nelson, who had restored the King to his throne. Ferdinand IV was not remarkable for showing gratitude to subjects and his treatment of Ruffo has been condemned as shabby and unworthy. Nelson and Hamilton, as Acton's letter shows, had interpreted the King's will correctly when they refused to recognise the capitulation, but they made no attempt to see the Cardinal's point of view or to meet him half-way on any issue they discussed. He was not given the trust usually accorded to any ally but was treated with suspicion and disrespect. Sir William, with his knowledge of the problems of diplomacy, should have appreciated Ruffo's difficulties but he gave in all too weakly to Nelson's brusque temper and ill-concealed dislike of the Cardinal. It is a pity that a man who in the past had so often lamented the lack of honest counsellors in the service of the King of Naples should have failed to recognise one in the person of Fabrizio Ruffo.

The letters from Palermo reached Naples on 28 June. As soon as they were read orders were issued from the *Foudroyant* that the transports in which the rebel soldiers from the forts had embarked were to be brought under the guns of the fleet and forbidden to sail. Those who had gone to their homes were told that they had twenty-four hours in which to surrender themselves to the King's mercy. The Cardinal saw with despair that his plan for a humane and reasonable settlement had been abandoned and he refused to take any further part in the operations in progress against the French at Sant' Elmo. At this point Hamilton wisely decided that the sooner the King appeared in person the better it would be. 'We are all of the opinion that without the presence of his Majesty the confusion will increase and no regular government can be established,' he wrote in reply to Acton. 'We could wish that both the King, Queen, and your Excellency could come *directly*, when in a very few days the material points of government might be settled. . . We trust no one with the secret of any probability of their Majesties coming, but should they so determine, we are firmly of opinion that they will by so doing place themselves on their throne of Naples with dignity and expedition; whereas leaving things in their present *mysterious* state, God knows how or when it may end.'[16]

Before the King arrived the work of punishment began. Maria Carolina had written to her 'Deputy' on 25 June laying down the general principles to be followed: 'The rebel patriots must lay down their arms and surrender at discretion to the pleasure of the King. Then, in my opinion, an example should be made of some of the leaders of the representatives, and the others to be transported under pain of death if they return into the dominions of the King, where a register will be kept of them; and of this number should be the Members of the Municipality, Chiefs of Brigade, the most violent Club members and seditious scribblers. No soldier who has served [republicans] shall ever be admitted into the army; finally, a rigorous severity, prompt and just. The females who have distinguished themselves in the revolution to be treated in the same way, and that without pity.' Her ideas for the future government of Naples showed rather more of a liberal spirit than this grim catalogue of penalties; she hoped that baronial privileges and jurisdictions would be abolished for ever 'in order to ameliorate the slavery of a faithful people who have replaced their King upon the throne from which treason, felony, and the culpable indifference of the nobles had driven him'. But in spite of this little flash of enlightenment the Queen ended her letter on a sombre note: 'Finally, dear Milady, I recommend Lord Nelson to treat Naples as if it were an Irish town in a similar state of rebellion.'[17]

The result of this letter was that the transports were searched for the most notorious republicans who were then confined in the holds of the British warships. After the arrival of the King they were handed over to a Tribunal of State from which it was but a short journey to the gallows. By ignoring the advice of Cardinal Ruffo the Neapolitan sovereigns made many martyrs for the republican cause.

Nelson, who believed in setting a stern example, had a suitable victim delivered into his hands when Commodore Francesco Caracciolo was brought on board the *Foudroyant* as a prisoner of war on the morning of 29 June. Caracciolo had served with distinction in the royal Neapolitan navy and his ship had sailed with Nelson's when the Royal Family had escaped. Since then he had returned to Naples and thrown in his lot with the republicans. He had commanded their small naval force and even fired on his own former flagship.

When he was captured he had been some days in hiding and was in such a sad condition that he was taken for an old man, though in fact he was no more than forty-seven years old. Nelson ordered a court martial to assemble the same day; it was composed entirely of officers in the Neapolitan service, though the prisoner had asked to be tried by British officers. There could be no doubt of Caracciolo's guilt but the trial was a summary affair; the prisoner was allowed no advocate nor was he able to call witnesses in his own defence. The court condemned him to death at midday and the sentence was confirmed by Nelson at one o'clock. He ordered the Commodore to be hanged from the yard-arm of his former ship, the Minerva, at five o'clock the same afternoon. Caracciolo's request to be shot instead of hanged, a privilege normally given to a person of his rank, was brushed aside. Both Sir William Hamilton and Count Thurn (who had presided over the court martial) begged Nelson for a stay of execution for twenty-four hours to give the unfortunate man time to prepare for death: he refused to grant it. Caracciolo was hanged at five o'clock in the evening as Nelson had ordered; at sunset the rope was cut and his body fell into the sea.

Caracciolo's execution had shaken Hamilton. For the first time since they had arrived in the bay he had attempted to stand up to Nelson. But when all was over he tried rather feebly to see it as being for the best, a sad but salutary example. 'Thurn represented it was usual to give 24 hours for the care of the soul. Lord Nelson's orders remain the same, although I wished to acquiesce with Thurn's opinion,' he told Acton when reporting the unhappy business to him, adding somewhat dubiously: 'All is for the best. . . Lord Nelson's manner of acting must be as his conscience and honour dictate, and I believe his determination will be found best at last.' One thing was certain to him, the King must come without delay. 'For God's sake', he concluded his letter, 'let the king come *at least on board the Foudroyant* and show his royal standard if he can.'[18] The presence of the King would relieve him of a heavy and increasingly unwelcome responsibility.

Emma, meanwhile, had been carrying her responsibilities with less heavy a heart. Standing at Nelson's side she assumed an amorous attitude which made it difficult for people to believe that she was much moved by the human tragedies that surrounded her. Many grotesque stories were told about her triumphing over the rebels, most of which were untrue, not least that which said that she and Nelson had had themselves rowed round the *Minerva* while Caracciolo was still hanging from the yard-arm. She exchanged lists of the condemned with the

Queen, discussing the merits of the various accused while the prisoners themselves, some of whom had formerly been her guests at the Palazzo Sessa, languished in the holds of the ships.

Maria Carolina's pent-up thirst for vengeance found an outlet at last as she sat in her palace at Palermo scanning these lists that Emma sent her, predicting the punishments or assessing the chances of reprieve of those whose names came under her eyes. Many of them had been her courtiers, some of them had been her friends, few were unknown to her. Many pleas for mercy found their way into Emma's hands and these, too, were passed on to her royal friend who was not always deaf to their appeals. The Queen also sent, interspersed with imprecations against her enemies, considerable sums of money for Emma to 'bestow as your benevolent soul suggests upon the unfortunate who need it, certain that it will be dispensed appropriately, for I know your heart'.[19] The complexities and contradictions in Maria Carolina's character had never been more apparent since her sister had died on the scaffold.

Ferdinand sailed from Palermo on 3 July; Acton came with him but the Queen remained behind. Writing to Emma she said: 'That has cost me many tears, and will cost me still more; but the King did not think it expedient that I should go for the short time he reckons on remaining.' This caused Emma to endorse the letter with another of her frenzied outbursts: 'This from my friend whom I love and adore. Yes, I will serve her with my heart and soul. My blood, if necessary, shall flow for her. Emma will prove to Maria Carolina that an humble-born English-woman can serve a Queen with zeal and true love, even at the risk of her life.'[20] Emma's life, of course, was not in the slightest danger, but the note shows that she was still very much in an euphoric state. Her two companions, fortunately, were now much calmer. Nelson had written to the King making some amends for the accusations of treason he had previously hurled at the Cardinal. 'I really do not believe that his Eminence has a disloyal thought towards overthrowing your Majesty's monarchy, but that his Eminence's wish was to have everything his own way,' he wrote with unconscious irony on 30 June, while Sir William assured Acton that 'although (as far as we can learn) the cardinal is surrounded by bad people, and has employed many that have served under the infamous republic and gives protection, as we are told, to some of the most conspicuous of noble Jacobin families—yet we do not believe his Eminency to have any direct treacherous design'.[21] This left the door open for some sort of a reconciliation between the King and the Cardinal.

On the evening of 8 July the Neapolitan warship *Sirena* which carried the King and Acton anchored off Procida for the night. The Cardinal was received on board and did his best to make his peace with Ferdinand, though Acton (strongly influenced by the letters he had received from Hamilton) was not so easily mollified as his master. The next day Acton sent a note to Sir William saying that 'Tomorrow the King shall enjoy Lord Nelson's agreeable cabin. We shall sail as soon as the wind permits—that is by 10 or 11 in the morning.'[22] Ferdinand was to make this 'agreeable cabin' his home for the month he remained in Naples. Trusting more in the safety of Nelson's flagship than his own ships or his own subjects he never left the *Foudroyant* until he stepped ashore again at Palermo. A few days after his arrival the French in the Castel di Sant' Elmo surrendered and the King had the satisfaction of seeing his royal standard fly from the battlements, but even this stirring sight did not encourage him to set foot on land. Sir William and Emma were more daring; they went up to the fortress to see the effect of the bombs. 'I saw at a distance our despoiled house in town and the Villa Emma that have been plundered,' Lady Hamilton told Greville, 'Sir William's new apartment—a bomb burst in it!'[23] The sight made them so low spirited that they had no desire to return. It was their last view of the Palazzo Sessa.

For the next month Naples was governed from on board a British man-of-war. Ferdinand's only moment of alarm was when Caracciolo's body was seen to rise to the surface and drift towards the ship. Something of the horror of the scene was allayed when it was suggested to the King that he had come to ask for Christian burial. The frightened monarch quickly granted the request. The episode cast a chill over the rejoicing at the King's return for those of his subjects who thought it an occasion for rejoicing, which by no means all did. For everyone the reappearance of the Commodore's body, which seemed to be swimming towards Naples, was a sinister and terrifying omen. It was a grim reminder, to Hamilton if not to anyone else, of an incident which he recalled with uneasiness and would gladly have forgotten.

The presence of the King and his chief minister relieved Hamilton of his heavy responsibilities and he was able to devote his attention to the long dispatch he sent to Lord Grenville.[24] His report to the Foreign Minister was dated 'On Board the *Foudroyant* in the Bay of Naples, July 14, 1799,' and gave a full account of all that had happened since he and Nelson had sailed from Palermo. It was a justification of the strong line they had taken against Ruffo's treaty which Sir William describes as 'shameful', declaring that if it had been carried into execution 'all the Chiefs of the Rebellion would have escaped and the others would have remained unmolested in the kingdom to propagate at their leasure the same pernicious maxims that have brought this kingdom to the brink of destruction—and their Sicilian Majesties would have remained for ever sullied by so unwarranted a stretch of Power of Cardinal Ruffo their Vicar General, whose ambitious views were certainly to favour the nobles, put himself at their head, re-establish the feudal system and oppress the People which is diametrically opposed to their Sicilian Majesties' intentions who wish to make the nobles feel their indignation for their late Treachery, ingratitude and disloyalty, and to caress and reward the people by whose Loyalty and bravery, with the aid of their good allies, the Kingdom of Naples has been so speedily recovered.'

While expressing very correctly the views of Ferdinand and Maria Carolina the dispatch presented a mere travesty of Ruffo's proposals and his view of the situation was never properly explained, which is perhaps not surprising as neither

Sir William nor Nelson made any attempt to understand it. The Cardinal is seen only from Nelson's biased standpoint which Hamilton had come entirely to accept. 'We found', he wrote, 'on our arrival in the Bay a general discontent of the people and of His Sicilian Majesty's most loyal subjects of the higher class complaining of the rapine and plunder committed daily at Naples by the Calabrese and the evident partiality shewn by the Cardinal to the Jacobin party whilst the Royalist and loyal people were brow-beaten and denied access to his Eminency at his head-quarters at the Ponte Maddalena in the suburbs of Naples; not that they accused him of being a Traitor, but that he was surrounded by Jacobins and venal evil councillors; in short, your Lordship can have no conception of the anarchy and confusion at Naples.' This was the best that Hamilton could bring himself to say about Cardinal Ruffo. One cannot help wondering what his opinion would have been if he had not given in so completely to the narrow and politically unenlightened views of Lord Nelson.

The date of this dispatch was, to the day, exactly a year since Sir William had walked round the rooms of the Palazzo Sessa making a catalogue of his pictures while Nelson searched the Mediterranean for Bonaparte's fleet which he would destroy on the first of August. Sir William's palace now lay despoiled and partly ruined, his collection dispersed and some of it destroyed. The past ten months had been spent constantly in the company of the Admiral whose courage and tactical brilliance he so much admired but whose opinions on political matters were reactionary in comparison with his own. He had long been subjected to Emma's parrot-like repetitions of the Queen's tireless invectives against the rebels. All these things had had their effect on him, adding their weight to the burden of age and ill-health. His old critical spirit had collapsed and he could no longer contend with younger, more vigorous, but less enlightened minds. As the representative of the civil power Hamilton should have attempted a mediation between the Cardinal and Nelson; instead he allowed himself to be swept along by Nelson's intransigence and Emma's thoughtless impetuosity. Their triumph over his liberality of mind can only be regretted.

Nelson's conduct in the bay of Naples was later on to be severely censured by Charles James Fox speaking on behalf of the opposition in the House of Commons in February 1800, but the immediate response of the Government to Sir William's dispatch was favourable. Writing from Downing Street on 20 August 1799, Lord Grenville replied: 'Your dispatch marked No. 22 containing an account of the surrender of the Fort of St. Elmo and of His Sicilian Majesty's return to the Bay of Naples has been received and laid before the King. You will not fail to convey to His Sicilian Majesty the Expression of sincere Satisfaction which has been occasioned by these interesting and important Events.'[25] When Sir William received this letter he was living once more in the Palazzo Palagonia. The King had left Naples for His Sicilian capital on August, sailing in Lord Nelson's flagship. Sir William and Lady Hamilton sailed with him and shared in the triumph of his return.

Emma was welcomed by the Queen with a positive cascade of diamonds. 'The goodness and affability of His Majesty was such as to enchant every officer and sailor on board,' Hamilton reported to Lord Grenville. 'On quitting the ship at Palermo His Majesty left a present of Two Thousand Three Hundred Ounces to be distributed among the Admiral Lord Nelson's servants and the Ship's Company. The King of Naples having remarked Lady Hamilton's zeal for his Service and the trouble she took in receiving the Neapolitan Ladies that came on board the *Foudroyant* to pay their Court to His Majesty during our stay in the Bay of Naples, and in keeping up a constant correspondence with the Queen of Naples at Palermo, was graciously pleased to present her with his Picture richly set with Diamonds on our return to Palermo, and the Queen of Naples has done Lady Hamilton the honor to present her with her Majesty's picture and hair set with Diamonds in bracelets with a pair of Ear Rings of Diamonds and Pearls, with an Egrette and Her Majesty's Cypher in Diamonds with a complete dress of the finest point lace.'[26] Nelson's reward was the Dukedom of Brontë with the feudal domains that went with it, which were said to be worth three thousand pounds a year, though it is doubtful whether the Admiral ever received anything like this sum from his new estates. Sir William had to be content with another diamond-set likeness of Ferdinand IV. The value of the presents showered on the Envoy and his wife by the grateful sovereigns was said to be in the region of six thousand pounds.

On the feast of St. Rosalia, the patron saint of Palermo, which fell on 16 August, the Queen gave a great fête in honour of her English friends. As a climax to the festivities, wax effigies of Lord Nelson, Sir William and Emma were crowned with wreaths of laurel and the nine-year-old Prince Leopold thanked the Admiral in the name of his parents for recovering his father's kingdom. The sight of these three waxen figures and the living originals who stood by them, the *Tria Juncta in Uno* as Emma liked to call them, had now a double meaning as amusing to the courtiers of Palermo as was the play on the motto of the Order of the Bath to Lady Hamilton, who saw in it a piquant parallel with the relationship between her husband, Lord Nelson and herself. Of these 'three joined in one' it was now common knowledge that Sir William Hamilton came very decidedly in the third place. Gossip was not confined to Palermo; there was talk at Gibraltar where Lady Elgin (on her way to Constantinople where her husband had been appointed Minister) discovered that 'they say there never was a man turned so *vain glorious* (that's the phrase) in the world as Lord N. He is now completely managed by Lady Hamilton.'[27] These rumours would soon be repeated in the London newspapers.

Lord and Lady Elgin were able to decide for themselves whether these rumours had any foundation in fact for early in October they were in Palermo and able to see things at first hand. They thought it prudent to decline an invitation to stay at the Palazzo Palagonia and put up instead with the Consul, Charles Lock, but an invitation to dine with the Hamiltons was not refused and Lady Elgin recorded her impressions of Emma and Nelson in a letter home. 'I must acknowledge she is pleasant,' she told her mother, 'makes up amazingly, and did all she could to make me accept of an apartment there, which I should have totally to myself. However I did not in the least scruple to refuse her Ladyship. She looked very handsome at dinner, quite in an undress;—my Father would say, "There is a fine Woman for you, good flesh and blood". She is indeed a Whapper! and I think her manner very vulgar. It is really humiliating to see Lord Nelson, he seems quite dying and yet as if he had no other thought than her. He told Elgin privately that he had lived a year in the house with her and that her beauty was nothing in comparison to the goodness of her heart.'

On 4 October Lady Elgin was taken by Emma to a fête at which the King and Queen and all their family were present. Emma had told her that it would be correct to go in 'a common morning dress' and then appeared herself blazing with diamonds in a gown of fine gold and coloured silk, putting the younger woman quite in the shade. This, Lady Elgin discovered, was 'a constant trick' of Lady Hamilton's, and one hardly likely to endear her to the rest of womankind. On this occasion Lady Elgin insisted on returning home, in spite of the Queen's polite protestations, and coming back in suitable attire in a dress that was 'most amazingly admired'. Commenting on this evening's fête she wrote: 'You never saw anything equal to the fuss the Queen made with Lady H., and Lord Nelson wherever she moved was always by her side. I am told the Queen laughs very much at her to all her Neapolitans, but says her influence with Lord N. makes it worth her while making up to her. Lady H. has made him do many very foolish things.'[28]

Emma was far from popular with the Locks, with whom Lady Elgin had been staying. Writing to his father Charles Lock complained: 'We have in Lady Hamilton the bitterest enemy you can imagine. Her wish to engross the conduct of affairs entirely, as I have before told you, prompted her to poison Sir William's mind against me; to this was joined a female vanity which could not bear that any English woman should be admired by her countrymen but herself. She has prejudiced the Court in a most unjustifiable manner against us, and she has taken occasion to insinuate that my wife's principles are republican. . . I have complained to Sir William and he has given me his word he will remove every impression of that kind on the first opportunity.' His picture of Hamilton was hardly encouraging: 'Sir William's health is very much broken and his frame is so feeble that even a slight attack of bile, to severe fits of which he has lately been subject, may carry him off. I am then totally in the dark if I have to take up the business; Sir William never takes copies of his letters but trusts to memorandums and foul copies, unintelligible to any but himself.'[29] Sir William had much trouble with his Consul, who had quarrelled with Nelson over the victualling of the fleet and had infuriated the King by wearing whiskers, a sure sign, in the eyes of Ferdinand, of rank republicanism.

Casanova, who had met Sir William many years before, said of him when he came to write his *Memoirs*: 'Hamilton was a genius, and yet he ended by marrying a mere girl who was clever enough to make him in love with her. Such a misfortune often comes to clever men in their old age.'[30] It was only now that his marriage with Emma began to take on the characteristics of a misfortune. Sir William was too much a man of the world to be ignorant of the situation that was developing between his wife and Lord Nelson and he cannot have been indifferent to the absurdity of his own position. Neither Nelson nor Emma gave it a thought as they paraded their infatuation before the inhabitants of Palermo; it was as though they found an added stimulation from the publicity of it all. Sir William had no place in this pantomime. His ill-health became a refuge from the humiliations he had to face in public. He has been described at this period as being senile,[31] but this was not so. Senility is a progressive condition and had he been senile then he would have been very much more so after his return to London when, in fact, he showed a great improvement in health. The ill-health and irritability that afflicted him in these months sprang from a different cause. His fondness for Nelson and such affection as he still felt for Emma would survive the strain they put on his generosity of spirit, but his health suffered in consequence.

Nelson's official duties took him away from Sicily more than once (during Lord Keith's absence he was acting commander-in-chief in the Mediterranean) but between visits to Malta and Minorca he always came back to the Palazzo Palagonia where he continued to dance attendance on Lady Hamilton. Even Troubridge wrote a tactful rebuke to Nelson for the talk his conduct was occasioning, begged him to give up 'nocturnal parties', and pointed out that Lady Hamilton's character would suffer, for nothing could prevent people from gossiping. Sir William had no option but to accept the situation with a good grace. He liked and admired Nelson who had originally been invited under their roof as his rather than as Emma's friend, and he had indulged his wife's extravagance and folly for too long to be able to put a stop to it now. To turn Nelson out of his house or (as a wild rumour circulating in Palermo whispered that he had already done) to challenge him to a duel, would only have added ridicule to a situation which already savoured too much of comic opera. Either action would in any case have been wholly out of character. Sir William had to summon all the diplomacy he could muster to his defence, present a bland face to the world, and pretend that nothing was happening. It was not an easy task; he lacked the insensibility of the other two; he must have known that behind his back the world was mocking him, though at this period he still believed their relationship to be essentially innocent.

Early in January 1800 Keith returned and Nelson was bidden to join him at Leghorn. The commander-in-chief had expressed the opinion that Lord Nelson (who had twice disregarded his orders) was now cutting an absurd figure for folly and vanity, and that he and Lady Hamilton were 'just a silly pair of sentimental fools';[32] under the circumstances it was not surprising that the meeting between the two admirals was chilly. They sailed together to Palermo where presentations were made to Ferdinand and Maria Carolina and after nine days in the Sicilian capital set sail for Malta. It was on this voyage that Nelson had the good fortune to meet and capture one of the few ships that had escaped him after the battle of the Nile. *Le Généreux* struck her flag after a sharp action in which the French admiral lost his life. The capture of this ship was some compensation for the disturbing news of Bonaparte's escape from Egypt and his proclamation, in December 1799, as First Consul of the French Republic. Cornelia Knight, whose muse had been listless of late, was inspired to add another verse to the National Anthem:

> While this we chant his praise,
> See what new fires blaze!
> New laurels spring!
> Nelson! thy task's complete;
> All their Egyptian fleet
> Bows at thy conqu'ring feet
> To George our King!

The new year which had added this fresh sprig of laurel to Nelson's fame brought Sir William another blow; he learnt that he had been recalled and that his successor was on his way to Palermo. Continued ill-health and Emma's irresponsible behaviour had been burdens enough without this additional one; he found the decision of the government very hard to accept. He had applied for leave as long ago as 1798 and had been hoping for an opportunity to come home, should events permit it, ever since then, but he was deeply hurt when it was given out that he was retiring at his own request. After thirty-seven years in Italy he could not believe that his recall was final and he tried to persuade himself as well as the Court that Arthur Paget, who had been appointed to succeed him, was coming only as a temporary replacement until he could return himself to his old post.

The Queen dreaded Sir William's departure; she referred to his successor as 'the fatal Paget'[33] and instructed the Neapolitan Minister to ask that Hamilton might be allowed to remain. This somewhat raised his hopes; at least he trusted that he might be allowed to decide for himself whether to stay in London or not. It was in this spirit that he wrote to his nephew on 25 January 1800. 'I have been induced, as you know,' he told Greville, 'to stay at my post because my conscience would not permit me to leave it. Without me Lord Nelson wou'd not stay here and without Lord Nelson their Sicilian Majesties wou'd think themselves undone. However, his Lordship having fairly reinstated them on their throne of Naples it is their fault if they don't keep fast there; all we cou'd do has been done, and all the efforts that I see are making to keep me on here by the Court will not surely prevail, but home I go in the spring. I realy now can serve them better in England than by staying here. The Queen is realy so fond of Emma that the parting will be a serious business. However, I say and mean not to resign my office—I go home to settle my affairs, which God knows are in much confusion, and to get a little relaxation. I do not give up my house at Naples; but, as I am 69 years old, it is nonsense to take any decided resolution about returning here or not. Shou'd England agree with me I think I may remain, but otherwise I can do no better than bask out the remainder of my days in the Naples sun, and in that case I would bring an active Secretary to write for me, for I cannot labour as I have hitherto without any assistance. It is certainly very flattering to me that after 37 years' residence at Naples all shou'd appear so very anxious that I shou'd remain with them.'[34]

The Queen certainly was anxious that he should remain. Maria Carolina had known no other representative of Great Britain since she had come to Naples from Vienna as a young girl thirty-two years ago; the thought of anyone else taking his place was obnoxious to her and she had no wish to lose so willing a collaborator as Lady Hamilton. But the British Foreign Secretary had made up his mind and it was only out of respect for Hamilton's feelings that he had said that he was recalling the Minister at his own request; he had determined to replace him anyway. The Queen urged Ferdinand to write personally asking that Sir William might stay but with a mixture of laziness and contrariness he did nothing about it. The King undoubtedly derived a certain pleasure from thwarting his wife's wishes and he no longer shared her enthusiasm for Emma.

The reason for Hamilton's recall was not hard to find. He was too old; he belonged to the old order which was fast disappearing. The new century and the new ideas that went with it required the presence of a younger man. A Minister who had been appointed when Louis XV was King of France and Maria Theresa still ruled at Vienna had no place in a Europe where Napoleon Bonaparte had just become First Consul. Sir William's age alone would have been a sufficient excuse for his retirement but there can be little doubt that the ugly rumours about Lord Nelson and Emma had seriously prejudiced him in the eyes of the government. Lord Elgin had considered it high time that Sir William went home, and he did not keep his ideas to himself. Charles Lock's complaining letters would also have been read in influential circles, for his wife was a first cousin of Charles James Fox and both enjoyed high patronage. The hint of scandal had also lost Sir William the most potent of his former supporters; he could no longer claim the friendly intervention of King George III.

Arthur Paget, who was the third son of Lord Uxbridge, reached Palermo at the beginning of the second week of April. General Acton was anxious to make his acquaintance and wrote to Hamilton on 9 April: 'I hear from your billet, my dear Sir, the arrival on horseback at Palermo of Mr. Paget. If I do not mistake, I found him riding yesterday with Mr. Lock. His likeness with Capt. Paget made me think it was the person you mention. I see that he has not brought you any other letters.'[35] Sir William took no notice of this hint. He showed no desire to introduce his young successor (Mr. Paget was only twenty-nine) to the Ministers of King Ferdinand's government or to present his own Letters of Recall. His reason for this, as he explained to the embarrassed Paget, was that he had no wish to remain in

Palermo as a private individual and unless Paget's instructions showed any reason to the contrary he would only present his Letters on the day before he left for England.

Sir William's rather peevish behaviour sprang from the resentment he felt at his recall and the speed with which Paget had arrived to take over from him. He was fighting a spirited but pointless rearguard action and it was to result in an angry exchange with his old friend General Acton, who had recently, at the age of sixty-four, amazed his friends by marrying his niece, a girl who was not quite fourteen years old. Hamilton heard that Acton had had private conversations with his successor without his own knowledge or consent and the news filled him with rage. The fact that Acton would have had no need to resort to this procedure (if indeed he had done so) had Hamilton himself been more prompt in presenting Mr. Paget carried no weight with the very provoked ambassador. He addressed a curt and furious note to the Minister on 15 April: 'Sir, Have you or have you not received in private Mr. Paget and allowed him to talk to your Excellency His Sicilian Majesty's Prime Minister upon affairs relative to our two Courts? A simple Yes or No will decide whether your Excellency has or has not betrayed your old and very sincere friend and at the same time offered the grossest insult to His Britannic Majesty's Envoy Extraordinary and Plenipotentiary accredited to this Court now upwards of Thirty Six Years.' The note was signed with an abrupt 'Wm. Hamilton' without any of the usual courteous flourishes.

At this stage, as sometimes happens on these fraught occasions, an improbable note of comedy was introduced, though it appeared as anything but amusing to the impassioned envoy. Sir William was waiting impatiently for the Prime Minister's reply when a messenger arrived at his house carrying an official letter bearing Acton's seal. Hamilton tore open the cover and discovered inside 'nothing more than two sheets of blank paper and a pencil'd drawing of a landscape and a temple'. His feeling of resentment against Acton was too strong for him to see this as anything but an added slight and he wrote to the Minister in even stronger terms: 'I now very seriously address myself to Your Excellency once more for an answer to my billet of yesterday, and if I do not receive one before ten o'clock tomorrow morning I shall go to His Sicilian Majesty and lay what I think my just complaints at His Majesty's feet. God is my judge that I have never acted a double part with your Excellency during our long acquaintance and, as I thought, sincere friendship, both of us acting for the mutual honour and interest of our respective Sovereigns; but when I think that I am trod upon either in my Public or private character I will not submit tamely to any man upon Earth. A thorough explanation therefore is absolutely necessary at this moment when Sir Wm. Hamilton has reason to suspect that he has been betrayed by his friend Sir John Acton at the same time that His Britannic Majesty's Minister at this Court has been highly insulted by the first Minister of His Sicilian Majesty.'

This second letter brought a measured and dignified reply from General Acton. 'I have received your letter last night and another this morning,' he wrote to Sir William. 'I begin to answer to the last by assuring you that I never sent you any letter last night, and I am surprised that a paper with my seal, as you tell me, but with Blanks alone should have been brought to you. Never any letter or commission from me to the two officers under my Orders as Secretaries could procure such an improper message. I shall enquire immediately on this business, and any person guilty of that strange blunder shall be conveniently punished. As to the letter of last night, I must tell you that I am perfectly conscious of having never forefeited in the least measure the duties of an old friend: I have never betrayed anybody by acting insincerely as a private person nor in ministerial capacity. I should not certainly have behaved improperly with a friend of above thirty years. I am on the contrary perfectly certain that I have constantly from the ancient date to the present day acted with candour, sincerity, and the most delicate regard in what ever concerns you. This is my answer and assertion on this article.

'As to your demand whether *or no* I have seen Mr. Paget as His Sicilian Majesty's Prime Minister, and received *in Private*, whether or no I have entertained him, or been entertained by him upon affairs relative to our two Courts, I refer myself first to my full assertion on the first article; I shall likewise be particular with you, Sir, and willingly open with you on the subject as I have ever been if you had thought proper to make me the same demand in another manner. But to a peremptory question made to His Sicilian Majesty's Minister, who may see, receive, and entertain any Person of any nation, and upon any subject and matter, without being answerable to anyone but to his Sovereign, I shall dispense myself to make even any answer. Your billet of this night confirms me in this determination.'[36]

Hamilton had to content himself with this reply. His irascible outburst sprang from the feeling of insecurity which recent events had created in his mind; his public office and his private dignity were both simultaneously threatened and it is not surprising that he should think himself 'trod upon' or that what seemed to him as a slight on the part of a very old friend should have resulted in this cry of anger and hurt pride. A betrayed husband becomes very sensitive of his honour. The ridicule to which Emma's behaviour laid him open, the resentment he felt at his summary recall after nearly thirty-seven years *en poste*, had both inflicted deep and painful wounds. He kept the wounds hidden but the slightest touch still made him cry out.

It was clear that the sooner he presented his Letters of Recall the better it would be. Lord Nelson provided him with the opportunity he looked for. The Admiral was also ready to go home and Maria Carolina, unable to bear the thought of Palermo without the presence of *le digne chevalier* or the protection of Lord Nelson, had decided to pay a long promised visit to her daughter and son-in-law the Empress and Emperor in Vienna. They would all leave together. But before they all went Nelson had decided to take the Hamiltons with him on a cruise to

Malta. 'My task is done, my health is lost, and the orders of the great Earl of St. Vincent are completely fulfilled,' he wrote, 'I hope the *Foudroyant* will be able to come here to carry us first to Malta and from thence, taking the Queen of Naples to Leghorn, proceed with us at least to Gibraltar, if not to England.'[37] He would be ready to embark his friends on 23 April.

Three days before embarking with Nelson, Sir William wrote to Acton (with whom he was now once more on friendly terms), to request a formal audience of King Ferdinand in order that he might present his Letters of Recall. He wrote in the third person as the solemnity of the occasion demanded: 'Sir William Hamilton. . . after having assured His Excellency General Acton of his best respects has the honor of acquainting His Excellency that he has received His Royal Master's gracious permission to return to England immediately on his private affairs, but that His Majesty not wishing to leave the Court of the Two Sicilies without a British Minister, has appointed Mr. Paget to that office during the absence of Sir William. Mr. Paget being already in Palermo Sir William begs the favour of General Acton to acquaint Their Sicilian Majesties of these circumstances and to entreat of Their Majesties that they will permit him to have the honor of presenting His Credential Letters to Their Majesties when ever it shall be most convenient to Their Majesties. Sir William cannot help adding that his sincere attachment to Their Majesties, their Royal Family, and their Kingdom is such, that if he was not fully persuaded that in a very few months he may have the satisfaction of returning again to the presence of Their Majesties, he shou'd at this moment be in the utmost despair. Sir William's ardent wish wou'd be to pass his few remaining Days in exerting himself in his endeavours to maintain and keep alive that perfect harmony which by the Grace of God so happily subsists at this moment between the Courts of Great Britain and the Two Sicilies.'[38]

Still clutching desperately to the forlorn hope that his recall might not be permanent Sir William took his official leave of the King and Queen on the morning of 22 April. Half an hour later the royal couple received Arthur Paget who presented his Letters as the new Minister of Great Britain to their Court. 'My taking leave at court yesterday was certainly a moving scene, and does me honour,' Hamilton wrote to Charles Greville the next day. His long diplomatic career was over.

1. Morrison, 411.
2. *Vide* O. Warner: *A Portrait of Lord Nelson*, p. 191.
3. Morrison, 405.
4. Morrison, 411.
5. Gutteridge: *Nelson and the Neapolitan Jacobins*, p. iii.
6. Idem: pp. 155-9.
7. B.M. Egerton MSS 2640, f. 265.

8.   Gutteridge: op. cit., p. 205.
9.   Nicolas: *Dispatches & Letters of Lord Nelson,* Vol. III, p. 385.
10. Morrison, 405.
11. Gutteridge: op. cit., p. 216.
12. *Vide* Morrison, 411.
13. Gutteridge: op. cit., pp. 231-2.
14. B.M. Egerton MSS 2640, f. 276.
15. Gutteridge: op. cit., p. 259.
16. Gutteridge: op. cit., pp. 269-70.
17. *Vide* Pettigrew: *Life of Nelson,* Vol. I. pp. 233-5.
18. Gutteridge: op. cit., pp. 279-80.
19. Jeaffreson: *Lady Hamilton & Lord Nelson,* Vol II., p. 101.
20. Gutteridge: op. cit., pp. 294 and 296-7.
21. Ibid., 286, 287-8.
22. Ibid., 305.
23. Morrison, 411.
24. B.M. Add. MSS 37077, ff. 107-14.
25. B.M. Add. MSS 37077, f. 123.
26. B.M. Add. MSS 57077, f. 120.
27. N.H. Grant: *The Letters of Mary. . . Countess of Elgin,* p. 17.
28. Ibid., pp. 22, 24.
29. Duchess of Sermoneta: *The Locks of Norbury,* pp. 179-80.
30. *Histoire de ma Vie* (Paris 1962), Vol. II, pp. 281-2.
31. cf. C. Oman: *Nelson,* p. 390.
32. W. Sichel: *Emma, Lady Hamilton,* p. 328.
33. *Vide* C. Knight: *Autobiography,* Vol. I, p. 143. The Queen
     sometimes varied this with the 'inevitable' Paget, 'in terms of
     pitiable distress'.
34. Morrison, 444.
35. B.M. Egerton: MSS 2640, f. 384.
36. B.M. Egerton: MSS 2640, ff. 386, 388 and 390.
37. *Vide* C. Oman: *Nelson,* p. 383.
38. B.M. Add, MSS 41200, f. 198.

CHAPTER XXIII

Back to England

Nelson's guests sailed from Palermo on 23 April. The party on board the *Foudroyant* consisted of Sir William and Lady Hamilton, Cornelia Knight, an unnamed English couple and an old Maltese nobleman. Their first port of call was Syracuse, which they reached on 1 May, and where two days were devoted to sightseeing. Late on the evening of 3 May the island of Malta was sighted and Nelson's ship joined the squadron blockading the port of Valetta, which was still in the hands of the French. They remained in Maltese waters until the twentieth of the month, sometimes going ashore to dine with the Governor, Captain Alexander Ball, or with General Graham, the military commander. Captain Ball, who said of Sir William 'he is the most amiable and accomplished man I know, and his heart is certainly one of the best in the world', addressed Emma gallantly as his 'sister' as both had recently been decorated with the cross of honour of the Order of Malta. Emma had been made *dame petit croix* on Nelson's recommendation to the Grand Master, the Czar Paul I of Russia, for helping to raise money and supplies to relieve distress on the embattled island, a task admirably suited to her abundant energy. 'I am the first Englishwoman that ever had it,' she told Greville proudly. 'Sir W. is pleased, so *I am happy*.'

Sir William had little enough to please him just then, least of all on this voyage. The atmosphere was hardly that of a party of pleasure in spite of Cornelia Knight's shrill cry of:

> Come, cheer up, fair Emma, forget all thy grief,
> For thy shipmates are brave, and a Hero's their chief.[2]

The hero, who became something more than a hero to Emma during the voyage, was himself very far from well, suffering from spasms which he thought to be heart-attacks, though Captain Ball attributed them to the effects of fatigue and anxiety. Emma, also unwell, retired below complaining of fever. Nelson ordered silence to be observed in all parts of the ship so that her repose might not be disturbed. The fact of the matter was that she had discovered herself to be pregnant.

The question must now be asked whether Emma had ever intended to give herself to Nelson as a lover in the fullest sense. When she first uttered the theatrical cry of 'Oh God! Is it possible?' and threw herself at him after the battle of the

Nile she was simply exploiting a dramatic situation for the sake of an effective scene, a thing she had done often enough before. After that she found the part of appearing everywhere as the hero's greatest friend a highly flattering and agreeable one which she could play with perfect complacency as she knew Nelson to be both a married man of honourable character and also devoted to her husband to whom he stood, on his own admission, in the relationship of a son. This gave her the public triumph of being Nelson's constant companion without running any of the private risks such a relationship might otherwise imply, a kind of *amitié amoureuse* in which romantic friendship rather than passion would be the predominant note. It was an attitude which had the advantage of being both exciting and safe.

It can be argued that Emma never expected that Nelson would demand more from her than she was herself prepared to offer, any more than it ever occurred to Sir William that he would be replaced in his wife's most intimate affections by the man upon whose integrity he would have staked his honour. It is certain that Emma had no wish to run any risks; she valued her new-found respectability far too highly and would cling to it, even to the point of ridicule, long after all the world knew it to be lost once more. Despite the many opportunities that Naples offered to a young and beautiful woman there is no evidence to suggest that she was ever unfaithful to Sir William until Nelson came to take his place in her life. It is possible that beneath a flamboyant and theatrical exterior she was not a very passionate woman. Nelson, however, was now deeply in love with her and she had played the part of adoring friend for far too long to be able to turn back. They had yet to realise the full implications of what had taken place. Emma had no desire to compromise the social position which she derived from her marriage to Sir William; Nelson did not realise that his own marriage was wrecked; neither of them was ready to face the realities of the situation. It would still be some time before Nelson would think of writing to Emma as 'my own dear wife, for such you are in my eyes and in the face of heaven'.

The *Foudroyant* was back in Palermo on the last day of May. For Hamilton, who was neither revengeful nor merciless, there were happy tidings waiting in the news that the day before, 30 May, Ferdinand IV had signed an edict of amnesty designed to suspend and cancel political sentences and to forgive those imprisoned on charges of *lèse-majesté*. Though the act was not exclusive it meant that the public execution of traitors, which had continued in Naples since the previous August, would now cease and the gallows be removed from the market-square where for the best part of a year they had stood as a symbol to the Neapolitans of what Nelson had called 'the clemency of their Sovereign'. To celebrate this somewhat overdue act of mercy the King had instituted a new Order of Chivalry dedicated to St. Ferdinand with the motto *Fedei et Merito*. Among the first to receive it was Lord Nelson who was awarded the Grand Cross, together with Marshal Suvarov and the Czar of Russia. Nelson greatly prized this decoration and in a Will made at sea before the battle of Copenhagen bequeathed its gold-and-silver star as well as the Collar of the Order of the Bath to his hereditary heirs 'in order that it may be recollected that there was once such a person as myself living'.[3]

For Sir William the last few days in Palermo can hardly have been happy. Though he kept up the pathetic pretence that he would be returning to his post he can have been under no serious illusion that his recall was not final. The climate of Sicily had never suited him and he had suffered almost continual ill-health, while his wife's conduct had exposed him to the sort of public ridicule that he had always secretly feared. References to old age and death had featured frequently in letters to his close friends. He had written gloomily on these subjects (but not without a touch of grim humour) when discussing his plans with Sir Joseph Banks the previous September when just back from the bay of Naples. He hoped, he told Sir Joseph, to return in the spring, 'when, alive or dead, I shall come home, for at my first wife's particular desire I am to lye by her in Selbeck Church when I am dead, and we shall roll soon together into Milford Haven for the sea is undermining that Church very fast.'[4]

Hamilton gave a grand dinner party at the Palazzo Palagonia on 5 June in honour of the birthday of George III. It was also his own farewell banquet. Among those present was Sir John Acton, the misunderstanding that had disfigured their last encounter now quite forgotten. Three days later Acton wrote: 'We have been true friends for a great number of years and you was almost the only one whom I found when called to this country, and a stranger, I found myself a Secretary of State which I little expected nor was wishing. We have since, my dear Sir, been agreeing together and constantly in whatever could be of real service and good for the two Countries, England and the Sicilies. We have been in continual agitation in these last troublesome times, and you did always friendly and warmly advise me in the disagreeable times with the true and active sense of Honesty and personal concern for the Country, the King's Service, and myself. My obligation shall be constant, and my wishes for ever directed to your welfare and satisfaction.'[5] The Queen reacted more emotionally than her Prime Minister at the thought of Sir William's departure. Even though she would be travelling with them as far as Vienna Maria Carolina felt obliged to beg Emma to 'tell the Chevalier I have never felt till now how much I am attached to him, how much I owe him. My eyes swim with tears. . . '[6] No record of the King's feelings appears to have survived, but as it was generally known that he could hardly wait to be rid of the Queen's company perhaps he considered Sir William's recall as a melancholy but necessary price to pay for this unexpected blessing.

Owing to the sudden panic of the Queen on hearing that Bonaparte was crossing the Alps intent on another invasion of Italy the sailing of the *Foudroyant* was delayed for three days. At length she came on board and early on the morning of 10 June Nelson was able to weigh anchor. With the Queen were her three unmarried daughters (future Queens of Spain, France and Sardinia), Prince Leopold, and a retinue of attendants numbering about fifty which did not make conditions on the ship exactly ideal for the other passengers. The Hamiltons were accompanied by Emma's mother (whom Lady Elgin had mistaken for their housekeeper in Palermo) and Miss Cornelia Knight. The latter, unresponsive to Maria Carolina's ecstatic cry of 'Leghorn! Leghorn!' as the ship put to sea, declared that for her part she left Sicily with great pain 'for it was also severing myself from Italy, where I had spent so many years of happiness.'[7] This can have expressed only a small part of what their final departure must have meant to Sir William after nearly thirty-seven years in Italy.

From Leghorn, after many delays, the party proceeded across land to Ancona. Bonaparte's victory over the Austrians at Marengo on 14 June put them in considerable peril and often their coach was only a few miles from the French outposts. From Ancona they took ship for Trieste, from where they continued in safety to Vienna.

For Sir William the journey home was a trial of strength which he only just survived. It lasted altogether four months, for the first of which he was in a state of nervous and physical prostration. Mrs. Cadogan and Miss Knight were seriously alarmed at his state of health but Nelson and Emma, absorbed in mutual admiration and eagerly enjoying the cheers that greeted them, seemed utterly indifferent to the fate of their elderly companion. A long letter, written in the form of a diary, which Cornelia Knight sent to Captain Berry, gives a pathetic account of Sir William's sufferings: 'July 2, 1800. Lord Nelson is well, and keeps up his spirits amazingly. Sir William appears broken, distressed, and harassed. . . July 16. Sir William says he shall die by the way, and he looks so ill, that I should not be surprised if he did. . . July 24. At Castel San Giovanni the coach in which were Lord Nelson and Sir William and Lady Hamilton was overturned; Sir William and Lady Hamilton were hurt, but not dangerously. . . poor Sir William suffered much when he left me at Arezzo. . . August 9 (Trieste). Sir William and Lady Hamilton and Lord Nelson give a miserable account of their sufferings on board. . . Poor Sir William Hamilton has been so ill that the physicians had almost given up; he is now better, and I hope we shall be able to set off tomorrow night for Vienna. . . How we shall proceed on our long journey is to me a problem; but we shall certainly get on as fast as we can; for the very precarious state of Sir William's health has convinced everybody that it is necessary he should arrange his affairs.'[8]

It might have been a good deal kinder to the ailing man if if they had thought of letting him rest for a week or more at Trieste instead of rushing him on to Vienna, but Emma and Nelson could not be held back. They had no sympathy for invalids as they enjoyed their triumphal progress. 'Great curiosity was expressed to behold the hero of the Nile at every place on the road to Vienna,' Miss Knight recorded, but she added that she did not herself enjoy the journey, 'for I was dreadfully fatigued, far from well, and uneasy on many accounts, besides being a good deal injured by the carriage being overturned in which I was travelling.' If this was how the journey affected the sturdy Cornelia, who was in her early forties, one can only imagine the sufferings of Sir William, in anguish of mind and body and well advanced in his seventieth year.

The journey back from Sicily to England was the worst ordeal Sir William ever had to face. His ills were not merely physical. He was now confronted by the unmistakable fact that his wife and his best friend were lovers and he had to decide how best to face the situation, a situation for which his own easy-going and tolerant attitude to life was partly to blame. He had, of course, been aware of the gossip about Emma and Nelson while they were still at Palermo, but he had felt sufficiently sure of himself there to ignore it or, despite some uneasiness, to postpone the taking of any determined line of action. This had been his mistake. A word of warning to Emma at the very beginning might have saved him from the humiliation of his later years; but Hamilton had never thought of warning her or of pointing out the dangers she courted so openly for the simple reason that he had never taken Emma very seriously as a woman. The gap in age between them was too great, especially as Emma was never able to enter on any footing of equality into his intellectual interests and pursuits. She was for pleasure and amusement after the serious work of the day was over, to be shown off in her 'Attitudes' like any other pretty work of art in his collection. Sir William had done a great deal for Emma in many ways but she had remained essentially shallow and vain. Even without Nelson's intervention he would have had to face the fact that his second marriage was a failure. That would have been a sad disappointment in his old age, but he was now faced with something very much worse. The cuckold was the butt of ridicule; the age in which Hamilton had thus far existed as so distinguished a figure was keenly aware of the absurdity that attaches itself to the elderly husband of an unfaithful young wife; it was a subject for much of its comic drama as well as for a great deal of hilarious private merriment. Sir William was well aware of the kind of talk that had proceeded him to England; he now saw before him every day the sort of conduct that had given rise to it; it was no wonder that Cornelia Knight found the old diplomatist 'broken, distressed, and harassed'.

It has sometimes been suggested that Hamilton did not disapprove of Nelson's role as Emma's lover. It is certain that he came to accept it but it is difficult to say that anyone exactly welcomes such an intervention. Hamilton had always feared that one day he would be superseded, but it is possible he hoped that when that time came he would know nothing about it. A lifetime spent in diplomacy had instilled in him a high regard for the virtue of discretion; he now saw discretion thrown to the winds. Whatever Sir William may have thought of the relationship between his wife and Lord Nelson (and in spite of at least one hint at a separation he certainly did come to accept it) he cannot but have deplored the public posturing in which both Nelson and Emma delighted, with the complete disregard for his own feelings which their behaviour implied. There was, in fact, nothing for him to do but to accept a *fait accompli*; he had no alternative. He had not protested in

Italy when he had believed the relationship to be innocent; he could not protest now because he must pretend it to be so. He had the months of their journey back to England in which to adjust himself to a role which at best was undignified and at the worst humiliating. For a man of Hamilton's character this was no easy task, and it accounts for the pathetic and at times absurd figure he struck in the wake of Nelson and Emma's flagrant progress across Europe.

Gossip travelled before and after them. Before they arrived in Vienna Lord Minto, an old friend and now British ambassador there, wrote to his wife that Nelson 'does not seem at all conscious of the sort of discredit he has fallen into, or the cause of it, for he writes still, not wisely, about Lady Hamilton and all that. But it is hard to condemn and use ill a hero, as he is in his own element, for being foolish about a woman who has art enough to make fools of many wiser than an admiral.' After the hero and his party had arrived Lady Minto passed on the message to her sister: 'He is devoted to *Emma*; he thinks her quite an *angel*, and talks of her as such to her face and behind her back, and she leads him about like a keeper with a bear. . . he is a gig from ribands, orders, and stars. . . [9] Hamilton had the consolation of meeting Josef Haydn in Vienna as, according to Miss Knight, all the best composers and performers were happy to be introduced to Sir William and Lady Hamilton. Haydn dined with them; his conversation was 'modest and sensible'. For the first time for some weeks Sir William was able to listen to a conversation after his own heart. It was here that his health began to show signs of improvement.

While in Vienna Sir William, who had last visited Schoenbrunn in the reign of Joseph II, was presented to the young Emperor Francis by the British Ambassador. Emma was introduced into the presence of the Empress by Lady Minto. She was eager to secure this honour for she could not forget, as she drew nearer to England, that she had not yet been presented at the British Court. Queen Charlotte's strict views were well known but Emma's hopes had been raised by Charles Greville who had written to his uncle during the previous summer to say how much Emma's conduct to the Queen of Naples had been admired at home. He had spoken on the subject to the Prince of Wales who, of his own accord, had assured him that 'all would be made pleasing to her when she arrived again in England'.[10] This, of course, was before rumours of Emma's conduct in another direction had found their way back to London and the Court.

It was also in Vienna that the Hamiltons and Nelson took their final leave of Maria Carolina. The Queen had already, at Leghorn, presented Nelson with a medallion of her own design and given yet another diamond necklace to Emma; this time she had only compliments and thanks to shower on her friends, gratitude to Sir William and the hero of the Nile; the assurance to 'Emma, dear Emma' that they would ever be friends and sisters. No doubt the impulsive Queen meant what she said, but involved as she always was in political intrigue of one sort or another she had little time to waste in the pleasures of idle correspondence. From time to time Emma received letters from her royal friend and sister but the intervals between each letter tended to grow longer and longer. At length the Queen gave up writing. An Emma in distant London, cut off from all influence and power, was no longer of any use to her.

The travellers left Vienna on 27 September and proceeded to Prague where they found their hotel illuminated in honour of Lord Nelson. This pretty compliment lost some of its charm, however, when they discovered that the host had added the cost of the lights to their bill. Here they met the Emperor's brother, the Archduke Charles Ludwig, another nephew of Maria Carolina. The Archduke, like Lord Nelson, was one of the few allied military leaders who had succeeded in fighting victoriously against the French, having defeated Jourdan at Amberg in 1796 and Masséna at Zurich in 1799. Since then ill-health had compelled him to retire temporarily from his military command and he had been appointed Governor of Bohemia. At a dinner given by the Archduke in celebration of Nelson's forty-second birthday Sir William noted with pride that he had the honour of sitting between the greatest military and the greatest naval commanders in Europe. His estimate was a patriotic one, for it took no account of General Bonaparte who was just then engaged in the reconquest of northern Italy.

Not every royal family showed the same readiness as the House of Habsburg to welcome the hero of the Nile and his interesting travelling companions. In Dresden, where Lord Minto's younger brother Hugh Elliot was Minister, the Elector of Saxony retired in confusion behind the walls of his palace at the approach of a trio whose reputation did not encourage him to play the gracious host. The Electress, less accommodating than the Empress of Austria, declined to receive Emma 'on account of her former dissolute life' and announced that there would be no Courts while Lady Hamilton remained in Dresden. When Nelson heard that the Elector did not intend to receive Emma he was foolish enough to say to Elliot; 'Sir, if there is any difficulty of that sort, Lady Hamilton will knock the Elector down,' a remark hardly calculated to ease an embarrassing situation. In order to discourage her great anxiety to be presented at Court the Minister's wife attempted to assure Emma that the experience would not amuse her, adding the information that the Elector never gave dinners or suppers, upon which the disappointed lady replied: 'What? no guttling!' It is hardly surprising that Emma did not make a very good impression in Dresden.

The source of this information was a sprightly and beautiful young widow called Melesina St. George.[11] Wholly unawed by either Nelson or Hamilton, Mrs. St. George viewed the party with an amused detachment. Emma she found 'bold, forward, coarse, assuming, and vain'. Her figure was 'colossal' but (with the exception of her feet, which Mrs. St. George declared to be hideous) well shaped. Her face reminded this severe critic of the bust of Ariadne, with finely shaped features and teeth 'a little irregular but tolerably white'. Of her eyes she noted that they were 'light blue, with a brown spot in one, which, though a defect, takes nothing away from her beauty or expression'. Lord Nelson was 'a little man, without any dignity. . . Lady Hamilton takes possession of him and he is a willing captive, the most submissive and devoted I have seen.' Sir William appeared old and infirm, 'all admiration of his wife and never spoke. . . but to applaud her'. So much for poor Hamilton's attempts to protect his wife's fragile reputation. Mrs. St. George seemed under no illusions about the relationship between Nelson and Emma. She listened to a performance of the songs Cornelia Knight had written in honour of Nelson sung by Lady Hamilton in the hero's presence. 'She puffs the incense full in his face', she noted, 'but he receives it with pleasure, and snuffs it up very cordially. The songs all ended in the sailor's way, with "Hip, hip, hip, hurra", and a bumper with the last drop on the nail, a ceremony I had never heard or seen before.' Mrs. St. George manages to give the impression that she had no wish ever to hear or see it again.

There was much to interest Hamilton in Dresden but unfortunately Mrs. St. George has nothing to say about the famous gallery which must have been one of Sir William's first places of pilgrimage, and though it is known that he visited it[12] no letter survives giving his impressions of the great works of art it contained. The party reached the Saxon capital on the evening of 2 October and stayed there for a week, during which time they visited the opera (where Nelson and Emma 'were wrapped up in each other's conversation during the chief part of the evening') and were also shown the Elector's collection of porcelain. This Sir William would be able to compare with the famous Capodimonte ware of Naples which had first been made in 1743 when craftsmen from Dresden had come to Naples at the request of the young Saxon wife of Charles III. Mrs. St. George was not much interested in Hamilton's activities; her sharp eyes were focused on his wife and Nelson. All she gives us is a pathetic glimpse of Sir William attempting to keep pace with Emma at a dance given by the Elliots, 'hopping round the room on his backbone, his arms, legs, star and ribbon all flying about in the air'.

The party left Dresden when Hugh Elliot brought the news that a frigate waited for them at Hamburg. They travelled by river, Cornelia Knight recalling in her Autobiography that 'the fine bridge was crowded with spectators to see Lord Nelson depart, as was the shore, and every window that commanded a view of the river'.[13] According to the tale the British Minister brought back to Mrs. St. George, the moment they were on board Lady Hamilton 'began bawling for an Irish stew and her old mother set about washing the potatoes, which she did as cleverly as possible'. This story, to which Elliot added various other details, including a brawl between Emma and her maid 'in language quite impossible to repeat', was probably due more to malice than truth, for even Emma was unlikely to behave in this way while the Envoy was still on board and the citizens of Dresden crowded to watch their departure. It shows, however, that her character was sufficiently compromised for her to be considered fair game for gossip of this sort. There is no doubt that the Elliots were glad to see her go. 'In the evening', wrote Mrs. St. George, 'I went to congratulate the Elliots on their deliverance, and found them very sensible of it. Mr. Elliot would not allow his wife to speak above her breath, and said every now and then, "Now don't let us laugh tonight; let us all speak in our turn; and be very, very quiet."'

There was no frigate at Hamburg. Elliot had been misinformed, though he had given them the message in good faith, for he had had it from a King's Messenger. On the last day of October the travellers boarded the mail-packet *King George* at Cuxhaven and reached Great Yarmouth on 6 November, after a stormy crossing. Here the victor of the Nile was given a hero's welcome. Lady Nelson was not there, she awaited her husband in London, so Emma was able to share his triumph without a rival. Sir William must have looked forward eagerly to reaching the capital and the end of their long journey, so taxing to a man of his age even in the best of circumstances. Not only did he look forward to meeting his old friends but he must surely have hoped that when Nelson and Lady Nelson were united once again what he would later come to describe as 'the nonsense I am obliged to submit to' would come to an end. Unfortunately for him it was only beginning.

They journeyed on towards London in ever more tempestuous weather, reaching the capital on Sunday, 9 November, when the city was being lashed by the worst storm it had suffered for ninety-seven years. To the accompaniment of rolls of thunder and flashes of lightning Nelson and his wife had a chilly reunion in the hall of Nerot's hotel in King Street, St. James's, at 3 o'clock in the afternoon. The admiral's aged father was also present. Later they were joined by the Hamiltons for dinner and Lady Nelson for the first time set eyes on her voluptuous rival. It can hardly have been a convivial meal.

While the dinner was in progress at Nerot's Cornelia Knight (who had installed herself with Mrs. Cadogan at an hotel in Albemarle Street) was approached by her old friend Sir Thomas Troubridge and strongly advised to drop an acquaintance which could only damage her reputation. 'He advised me', she wrote, 'to go to my friend Mrs. Nepean, whose husband was Secretary to the Admiralty, and who, on the following day, made me take possession of a room in her house.'[14] Perhaps one reason why Sir Thomas and her other friends were so quick to warn Cornelia of the dangers of a scandalous connection was because, the day before, her lines to 'fair Emma' had been fully quoted in a London newspaper. Her additional verses to the National Anthem were already generally known. Not so well known, fortunately, was a parody of them which Lord Palmerston had copied into his anecdote book:

> Also huge Emma's name
> First on the role of fame,
> And let us sing.

Loud as her voice, let's sound
Her faded charms around
Which in the sheets were found,
God save the King.
Nelson, thy flag haul down,
Hang up thy laurel crown,
While her we sing.
No more in triumph swell,
Since that with her you dwell,
But don't her William tell—
Nor George, your King.[15]

King George, as Hamilton and Nelson were soon to discover, did not need to be told of a situation which for some months had been the talk of London. On Tuesday, 11 November, the day after Nelson had been presented with a jewelled sword at a banquet given by the Lord Mayor of London, the two men, one in the full dress uniform of a Rear-Admiral, the other arrayed as a member of the Privy Council, both wearing their stars and ribands, presented themselves at St. James's Palace for His Majesty's *levée*. The King entered the room, talking in his voluble way to the crowded courtiers. He came to the spot where stood his old foster-brother the retired Minister to the Court of Naples and Lord Nelson, the victor of the Nile. The King expressed the hope that his Lordship's health was improved and without waiting for an answer turned to an obscure military officer who stood next to them and engaged him in conversation for half an hour, while Nelson and Sir William had nothing else to do but gaze at the broad back of their sovereign very ostentatiously turned upon them. It was not only a crushing royal snub to Nelson and Hamilton, it was also a final blow to all Emma's hopes of being presented to Queen Charlotte. That evening Nelson appeared in so black a humour at a dinner party at Admiralty House that his wife was reduced to tears.

Poor Lady Nelson had good reason to weep. For a time there was a sort of public duel between the two women in which Frances Nelson was a most reluctant contestant. Her husband insisted on going everywhere with the Hamiltons, his excuse being, according to Miss Knight, that as so much was said of his attachment to Lady Hamilton 'he felt irritated, and took it up in an unfortunate manner by devoting himself more and more to her, for the purpose of what he called supporting her,'[16] an attitude which resulted in his wife's public humiliation. But Nelson seems to have had no more regard for his wife's feelings in London than he had shown for Sir William's in Palermo. Lady Nelson, however, was not a woman of the world, she could not take refuge in 'philosophy'. When her husband went to the theatre and expected her to sit in the box with Emma she could not brazen it out with her rival but, as the *Morning Herald* informed its readers next morning, 'about the end of the third act Lady Nelson fainted away and was obliged to be carried out of her box'.

Nelson's wife was in a difficult and most unenviable position. Though there was nothing in her past relations with her husband about which she need reproach herself it was being made abundantly clear that she had lost his affection. She had never met the Hamiltons before; she had no cause to like Emma; while Sir William, kindly and understanding as he usually was, seems to have done little to make her position any easier. It was most unreasonable of Nelson to expect her to embrace Emma as a friend. Hamilton for his part had had the months of their journey home in which to adjust himself to a situation which he would certainly rather have avoided, nor was his dilemma in any way comparable to Lady Nelson's, for he liked and admired his rival; indeed, before his death he came to enjoy Nelson's company more than his wife's, for Emma's increasing loudness and vulgarity began to grate on his nerves. He had another reason for turning a blind eye on his wife's behaviour now that they were back in London. He had married Emma in the face of a good deal of hostile criticism, both public and private; to give her up now would amount to an admission that his critics had been in the right. It was very much a question of *amour-propre*.

The Hamiltons' first London House was No. 22 Grosvenor Square, which had been lent to them by William Beckford. It was here that Lord Palmerston visited them just over a fortnight after their return home. 'I have been out this morning and called on the Hamiltons, whom I found at home', he recorded on 25 November 'He is still thinner and yellower than he was when we saw him but in other respects seems much the same and seems occupied with the same pursuits as usual. She is grown much larger and her face broader and her features stronger than they were. She was dressed in a white wrapping gown which made her look of very large dimentions, but so completely took away all shape that I cannot judge what her figure would be in a common dress.' Emma's 'large dimentions' and her ingenious attire were due, of course, to the fact that she was in an advanced stage of pregnancy. She was now naturally of such big proportions that she managed to conceal her condition with complete success. 'She has', Lord Palmerston concluded, 'a little more conceit and affectation than she had, which is very natural, but she has the same good humoured manner that she used to have. Her attentions to Sir William do not seem to have relaxed in any degree and they both talk of Lord Nelson in every other sentence. His bust is in the room and Sir William says his friendship and connection with him is the pride and glory of his life.'[17]

Once back in England Sir William calmly accepted the fact that his diplomatic career was over. There was no more talk of returning to Palermo or Naples after he had called on Lord Grenville at the Foreign Office on 10 November; his energies were now directed to the business of securing his pension and trying to reach some settlement on the old issue of 'extraordinary expenses' which had so often caused him anxiety in the past and had grown out of all proportions during his last few years in office. Nelson helped to draw up his claim and prepared a memorandum on the subject. Headed 'Facts' and written in Nelson's hand, this document declared: 'For four years past Sir William Hamilton had permission to come to England to settle his private affairs, and would have come with all his effects if the embroiled state of Italy, and the arrival of the King's fleet in the Mediterranean had not made him determine, whatever the inconvenience he might suffer, to remain at his post. In October 1798, part of Sir William's valuable effects were sent home in the *Colossus*. By the accident which happened to that ship he suffered a loss of several thousand pounds. In December of the same year, except some pictures and vases which Lord Nelson had placed on board a transport, the whole of Sir William's effects at Naples were lost; for although much might have been saved had his thoughts been only turned towards his own property, yet self was absorbed in attending to the preservation of a whole Royal family, therefore not an atom of furniture was removed, excepting one couch, no, not even a bed. It can readily be conceived what mounting of such a house (as every person who has travelled in the country can testify) must have cost. On Sir William's arrival at Palermo, although the Queen did more than could be expected, it became necessary to arrange a new establishment consistent with his public character, and from the emigrated English from Naples and Tuscany, with many other people of high rank in the world, together with the constant communication with the Navy, necessarily brought on a very heavy expense, for there was no house for these persons to resort to, but the British Minister's. The settling this new establishment, together with the closing the accounts on his being superseded, cost, by bills drawn upon London, £13,213 between August 1799 and June 1800, besides all losses, which cannot be estimated less than £10,000 sterling.'[18]

Nelson had good reason to help his friend in this matter, for by the time they reached London Sir William was in his debt to the extent of £2,276, consisting of sums lent in Palermo and half the expenses of the journey from Leghorn.[19] Hamilton was, as usual, in considerable financial difficulties even without taking Emma's incorrigible extravagance into consideration. The banker Coutts told Henry Swinburne in January 1801 that Sir William's estate in Wales did not bring in above a thousand pounds a year which, with a pension of two thousand, would not be enough to keep up their establishment. (This was after the Hamiltons had moved to their own house at 23 Piccadilly, overlooking the Green Park.)[20] Sir William's pension, in fact, fell a good deal short of the banker's estimate. It was settled at £1,200 per annum and was to terminate at his death. The Government, which had never recognised Sir William's wife, made no provision for his widow. As for any compensation for his 'extraordinary expenses' and other losses, he would still be involved in fruitless negotiations on this unhappy issue when his death closed the account.

Lord Nelson was not the only person to take an interest in the settlement of Sir William's affairs. William Beckford had never fully reconciled himself to the loss of the peerage which would have been bestowed on him had not scandal intervened over fifteen years before. He now conceived a scheme as improbable as anything in his oriental fantasy *Vathek*. Sir William first heard of the plan in a letter dated 15 November from Beckford's steward Nicholas Williams. It was proposed that he should apply for a peerage, which might be considered his due after representing his sovereign for nearly thirty-seven years at a foreign court, and that his distant cousin William Beckford would make up by a life annuity whatever sum fell short of Hamilton's expectations from the Government in relation to his claims on the condition (as Williams expressed it) that 'a peerage should be offered and you could arrange it so that the grant may be made to yourself with remainder to Mr. Beckford and his heirs'.[21] The idea did not commend itself to the authorities and there is no evidence to suggest that Sir William ever took it very seriously, though there was some feverish correspondence on the subject between Beckford and Emma. 'You know me and can well imagine that a Peerage would not flatter my vanity,' Hamilton later told the Marquis of Douglas, 'but the offered increase of income would certainly put me more at my ease than I am at present.'[22] The matter was still being canvassed by Beckford when Hamilton's death put an end to his scheme.

This, no doubt, was one of the reasons why Beckford invited Sir William and Emma to spend the Christmas of 1800 with him at Fonthill in Wiltshire where he was nearing the completion of the great gothic 'Abbey' which was to replace the country house he had inherited from his father. Hamilton had been invited to inspect this spectacular folly as long ago as December 1799 when Beckford had written to him at Palermo to express 'how eagerly I long to see you and the tutelary Divinity of the Two Sicilies once more'. He had commiserated with Sir William over the loss of his collection: 'I who have bowels for works of art know how to feel the sad loss you experienced by the wreck of the *Colossus*,' and spoken of his own creative activities in the phrase, 'the Abbey will astonish you.'[23] To someone like Sir William, brought up in the classical tradition and nurtured on antiquity, astonishment was certainly more likely than approval on first seeing Beckford's pinnacled and crenellated pile, its central tower rising to a height of two hundred and seventy-six feet, with its cloisters, turrets and buttresses, like some monstrously expanded version of Walpole's Strawberry Hill. As an added inducement Beckford now included Nelson in the invitation. 'I exult in the hope of seeing Fonthill honoured by his victorious presence,' he told Emma, 'and if his engagements permit his accompanying you here, we shall enjoy a few comfortable days of repose—uncontaminated by the sight and prattle of drawing-room parasites.'[24] Lady Nelson, rather pointedly, was not asked to join the party.

In order that his Abbey should be ready for the reception of his guests Beckford ordered the work to continue on it by night as well as by day. 'A novel scene was presented in the winter of 1800,' according to one account. 'During the dark and inclement season of November and December in that year, it is related that nearly five hundred men were successively employed night and day to expedite the works; and in the darksome and dreary nights of those months, they prosecuted their labours by torch and lamp light. The prospect of an illuminated edifice, as seen from a distance with flitting lights and busy workmen, must have produced a singular and mysterious effect.'[25] It was exactly the sort of effect that Beckford delighted in producing. His temperament had changed very little (except perhaps for the worse) since the days when he had exchanged romantic letters with Sir William's first wife.

The guests assembled on 20 December, Nelson and the Hamiltons coming by way of Salisbury where the admiral was presented with the freedom of the city. Beckford had also invited James Wyatt, the architect of his abbey, and Benjamin West, the President of the Royal Academy, an artist who had studied in Rome just before Hamilton had first gone to Italy and who shared his interest in Greek and Roman antiquities. As a compliment to Emma, Beckford had asked the singer Madame Banti whom she had known in Neapolitan days. It was this *diva*, the reader will recall, who had exclaimed 'Just God, what a voice!' after first hearing Emma's full-throated soprano in 1787. Her presence was a guarantee that both ladies would be able to exercise their lungs in some spirited duets for the Banti was celebrated for the phenomenal size of her larynx and her voice, in combination with Emma's, would have no difficulty in filling a room even the size of some of those at Fonthill Abbey, the hall of which measured sixty-eight feet in length and twenty-eight feet in width with a ceiling seventy-eight feet above the floor. Less happy was the choice of Dr. John Wolcot whose name completed the list of guests, for he was none other than 'Peter Pindar' whose malicious verses had more than once been written at the expense of Sir William and his second wife. Neither Sir William nor Emma, however, seem to have resented his presence in the Christmas house party.

The climax of the visit to Fonthill came on the evening of 23 December when what was quaintly described as a 'monastic fête' was given at the Abbey. 'A procession of carriages, horses, soldiers, etc., moved from the old house to the abbey in the evening,' we are told. 'Flambeaux, torches, and many thousand lamps were distributed on the sides of the road among the woods; whilst bands of music and files of soldiers were stationed in different places to greet and charm the company as they passed. Everything, indeed, was provided to steal upon the senses, to dazzle the eye, and to bewilder the fancy. After passing through a long, winding, umbrageous avenue—after hearing the sounds of distant, near, and varied instruments, with their reverberations among the woods and dells, and contemplating the vivid and solemn effects of bright lights and deep shadows, the company was conducted to the abbey, where a new, impressive, and mystical scene, or succession of scenes, were presented.'

The guests were led through the groined gothic hall to a room called the Cardinal's Parlour where a meal was waiting in 'one long line of enormous silver dishes'. The greedier of the guests (and among these must be counted Emma with her love of 'guttling') may have been a little disappointed when they discovered that the food was as monastic as the surroundings and was 'unmixed with the refinements of modern cookery'. After dinner the company went to the other completed apartments of the Abbey, climbing a staircase illuminated by large wax torches clutched by 'certain mysterious living figures dressed in hooded gowns'. After being conducted through the library and shown a beautiful statue of St. Anthony in marble and alabaster which occupied a special shrine they were entertained by more earthy delights, including an 'attitude' by Emma who appeared before them in the character of Agrippa bearing the ashes of Germanicus in a golden urn. After this dramatic interlude, which drew tears from some of the company, the party returned to old Fonthill house where a supper was prepared for their final refreshment.[26]

The party broke up on 26 December and Beckford's guests returned home to face the realities of ordinary existence. For Nelson this meant the final break-up of his marriage. After an unpleasant scene with his wife, who was conscious herself of never having failed in her fidelity to him but had become tired and exasperated by his unending praise of 'dear Lady Hamilton', the couple parted and were never to live together again. Immediately afterwards Nelson left for Plymouth where he took up a new command on 17 January. On New Year's day he had been promoted Vice-Admiral of the Blue, and he now hoisted his flag in the *San Josef* as second-in-command of the Channel Fleet. His departure was the occasion for Gillray's malicious caricature of Emma called *Dido in Despair*. The drawing shows an immense Emma rising from a bed in which a wizened Sir William still slept. Her arms are flung out despairingly towards an open window through which the ships of Nelson's fleet can be seen sailing towards the horizon. Below this picture were printed four lines of verse:

> Ah, where, and oh! where is my gallant sailor gone?
> He's gone to fight the French for George upon the throne.
> He's gone to fight the French, t'lose t'other arm and eye,
> And left me with old Antiquity, to lay me down and cry.

Sir William and Emma had returned to their new house in Piccadilly where, towards the end of January 1801, it was announced that Lady Hamilton was suffering from a very bad cold and had retired to bed. Her old mother took command of the sick-room. Here, between the 28th and 30th of January Emma gave birth to a daughter. Nelson, when he heard the news, wrote that he would go mad with joy.[27] A few days later the child was removed from the house and put out to nurse, and within the week Lady Hamilton was seen at a concert given at the Duke of Norfolk's house in St. James's Square. The secret was so well kept that the world remained in ignorance of an event which would have shocked some and entertained many. Sir William had decided that he would know nothing about it.

1. *Vide* H. Tours: *Life & Letters of Emma Hamilton*, p. 147.
2. In Miss Knight's *Autobiography* (Vol. I, p. 147) the name 'Delia' is discreetly substituted for that of Emma.
3. Morrison, 547.
4. B.M. Add. MSS 34048, f. 95.
5. B.M. Egerton MSS 2640, f. 398.
6. W. Sichel: *Emma, Lady Hamilton*, p. 328.
7. C. Knight: *Autobiography*, Vol. I, p. 148.
8. C. Knight: op. cit., Vol. I, pp. 319-23.
9. *Life and Letters of Lord Minto*, Vol. III, pp. 114 and 147.
10. Morrison, 396.
11. Afterwards Mrs. Richard Trench. *Vide Remains*, pp. 105-112.
12. *Vide* Pettigrew: *Memoirs of Lord Nelson*, Vol. I, p. 388.
13. C. Knight: op. cit., Vol. I, p. 154.
14. C. Knight: op. cit., Vol. I, p. 158.
15. *Vide* B. Connell: *Portrait of a Whig Peer*, p. 417. The penultimate line is a pun on the name of the French warship *William Tell* captured after the battle of the Nile, from which it had escaped.
16. C. Knight: op. cit. Vol. I, p. 162.
17. B. Connell: Portrait of a Whig Peer, p. 436.
18. Vide, Pettigrew, op. cit., Vol. I, pp. 401-2.
19. Morrison, 538.
20. H. Swinburne: *The Courts of Europe at the Close of the Last Century*, Vol. II, p. 260.
21. Pettigrew: op. cit., Vol. I, pp. 402-3.
22. Morrison, 673.
23. Morrison, 438.
24. J. W. Oliver: *Life of William Beckford*, p. 240.
25. J. Britton: *Illustrations of Fonthill Abbey*, p. 28.
26. *Vide* J. Britton, op. cit., pp. 29-31.
27. Morrison, 504.

CHAPTER XXIV

The Final Years

The remainder of Hamilton's life (he had little more than two years to live after the birth of Emma's daughter) was to be a gradual *diminuendo* against the rising *crescendo* of his wife's public notoriety. He took refuge in his old pursuits, visiting the sales of pictures and works of art, frequenting the British Museum where his first collection of vases was displayed, and attending the meetings of the Society of Antiquaries and the Royal Society. No longer able to hunt, as he had done in his younger days, he became an enthusiastic angler and passed many tranquil hours fishing the Thames. When he went on visits to his relations or to his estates in Wales he now travelled alone; his wife remained in London. He found Emma's conduct increasingly tedious and boring and only put up with it because he had no wish to upset a man whose character he respected and whose friendship he still valued above all others. 'It is but reasonable, after having fagged all my life, that my last days should pass off comfortably and quietly,' he wrote to Charles Greville in January 1802.[1] 'Nothing at present disturbs me but my debt, and the nonsense I am obliged to submit to here to avoid coming to an explosion, which wou'd be attended with many disagreeable effects, and would totally destroy the comfort of the best man and the best friend I have in the world. However, I am determined that my quiet shall not be disturbed, let the nonsensicall world go on as it will.'

Sir William, who had always been stimulated by the company of younger men of ability and intelligence, by now much preferred the friendship of Nelson to the waning charms and waxing impetuosity of his wife. Nelson did not return this friendship in the same degree. His passion for Emma and the jealousy he felt for her made him a prey to ungenerous and acrimonious feelings towards the man he had once referred to as 'good Sir William'. In the 'Thompson' correspondence (in which Nelson and Emma, in order to discuss their own daughter, had invented a fictitious Thompson who served in Nelson's ship and whose 'wife' was under Lady Hamilton's protection) there are some unflattering references to Hamilton who features in the letters as the 'uncle' of Mrs. Thompson.

Nelson showed no hesitation in this impassioned correspondence in wishing the 'uncle' out of the way. 'Your dear friend, my dear and truly beloved Mrs. T., is almost distracted,' he wrote from sea early in 1801, 'he wishes there was peace, or that if your uncle would die, he would instantly then come and marry you, for he doats on nothing but you and his child. . . ' In February he assures her that 'Your most dear friend [Thompson] desires me to say that he sincerely feels for you, and that if your uncle is so hard hearted as to oblige you to quit his house, that he will instantly quit all the world and its greatness to live with you a domestic, quiet life.' When he thought the Prince of Wales was going to dine at Sir William's and Emma might be exposed to the advances of that amorous prince he wrote in a frenzy of jealousy and alarm to expostulate against the 'shocking conduct of your uncle' for allowing so dangerous a situation to occur.'[2] At the, thought of it his latent distrust of Emma and fury at Hamilton reached almost hysterical proportions. 'I have had a letter from Sir William,' he wrote to Emma on 8 February, 'he speaks of the Regency as certain, and then probably he thinks you will sell better—horrid thought.' It was a thought, it should be added, that was entirely Nelson's; it had never so much as entered Hamilton's head, and in fact the Prince's visit never took place. But Nelson could not escape from his morbid fears. 'Does Sir William want you to be a whore to the rascal?' he asked a few days later.[3] No one would have been more surprised (or more deeply wounded) than Hamilton had he known of this extraordinary suggestion.

Nelson had now come to look upon Emma as his wife. He wrote to her on 1 March calling her 'my own dear wife, for such you are in my eyes and in the face of heaven. . . I love, I never did love anyone else. I never had a dear pledge of love till you gave me one, and you, thank my God, never gave one to anybody else.'[4] In allowing Nelson to believe this Emma was, of course, grossly deceiving him. Her other 'pledge of love', born at the time Charles Greville took her into his protection, was now a young woman of about nineteen years of age living in obscurity near Chester under the name of Emma Carew. Mrs. Cadogan occasionally visited her; her mother rarely if ever did so. Nelson was never to learn of her existence.

While these exchanges were taking place behind his back Hamilton was busily occupied with the problem of his debts. Within a short time of his return to England he told a correspondent that he was 'totally taken up in endeavours to save from the late wreck at Naples as much as I can of my property and to induce Government if possible to make me some amends and give me honourable retreat after 37 years services abroad and having suffer'd heavy losses and been at most Extraordinary Expenses owing to the Cursed French Revolution at Naples.' He was already becoming disillusioned at the prospect of success. 'But wou'd you think it?' he continues, 'altho' I am here two months I am still in the dark, and altho' my successor Paget was appointed without my knowledge as Consul so that until something is done I must appear in the Eye of the World as a disgraced man, and yet I have as far as words go received the full approbation of the K[ing] and his ministers. . . ' After stating that his pictures (saved by Lord Nelson on board the *Foudroyant*) were all now in London though not yet unpacked, he ended his letter: 'I believe you are as much tired of the Diplomatic Line as I am. It is a ruinous business at all times but worse now.'[5]

Early in 1801 he decided that he would have to sell some of the pictures which had formed part of his collection at the Palazzo Sessa. Arrangements for the sale were made with Christie and 150 pictures came under the hammer (75 each day) on 27 and 28 March. Most of his best canvasses were sold, including Tintoretto's Flagellation of Christ, Titian's portrait of a man of the Barbarini family, Rubens' sketch of one of his wives, Velasquez's portrait of a Moorish slave, Van Dyck's martyrdom of St. Sebastian and the Laughing Boy attributed to Leonardo da Vinci. Hamilton was satisfied with the results and wrote to Greville on 31 March: 'I was yesterday with Christie; he gave me in writing the produce of the sale, with my ballance much greater than I thought, altho' many mistakes have been made, and pictures bought in for me that went beyond the limits I had set in the Catalogues.

> Bought in to the value of £636
> Total of the sale produced £5760-14s
> Actually sold to the value of £5025-13s

Mr. Christie's room will be ready for my next sale the 21st of April, and he proposed the 2nd and 3rd of May for the 2 days' sale, so that we may have 10 days of private and public views.'[6]

The second sale in fact took place on 17 and 18 April, when 184 pictures were sold (92 each day). Among the highest prices bid were twelve guineas for two views of Venice by Canaletto and eighteen guineas for two landscapes by Zuccarelli. For the rest this sale consisted mainly of copies of old masters and works by contemporary artists such as Hackert, Fabris and Vigée Le Brun. The total proceeds amounted to seven hundred and seventeen pounds six shillings and sixpence. In a general sale of pictures held on 13 November were two more from Hamilton's collection. A 'land storm' by Salvator Rosa went for twenty-five pounds, and 'six original heads, cartoon for the Last Supper' attributed to Leonardo da Vinci was sold for the sum of thirty pounds.[7] The thought that Sir William might be selling a picture of Emma as well as parading the original before the libidinous gaze of the heir to the throne threw Nelson into another fit of jealous rage. 'I see clearly, my dearest friend, you are on SALE,' he wrote to Emma from on board his flagship on 11 March. 'I am almost made to think of the iniquity of wanting you to associate with a set of whores, bawds, and unprincipiled lyars. Can this be the great Sir William Hamilton? I blush for him'[8] The idea of anyone else possessing Emma, even on canvas, was repulsive to him and resulted in the wildest accusations against Sir William.

The unpacking of Hamilton's works of art and pictures brought to light a most fortunate piece of luck. The day after Nelson had written to Emma implying the very worst motives to her husband's conduct Sir William himself, innocent of both the fact and the knowledge of what Nelson imputed to him, was writing happily to his friend: 'It is quite beyond all expectations that I have found so many of my fine vases; fortunately some cases of the worst were taken on board the *Colossus* by mistake, when I thought the eight best cases were gone.'[9] These precious cases, or at least some of them (for Hamilton does not specify the number), were now discovered to have been put on board the *Foudroyant* with his other belongings and were now arrived safe and sound. Glad as he was that some of his collection had so miraculously survived, Hamilton was compelled none the less to sell what remained, as, indeed, he had always intended to do. Once again Christie was approached and a sale arranged, when a private purchaser appeared on the scene. 'This morning Mr. Thomas Hope came to me,' Sir William informed Charles Greville on 3 April, 'and having offered the round sum of four thousand pound down for my whole collection of vases for which I had asked £5,000, finding that I could get no more, and considering trouble, risk, and then a little vanity in the collection being kept entire which I made with such pains, I struck with him . . .' What particularly pleased Hamilton was the fact that his vases would not be dispersed but would remain together for what he described as 'the inspection of the learned antiquaries and artists' which he had always considered as one of the chief purposes of such a collection. 'I saw Christie was much disappointed, but upon the whole I have, I believe, done prudently,' he concluded. 'At least, my mind is made easy at once and much trouble avoided, which counts much with me. Risk of breakings, selling ill, and auction expenses would, I believe, have run my ballance below what it now is.'[10]

While Hamilton was engaged in these matters Nelson, once more in what Lord Minto had rightly called his own element, had transferred his flag from the *San Josef* to the *St. George* and was sailing towards the Baltic as 'the champion of England in the north.' On 2 April he fought and won his second great victory in the terrible and hard-fought battle of Copenhagen. The news of this great action did not reach England until 15 April, when the Hamiltons celebrated their friend's victory by giving a dinner party at their house in Piccadilly. The guests included the Dukes of Gordon and Queensberry, Lord William Gordon, Monsieur de Calonne (who had been the French controller-general of finances under Louis XVI), Charles Greville, the Duke of Noia (a Neapolitan nobleman) and Sir Nathaniel Wraxall. 'Lady Hamilton', Wraxall later wrote, 'inspired by the recent success of Lord Nelson against the Danes. . . after playing on the harpsichord and accompanying it with her voice, undertook to dance the "Tarantella". Sir William began it with her, and maintained the conflict, for such it might well be esteemed, during some minutes. When unable longer to continue it, the Duke of Noia succeeded to his place, but he too, though nearly forty years younger than Sir William, soon gave in from extenuation. Lady Hamilton then sent for her own maidservant, who being likewise presently exhausted, after a short time another female attendant, a Copt, perfectly black, whom Lord Nelson had presented to her on his return from Egypt, relieved her companion.'[11] The admiral's elder brother William, a bulky and very worldly clergyman who was also present on this evening of festivity, so far forgot the gravity of his calling as to dance round the dining room table. He had good reason to perform this jig, for thanks to his brother's success he was soon to dance his way into a prebendal stall at Canterbury cathedral.

The admiral himself was raised in the peerage to the degree of Viscount and, as he had no legitimate heir, a new barony of Nelson was created with remainder to the sons and daughters of his father. In giving his consent to this new creation King George wrote to his Prime Minister, Henry Addington: 'The King is so thoroughly satisfied with the services and ardour of Viscount Nelson, that he cannot make the smallest objection to the preservation of the Barony in his Father's family.'[12] This gracious action on the part of his sovereign made some amends for the frigid reception Nelson had been given at St. James's on his previous return from a victorious campaign. The new barony, with the addition of an earldom, would eventually be enjoyed with evident relish by his clergyman brother. Emma and Sir William were of the opinion that their friend had already merited an earldom after the battle of Copenhagen; in their eyes no honour was too great for the returning hero. The Government, however, were in some embarrassment over rewards, not least because Great Britain was not officially at war with Denmark when this 'preventative' action was fought. To Nelson's lasting regret no special medal was struck to honour his fellow officers and men.

The *Tria Juncta in Uno* were reunited when the admiral returned home on 1 July. He was to enjoy less than a month's leave, for on 26 July he was appointed commander-in-chief of a squadron responsible for coastal defences against the still very real threat of a French invasion.[13] Nelson was given this post by a Government anxious to reassure public opinion that they were alive to the seriousness of the situation and also (or so Nelson believed) in response to private pressure from Lord St. Vincent and Sir Thomas Troubridge who deplored the baleful influence of Emma and were concerned to keep the lovers separated. There was time, however, for Nelson to meet Sir William and Emma for a brief fishing holiday on the river at Shepperton near Staines where they were joined by William Nelson and his family. Hamilton, who was himself in anecdotal mood on this occasion, found the presence of this ponderous cleric something of a bore. Sir William's catch was not always to Nelson's taste. Later in the year when discussing the property he had bought at Merton he told his old friend: 'I shall buy fish out of the Thames to stock the water, but I bar barble. I shall never forget the one you had cooked at Staines.'[14]

On 20 July, Nelson was called to the Admiralty and the party at Shepperton broke up. A week later he took over his new command but not before he had received, and ignored, a touching letter from Lady Nelson congratulating him on his victory and assuring him that no wife ever felt greater affection for a husband than she did. As though to emphasise the completeness of his break with the past he asked Lady Hamilton to look out for a country house for him. It would be run on the lines of the joint household they had maintained at the Palazzo Palagonia, but with one difference: it would be Lord Nelson's own. Hamilton, of course, would be welcome (indeed, it would be impossible for Emma to go there without the protection of her husband's presence, for she still clung desperately to the pretence of respectability), but Nelson wrote very firmly, when a suitable property had been found, that he did *not* wish to have any of Sir William's books there, nor any of his servants either.[15] Nelson had something quite simple in mind, and should have known better than to leave the negotiations to someone of Emma's extravagant ideas. Merton Place, when bought, was not an imposing country house in the grand style but it was a good deal more impressive than the 'little farm' its purchaser had expected. Furthermore it cost more than he had bargained for and the fact that it lay near the road to Brighton awoke new fears that the Prince of Wales might arrive and carry off Emma, though he tried to reassure himself with the thought that she would never let the Prince into the premises.

Hamilton took the opportunity to visit his Welsh estates while Emma was inspecting country properties in the neighbourhood of London on Nelson's behalf. There seems to have been no question of her going to Wales with her husband. By 19 August he was back in London in time to receive an invitation from Nelson asking them both to visit him at Deal. 'My movements,' Nelson wrote, 'are as uncertain as the wind, or rather are directed by the damned French. . . [but] if any place may be called stationary for me, it is the Downs.' Lady Hamilton, he added, could take the benefit of sea bathing.[16] Rooms were engaged for his visitors at the Three Kings inn and excursions organised to Ramsgate, Walmer, and Dover castle, while Nelson saw to it that Sir William had time for some fishing. Early in September the visitors returned to Piccadilly leaving a distracted admiral behind them, desolate at parting from Emma and saddened by the mortal illness of a young fellow-officer wounded in a recent raid on the French coast. 'My dearest wife, how can I bear our separation?' Nelson wrote to 'Mrs. Thomson, care of Lady Hamilton' soon after his guests' departure. 'Good God, what a change! I am so low that I cannot hold up my head. When I reflect on the many happy scenes we have passed together, the being separated is terrible, but better times *will* come, *shall* come, if it please God. . .'; whether one of the conditions for 'better times' still included the removal of the 'uncle' to a better world Nelson did not, on this occasion, specify in so many words, but to write to Emma as his 'dearest wife' so soon after entertaining her husband does not suggest that Hamilton was expected to continue in this inconvenient rôle for very much longer.[17]

The 'farm' which Emma had selected as Nelson's country home was situated near Wimbledon, almost exactly an hour's carriage drive from London. It was a two-storey brick building built about a hundred years before the time of Nelson's purchase, standing in seventy acres of land, and cost the admiral nine thousand pounds. He was obliged to raise a loan to meet the cost, (he could only 'command' three thousand pounds at that time), but flatly refused to borrow from

Sir William. 'I could not do it,' he told Emma, 'I would sooner beg.' Whether this refusal sprang from delicacy or from a feeling of guilt does not transpire, but it is doubtful if Hamilton would have been able to help him even if asked, for Emma's extravagance and the Government's delay in defraying his expenses continued to embarrass him, and in October he confessed to Greville that he had received a bill for wine, since they came home, of four hundred pounds. Emma could never bring herself to understand that they could no longer afford to entertain on the scale they had been used to at the Palazzo Sessa. Furthermore Hamilton had insisted on paying his share when they were all to be together at Merton and this, when he had a house of his own to keep up in London, would be an additional and unnecessary burden on his purse.

Sir William left Emma to her own devices while the final negotiations for the purchase of Merton were taking place, and towards the end of September set out on a visit to his nephew the Earl of Warwick. The report he sent to the Earl's younger brother Charles Greville shows that he had lost nothing of his sense of humour and interest in the oddities of human behaviour, even under the most trying circumstances. 'Your brother often spoke of you with affection, and I told him you did so of him,' he wrote on 9 October. 'However, *entre nous*, altho' I was delighted with the local and the charming family, I was bored to death by his Lordship's eternal talk and stories, chiefly of himself, as to strength, bravery, knowledge of improvement, so as to be actually now one of the richest men in England, having paid all his father's and his own debts, and then by a parenthesis (except one to me, which by accident was yet unpaid), and then went on with great composure in the same rhapsody of incoherent boasting. In short, I should be ungrateful if I did not feel the affection shown me during this visit from all the family, but it would drive me mad was I obliged to live a month with him; he does not give an echoe fair play. I gave him, however, 2 or 3 hints that he should allow other people to say a word now and then, by which I got in a good story or two of mine, but alas! I fear he is on that part incorrigible, and, as he sees only persons that are bound to listen to him, he will go on talking to all eternity.'[18]

While Hamilton was still at Warwick Castle news came through that preliminaries of peace had been signed with the French republic. Emma informed her husband by express from London so that Lord Warwick was able to give the town corporation the good news ten hours before the regular arrival, though Sir William had to pay for the express. He returned to London and soon joined Emma at Merton Lodge which she had been preparing for the hero's arrival. Nelson himself applied for leave, not only because his task was now complete and he could tell the Admiralty that not so much as a boat had been captured by the enemy during the period of his command, but also because his state of health required repose on shore.[19] Before his request was granted he received a letter from Sir William describing his new property, for Nelson had not yet set eyes on his 'farm' at Merton. 'A seaman alone,' Hamilton wrote in jest, 'could have given a fine woman full power to chuse and fit up a residence for him without seeing it himself. You are in luck, for in my conscience I verily believe that a place so suitable to your views could not have been found, and at so cheap a rate, for if you stay away 3 days longer I do not think you can have any wish but you will find it compleated here, and then the bargain was fortunately struck 3 days before an idea of peace got abroad. Now every estate in this neighbourhood has increased in value, and you might get a thousand pounds tomorrow for your bargain.'[20]

'You have nothing but to come and enjoy immediately,' Sir William's letter continued, 'you have a good mile of pleasant dry walk around your own farm. It would make you laugh to see Emma and her mother fitting up pig-sties and hen-coops, and already the Canal is enlivened with ducks, and the cock is strutting with his hens about the walks. Your Lordship's plan as to stocking the Canal with fish is exactly mine. I will answer for it, that in a few months, you may command a good dish of fish at a moment's warning. . . I think it quite impossible that they can keep you at Deal more than 3 or 4 days longer. It would be *ridiculous*.' A week after this letter was written, on 23 October, Lord Nelson arrived in the early hours of the morning, having driven all through the night in his post-chaise from Deal. Merton was now to be his head-quarters, but he expected Emma to be the presiding goddess of his little domain. Some weeks before he had written to her: 'You are to be, recollect, Lady Paramount of all the territories and waters of Merton, and we are all to be your guests, and to obey all lawful commands.'

The situation of the house in the neighbourhood of Wimbledon had certain advantages, for it was close enough to London to make business visits easy, yet far enough away for Nelson to live the secluded life which he now declared to be his wish. He had no desire to visit in the neighbourhood and gave it out that he wished to 'live retired'. The reason for this was not hard to find. It did not spring from any lack of sociability on his part but rather because fashionable society though fascinated to gossip about the interesting *ménage* at Merton, was not over anxious to call. Emma had already discovered, even in her husband's house, that though his men friends enjoyed his hospitality their wives preferred to stay at home. For female company the former friend of the Queen of Naples had now to make do with Mrs. Powell, the Drury Lane actress, (a companion of the distant days when both had worked in Dr. Budd's house in Blackfriars), with Brigitta Banti of the prodigious voice, and with women whose conduct was motivated more by curiosity than exclusiveness. She made new friends among Nelson's relations both male and female who, seeing the way the wind was blowing, quickly abandoned the unfortunate Frances Nelson in favour of Lady Hamilton. Nelson's old father alone continued to visit his daughter-in-law, though even he was prevailed upon, rather reluctantly, to meet her successor.

Lord Minto visited Merton in March 1802 and left a vivid account of the household. 'I went to Lord Nelson's on Saturday to dinner, and returned today in the forenoon,' he told his wife.[21] 'The whole establishment and way of life is such as to make me angry, as well as melancholy; but I cannot alter it, and I do not think myself obliged or at liberty to quarrel with him for his weakness, though nothing shall ever induce me to give the smallest countenance to Lady Hamilton. She looks ultimately to the chance of marriage, as Sir W. will not be long in her way, and she probably indulges a hope that she will survive Lady Nelson; in the meanwhile she and Sir William and the whole set of them are living with him at his expense.' Here Lord Minto wronged his old friend and colleague, for Hamilton was meticulous in bearing his half-share of the expenses while he and Emma were under Lord Nelson's roof.[22] 'She is in high looks,' Lord Minto declared of the thirty-seven-year-old Emma, 'but more immense than ever. She goes on cramming Nelson with trowelfuls of flattery, which he goes on taking as quietly as a child does pap. The love she makes him is not only ridiculous, but disgusting: not only the rooms but the whole house, staircase and all, are covered with nothing but pictures of her and him, of all sizes and sorts . . . '

It was not a very prepossessing picture and it is no wonder that Hamilton grew a little disenchanted with his wife's constant singing of the hero's praise. It would be some months yet before he would feel it necessary to issue some words of warning, though he had already complained to Charles Greville. Once again he fell back on the old excuse of anything for peace and quiet. He was now over seventy, was conscious of the fact that he had only a little time left, and was indifferent to the opinion of 'the nonsensical world'. He would no doubt have preferred to remain in his house in Piccadilly, surrounded by his books and such pictures and works of art as he still possessed, within easy reach of the Museum, the Royal Society, and his old friends, antiquarians, connoisseurs, and men of science like himself. Instead he had to content himself with occasional visits to London, making the best of such time as he could snatch for the pursuit of his own affairs. Friendship for Nelson still drew him to Merton as well as the desire to protect his wife's reputation (and his own) in so far as this was still possible, but his heart was no longer in the *comedietta* that went by the name of *Tria Juncta in Uno*.

Christmas was spent at Merton and there was a good deal of going to and fro between Wimbledon and Piccadilly in the early months of 1802. The Peace of Amiens, signed on 24 March, introduced the period of 'experimental peace' with republican France that was to last until just after Hamilton's death. With the end of hostilities Sir William applied once more for the settlement of his extraordinary expenses and once again met with the prevarication which was becoming a depressingly familiar feature of his negotiations with Government since his retirement. By June he had still made no progress, and after a humiliating visit to Whitehall he wrote a dignified letter of protest to the Foreign Secretary,[23] Lord Hawkesbury, dated 12 June:

My Lord

I have had the honor of waiting upon your Lordship at your office twice without having had the good fortune of finding your Lordship at leasure to give me an audience. I went again to the office this day at half-past 12 o-clock and sent up a billet to your Lordship entreating a moment's audience and for which that I wou'd wait below your Lordship's conveniency. After two hours a message came from your Lordship that you was too much engaged to see me this day and desired that I wou'd return some day next week. As my business depended entirely on the notice of your Lordship's office I enquired for either Mr. Hammond or Lord Hervey, your Lordship's first Secretaries, and Lord Hervey was so good as to send for me soon after. My business was simply to request that as Lord Grenville had neglected when he went out of office the passing of some of the usual Bills of Extraordinarys due to me as the King's Minister at the Court of Naples, that they might be sent to the Treasury properly authenticated by your Lordship and without which I can not receive from the Treasury what has long been my due.

I must own, my Lord, feeling my situation as having the honor of being of His Majesty's Privy Council and having served his Majesty as His Minister at the Court of Naples to the best of my ability for 37 years, that I felt myself humbled by waiting so many hours as I have done in your antichamber, and as I am not sensible of having been wanting in attention or civility to your Lordship (the son of my old and worthy friend Lord Liverpool) when you visited Naples, I hope your Lordship will excuse the Liberty I now take of expressing my feelings and that you will grant the just request I have made to-day to your Lordship through the channel of Lord Hervey.

I have the honor to be

My Lord

Your Lordship's most obt. and most humble servt.

WILLIAM HAMILTON[24]

The Foreign Secretary's answer to this letter has not survived. It is to be hoped that the rebuke stung him to some action, but the unhappy business of reimbursement was still unsettled at the time of Hamilton's death and was to be taken up at various times, with even less success, by his widow under the encouragement of Lord Nelson, and later of less scrupulous advisers. Meanwhile Beckford had returned to the peerage question which he had raised with Sir William more than a year before. He now hoped to enlist the help of the Duke of Hamilton, as head of the family, and his son the Marquis of Douglas. Sir William laid the matter before his relations and was probably more relieved than anything else when Lord Douglas replied: 'The plan you state to me, my dear Sir William, I should fear never could possibly succeed, for, however unreasonable may be the objections to it, they are such as weigh very much with the individuals of this country. Were it in my power to second any wish of yours, I am sure I should feel happy beyond measure to do it, but my political interest can be of no avail, and the asking would only subject us both to a refusal, which would certainly come, from the final clause in the object in question being of so peculiar a nature, and so little consonant with the feelings and tempers of people.'[25] With this ended Beckford's hopes for a peerage as well as Hamilton's for an additional two thousand pounds a year. As far as the peerage was concerned he had no regrets, but the money, as he somewhat wistfully pointed out to Lord Douglas, would certainly have put him more at his ease than he was at present.

As a distraction from these worrying financial preoccupations Sir William set out towards the end of July on a long progress across the west of England and Wales in the company of Nelson and Emma. The journey had two objectives: a visit to Oxford where both the town and the university were to honour their distinguished visitors, and a tour of inspection of Hamilton's property at Milford Haven which he hoped, with Nelson's interest and encouragement, might be developed into a flourishing port. The admiral's elder brother and his wife were also of the party which soon developed into a triumphal progress for the hero of Copenhagen and the Nile.

Oxford was reached on 21 July and the travellers put up at the Angel Inn in High Street where two more of Nelson's relations, his youngest sister Catherine and her husband George Matcham, attached themselves to the party. The following day the freedom of the city was presented to the admiral in a golden box. On the twenty-third, a Friday, the university in full Congregation bestowed the honorary degree of Doctor of Civil Law upon both Lord Nelson and Sir William Hamilton, who were presented by the Vinerian Professor of Law. The egregious William Nelson, ever ready to benefit from his brother's fame, was made a Doctor of Divinity, while Emma enjoyed the possibly unique distinction of seeing her husband and her lover being honoured simultaneously by England's senior university.

From Oxford the party proceeded to Woodstock where they spent the night. The next day they set out to view the splendours of Blenheim Palace, but here they met with a rebuff. The Duke of Marlborough, sulkily recovering from a recent scandal involving his heir and the wife of a Member of Parliament, flatly declined the honour of meeting a celebrated *ménage à trois* whose activities provided such interesting copy for the less respectable news-sheets and journals. The announcement of their arrival produced only an embarrassed silence followed at length by the information that refreshments would be served for them in the park but not beneath the frescoed ceiling of the ducal diningroom. Sir William's surprise at an apparent affront was mixed with disappointment at being unable to explore Vanbrugh's architectural masterpiece. Emma gave loud expression to wounded pride, and Nelson coldly refused the offered refreshments. The travellers returned to their carriage in varying degrees of wrath and drove on to Burford.

They continued by way of Gloucester, Monmouth and Carmarthen, at all places on the road large crowds gathering to cheer the hero. They were greeted in the towns by bands, robed representatives of the corporation, and the inevitable addresses of welcome. Milford was eventually reached and Sir William was allowed, for a while, to take the centre of the stage. Charles Greville, who had managed the property for so many years, was waiting to receive them. The party visited a fair, witnessed a rowing match and inspected a cattle show, rural pleasures that were something of a novelty for an admiral and an ex-ambassador. Sir William, in his capacity as landed proprietor, laid the foundation stone of a new church. The anniversary of the battle of the Nile was the occasion for a banquet attended by the Lord Lieutenant of the county and a distinguished company of guests. Before they took the road once more Nelson surveyed the harbour and pronounced it to be one of the best he had seen, comparing it favourably with Trincomalee in Ceylon. As a parting gesture Sir William presented a portrait of Lord Nelson to the host of the New Inn, which the party had used as their headquarters during their stay in Milford.

The journey back was no less arduous for a man of Hamilton's age. At Swansea a tour was made of the porcelain factory before a return visit to Monmouth. There was a welcome break at Downton Castle near Ludlow, the home of Richard Payne Knight, an old friend of Hamilton's, a fellow antiquarian who had twenty years ago shared his interest in the curious and amusing cult of the great toe of St. Cosmo, and who now lived in retirement behind his recently constructed gothic battlements. A friend of Goethe's and a familiar traveller in Italy, he and Sir William would have had much to talk about. From the peace of Ludlow they continued on to Worcester, Birmingham and Warwick where Hamilton had to listen to more stories from his garrulous nephew. It was September before they were back at Merton. The journey had taken very much longer than any of them had intended; it had also cost four hundred and eighty-one pounds, of which sum Sir William had to provide one half.

Almost immediately upon their return Emma decided that she was in need of sea bathing, and though the season was well advanced insisted upon dragging her husband to Ramsgate. Sir William was irritated at being hustled away so soon after their long and tiring journey and made no secret of his desire to leave a resort that had nothing to offer an elderly antiquarian whose days of sea bathing were long past. He felt that his time was being wasted and he was sadly conscious that time was no longer on his side. Emma, long accustomed to having her own way, responded with equal irritation. She sent her husband an abrupt note which declared: 'As I see it is a pain to you to remain here, let me beg of you to fix your own time for going. Weather I dye in Picadilly or any other spot in England, tis the same to me; but I remember the time when you wish'd for tranquility, but now all visiting and bustle is your liking. However, I will do what you please, being ever your affectionate and obedient E.H.'

Hamilton, with a reasonableness and courtesy that the letter hardly deserved, replied upon the back of Emma's note: 'I neither love bustle nor great company, but I like some employment and diversion. I have but a very short time to live, and every moment is precious to me. I am in no hurry, and am exceedingly glad to give every satisfaction to our best friend, our dear Lord Nelson. The question, then, is what can we best do that all may be perfectly satisfied. Sea bathing is usefull to your health; I see it is, and wish you to continue it a little longer; but I must confess that I regret, whilst the season is favourable, that I cannot enjoy my favourite amusement of quiet fishing. I care not a pin for the great world, and am attached to no one so much as to you.' Emma's temper was not calmed; her mood remained angry as she scrawled on the fly-leaf: 'I go when you tell me the coach is ready.' It was the reply of a bad-tempered school girl, and drew from Sir William the calm rejoinder: 'This is not a fair answer to a fair confession of mine.'[26]

Emma was not one to remain long in a bad humour and the storm passed. No doubt there were others, for the strain of the life they were leading was beginning to tell, and Hamilton decided that there was a limit to what he was prepared to endure. Emma's life was centred more and more at Merton; she flung money away on lavish entertainments; her husband's interests were neglected and if he complained there were 'silly altercations.' Nelson, who had so many of the qualities of greatness, seems to have lacked a sense of humour. His complacent acceptance of Emma's 'trowelfuls of flattery' must have become wearisome to someone who had to witness it almost every day, even when that person admired him as sincerely as Sir William did. Though he was unaware of the existence of the 'Thompson' letters he must have recognised that so far as the *Tria Juncta in Uno* were concerned he had become something of a supernumerary. The man who had made so many concessions in the interests of peace and quiet now decided that he must have some peace and quiet for himself, and he delivered what might be called his ultimatum to Emma.

'I have passed the last 40 years of my life in the hurry and bustle that must necessarily be attendant on a publick character,' he began.[27] 'I am arrived at the age when some repose is really necessary, and I promised myself a quiet home, and altho' I was sensible, and said so when I married, that I shou'd be superannuated when my wife wou'd be in her full beauty and vigour of youth. The time is arrived, and we must make the best of it for the comfort of both parties. Unfortunately our tastes as to the manner of living are very different. I by no means wish to live in solitary retreat, but to have seldom less than 12 or 14 at table, and those varying continually, is coming back to what was become so irksome to me in Italy during the latter years of my residence in that country. I have no connections out of my own family. I have no complaint to make, but I feel that the whole attention of my wife is given to Ld. N. and his interest at Merton. I well know the purity of Ld. N's friendship for Emma and me, and I know how very uncomfortable it wou'd make his Lordship, our best friend, if a separation shou'd take place, and am therefore determined to do all in my power to prevent such an extremity, which wou'd be *essentially detrimental* to all parties, but wou'd be more sensibly felt by our dear friend than by us. Provided that our expences in housekeeping do not encrease beyond measure (of which I must own I see some danger), I am willing to go on upon our present footing; but as I cannot expect to live many years, every moment to me is precious, and I hope I may be allow'd sometimes to be my own master, and pass my time according to my own inclination, either by going to my fishing parties on the Thames or by going to London to attend the Museum, R. Society, the Tuesday Club and Auctions of pictures. I mean to have a light chariot or post-chaise by the month, that I may make use of it in London and run backwards and forwards to Merton or Shepperton, etc. This is my plan, and we might go on very well, but I am fully determined not to have more of the very silly altercations that happen but too often between us and embitter the present moments exceedingly. If realy one cannot live comfortably together, a *wise* and well *concerted separation* is preferable; but I think, considering the probability of my not troubling any party long in this world, the best for us all wou'd be to bear those ills we have rather than flie to those we know not of. I have fairly stated what I have on my mind. There is no time for nonsense or trifling. I know and admire your talents and many excellent qualities, but I am not blind to your defects, and confess having many myself; therefore let us bear and forbear for God's sake.'

The result of this ultimatum was that Hamilton's remaining months of life were passed in peace. The tragedy was that he had so short a time left in which to enjoy his freedom. Money worries still assailed him. In December he told Greville that if the Treasury did not pay him soon he would apply directly to the Prime Minister, adding 'it is most shamefull'. Emma's extravagance did not help him. He probably did not know the full extent of her debts, which were thought to be in the neighbourhood of seven hundred pounds, but before Christmas he made over £450 towards their settlement.[28] The woman whose mind he had tried to form in Naples was already beginning to go downhill. His namesake William Hamilton the artist who saw her in 1801 declared that 'she is bold and unguarded in her manner, is grown fat and drinks freely;'[29] a year later Lord Minto expressed his opinion more briefly: 'she is horrid'. Sir William's rapid deterioration in health in the spring of 1803 saved him from witnessing her further decline in character and reputation.

In October 1802 Hamilton was able to enjoy his last fishing expedition on the Thames. Later in the autumn he went with Lord Nelson to some meetings of the Literary Society and in December, when Sir Joseph Banks was ill, he took the chair at a meeting of the council of the Royal Society. Christmas was spent at Merton; there was a great gathering of Nelson's relations and Emma gave a ball for the children. After the festivities were over Sir William returned to his house in Piccadilly and in January made his last appearance at Court for the Queen's birthday Drawing-Room. In March his health began to give cause for anxiety. Nelson's sister Mrs. Bolton wrote to Emma on the twenty-first: 'This mild weather must be greatly in his favour. I sincerely hope he will be restored to you.'[30] Three English winters, however, were to prove too much for a man who had spent thirty-seven years under the Italian sun. There was no rallying; on the morning of 6 April, 1803, at ten minutes past ten o'clock, Sir William Hamilton died 'without a sigh or a struggle.'[4] Emma and Nelson were by his bedside; he died in his wife's arms while Lord Nelson held his hand.

The first direction made by Hamilton in his Will was that he was to be buried beside his first wife, Catherine Hamilton, 'to fulfil the promise I made'. The second was that his funeral was to be conducted 'in as private a manner as decency and propriety will admit'. He left Emma the sum of three hundred pounds to be paid immediately after his death, and a further hundred to her mother, Mrs. Cadogan. Emma also received an annuity of eight hundred pounds of which the sum of one hundred was again assigned to Mrs. Cadogan. The annuity, clear of all deductions, was to be paid quarterly. The residue of the estate, in fulfilment of the agreement made eighteen years before, was left to Charles Greville. Lord Nelson was mentioned in a codicil: 'The copy of Madame Le Brunn's picture of Emma in enamel, by Bone, I give to my dearest friend Lord Nelson, Duke of Bronte, a very small token of the great regard I have for his Lordship, the most virtuous, loyal, and truly brave character I ever met with. God bless him, and shame fall on those who do not say amen.'[32]

In April 1799 Sir William had written to Greville: 'I love Lord Nelson more and more—his activity is wonderful, and he loves us sincerely.'[33] The reference to the admiral in his Will was less ingenuous; it might have been written in irony or bravado. Sarcasm was not in Hamilton's line, but there is certainly a hint of ambiguity in the words, which was perhaps what he intended. It was almost superfluous to present a picture (and a copy at that) to the man who already possessed the original. Nelson's own reaction to Sir William's Will was expressed in a letter to the Queen of Naples: 'The good Sir William did not leave Lady Hamilton in such comfortable circumstances as his fortune would have allowed. He has given it among his relations. But she will do honour to his memory although every one else of his friends calls loudly against him on that account.'[34] The letter was most ungenerous to Sir William's memory. The annual sum he left Emma was ample provision, by the monetary values of the day, for a widow of her rank, and there is no record of anyone except Nelson calling loudly against him on this aspect of his Will. He certainly knew better than to give Emma access to capital which she would very rapidly have squandered. If she was to be in uncomfortable circumstances it was due, not to Sir William's lack of provision, but to her own wild extravagance.

It is difficult to know what Emma herself felt when her husband died. The inevitable note of self-dramatisation was struck when she wrote: 'Unhappy day for the forlorn Emma. Ten minutes past ten dear blessed Sir William left me!' Perhaps she had ceased to be able to distinguish genuine feeling from histrionic effect. This, at least, is the kindest interpretation to put upon an anecdote related some years later by Sir William Gell of a scene which he may well have witnessed himself:

'A gentleman passing along Piccadilly saw a crowd of people at Sir W. Hamilton's door, where they were putting the coffin into the hearse; but seeing everybody looking up at the window, he looked also, and there was to be seen Lady Hamilton in all the *wildness of her grief*. Some said her attitudes were fine; others that they were affected; others that they were natural. At last, as the gentleman was leaving this motley group, some of whom were crying and others laughing, he heard a child go up to its mamma, and say, "Ma, mamma, don't cry, pray don't cry, for they say as how it's all *sham*."[35] Sham or not, her grief had to be expressed dramatically, and when she appeared in public it was noticed that Emma now wore her hair *à la Titus*, a classical style that was considered fashionable for widows.

Reports of Hamilton's death caused no great stir in the newspapers which were full of news of the First Consul's court where, since the Peace of Amiens, British visitors were being received for the first time. The *Times* informed its readers on 7 April that Sir William 'expired without a groan.' It mentioned the patronage he had enjoyed as foster-brother of the King, but had little to say of his diplomatic career except that 'he maintained the most perfect harmony between the two Courts at a period when it required all his influence and address to counteract the designs of those who had interest in a breach of amity that so happily subsisted.' The obituary notice rightly laid emphasis on his activities in the world of art and scholarship. 'Sir William', the *Times* concluded, 'was a man of extraordinary endowments, and his memory will be dear to the literary world by the indefatigable exertions which he made through life to add to our stock of knowledge and of models in the fine arts.' The *Sun* took a similar line in its edition of 9 April. 'The late Sir William Hamilton', it recorded, 'though by no means wanting in political knowledge and diplomatic address, was principally distinguished by his taste in the Fine Arts. It was chiefly owing to his zeal, assiduity, and encouragement, that a prodigious number and variety of the remains of ancient art were discovered; and the accounts which he published of these interesting and valuable remains have in a great measure diffused a taste for *virtù* and a knowledge of antiquity, not only throughout this country but all Europe. To Sir William, indeed, we are in a great degree indebted for those classical ornaments which appear in the interior of our higher mansions and in the style of our furniture, as well as in the general improvements of design in all that relates to the Arts.'

On 12 April Hamilton's remains were taken from the house in Piccadilly where he had died and started on the last journey to Wales. He was buried beside his first wife in Selbeck Church. It was appropriate that he should return to the mild, loving and selfless Catherine after the garish interlude as Emma's husband. It was in this latter rôle, however, that history would continue to remember him. Sir William Hamilton's diplomatic career was of no great significance. His post was not an important one, and though he filled it with distinction for many years it did not become for him (as he had at one time hoped) a stepping-stone to a position of more influence and power. His success lay in the personal sphere, in the happy *rapport* he established and maintained with the Neapolitan Court and in the position he achieved for himself as a figure of European reputation in the world of art and scholarship. It was not to meet a Minister to a minor Court that scholars, artists, musicians, connoisseurs and literati flocked to the Palazzo Sessa when they visited Naples; it was to meet a man who was an acknowledged authority in those undiplomatic activities upon which his fame rested: the observation and exploration of volcanoes, the excavation of archaeological sites, the study of the history and origins as well as the form and beauty of Greek vases, the collection of pictures, the patronage of painters, and the appreciation of music and the civilised arts in general. He was fortunate to live at a time before excessive specialisation made it impossible for one man to excel in so many fields. He was a worthy citizen of that international republic of learning which was one of the happier features of the Age of Reason.

Hamilton would probably have considered that his most important work consisted in the influence he brought to bear on young artists and through their work upon the taste and culture of the times in which he lived. It was for this reason that he formed his collections and issued the volumes illustrating them. The catalogues which he made show that as a collector of pictures he was not in any sense an innovator; his gallery very much reflected the informed taste of his day. Its interest now lies in the contemporary artists he patronised. The illustrated volumes of his collections of vases had a direct influence on the neoclassical painters, drawing their attention to Greek themes and emphasising purity of line; while the illustrations to his *Campi Phlegraei* show the peculiarly Neapolitan *genre* of view-painting at its most felicitous. It is therefore not surprising that it was the painters of these schools whose works found a place on the walls of the Palazzo Sessa. Of the first group were established figures like Gavin Hamilton (a disciple, as was Sir William, of Winckelmann), and those who may be said to have come under Sir William's own influence like Tischbein, John Flaxman and David Allan, the latter also a pupil of Gavin Hamilton. The view-painters were represented by the spacious canvasses of Philip Hackert and the more intimate scenes painted by Pietro Fabris and the lesser known Xaviero della Gatta. Sir William included no less than fifteen works by his protégé Fabris among the pictures he shipped home to England.

The influence in the third group of contemporary artists he patronised derives not from Sir William's own published works but from his taste in another direction. These were the portrait painters whose works adorned his walls chiefly from their skill at delineating the features of his second wife. Some, like Angelica Kauffmann, might also be described as neoclassics (she was influenced by Hamilton's second vase book), and Rosalba, though a charming portraitist, was in fact represented by a 'Venus and Cupid'; but Reynolds, Romney and Vigée Le Brun, as well as Angelica, were all represented by their various pictures of Emma. It is doubtful whether the art of portraiture would have featured so largely in Sir William's gallery of pictures had he not married for a second time.

Hamilton's reputation as a collector was established not by his pictures but by his two great collections of Greek vases. Though not a pioneer in this field (although one of the first to distinguish between Greek and Etruscan) it was he, as Michaelis pointed out, who first appreciated their artistic merit and saw their possibilities as an influence on contemporary taste, a discovery which was to have a profound effect on the work of Josiah Wedgwood and on artists like Flaxman and Henry Fuseli. Of these collections the second (or such of it as survived the wreck of the *Colossus*), generally considered to have been the best of the two, has been dispersed through the sales of those that escaped ship-wreck and were bought from Sir William by Thomas Hope, though some of the vases from this collection have since joined those of the first in the British Museum after passing through various hands. The first collection itself no longer exists as a separate entity, having been absorbed into the main collection probably at the time when the present museum was built, so that its distinctive existence as the Hamiltonian Collection has been lost. Sir William's vases can still, however, be identified by the letter 'H' in white which marks many of them or by reference to the plates illustrating d'Hancarville's volumes. Those familiar with these plates will easily recognise the originals, a final justification of the care and expense lavished by Hamilton on the production of these four exquisite folios.

These books, with the others he produced, are themselves works of art and are Sir William Hamilton's chief memorial. The volumes devoted to his two collections of Greek vases are still of value to the scholar, the aesthetic theory he maintained has not lost its validity, and the plates remain a delight to the eye. The three volumes of *Campi Phlegraei* have a double attraction; for while Hamilton's descriptions of his volcanic observations remain fascinating to read, the plates produced by Pietro Fabris under his direction give an extraordinarily vivid and unique picture of Naples and its surrounding countryside in the decades immediately before the French revolution. Hamilton intended it as a scientific work, and would probably have been rather shocked to think that it would one day become a collectors' piece (something he claimed to despise), but it remains a work of absorbing interest, using the skill of the artist in the exposition of scientific theory for the greater edification of mankind, an ideal which lay at the heart of Sir William's philosophy of life.

Hamilton belonged essentially to the period before the French revolution. He never adjusted himself to the new ideas which flowed from Paris in the years after 1789, and his idolising of Nelson was not unconnected with the fact that the battle of the Nile was the first major check to the advances of revolutionary power as it was exemplified by the victorious armies of France. He was a man of the Enlightenment. He stood for those civilised virtues of tolerance and urbanity combined with a sense of discipline, order, and proportion which depend for their existence upon a tranquil state of society. The destruction of that tranquillity in the world at large was reflected in his private life by the confusion that attended the last years of his second marriage. When his life is viewed as a whole, however, Sir William may be considered as a worthy example of these essentially eighteenth-century virtues which, in conjunction with a cultivated mind and an equitable temperament, made him (in the words of his old friend Sir Nathaniel Wraxall) for so many years 'the delight and ornament of the Court of Naples'.

Just over a month after Hamilton's death war broke out again between France and Great Britain. Nelson was appointed to the Mediterranean command and on 18 May, 1803, the day hostilities began, hoisted his flag in the *Victory*. For the brief span of life that remained to him (during the greater part of which he was away at sea) he continued the devoted lover of Emma Hamilton. His campaign ended in the defeat of the combined French and Spanish fleets off Trafalgar on 21 October 1805. Nelson's death in the hour of victory left Emma the last survivor of the *Tria Juncta in Uno*. Death was busily clearing the stage of those who had taken part in her adventurous career. In 1809 Charles Greville died, still a bachelor, and the following year Mrs. Cadogan ended a long and curious life.

In a Will made before the battle of Trafalgar Nelson had bequeathed his mistress to his King and Country—a bequest which neither nation nor monarch were prepared to accept—in the hope that a pension might be secured for her. He also made further financial provision for her out of his own estate, as well as for the child she had given him. Emma, however, was too deeply in debt for any additions of income to make much difference. The pension never materialised; extravagance and gambling brought about the ruin which many had foreseen but few warned her against; her attempts to save the situation were often desperate, not always honest, and never successful. In 1813 she was imprisoned for debt, and in 1814 after peace was restored, fled to France to avoid the further attentions of the debt-collector. She died in Calais on the 15th of January 1815 at the age of fifty. Her daughter survived her by many years, dying at the age of eighty-one. She was aware that she was Lord Nelson's daughter but remained all her life uncertain of the name of her mother. It was a secret which Emma had kept to herself.

1. Morrison, 651.
2. *Vide* Morrison, 513, 519 and 526.
3. Ibid., 511 and 521 (19 February 1801).
4. Morrison, 532.
5. Letter to Richard Worsley (Lincolnshire Record Office: Worsley MSS 55) [F].
6. Morrison, 550. No priced catalogue of the sale of March 27-8 appears to have survived.
7. The author is grateful to Messrs. Christie's for these details.
8. Morrison, 543.
9. Morrison, 544.

10. Morrison, 552. Thomas Hope (1770-1831) author, antiquarian and patron of the arts, sold part of the collection (180 specimens) in 1805. More were sold in 1849 and Hamilton's second collection ceased to be 'kept entire' as he had wished.
11. Wraxall: *Historical Memoirs*, pp. 164-5.
12. Nicholas: *Letters & Dispatches of Lord Nelson*, Vol. IV, p. 424.
13. The peace of Luneville, (February 1801) between Austria and France had brought hostilities to an end on the continent and it was thought that Bonaparte would concentrate his forces on an invasion of southern England.
14. Morrison, 635.
15. Ibid., 626.
16. Ibid., 616.
17. Ibid., 621. Nelson uses the spelling 'Thompson' and 'Thomson' indiscriminately in this correspondence.
18. Morrison, 633.
19. Nicolas: *Letters & Dispatches of Lord Nelson*, Vol. IV, p. 511.
20. Morrison, 638.
21. *Life & Letters of the Earl of Minto*, Vol. III, p. 242.
22. *Vide The Farington Diary*, Vol. I, p. 344: 'Edridge has been at Merton with Sir Wm. Hamilton and Lady Hamilton, and Lord Nelson who live constantly together, bearing the expenses jointly and settling once a month.'
23. Foreign Secretary 1801. Later second Earl of Liverpool and Prime Minister.
24. B.M. Add. MSS 41200, f. 219.
25. Morrison, 678. Lord Douglas (later tenth Duke of Hamilton) subsequently married Beckford's second daughter and co-heiress.
26. Morrison, 679, 680.
27. Morrison, 684.
28. Morrison, 694. He had only paid about half of this sum at the time of his death.
29. Farington *Diary*, Vol. I., p. 307.
30. Morrison, 706.
31. Nelson to Alexander Davison: *Vide* Rawson, *Nelson's Letters*, p. 372.
32. *Vide* Morrison, Vol. II, Appendix E, pp. 418-24. This picture is now in the Wallace Collection, London.
33. Ibid., 381.
34. *Vide* E. Edwards: *Lives of the Founders of the British Museum*, Vol. I, p. 361.
35. Lady C. Bury: *Diary of the Times of George IV*, Vol. IV, p. 130-1.

APPENDIX
Sir William Hamilton's Collection of Pictures
(from the manuscript catalogue in the Fitzwilliam Museum, Cambridge)

Catalogue
of Pictures, Marbles, Bronzes &c.
The property of The Right Honble.
Sir William Hamilton, K.B.
&c. &c. &c.
Packed at Naples in Octr Nov^r & Decr 1798
Under the Direction of
Sir William's
much obliged
and most obedient humble Servant
JAMES CLARK[1]

The following Measurements are in Neapolitan *Palme* and *Once*, twelve of which last are equal Ten Inches and one third English measure.

Case No. 1

No.		Height		Breadth or Length	
1 to 16	Contains Sixteen pictures in Oil Colours being views of Venice by Cannaletti, each measuring 2 palms 4 once in height, by 3 palms 8 once in length, viz.	2	4	3	8

Case No. 2

No.		Height		Breadth or Length	
	Containing the following Twenty four Pictures viz.				
1	By VANDERWERF, A Sea picture with shipping etc., on Canvas	1	7	1	6
2	By Do. Do. On Board	1	6	1	3
3	WOUVERMAN, A landskip with figures, horses, etc.	1	5	D°	D°
4	POLENBURGH, A landskip with satyrs, Fawns, Nymphs, Ruins, etc.	1	3	1	7

No.		Height		Breadth or *Length*	
5	RUBENS, Sketch of a Holy Family—five figures	1	6	1	3
6	Augustine CARACCE—Bust of a Friar in white	1	9	1	4
7 & 8	DEANE, Two Landskips, companions, oval frame each,	1	4	1	9
9	Clouds—Landskip background *Mola*	1	9	–	11
10	POLIDOR DA CARAVAGGIO - Adoration of the Shepherds, with 7 principal figures - in the clouds several angels, on Board	2	4	1	6
11 & 12	LANFRANCS & *Guido*, Two heads, sketches, companions, each	1	6	1	2
13	Flemish School - Bambacciato - A woman with three children, copper vessels, cabbage, etc *Chardon*	1	7	1	3
14 & 15	Two Landskips Companions - one a view of Messina, & the other an Eruption of Vesuvius, on Copper	–	10	1	7
16	FABRIS Landskip with a Grotto & Ten Figures	1	5	2	–
17 & 18	FABRIS Two Landskips Companions, each with Capuchin Hermits	1	6	1	2
19	TADEO ZUCCHERI, Adoration of the Magi—Angels in the Clouds	1	7	1	4
20	*Teniers* Landskip with six ducks on Board	1	–	1	4
21	*Paul Veronese* Madonna & Child with many Cherubs	1	6	1	3
22	POLLIDOR DA CARAVAGGIO A Monte Calvario or Christ bearing his Cross, with many figures, on Board	1	–	1	5
23	Copy of the celebrated St. Jerom by Coreggio in the Academy of Parma	1	3	–	9
24	PETER NEFFS Perspective view of the interior of a Gothic Church	1	2	2	–

N.B. The above 24 pictures were packt the 26th Oct. 1798.

Case No. 3

No.		Height		Breadth or *Length*	
	Containing the annexed Eighteen pictures, viz.				
1	TITIAN *or Bellini* A Madonna & Child, painted on Board	2	4	1	8
2 & 3	PAUL BRILL, Two Landskips, Companions, each	1	8	2	3
4 & 5	A. CARACCE, Two Busts Companions Portraits of Calvin & Luther	2	–	1	10
6 & 7	*Morone* Two Busts, Companions – one of a man with a Book, The other of a Girl with a circular machine, each	2	–	1	8
8	*Hackert* Landskip with Greyhound, two Spaniels, etc.	1	8	2	1
9	*Fabris* The Marriage of Cupid & Psyche, 5 Figures	1	9	2	3
10	*Copy from Titian, Werling* Danae & an old woman catching the Gold	1	6	2	1
11 & 12	FABRIS, Two Snow-Pieces, Caminions – Each	1	6	1	10
13 & 14	*Fabris*, Two bambacciate of a Cobler, a Tinker & their families	1	11	1	6
15 & 16	Morone, Two Busts, Companions, One a Girl with her Mask and Fan, the other, a Girl with a Basket, Each	2	–	1	8
17	FABRIS, Landskip—the Ferry at Chajazza	1	4	2	3
18	BENVENUTO GAROFOLO – Holy Family, Landskip background	1	4	1	11

N.B. The above 18 Pictures were packt the 26th. Oct[r] 1798

Case No. 4

No.		Height		Breadth or *Length*	
	Containing the following Twelve Pictures, viz.				
1	VERNOIS, A Sea-Piece, A Cabin with Shipping etc.	2	–	3	–
2	VANDERWERF Do. Do. Do.	1	11	2	5
3 & 4	CANALETTI Two Views of Venice – Companions – each	2	2	2	9

No.		Height		Breadth or Length	
5 & 6	MICHELANGELO delle BATTAGLIE, Two Battlepieces ——	2	2	2	9
7	Do.　　　Do.	2	–	2	6
8	TINTORETTO, A Pietà, with seven Figures	2	–	2	10
9	Portrait of a Man with black Drapery, flowing hair & a scrol in his left hand, Half Figure	2	7	2	2
10 & 11	FABRIS, Companions, two Night-Scenes with Torch, light on sea shore by the Hermitage at Pausilipo, each	2	–	2	6
12	LUCA GIORDANO[2] in imitation of P. Veronese, A naked Jesus reclining with a Cross in his left hand	1	6	2	–

N.B. The above 12 pictures were packt the 29th. Octr 1798.

Case No. 5

Containing the annexed twelve Pictures, viz.

No.		Height		Breadth or Length	
1	MADE. LE BRUN, Portrait of Lady Hamilton—a Bust with Turbant and Scroll *in the character of a Sybil*	3	4	2	3
2	Sir JOSHUA REYNOLDS, Portrait of Lady Hamilton, Half Figure – on Board	3	–	2	6
3	ANDREA SACCHI—St. Jerom full length Figure with a Crucifix, Scull, Book & Landskip Back-Ground	2	3	3	–
4	ROMNEY, Portrait of Lady Hamilton, Half-Figure with a Dog	3	–	2	5
5	D° Portrait of The Honb^{le} Charles Greville—a Bust	3	5	D°	D°
6	FURINO Sophonisba with the Heart of Sigismondo on a Vase. H. Fig^e.	2	10	2	4
7	RUBENS Portrait of one of his Wives—a Bust	2	8	2	4
8	WOUVERMAN, A Battle-Piece	1	10	2	6

No.		Height		Breadth or *Length*	
9	MENGS, Portrait of Himself with Pallet & Pencils	2	11	2	5
10	BERGHEN,[3] Landskip, with Milk-Maid, Clown, Cattle &c. on Bd	1	6	2	–
11	Portrait of Mad[e]. Pompadour, a Bust	2	5	2	–
12	VERNOIS, A Sea-Piece with Figures, Shipping Rocks	2	3	3	4

N.B. The above 12 Pictures were packt the 30th. Oct[r] 1798.

Case No. 6

	Containing the following Ten Pictures, Viz.				
1 & 2	VIVIANO Architectual Ruins, Companions each	2	11	4	–
3	WALLIS Landskip with a Cataract &c.	3	10	2	11
4	VANDYKE, A crucifixion—painted on Board	4	–	2	10
5	IOLE The interior of St. Peter's Church at Rome	3	1	4	3
6 & 7	GAVIN HAMILTON The Genii of Painting & Poetry, two half figures, Companions	3	10	2	11
8	GIORGIONE, Portrait of D. *Piombino* half Figure—Spanish Dress, painted on Board	3	9	3	–
9	D. TENIERS. Three peasants with Landskip Background	3	6	2	8
10	RUBENS, Portrait of a Woman, Half-Figure in Black Drapery	3	–	2	6

N.B. The above 10 Pictures were packt the 30 & 31st. Oct[r] 1798.

Case No. 7

	Containing the following Fourteen Pictures, viz.				
1	*Tintoret* Pilate acquitting Christ with many Figures	3	11	3	–

No.		Height		Breadth or *Length*	
2	CLAUDE LORAINE A Sea Piece with the setting sun, etc.	2	9	3	9
3 & 4	FABRIS, Companions, Two Views, Eruptions of Mount Etna and Stromboli, Each	–	–	–	–
5 & 6	IOLE Companions—Two Views, Ruins of Temples at Paestum	3	–	3	11
7 & 8	*Mola*⁴ Companions—Two Landskips with Friars of whom one is St. Bruno & the other St. Romualdo	2	9	3	8
9 & 10	FABRIS, Two views of Pausilipo – Bambacciate Subjects with many Figures, each	2	9	3	9
11	BERGHEM Landskip with Cattle, an Arch & distant View	2	6	3	–
12	VELASQUEZ Portrait of a Man, Half Figure, Spanish Dress	3	1	2	8
13 & 14	ZUCCARELLI, Two Landskips, Companions, each	2	5	3	8

N.B. The above 14 Pictures were packt the 3 Novr 1798.

Case No. 8

Containing the following Ten Pictures, viz.

No.		Height		Breadth or *Length*	
1	FABRIS View at Pausilipo, many Figures	3	10	5	10
2	D° View at Sea La Madonna dell'Areo, with Many Figures	D°	D°	D°	D°
3	D° View at Pausilipo also with many Bambacciate Figures	D°	D°	D°	D°
4	D° A Night Scene	D°	D°	D°	D°
5	D° Eruption of Vesuvius in Aug. 1779 by Night	D°	D°	D°	D°
6	SALVATOR ROSA. A Magician with various Impliments of Sorcery	5	8	3	9
7 & 8	PHILIP HACKERT, Two Landskips with a View of the English Garden at Caserta & the other his own Composition. Each	3	9	5	3
9	POMPEO BATTONI. Portrait of Prince Ferdinand o Brunswick	5	2	3	10

No.		Height		Breadth or Length	
10	A CARACCE[5] (in the style of) The Virgin, Jesus, & St. Joseph	4	8	3	8

N.B. The above 10 Pictures packt the 5th. Nov[r] 1798.

Case No. 9

	Containing the following Eight Pictures, viz.				
1	Copy by Ja[s]. CLARK after SCHIDONI'S large Holy Family in the Royal Collection at Capo di Monte	4	2	3	4
2	GUIDO CAGNACCIO, Lucretia stabbing herself	4	4	4	0
3	ROMNEY, Portrait of Lady Hamilton in black	4	10	3	10
4	D° D° in the Character of Baccante	4	10	3	10
5	TITIAN Portrait of a Man, Half-Figure, in black by a Table on which a Carpet is spread etc.	4	–	3	4
6	LUCA GIORDANO, A Man playing on the Calascione, with the auditors, an Ass, a Ram, a Parrot & a Monkey	4	10	3	10
7	GUIDO, David with the Head & Sword of Goliath, Half Figure	3	10	4	5
8	TITIAN. A Concert of Musick – five Half-Figures	3	9	4	4

N.B. The above 8 pictures were packt the 6th. Nov[r] 1798.

Case No. 10

	Containing the following Six Paintings, viz.				
1 & 2	SALVATOR ROSA, Two Pictures, Companions, one representing a Storm by Sea, the other a Tempest by with Land Lightning	5	2	8	2

No.		Height	Breadth or Length
3	GAVIN HAMILTON, A Sleeping Venus & Cupid with a Lyre	5 –	8 –
4	VANDYKE, The Martyrdom of St. Sebastian shot with arrows full length, with two Angels & Landskip Back Ground	– –	– –
5 & 6	FABRIS, Two Bambacciate Companions, one a Night-Piece with many Lazaroni sitting by a fire; & the other a popular Feast at Monte Virgine. Each	7 –	5 –

N.B. The above 6 Pictures packt the 9 Nov.ʳ 1798.

Case No. 11

		Height	Breadth or Length
	Containing the following eleven Pictures, Viz.		
1	Copy of SCHIDONIS Small Charity after the Original at the Royal Collection of Capo di Monte, Naples	4 9	3 3
2	GUIDO, St. Francis, Half-Figures with a Skull & Book	4 –	3 –
3	D. TENIERS Landskip with a Shepherd & Shepherdess on a Hillock, & Cattle below	2 6	3 3
4	REMBRANDT, Portrait of his Mother with a book on her knee	3 3	2 9
5	Giacomo BASSANO, Descent from the Cross, Seven figures	2 6	2 10
6	ANDREA SACCHI, Four figures & a Head from Miracle *of the true Cross*	2 6	3 1
7	VOLAIRE, Eruption of Vesuvius by Night in Aug 1779	3 1	1 11
8	TITIAN, A masterly outline on unprepared Canvas of a Young Man holding a Shoe whilst a Shoemaker is taking his Measure	2 3	1 8
9	P. VERONESE, A Sketch of three Heads—much expression	2 6	1 10
10 & 11	ZUCHARELLI, Two Landskips, Companions—each	2 7	4 3

N.B. The above 11 Pictures pakt the 27th. Nov.ʳ 1798.

No.		Height		Breadth or Length	

Case No. 12

No.		Height		Breadth or Length	
	Contains the following Fifty-three pictures, viz.				
1	JORDANS, *Twelfe nights* A burlesque Festivity with many figures	6	–	8	–
2	Mad^e. LE BRUN, Portrait of Lady Hamilton Full length	5	4	6	–
3	GUIDO, Cupid asleep and Psyche with the lamp	5	3	7	–
4	PALMA GIOVANI, A Satyr rapturously admiring a sleeping Venus – Cupid presiding. In Chiaro Oscuro	5	3	4	6
	N.B. Within this Case is also packt a large slight Box to the Bottom and Cover of which are strewed the following Forty nine small pictures, viz:				
5	SCHIDONI A Holy Family consisting of the Virgin, Jesus, St. John & St. Joseph, painted on Board	1	5	1	2
6	SCHIDONI, The Virgin, Jesus and St. John, on Board	1	3	1	–
7	CARACCE, Head of a young Man with Whiskers	1	5	1	1
8	Copy of the Marriage of St. Catherine after Correggio in the Royal Collection of Capo di Monte	1	1	–	11
9	TENIERS, Head of an Old man upon paper pasted on a Canvas	1	4	1	2½
10 & 11	GUEREINO, Two Drawings in Bistre, Companions, of which one is the Prodigal Son & the other a Woman & Boy with their Rosaries asking Charity of a young Man in a Spanish dress with his Sword	–	10	1	–
12	*Lodovico* CARACCE, St. Agatha with a Book, a Boy with a Vase & lighted Torch, and an Old Man	1	7	1	2

No.		Height		Breadth or Length	
13	RUBENS, A Sketch in Chiaro Oscuro of Figures, Horses, slightly painted but with much spirit & expression, on Board	1	2½	1	9
14	MENGS, *Study for the Christ's head at Oxford* on paper	1	9	1	4½
15	Crayon HAMILTON, Three Busts forming one picture being Portraits of Lady Hamilton – in crayons, on paper	1	5	1	8
16	GUIDO, La Madonna del Rosario with Jesus in the Clouds and San Lorenzo, S. Domenico & St. Francisco with three female Saints below—painted on Copper	1	–	–	9
17	TINTORETTO, The Flagellation of Christ, Six figures, on board,	1	1	–	7
18	D°. Adoration of the Shepherds, ten Figures on Alabaster	–	10½	–	8
19	Crayon HAMILTON, Bust in profile, a Portrait of Lady Hamilton in crayons, on Paper	1	4½	1	½
20 & 21	JOHN HACKERT, Two Landskip companions in Water Colours (Distemper) on Paper	–	11	1	2
22	TENIERS, An old Woman with a Vase, Half Figure	–	6	–	5
23 & 24	ALLAN. Two Bambacciati Companions One representing a Painter of the Rue Catalana with his wife and Child, & the other Two Zampognari playing before the Virgin	–	10	–	9
25 & 26	BORGOGNONI, Battle pieces, Companions, on Copper	5 ½		–	9 ½
27	GARBI, Portrait of Lady Hamilton, Half Figure	1		–	9
28	Landskip, Evening, warm tint— with St. Bruno meditating on Mortality	10		–	9 ½
29 & 30	ROSALBA Venus, Cupid & Doves in Miniature. On the Reverse of this is a Landskip with a bridge across a Cataract, also in miniature of the same size, oval frames.	4		–	3

No.		Height	Breadth or *Length*
31	FABRIS, Susanah & the two Elders—on Copper	6	– 5
32	Copy in Miniature of the Madonna della Sedia after Raphael	4	– 4
33	COLTELLINI, Portrait of the Countess Scawronski in miniature	5 ½	– 4 ½
34	*Gobbo Caracci*, Landskip with Ruins & a Temple, on lead	5 10	– 4 ½
35	*Cooper*, Portrait Oliver Cromwell, a Bust, miniature	4	– 3
36	Portrait, a Bust in Spanish Dress, Miniature	3 ½	– 3
	N.B. The following Seventeen Pictures are screwed to the cover of the Box, Viz:		
37	Portrait of Lady Hamilton, a Bust with a Shawl and White Drapery. Oval with a black square Frame	7 ½	– 6
38	Portrait of a Painter with an Easle Half Figure with both hands, on Copper	10	– 7 ½
39	Portrait of a young Girl, a Bust miniature, Oval in broad ebony Frame	4 ½	– 3
40	Portrait of a young Man with Whiskers, a ruff, & black dress	– –	– –
41	Architectual of Palaces with columns etc., many figures	– 9	1 1 ¾
42	Three busts in Mezzo Relevio in coloured wax, being Portraits of Masaniello and his two Lazzaroni Counsellors Perrone and Genuino, in one Frame	– 8 ½	– 9½
43	Portrait of a woman being a Bust in Profile of Coloured wax	– 2 ½	– 2
44 –46	CIPRIANI, Three Drawings in Chiaro Oscuro of Sir William Hamilton's celebrated Barberini Vase,[6] each	– 8	1 1
47	The Virgin Mary with four angels & a Saint in adoration	2 11	1 7
48	Painted on a gilt ground . . . two scenes of which the lower one		

No.		Height	Breadth or *Length*

represents the virgin sitting with Jesus in her lap, attended by 3 male and 3 female saints standing. The upper . . . God the Father in Heaven, Jesus nailed to the Cross and the s Marys standing by disconsolate. Painted on Board & finishing at top in an acute angle — 1 9 — – 10

49 *Benefiali*, St. Benedict fed by a Raven, Landskip background — 1 – — – 9

50 – 53 Four pictures painted on the principles of Caloptricks. *to be seen in cilanders highly polished.* — 1 11 — 2 6

N.B. The above 53 Pictures were packt the 24th., 25th., 26th., & 27th., of November, 1798.

Case No. 13

Consisting of the following Ten Pictures & Nine Drawings Viz.

1 MARONNE, Portrait in full length of Sir William and the late Lady Hamilton — 9 9 — 7 –

2 TITIAN *or rather Schiavoni* Landskip with six figures of whom two on the foreground are, a young Man in a Spanish dress playing on the violin and a young Woman behind him — 8 7 — 6 –

3 IOLE A Piece of Perspective with Arcades, Water, etc. — 9 7 — 6 –

4 LUCA GIORDANO The Virgin Mary in the Clouds spouting her milk upon a groupe of White Friars etc. — 5 4 — 7 6

5 D°. Companion to the last. The Virgin in the Clouds & a Bishop or Pope by an Alter interceding with her for the Souls in Purgatory — 5 4 — 7 6

6 *Simonelli*, The Virgin in the Clouds dispensing Garments to the White Friars etc. — 7 5 — 5 3

		Height	Breadth or Length
No.			
7	*Simonelli*, Companion to the last. A young Woman, probably some Saint, in conference with White Friars. The Virgin Mary in the Clouds at the top of a Ladder or Stairs, with Angels round her, etc.		

N.B. The above Seven pictures were packt the 28 Dec[r].

		Height	Breadth or Length
8	Madame Angelica KAUFFMANN, Portrait of Lady Hamilton, a three quarter length	5 –	3 10
9	SOLIMENA, A naked sleeping Venus with Cupids	3 9	5 2
10	CALABRESE, The departure of Hagar with the Boy her son. Four Half Figures	5 6	5 6
	Nine drawings. Copies in Watercolour after the Antique paintings of Herculaneum, Pompeia and Stabia.		

N.B. The above 4 Pictures and 9 Drawings were packt on the 29th. December, 1798.

Case No. 14

Mr. Clark having been confined to his house very ill for the fifteen days of this year (1799) he therefore could not supervise the package of this case. He knows however that it containes several copies by Francesco Candido of the Dancing Baccante etc. after Antique Paintings of the Herculaneum.

N. B. These came from Caserta.

LIST OF SOURCES

MANUSCRIPT SOURCES

London: British Museum
      Department of Manuscripts: Add. MSS. 34048, 37077, 41197—
      41200, 42069, 42071, 42096
      Egerton MSS. 2634—2637, 2639—2640, 2641
      Dept. of Greek and Roman Antiquities: Hamilton Papers
Cambridge: Fitzwilliam Museum
      Percival Bequest MSS.
Edinburgh: National Library of Scotland
      MS. 3942

BIBLIOGRAPHY

Acton, Harold, *The Bourbons of Naples*, London, 1957

Alexander, Boyd, *England's Wealthiest Son*, London, 1962

Annual Register for 1803

Anspach, Margravine of, Memoirs, Vol. 1. London, 1826

Anson, E. & F., *Mary Hamilton*, London, 1925

Bearne, Mrs., *A Sister of Marie Antoinette, The Life Story of Marie Caroline, Queen of Naples*, London, 1907

Beckford, William, *Italy, Spain and Portugal*, London, 1840

Bickley, Francis, (ed.), *Diaries of Lord Glenbervie*, Vol. I. London, 1928

Bindoff, S. T., *British Diplomatic Representatives*, 1789-1852 (Camden Third Series, Vol. L.) London, 1934

Boigne, Comtesse de, *Memoirs*,(Trans. S. de Morsier-Kotthaus), London, 1956

Bonney, T. G., *Volcanoes, their Structure and Significance*, London,1902

Bowen, Marjorie, *Patriotic Lady: A Study of Emma, Lady Hamilton and the Neapolitan Revolution of 1799*. London, 1935

Britton, John, *Graphical and Literary Illustrations of Fonthill Abbey*, London, 1823

Brockman, H. A. N.: *The Caliph of Fonthill*, London, 1956

Bullard, F. M., *Volcanoes in History, in Theory, in Eruption*, Edinburgh, 1962

Burney, Dr. Charles, *Musical Tour in France and Italy* (ed. Percy A. Scholes), Vol. I. London, 1959

Bury, Lady Charlotte, *Diary Illustrative of the Times of George IV*, (ed. John Galt), London, 1839

Caidora, Umberto, (ed.), *Diario di Ferdinando IV di Borbone*, (1796-1799). Naples,

1965

Cameron, H. C., *Sir Joseph Banks*, Sydney, 1952

Chapman, Guy, *Beckford*, London, 1937

Childe-Pemberton, W. S., *The Earl Bishop*, 2 Vols. London, 1925

Coke, Lady Mary, *Letters and Journals*, Vols. III & IV. Edinburgh, 1892-6

Colletta, Gen. Pietro, *History of the Kingdom of Naples 1734-1825* (Trans. S. Homer), Edinburgh, 1858

Collison-Morley, Lacy, *Naples through the Centuries*, London, 1925

Conneli, Brian, *Portrait of a Whig Peer*, (2nd Viscount Palmer ston). London, 1957

Croce, Benedetto, *La Rivoluzione Napoletana del 1799*, Bari, 1912

Cust, Lionel, *History of the Society of Dilettantti*, London, 1898

D'Auvergne, Edmund B., *The Dear Emma: The Story of Emma, Lady Hamilton, her Husband and Lovers*, London, 1936

D'Hancarville, (P. F. Hugues), *Collection of Etruscan, Greek and Roman Antiquities from the Cabinet of the Hon. Wm. Hamilton*, 4 Vols. Naples, 1766-7

Edwards, Edward, *Lives of the Founders of the British Museum*, 2 Vols, London, 1870

Farington, Joseph, *The Farington Diary*, Vols. I & II. (ed. James Greig). London, 1922

Finer, A. & Savage, G., *Selected Letters of Josiah Wedgwood*, London, 1965

Fremantle, Anne (ed.), *The Wynne Diaries, 1789-1820*, Oxford, 1952

Gamlin, Hilda, *Nelson's Friend*, 2 Vols, London, 1899

Giglioli, C. H. D., *Naples in 1799*, London, 1903

Goethe, Johann Wolfgang, *Travels in Italy* (Italienische Reise) Trans. A. J. W. Morrison & C. Nisbet, London, 1892

Gordon, Pryse Lockhart, *Personal Memoirs*, 2 Vols, London, 1830

Gordon, T. Crouther, *David Allan of Alloa*, Alva, 1951

Grant, N. H., *The Letters of Mary Nisbet of Dirleton, Countess of Elgin*, London, 1926

Gunn, Peter, *Naples, A Palimpsest*, London, 1961

Gutteridge, H. C., *Nelson and the Neapolitan Jacobins*, Navy Records Society, Vol. XXV. London, 1903

Hamilton, Sir William, *Observations on Mount Vesuvius, Mount Etna, and other Volcanos in a Series of Letters addressed to the Royal Society*, London, 1772

—*Campi Phlegraei, Observations on the Vokanos of the Two Sicilies as they have been communicated to the Royal Society of London*, 2 Vols, Naples 1776, Supplement, 1779

—*Collection of Engravings from Ancient Vases mostly of Pure Greek Workmanshzp discovered in Sepulchres in the Kingdom of the Two Sicilies*, 4 Vols, Naples 1791-5

Harcourt-Smith, Sir Cecil, *The Society of Dilettanti, its Regalia and Pictures*, London, 1932

Harrison, James, *Life of Horatio, Lord Viscount Nelson*, 2 Vols. London 1806

Herbert, Lord, *Henry, Elizabeth and George (1734-80). Letters and Diaries of Henry, 10th Earl of Pembroke and his Circle*, London, 1939

—Pembroke Papers (1780-94), London, 1950

Hilles, F. W. (ed.), *Letters of Sir Joshua Reynolds*, Cambridge, 1929

Horn, D. B., *British Diplomatic Representatives 1689-1789*, (Camden Third Series, Vol. XLVI), London, 1932

Ilchester, Earl of, (ed.), *Journal of Elizabeth, Lady Holland*, Vol. I. London, 1908

Irwin, David, *English Neoclassical Art*, London, 1966

Jeaffreson, J. Cordy, *Lady Hamilton and Lord Nelson*, 2 Vols. London 1888

—*The Queen of Naples and Lord Nelson*, 2 Vols. London, 1889.

Jones, Thomas, *Memoirs*, Walpole Society, Vol. XXXII, London, 1951

Kelly, Michael, *Reminiscences*, Vol. I, London, 1826

Knight, Cornelia, *Autobiography*, Vol. I, London, 1861

Lee, Vernon, *Studies of the Eighteenth Century in Italy*, London, 1907

Lewis, Lesley, *Connoisseurs and Secret Agents in Eighteenth Century Rome*, London, 1961

Lobley, J. Logan, *Mount Vesuvius*, London, 1889

Mankowitz, Wolf, *The Portland Vase and the Wedgwood Copies*, London, 1952

—*Wedgwood*, London, 1953

Melville, Lewis, *The Life and Letters of William Beckford of Fonthill*, London, 1910

Michaelis, Adolf, *Ancient Marbles in Great Britain*, Cambridge, 1882

Miller, Lady Anne, *Letters from Italy in the Years 1770 and 1771*, 3 Vols. London, 1776

Minto, Countess of, (ed.), *The Life and Letters of Sir Gilbert Elliot, 1st Earl of Minto, from 1751 to 1806*, 3 Vols. London, 1874

Moore, Dr. John, *A View of Society and Manners in Italy with Anecdotes relating to some Eminent Characters*, Edinburgh, 1820

Morrison, Alfred, *The Hamilton and Nelson Papers* (Morrison MSS), 2 Vols. Privately printed 1893-4

Nicolas, Sir N. H., *Dispatches and Letters of Vice-Admiral Lord Viscount Nelson*, (Vols. 1-5), London, 1845

Oliver, J. W., *The Life of William Beckford*, London, 1932

Oman, Carola, *Nelson*, London, 1947

Pettigrew, T. J., *Memoirs of the Life of Vice-Admiral Lord Viscount Nelson*, 2 Vols. London, 1849

Piozzi, Mrs., *Glimpses of Italian Society in the Eighteenth Century*, London, 1892

Rawson, Geoffrey, (ed.), *Nelson's Letters*, London, 1960

Scholes, Percy A., *The Great Dr. Burney*, Oxford, 1948

Sedgwick, Romney, (ed.) *Lord Hervey's Memoirs*, Vols. II & III, London, 1931

Sermoneta, Duchess of, *The Locks of Norbury*, London, 1940

Sichel, Walter, *Emma Lady Hamilton*, London, 1905

Stendhal, *Rome, Naples and Florence*, (Trans. Richard N. Coe) London, 1959

Swinburne, Henry, *The Courts of Europe at the Close of the Last Century*, 2 Vols. London, 1895

Tours, Hugh, *The Life and Letters of Emma Hamilton*, London, 1963

Trench, Mrs. Richard (Mrs. St. George), *Remains*, London, 1862

Walpole, Horace, *Letters*, (Ed. P. Cunningham), Vols. Ill-IX, London, 1857-59
Warner, Oliver, *A Portrait of Lord Nelson*, London, 1958
—*Emma Hamilton and Sir William*, London, 1960
Whitley, William T., *Artists and Their Friends in England, 1700-1799*, London, 1928
Wraxall, Sir Nathaniel, *Historical and Personal Memoirs*, Vol. I, London, 1884

ARTICLES AND MONOGRAPHS

Ashmole, B., 'A New Interpretation of the Portland Vase'. (*Journal of Hellenic Studies*, Vol. LXXXVII) London, 1967
Deutch, 0. E., 'Sir William Hamilton's Picture Gallery'. (*Burlington Magazine*, Vol. LXXXII) London, 1943
Haynes, D. E. L., *The Portland Vase*. London, 1964
Hamilton, Sir William, 'An Account of the Late Eruption of Mount Vesuvius by the Rt. Hon. Sir W. Hamilton K.B., F.R.S. Dated Naples Aug. 25, 1794.' (*Philosophical Transactions of the Royal Society of London*, Vol. XVII) London, 1809
—'Of the Earthquakes which happened in Italy from February to May 1783.' (*Philosophical Transactions of the Royal Society of London*, Vol. XV) London, 1809
Penzer, N. M., 'The Warwick Vase'. (*Apollo*, Vol. 62, Dec. 1955) London, 1955
Skinner, Basil, *Scots in Italy in the Eighteenth Century*, Edinburgh,   1966
Waterhouse, Ellis K., 'The British Contribution to the Neo-Classical Style in Painting'. (*Proceedings of The British Academy*, Vol. XL., 1954) London, 1955

INDEX